Mastering SAP ABAP

A complete guide to developing fast, durable, and
maintainable ABAP programs in SAP

Paweł Grześkowiak
Wojciech Ciesielski
Wojciech Ćwik

BIRMINGHAM - MUMBAI

Mastering SAP ABAP

Commissioning Editor: Aaron Lazar
Acquisition Editor: Shahnish Khan
Content Development Editor: Akshita Billava
Technical Editor: Ashi Singh, Neha Pande
Copy Editor: Safis Editing
Language Support Editor: Storm Mann
Project Coordinator: Vaidehi Sawant
Proofreader: Safis Editing
Indexer: Pratik Shirodkar
Graphics: Jisha Chirayil
Production Coordinator: Aparna Bhagat

First published: May 2019

Production reference: 1280519

Published by Packt Publishing Ltd.
Livery Place
35 Livery Street
Birmingham
B3 2PB, UK.

ISBN 978-1-78728-894-2

www.packtpub.com

I would like to dedicate this book to my fiancée, Natalia, for her support
and unlimited level of patience.

— Paweł Grześkowiak

To my wife, Anna, for being my loving partner throughout our joint life journey.
To my mother, Danuta, and to the memory of my father, Bogumił, for their sacrifices and
for exemplifying the power of determination, love, support, and inspiration;
and to my sister, Ewelina, for her smile and for not giving up.

— Wojciech Ciesielski

I dedicate this book to my wife, Jagoda, for her love, faith, support, and for being
an invaluable life companion.

— Wojciech Ćwik

`mapt.io`

Mapt is an online digital library that gives you full access to over 5,000 books and videos, as well as industry leading tools to help you plan your personal development and advance your career. For more information, please visit our website.

Why subscribe?

- Spend less time learning and more time coding with practical eBooks and Videos from over 4,000 industry professionals

- Improve your learning with Skill Plans built especially for you

- Get a free eBook or video every month

- Mapt is fully searchable

- Copy and paste, print, and bookmark content

Packt.com

Did you know that Packt offers eBook versions of every book published, with PDF and ePub files available? You can upgrade to the eBook version at `www.packt.com` and as a print book customer, you are entitled to a discount on the eBook copy. Get in touch with us at `customercare@packtpub.com` for more details.

At `www.packt.com`, you can also read a collection of free technical articles, sign up for a range of free newsletters, and receive exclusive discounts and offers on Packt books and eBooks.

Contributors

About the authors

Paweł Grześkowiak has been passionate about programming from his early years, and since 2012 he has been a SAP technical consultant—mainly in the ABAP area. He has expertise in boosting implementations in the rail transport industry, the chemical industry, media, government administration, the wood industry, and banking. Currently, he designs extensions to SAP S4/HANA systems in ABAP and Java. He is an active member of the SAP community and a three-time SAP Inside Track conference organizer.

I would like to thank all my colleagues from Capgemini who helped make this book better: Krzysztof Bulanowski, Daniel Iwanowski, Bogdan Brzozowski, Mateusz Skadorwa, Marcin Maciejewski, Piotr Roszak, and Marcin Bielecki. Special thanks to Anna Wilk for checking all the examples carefully and for her brilliant review. Last but not least, many thanks to my Capgemini mentor, Paweł Gaura, for his support in my career and development.

Wojciech Ciesielski graduated from the Wroclaw University of Technology with an Engineering degree in Automation and Robotics, and he has a master's degree in Management in WSB Universities. Since then, he has been tightly connected with the SAP environment, working as an ABAP consultant. He has several years of business background in ABAP development and the use of modern technologies in business. He is experienced in working with ERP and CRM systems and integrating them with third-party solutions—from single companies to multinational corporations. He is a co-creator of innovative solutions delivered to the wide international audience of SAP events. He is currently focused on new technologies and solutions in the SAP portfolio: SAP Cloud Platform, Internet of Things, and artificial intelligence; but he is also increasing his expertise in development with other languages.

Wojciech Ćwik has been a certified ABAP consultant for several years, with a specialty in mobile solutions, especially in creating interfaces between SAP and frontend solutions from Fiori and third-party platforms; he also enjoys creating architectures in SAP ERP ecosystems. He is a co-originator of an unconventional system linking new solutions from the SAP portfolio such as IoT, SAP Cloud, and SAP blockchain services.

About the reviewer

Dariusz Pacynko graduated from Wroclaw University of Technology with an MSc degree in Optical Engineering. Since then, he has been tightly connected with the SAP environment, working as an ABAP consultant. He has multiple certifications, such as ABAP with SAP Netweaver 7.40 Development Associate, and several years of business background including experience with ABAP development, OData services, and SAPUI5 applications. He is experienced in working with ERP and CRM systems, integrating them with third-party solutions, and opening them to the mobile philosophy. He is a co-creator of innovative solutions delivered to the wide international audience of SAP events. He is currently focused on the new technologies and solutions in the SAP portfolio, such as SAP Cloud and IoT, but he is also increasing his expertise in Fiori development.

Packt is searching for authors like you

If you're interested in becoming an author for Packt, please visit `authors.packtpub.com` and apply today. We have worked with thousands of developers and tech professionals, just like you, to help them share their insight with the global tech community. You can make a general application, apply for a specific hot topic that we are recruiting an author for, or submit your own idea.

Table of Contents

Preface

Advanced Business Application Programming (**ABAP**) is an established and complex programming language in the IT industry. This book will be your guide to becoming an industry expert in **Systems, Applications, Products** (**SAP**) ABAP. You will learn how to write custom code that is suited for the latest version of SAP ABAP as well as the older versions of SAP. By exploring practical examples, you will learn how to make user-friendly interfaces and will uncover various ways to optimize your ABAP code.

Who this book is for

This book is for developers who want to learn and use ABAP skills in order to become an industry expert. Familiarity with object-oriented programming concepts is expected.

What this book covers

Chapter 1, *Creating Custom Code*, focuses on available actions for changing SAP systems within the modern and ever-changing SAP wold.

Chapter 2, *The Basic Structure of ABAP*, focuses on the distinction between ABAP and modern programming languages.

Chapter 3, *Database Access in ABAP*, describes how to extract data from a database in ABAP.

Chapter 4, *Import and Export to Document Formats*, focuses on the toolset the ABAP developer has for importing and exporting data to/from different environments.

Chapter 5, *Exposing Data to Print Forms*, explains how to represent extracted data in a user-friendly print form, how to make it clearly readable, and how to make its maintenance less time-consuming.

Chapter 6, *ABAP and XML*, deals with the different tools ABAP has for XML manipulation, their performance features, and what real-life scenarios they are intended for.

Chapter 7, *Building User Interfaces*, focuses on how to build classical Dynpro with the help of ABAP tools. It explains what screen types exist and how they are interconnected with each other, what GUI controls ABAP developers have in their toolset, and which of them are recommended and which are not. It also describes **ABAP List Viewer** (**ALV**) controls and the ALV component model.

Chapter 8, *Creating Stunning UI5 Interfaces*, places UI5 in the family of SAP interfaces and explains how to use it in the most efficient way.

Chapter 9, *Business Object Processing Framework*, gives an overview of **Business Object Processing Framework** (**BOPF**) and explains why it is important in SAP environments for the acceleration of development, easier maintenance, and supportability.

Chapter 10, *Modification and Customization Techniques*, describes the customization techniques across SAP modules, explaining which techniques are recommended to use and which are outdated.

Chapter 11, *Handling Exceptions in ABAP*, covers testing exceptions in ABAP, the types of exception that have existed from the beginning, and the types we have now. It also recommends the proper way of handling exceptions, explaining in which situations it is strongly required, and those in which it is not recommended.

Chapter 12, *Testing ABAP Programs*, explains how to test ABAP programs for performance without sacrificing the clarity of ABAP code and how to use the ABAP Debugger correctly to find bottlenecks and speed up ABAP programs.

Chapter 13, *Advanced Techniques in ABAP Objects*, deals with the advantages ABAP objects bring to the development process.

Chapter 14, *Integrating SAP with Third-Party Systems*, focuses on how to build a stable and error-prone connection of a SAP system with non-SAP software.

Chapter 15, *Background Processing of ABAP Programs*, reveals all the ins and outs of background data processing in SAP that you may face, and the approaches that are used to handle with them.

Chapter 16, *Performance and Optimization of ABAP*, provides a thorough review of the available ABAP toolset for testing the performance of ABAP apps and tuning their execution. It also gives some best practice tips and tricks of internal ABAP statements and focuses on tracing and tuning OpenSQL selections.

To get the most out of this book

The reader should know the basics of programming, as well as the basics of SQL and operations on databases. Basic knowledge of business processes will also be helpful. This book also deals with the subject of UI5; therefore, it is worth the reader knowing the basics of JavaScript.

To create code in ABAP, the readers also need access to SAP systems with the developer key.

To create applications in UI5, the readers should create a trial account in the SAP Cloud Platform. The SAP Web IDE Full-Stack developer environment is available there. The programming environment allows you to create and extend SAP applications on a full stack for browsers and mobile devices.

Download the example code files

You can download the example code files for this book from your account at www.packt.com. If you purchased this book elsewhere, you can visit www.packt.com/support and register to have the files emailed directly to you.

You can download the code files by following these steps:

1. Log in or register at www.packt.com.
2. Select the **SUPPORT** tab.
3. Click on **Code Downloads & Errata**.
4. Enter the name of the book in the **Search** box and follow the onscreen instructions.

Once the file is downloaded, please make sure that you unzip or extract the folder using the latest version of:

- WinRAR/7-Zip for Windows
- Zipeg/iZip/UnRarX for Mac
- 7-Zip/PeaZip for Linux

The code bundle for the book is also hosted on GitHub at https://github.com/PacktPublishing/Mastering-SAP-ABAP. In case there's an update to the code, it will be updated on the existing GitHub repository.

We also have other code bundles from our rich catalog of books and videos available at https://github.com/PacktPublishing/. Check them out!

Download the color images

We also provide a PDF file that has color images of the screenshots/diagrams used in this book. You can download it here: `https://www.packtpub.com/sites/default/files/ downloads/9781787288942_ColorImages.pdf`.

Code in action

Visit the following link to check out videos of the code being run: `http://bit.ly/2M4ILyK`.

Conventions used

There are a number of text conventions used throughout this book.

`CodeInText`: Indicates code words in the text, database table names, folder names, filenames, file extensions, pathnames, dummy URLs, user input, and Twitter handles. Here is an example: "In the **Details** window, create lines `%C1` and `%C2` with the values that are shown in the following screenshot."

A block of code is set as follows:

```
<script
    id="sap-ui-bootstrap"
    src="resources/sap-ui-core.js"
    data-sap-ui-libs="sap.m"
    data-sap-ui-theme="sap_belize">
</script>
```

When we wish to draw your attention to a particular part of a code block, the relevant lines or items are set in bold:

```
data-sap-ui-bindingSyntaxt="complex"
data-sap-ui-resourceroots='{ "my.namespace":"./" }'
```

Any command-line input or output is written as follows:

```
$ mkdir css
$ cd css
```

Bold: Indicates a new term, an important word, or words that you see onscreen. For example, words in menus or dialog boxes appear in the text like this. Here is an example: "Select **System info** from the **Administration** panel."

Warnings or important notes appear like this.

 Tips and tricks appear like this.

Get in touch

Feedback from our readers is always welcome.

General feedback: If you have questions about any aspect of this book, mention the book title in the subject of your message and email us at customercare@packtpub.com.

Errata: Although we have taken every care to ensure the accuracy of our content, mistakes do happen. If you have found a mistake in this book, we would be grateful if you would report this to us. Please visit www.packt.com/submit-errata, selecting your book, clicking on the Errata Submission Form link, and entering the details.

Piracy: If you come across any illegal copies of our works in any form on the Internet, we would be grateful if you would provide us with the location address or website name. Please contact us at copyright@packt.com with a link to the material.

If you are interested in becoming an author: If there is a topic that you have expertise in and you are interested in either writing or contributing to a book, please visit authors.packtpub.com.

Reviews

Please leave a review. Once you have read and used this book, why not leave a review on the site that you purchased it from? Potential readers can then see and use your unbiased opinion to make purchase decisions, we at Packt can understand what you think about our products, and our authors can see your feedback on their book. Thank you!

For more information about Packt, please visit packt.com.

1
Creating Custom Code

The chapter is an introduction to the **Systems, Applications, Products (SAP)** system. You will learn how to organize their daily work, how to act within SAP systems, how to add custom code, and how to change software features of SAP systems. This chapter presents modern techniques of cooperation within a company. Basic knowledge of these issues is required to work with the SAP system. This chapter is an introduction to the more complex and difficult topics contained in this book.

The following topics will be covered in this chapter:

- Making changes
- Design thinking
- **Big Design Up Front/Little Design Up Front (BDUF/LDUF)**
- Designing for quality and use
- Designing the **User Interface (UI)**
- Designing the services
- Designing the business logic
- Designing the database
- Agile principles
- DevOps
- Continuous Delivery

Technical requirements

This chapter does not have complex technical requirements. To check the solutions and examples, it is worth having user access to the SAP system. Other information (for example, agile designing the UI) can be better understood by IT employees. However, it is worthwhile for everyone who's interested in working with SAP systems to read the information contained in this chapter.

All the code used in this chapter can be downloaded from the following GitHub link: `https://github.com/PacktPublishing/Mastering-SAP-ABAP/tree/master/Chapter01`.

Making changes

There are several ways in SAP to make changes. Some of them are configuration changes, and some are purely programmatical changes.

SAP systems can be enhanced in five ways:

- **Customizing**: Specific business and functional process configuration according to the implementation guide. The need to make these changes is predicted by SAP and the procedure of implementation has been developed.
- **Personalization**: Setting up global attributes to display certain fields (such as default values or switching off the display of a field).
- **Modification**: These are changes SAP Repository objects make at the client side. SAP also can deliver a new version of those objects, and customers need to reflect these changes in the system. Before version 4.0B, customers needed to make this adjustment manually using upgrade utilities. From 4.5A, customers can use the Modification Assistant to automate this procedure.
- **Enhancement**: Creating a repository object inside a standard SAP program. More details about enhancement will be in `Chapter 10`, *Modification and Customization Techniques*.
- **Custom development**: This means creating objects that are unique to the client repository, which is created in the specified namespace, such as `Y*` or `Z*`, for all new objects.

In your daily work as an ABAP programmer, your most common work is creating custom developments and enhancements. Since we have a chapter on enhancements, we will focus here on custom development.

In custom development, we can create a custom program and dictionary elements. There will be more about creating dictionary elements in `Chapter 2`, *The Basic Structure of ABAP*.

As an example, we will show you how to create one of the most basic programs: *Hello World*.

In the first step, we need to open one of the most commonly used transactions in our daily work—SE80. This transaction is called **Object Navigator**, and is a transaction where we can create, change, and delete most ABAP objects.

The main window for the SE80 transaction looks like this:

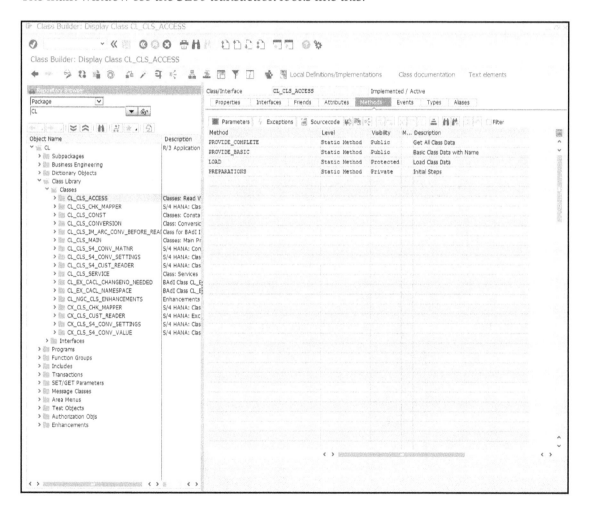

First, to open the SE80 transaction, we need to put the name of the transaction in the search box, as shown in the following screenshot:

Press *enter*, or click on .

After opening a transaction, we need to choose the **Program** option in the drop-down list on the left and enter the name Z_HELLO_WORLD in the window, as shown in the following example, and press *Enter*:

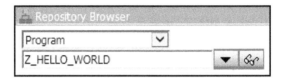

In the next window, choose **Yes**:

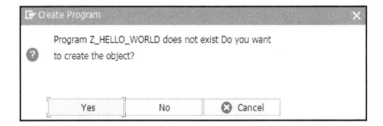

Confirm the name of a new program in the next window. Click on or press *Enter*:

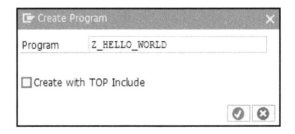

In the next window, define the attributes of the program, and now press *Enter* or click on
Save:

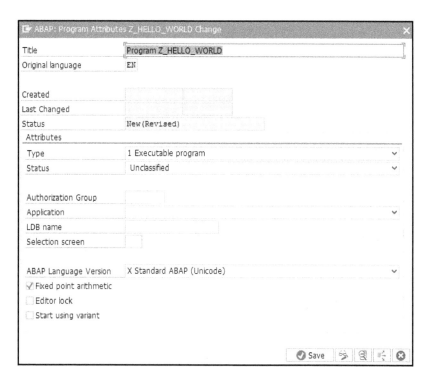

After this, choose a package. We need to create a program as a local object, so click on
Local Object:

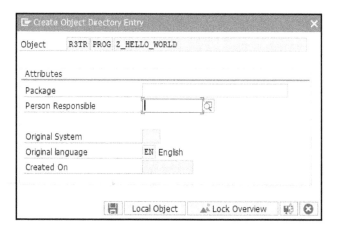

After this, we get a window like this:

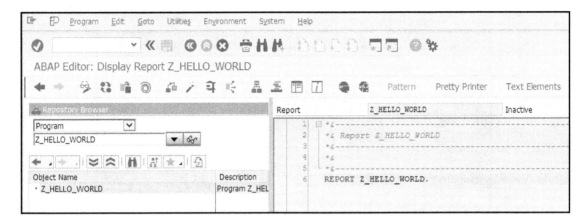

Now change the mode to **Change** by clicking on the icon or pressing *Ctrl + F1*. The background color of the window with the code will change to white. Now we put the code there.

To print `Hello world` on the screen, we just need to add this:

```
WRITE 'Hello World'.
```

> Remember! All ABAP custom programs needs `REPORT NAME_OF_PROGRAM` at the beginning.

The program looks similar to the following screenshot:

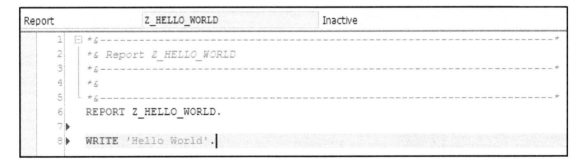

The program now needs to be activated. To activate it, click on ✐ or press *Ctrl + F3*. When an object has been activated, a message will be shown: ✔ Object activated .

To execute the program, click on ⬕ or press *F8*:

The result of the program is shown in the preceding screenshot.

Design thinking

Design thinking is a method of creative problem-solving. This method is designed to deliver innovative solutions by using a specific work method. The motto of this method is *doing, not talking,* so going over every detail of the project is changed into a multi stage division of tasks in order to extend and refine subsequent tasks.

The process of design thinking is divided into five steps:

1. **Empathy**: All of the new solutions are created for people. Therefore, the needs of a given group of people should be known, and this is why empathy is the starting point of all projects created by design thinking. To find the optimal solution, we need to see how this solution will help the common user.

2. **Define the problem**: In this stage, we need to define the exact problem to solve. We need to remember not to define problems in too narrow or too wide a range so that the solution will not be limited by rigid frames.

3. **Ideas**: This stage consists of creating as many ideas as possible for solutions relating to the previously defined problem. In this step, a brainstorm is very useful. The important thing is not to stick to your own ideas, and not to judge others. These sessions should be ended by choosing a concrete solution, which will be picked from the previously selected ideas.

4. **Prototypes**: Creating the prototypes is an indispensable step. Building prototypes should not be a very complicated process. The most important thing is to make a preliminary visualization of the idea, because only in that way can the idea be tested naturally. Every subsequent prototype should be created by thinking of the user and answering concrete questions.

5. **Tests**: This step is extremely important. In this step, the product is tested in a real environment, so you can check that it functions correctly. Every prototype can be evaluated by the group (for example, the project group), and the best one will be chosen for further improvements. Testing should be repeated until a satisfactory result is obtained.

BDUF/LDUF

LDUF is the process of modeling a small subsystem before coding, and BDUF is also a process of modeling, but in BDUF, the whole system needs to be modeled before implementation. BDUF can also be an anti-pattern for many reasons, but LDUF (or many occurrences of LDUF within a project) is often helpful.

BDUF occurs in one of two categories:

- A document of the high-level architecture, which determines the key features of architecture, but the rest of the things are unspecified and/or unclear.
- General documentation should describe everything from high-level architecture to the smallest detail of the system. These documents are often incoherent as there are no automatic ways to cross-check them.

LDUF can be precise and concise, and many programmers/architects can check/verify LDUF and detect any inconsistencies.

Generating and changing BDUF is often hard and expensive. It requires teams of analysts, consultants, and architects, and support from many layers of management. LDUF is light and informal—often, a programmer can do a mock-up, and if it's checked, it can be checked by a small team.

These are the main aspects of LDUF:

- Highly informal; it can be made by yourself or with a small team of programmers.
- Code is created in a small subsystem, which can be as small as even one class, function, or package.
- Often not prescriptive—the results are to be used as advice, not requirements.

BDUF is prescriptive—the code must be consistent with the paper project; all exceptions require management intervention. Additionally, it is anti-productive for many of the reasons mentioned in the preceding points.

Designing for quality and use

When designing new software, it is not only a matter of creating functional code. The eventual outcome is going to be a product that serves its purpose, but is also possible to improve, is robust, is easily maintained, and can be used for a long time. From the user's perspective, once the product is paid for, it won't require much more cost in terms of funds, man effort, or any other measurable value.

In order to fulfill these goals and achieve user satisfaction, the philosophy of quality engineering was introduced. In principle, it defines product quality as the ratio of the result of efforts and the total cost; however, in detail, it considers various factors, such as reliability, maintainability, continuous improvement, corrective actions, and risk management.

Particularly in software engineering, there is a need to estimate the quality through an *end-to-end* view. It requires the collaboration of various actors, whose roles are mostly independent—business architects, security officers, project managers, and more.

One of the basic steps in designing for quality is to determine quality objectives that describe the requirements for software quality. The software quality should be considered in two areas:

- How it complies with functional requirements—whether the developed product is actually doing what it is supposed to do
- How it meets the non-functional requirements—whether it reaches its goals in the correct way

Once the objectives are defined, they can be measured with help of appropriate models and various methods, such as **Goal Question Metric (GQM)**, **Balanced Scoreboard (BS)**, or **Practical Software Measurement (PSM)**.

There is no universal way to measure and control the value of quality in all environments. From the vast list of factors, several apply to SAP systems, and should always be considered when developing new code:

- **Understandability**: Both the code and all the documentation should be readable by peers.
- **Conciseness**: Not only should the code be kept small, but it also should not process unnecessary data.
- **Consistency**: The software should follow the notation conventions present in the system.
- **Maintainability**: It should be well documented and not complex (modularized as needed) to allow for future updates.
- **Testability**: The software should be written in a way that allows tests to check its correctness and performance.
- **Reliability**: The code should behave properly (non-erroneously) in all conditions.
- **Security**: It should always consider preventive measures to avoid unauthorized access to important data.

Depending on the level of interaction with the user, there are several additional factors that should be considered:

- The intuitiveness of the UI
- Ease of use
- Sensibleness of messages, for example, errors
- Responsiveness of the interface

Although these terms tend to be subjective and, in general, hard to determine in the design phase, they have a major impact on the quality of the software as seen by the end user, and therefore, cannot be neglected.

Designing the UI

The practical approach of building and implementing user interfaces will be shown in `Chapter 7`, *Building User Interfaces*, and `Chapter 8`, *Creating Stunning UI5 Interfaces*. There are, however, some ground rules and guidelines that should be followed when designing UIs:

- **Use written words**: As a rule, the software should be as self-descriptive as possible. Although graphical interfaces use images or any other means of communication, it is still encouraged to give the user appropriate and relevant information with text.
- **Use the user's language**: All messages, field names, and texts should be defined in the user's language (if possible).
- **Use consistent terminology**: The same objects should be named the same way throughout the environment.

Creating a user interface for R/3 transactions requires a few decisions to be taken up front. One of the most important decisions is to determine the basic type of application:

- **With screen changes**:
  - None, or a few areas on the page
  - Simple, sequential navigation
- **With multiple areas**:
  - Few or no changes to the main screen; several areas with lot of interaction between them
  - Provides stable context

Both types have pros and cons, and the choice depends on several criteria—length of processing, the amount of detail required, the user type (such as casual or expert), and the data type (such as a flat structure or volume).

The main goal of the design is to facilitate the user's focus on the current task, while more or less ignoring irrelevant details. In order to do so, use expand and collapse areas and splitters.

When designing R/3 screens in detail, there are several effects—psychological principles—that should be considered to improve the perception of information:

- **The effect of proximity**: Items that are close together tend to be *grouped* in our perception.
- **The effect of similarity**: Items of the same size, shape, or quality are likely to be viewed as a group or pattern.
- **The effect of closure**: Lines that enclose areas are perceived as units.
- **The effect of continuity**: Items arranged into a unified layout are perceived as a unit.

Designing services

Services, in principle, are meant to be consumed by some other part of the system, or even by an external system. It is required to keep in mind that the service may not, and most likely will not, be able to determine where and when it is used. This is why this type of development needs to be particularly robust and reliable, as various areas of the system may depend on its correct functioning.

When designing the services, aside from their scenario-specific implementation needs, there are several things that should be considered in order to minimize upgrade and maintenance costs:

- **Keep services singular-task oriented**: Even if the service is supposed to perform many actions on the system, one entry point should perform one consistent end-to-end task (for example, creating a business object, or deleting one). Avoid mixing multiple tasks in a single service call.
- **Avoid direct database manipulation in services**: Delegate all logic to the business logic layer.
- **Expect, but check**: Do not assume that all the required data is provided by the caller, and always verify its consistency.
- **Provide consistent and explanatory responses**, especially when errors occur, so the caller can react accordingly.
- **Keep the service well documented**, so it is clear from the consumer's perspective what to expect when calling a particular part of it.
- **If possible, keep the service's interface unchanged**: Even small changes to the interface will require adjustments in the consumer's implementation. Utilize optional parameters to keep backward compatibility.

Designing the business logic

The business logic layer is meant to handle business objects and the interaction between them. Decouple it from the service and database layers—it should know as little about the database access or user interaction as possible, yet exchange information with them as needed using a level of abstraction, such as interfaces or base classes. The business logic should focus on transforming and calculating data, leaving other tasks to other layers.

Minimize the complexity of the business logic itself by separating concerns into different areas. Keep the processing, workflow, and business entities separated and loosely coupled. The separation will make the implementation easier to follow, whereas loose coupling will allow modification with a relatively low cost. Then, make sure you avoid the duplication of functionalities in different areas by reusing common parts of business logic.

Identify the consumers of the business layer so that the data can be exposed in the desired way. This will prevent the additional effort of converting data from one format to another. Having consumers in mind, make sure you have prepared not only the functional logic, but also various auxiliary aspects, such as security requirements, validations, exception management, and concurrency—keep them consistent and manage them centrally if possible.

Do not forget about unexpected situations and audits—use logs to store the history of critical changes or errors, yet without business-sensitive data. Ensure that errors in the logging process itself do not affect the normal functionality of the system—keep it as a separate logical unit. Make sure that the logged information is sufficient to track the root causes of any problems.

Designing the database

Designing the database is an essential part of the company's organization. This is a definition that covers data organization according to the model adopted. Designing the database prepares how data is to be linked in tables. It is also necessary to specify which data should be stored. Designing the database provides easier design, expansion, and maintenance of the SAP system. The correct design of the database greatly influences the optimization and quality of the system.

Creating logical and physical models of the database system is the target in designing databases. It is a complicated and complex process due to the use of relational databases in SAP systems. This architecture has its own great advantages, and a proper design simplifies the implementation of the ABAP language.

The logical model contains information on data storage, but there is no information on how it will be stored. This model makes it easier to analyze the structure of an information system that's unrelated to a specific database implementation. A physical data model enables us to analyze the tables, views, and other objects in a database. The physical data design model includes changing the logical database design to a physical layer. The designer uses software systems for this purpose, such as **database management systems** (**DBMSes**). A DBMS is system software for creating and managing databases.

In the SAP system, it is possible to graphically show connections using foreign keys. Using this tool is extremely simple. The user enters the table, for example, through SE11 transactions.

After clicking on the button shown in the following screenshot, the SAP system will display the tool in a separate window:

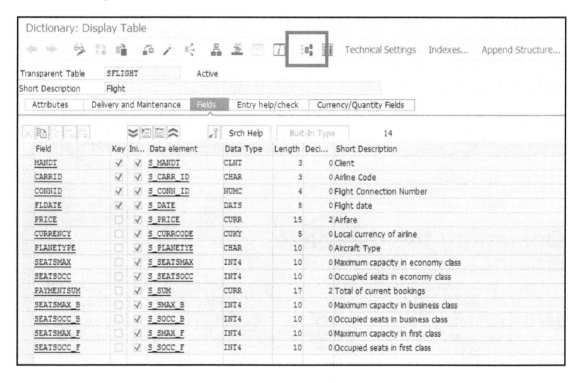

An example of how to connect to the **SFLIGHT** table is shown in the following screenshot:

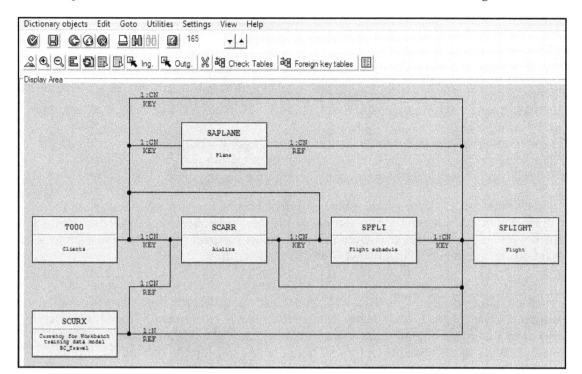

This allows the user to view all the tables that are associated with a foreign key. A double-click on one of the related tables moves the user to this table. Information on the types of relationship between tables is also included here.

Agile principles

In 2001, the *Manifesto for Agile Software Development* was created. This is an alternative to the cascaded way of generating software. The manifesto describes agile as a philosophy for carrying out various projects, including IT projects.

The basis of the Agile Manifesto includes four basic principles:

- Individuals and interactions over processes and tools
- Working software over comprehensive documentation

- Customer collaboration over contract negotiation
- Responding to change over following a plan

The manifesto means that the values described on the left are more important than the ones on the right. It's no coincidence that people are placed first. The success of each project depends on them. If the team has the right skills and a lot of commitment, there is a good chance that each project will be successfully completed. Interactions between team members speed up the work and allow the use of maximally positive aspects of teamwork.

The second point indicates what is most important from the point of view of the software recipient. Even the best documentation cannot replace properly working software. The working end product is the basis for considering whether the project has been successful.

A quick response to changes causes the team to be able to deliver the ideal product to the recipient. It builds a sense of professionalism and can contribute to the expansion of business cooperation with the current investor. Agile is a great project management tool that helps to eliminate the likelihood of an IT project failure.

Work based on agile methodologies takes advantage of an iterative and incremental approach. This means that the team of programmers is focused on the fast, cyclic, and orderly delivery of product elements. The result of this is greater flexibility. This is very important due to the high frequency of changes, along with building solutions. Agile methodologies of software development do not have rigid conditions and assumptions regarding every aspect of the project.

DevOps

DevOps is an organizational culture whose assumption is to combine the work of software development teams and operations teams. DevOps is an innovative approach to software development. The benefits of using this approach are, among others, as follows:

- Time and cost savings
- Shortening the time of product implementation
- Quick changes in products
- Better-fitting functionalities
- More accurate verification of correctness
- Advantage over competitors
- Better team cooperation

DevOps uses iterative work growth in accordance with agile methodologies. This gives the product recipient the opportunity to quickly read the results of the work. DevOps characterizes a fast and visible change in the company's operations. Teams carry out projects that are more suited to the needs of users.

DevOps assumes smooth communication between technical teams and, at the same time, assumes the following:

- The product is built from the perspective of the whole.
- Accurate testing from the initial functionality.
- Relying on reliable data.
- Reducing the time of software development.

Continuous delivery

Continuous delivery is a concept of software development. It is based on the assumption that software is created in short intervals of time. This approach allows you to create solutions tailored to the current business needs of recipients. A very important feature of this method of sharing the finished product is the need to accept the possibility of running the software on the main (production) system. The remaining elements of the implementation process are automated. The process is also characterized by a repetitive delivery cycle.

Continuous delivery is similar to the method of **continuous implementation**, in which software is also produced in short cycles, but with the help of an automatic process in terms of production transfer.

Summary

This chapter describes how the user can organize their daily work and operate in a broader context. We've looked at some ideas for becoming a more attentive developer or architect. At an advanced level, readers will be able to organize several topics within complex projects, including managing stakeholders. At a basic level, the user should be familiar with the daily activities of a project manager or architect and has learned how to integrate with the complex configuration of the project.

The next chapter will describe the world of modern SAP systems, with a basic outline of the ABAP language and gives you a view on older syntactic data and their equivalents, which are used in modern ABAP systems.

Questions

The following questions will allow you to consolidate the information contained in this chapter:

1. What are the positive aspects of using agile methods?
2. What are the principles of the agile manifesto?
3. What is the difference between a logical model and a physical model when designing a database?
4. List the possible programming changes in SAP.
5. What is the motto of design thinking, and why is it coherent with the design thinking methodology?
6. In which categories does BDUF occur?
7. What aspects of development impact the quality of the design?
8. Why should business logic be loosely coupled?

The Basic Structure of ABAP 2

This chapter will provide you with a quick introduction into the world of modern **systems applications products** (**SAP**) systems, along with a basic outline of the **advanced business application programming** (**ABAP**) language. We will take a look at legacy syntax figures and their counterparts, which are often used in modern ABAP systems.

In this chapter, we will explain basic data structures, the principles of data manipulation, and also typical hardware and software features of SAP systems. This knowledge is necessary for navigating the SAP system and creating applications.

In this chapter, we will cover the following topics:

- The Data Dictionary
- Domains
- Data elements
- Structures
- Table types

Technical requirements

All the code used in this chapter can be downloaded from the following GitHub link: `https://github.com/PacktPublishing/Mastering-SAP-ABAP/tree/master/Chapter02`.

The Data Dictionary

The Data Dictionary is a set of information describing the objects of a database and the relationship between its elements.

The Data Dictionary is used to control access to and manipulation of the database.

The **Data Dictionary** includes a domain, **Types** (**StRUCTURES**, **DATA TYPE**, and **TABLE TYPE**), tables, views, search helps, and lock objects.

The following diagram explains the division of objects in a **Data Dictionary**:

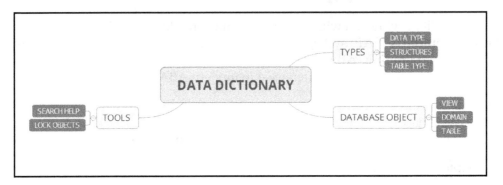

To create an object for the Data Dictionary, we need to use the SE11 transaction. The transaction code is usually only a few characters long and guides you directly to the screen of the task that the user wants to perform. This screen is shown in the following screenshot:

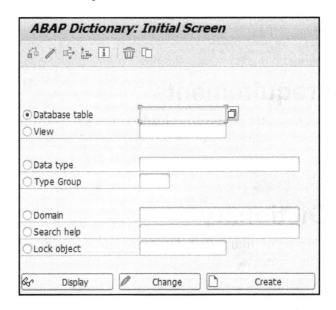

Domains

A domain is an object that describes various technical attributes, such as the data type length of a table field. A domain is assigned to a data element. One domain can be assigned to many data elements.

Creating a domain is very easy and quick. We don't need specialized knowledge. The following is the typical procedure for creating the data element:

1. Go to **Transaction SE11**, select the radio button for **Domain**, and enter the name you wish to give it, preferably something you will remember when you see it. Then, click on **Create.** It is important that the names of the domains follow the convention of Z (or Y) prefixes:

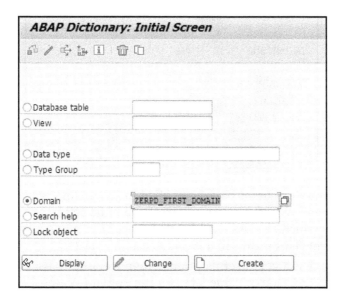

2. The **Definition** tab defines the technical data. The user enters the description of the data. In this step, we must select the data type (what kind of data this is), as well as the number of characters. Fortunately, the SAP environment is very friendly. If we forget to fill in a field that's mandatory, the system will not allow you to save the changes. We have the option to enter a decimal place if we choose a numeric data type. Conversion is the procedure that SAP uses to normalize the data held in the various tables, but it is not obligatory. There are two methods in a conversion routine. The first adjusts the data to the variable, while the other changes the data so that it's in a more readable output form.

In summary, this is a way we can adjust the values to variables. The **Lower Case** checkbox allows you to store lowercase characters (as stated by its label). By default (when it is not checked), the values are stored in uppercase. The following screenshot explains what fields you need to fill in to create a domain:

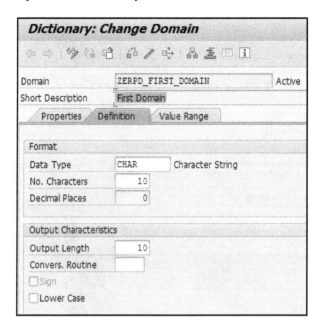

3. All the mandatory fields have been filled in so we can save our domain. In the SAP system, if we want to use an object, we must activate it. Activation is the process by which execution causes the object to be made available to the runtime environment. This means that it can be used or started.

4. **Value Range** is a very useful option. Often, we need to use specific data. We can define a single value or value table for the domain. **Value Table** is one of the properties of a semantic domain and contains the default values of the field control table. Only the values contained in this table can be used. The following screenshot explains how to *define a value in a domain*:

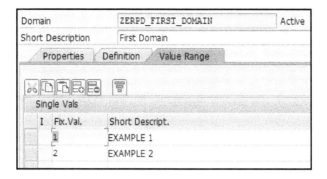

If we want to check or use this data, we can use a simple program:

```
DATA: lt_value_domain TYPE TABLE OF dd07v.

CALL FUNCTION 'DD_DOMVALUES_GET'
  EXPORTING
    text      = 'X'
    domname   = 'ZERPD_FIRST_DOMAIN'
  TABLES
    dd07v_tab = lt_value_domain.
```

The result of the preceding program is a table with values:

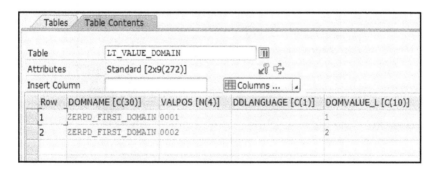

Now let's move on to the next section.

Data elements

Data elements are objects that describe the unitary fields in the Data Dictionary. It should be emphasized that the domain is used to define technical parameters, while the data element is more function-oriented (because it has labels explaining its purpose). This object is used to define the type of the table field, as well as the structure of the component.

Follow these steps to create a data element:

1. Go to **Transaction SE11**, select the radio button for the **Data Type** element, and enter a name for it. Then, click on **Create**:

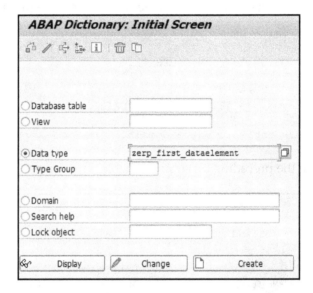

2. Choose the **Data element** checkbox and press *Enter*:

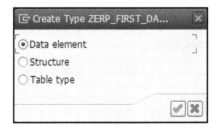

3. Enter a short description and assign the element with the type. The user can assign one of the following types to the data:
   - Domain
   - Elementary type
   - Reference type

The following screenshot explains the data element creation screen:

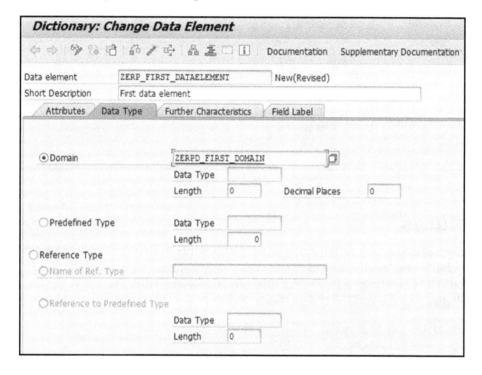

4. Enter the fields for **Short** text, **Medium** text, **Long** text, and **Heading** in the **Field Label** tab, as shown in the following screenshot. Then, save and activate your changes:

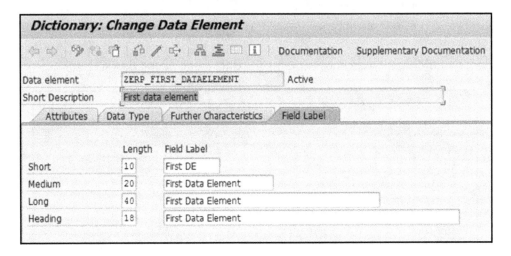

Structures

The structure is a data object that consists of components or fields. This data object can be created globally and locally. The user can create a global structure using the SE11 transaction. The creation of a local structure can be implemented in two ways. The first way is by implementing the code in the method:

```
TYPES: BEGIN OF tt_type,
         first_data  TYPE string,
         second_data TYPE i,
         third_data  TYPE c,
       END OF tt_type.
```

This solution has the limitation that it is only implemented in one method. If we want to use a structure in another class, we must create types in the class editor:

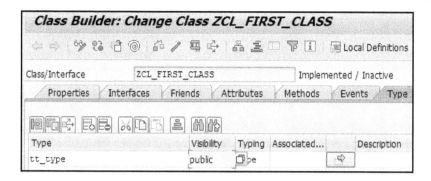

When we enter **Direct Type Entry**, we develop the preceding code.

A structure can be used in classes, report programs, interfaces, and module pools. If we create a table, we use a structure to determine what fields will be used. A structure may have only a single record at runtime.

The creation of a structure in the SAP system can also be performed using SE11 Transaction.

In the **Data type** field, the name of the created structure is entered and the **Create** button must be pressed. The window of this transaction with the structure name entered is as follows:

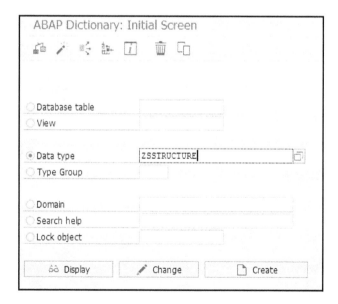

The system asks what type of data the user wants to create. The user should choose **Structure**. After entering the creation screen, enter a short description of the structure being created. In the window that appears, you can enter any variable names and specify their type. There are two ways of declaring variables in the structure. The first option is to use existing data types. The user can also use predefined data types. For example, the completed fields of the structure are shown in the following screenshot:

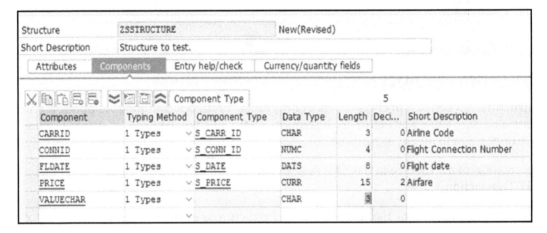

In the **Attributes** section, information about the structure creator, last change time, and the package is available. This information is useful when the structure needs to be expanded and there is a need to consult its creator. To use the created structure, the creator should save and activate it. A structure that's created in this way can be used in any program in the SAP system.

Search helps

One of the most important elements of the Data Dictionary is its ability to help you implement search helps. It allows you to find all the required values. Of course, if we need to narrow down our search, we can do that. Creating a search help in SAP is very simple and is used often.

There are two types of search helps in the SAP system:

- A collective search help
- An elementary search help

A collective search help is a combination of several elementary searches. This search help object specifies a series of search process paths for the object. This category has an interface that carries values because the results are transferred between the basic search help and the input template.

An elementary search help is used to display the possible entries of values into the field. This helps in completing the fields as we can select values from the list.

In order to create a search help, the user should select SE11 transactions and select the appropriate checkbox. The next step is to enter a name and press the **Create** button. In the next window, the system will ask what category the user wants to choose. For the example shown, **Elementary srch hlp** was selected. After accepting this type of category, the system will display the creation screen, as follows:

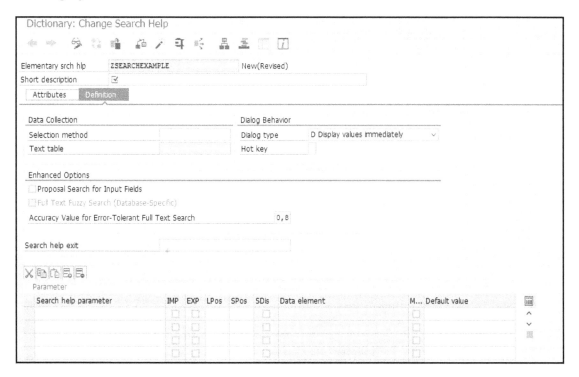

Just like many other objects in the SAP system, a short description is obligatory. In the **Selection method** field, the user can enter tables that values will be collected from. The type dialog is used to specify the appearance of the limiting dialog box. To use the search help tool, the system requires the selection of the parameters that will be used. The user can do this in the parameter section. In the parameter section, it is possible to fill in the following fields:

- Import (**IMP**): Determines whether the parameter is imported
- Export (**EXP**): Determines whether the parameter is exported
- **LPos**: Entering the value determines where the field will appear in the selection list
- **SPos**: Entering the value determines where the field will appear in the restrictive dialog box

An example screen with completed data is as follows:

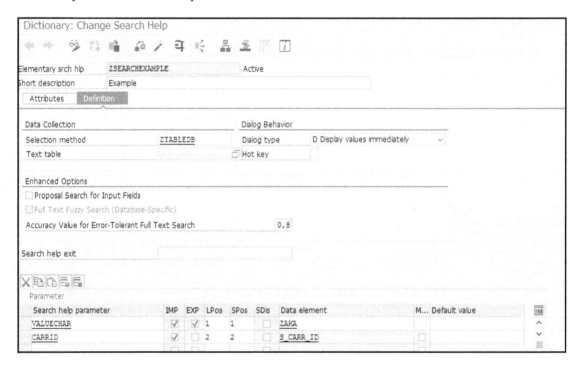

After creating, saving, and activating, it is possible to test the search help tool that was created. In this example, the search help is as follows:

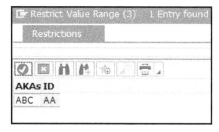

As we can see, the search help works without any problems.

Table types

The table type is one of the elements of the ABAP dictionary in the SAP system. Its main purpose is to defend the internal table and the sourcing of structures. Like the other elements, it is created in Transaction SE11. A table type created by this transaction is available globally. This means that, once created, an object can be used in many programs, not depending on the place. Changes in these objects must be thought out because they can affect many processes and cause their incorrect operation. The second way to create a type table is to create it locally. It is then included in the program's code and is only available in this area.

During the creation of a types table in a SE11 transaction, the user can choose one of the following types of data access:

- A standard table
- A sorted table
- A hashed table
- An index table
- Not specified

Databases

In most cases, business processes in the SAP system are based on recorded data. For this purpose, a model based on relational data is used. A database table is, therefore, an object for storing data. It offers many possibilities to support the work of a programmer.

Creating a table is as simple as it is in the other objects of the dictionary. The user starts this process in the SE11 transaction—they select the **Database table** checkbox and enter a name (which must start with the character Z or Y), as shown in the following screenshot:

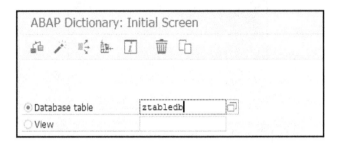

Then, they need to click on the **Create** button. The SAP system will take the user to a screen where they can choose some options. A short description should be entered as it is an obligatory field. The screen the user will see is as follows:

As we can see, there are two fields to fill in at this stage. The first one (**Delivery Class**) determines what kind of data will be stored. The following entries are available:

- **A**: An application table (master and transaction data)
- **C**: A customization table, maintenance only by the customer, with no SAP imports
- **L**: A table for storing temporary data. This is delivered empty
- **G**: A customer table, protected against SAP updates

- **E**: A control table where SAP and customers have separate key areas
- **S**: A system table, where maintenance is only performed by SAP
- **W**: A system table whose contents can be transported through separate **Transport Request (TR)** objects

Selecting one of these options controls how the data is transported. It is also used in the extended table. The second option specifies the ability to display and make changes to the database table in the following ways:

- **Display/Maintenance** allowed with restrictions
- **Display/Maintenance** allowed
- **Display/Maintenance** not allowed

After selecting the appropriate options for the database, the user can go to the **Fields** section. For example, a table filled with fields is shown in the following screenshot:

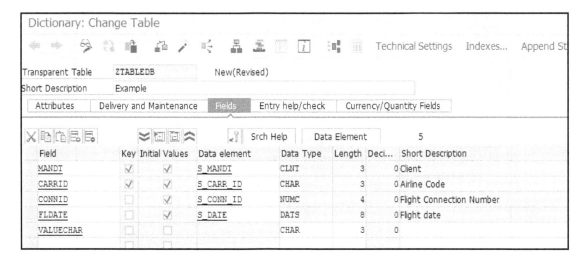

When a field is added to the table, the user must specify its name and type. The item data can be used to determine the type. You can use its attributes, such as a description, for this. The use of basic types is also allowed. However, the system forces you to select the number of characters. The user can specify which fields will represent the key in the table and whether the values in the fields must be non-initial.

An important part of creating an object is defining its technical settings. It isn't possible to activate the database table without specifying these conditions. After selecting this option, the system will move the user to a screen like the following:

In the **Data Class** option, the user can choose what data is stored in the table and the transport system. Each of the available classes determines the physical area in which the system stores data. The available choices are shown in the following screenshot:

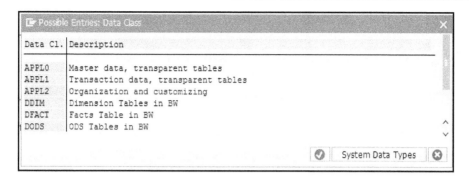

Another option is to specify the number of records stored in the database. The ranges are as follows:

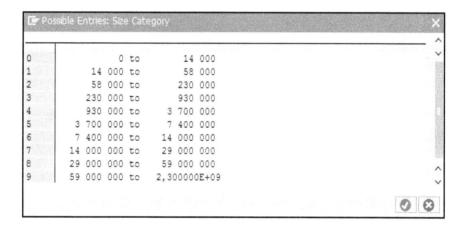

In this section, the options for caching and saving the change log are also available. To make the table available, save it and activate it.

Data declaration

After learning about the objects in the Data Dictionary, we can start talking about the syntax declaration in ABAP. The easiest way to declare variables is as follows:

```
data: lv_first_variable TYPE c.
```

Variables are named data objects that are used to store values within the allotted memory area of a program. It is good practice to properly name local variables. It is assumed that the first two characters in the variable name determine its use. The first letter indicates whether the variable is global or local. If the local variable starts with l, then in the case of global variables, g is the first letter. The second character determines what type the object is:

- **Variable**: v
- **Line**: s
- **Internal table**: t

Each variable must have a type that describes what is stored inside. A variable may have the following types:

- Elementary types
- References
- User-defined types
- Generic ABAP types

In the ABAP language, you can use predefined types to define local data types and objects in a program and to specify the type of interface parameters and field symbols. These are divided into numeric types, character types, and hexadecimal types. These types can be defined globally in the ABAP Data Dictionary or locally in an ABAP program. Some data types are already defined in the ABAP Data Dictionary. Variables are also divided by type. The first type is static variables, which are declared in subroutines, function modules, and static methods.

The elementary types are mentioned in ABAP. They can be used directly to define a variable. User-created types are also based on elementary ones. The SAP system has the following elementary types:

- Type c: Its initial size is 1, and the range of characters it can accept is 1-65535. The initial value is space. It accepts alphanumeric characters. It's used to process text.
- Type N: This type of variable contains strings of digits. It is like the c type variable since it has an initial size of 1 and a maximum of 65535. Its initial value is 0, and it is used to express identifying numbers.
- Type D: This is an eight-character variable. The type used for the date. The initial value is 00000000.

- Type T: This is a six-character variable. The type used for the time value. The initial value is 000000.
- Type I: This is used to store integers, and the initial value is 0. The range of values is $+2^{31}$ to -2^{31}.
- Type F: This is a floating-point number, where the accuracy range is approximately 15 decimals. The range of values is 10^{307} to -10^{307}.
- Type P: Numbers are stored in compressed formats; they are a maximum of 31 digits.
- Type STRING: Like type C, there is no defined length.
- Type XSTRING: Like type X, there is no defined length.

For the C, N, D, I, and F variables, the programmer can define a length. If they don't, the variables will take the minimum number of characters. The user can also specify their initial values, other than standard values. An example initialization of a variable that has 3 characters with the initial value, 'ABC', is shown in the following code:

```
data: lv_first_variable(3) TYPE c VALUE 'ABC'.
```

As we can see, the number of characters is written after the variable name in brackets. Adding the word VALUE at the end of the initialization adds the initial value.

Field symbol

A **field symbol** is an instrument in which applications are created with elasticity. Field symbols do not have any memory; instead, they will be pointing to a memory location. An element can be compared to a pointer from other programming languages.

The following code will help you to declare field symbols using different typing methods:

```
TYPES: BEGIN OF ts_type,
         first_data  TYPE string,
         second_data TYPE i,
         third_data  TYPE c,
       END OF tt_type.

DATA : ls_type TYPE tt_type,
       lt_type TYPE STANDARD TABLE OF  tt_type.

FIELD-SYMBOLS: <fs_type1> TYPE c,
               <fs_type2> TYPE tt_type,
               <fs_type4> TYPE data,
               <fs_type5> TYPE any,
```

```
                          <fs_type6> TYPE ANY TABLE,
                          <fs_type7> LIKE ls_type,
                          <fs_type8> LIKE LINE OF lt_type.
```

In order to use a field symbol, we must assign it to the object value. This results in the o element not reserving a physical data field space:

```
ASSIGN lv_value TO <fs_value>.
```

Field symbols can also be used to reference internal table variables, as follows:

```
TYPES: BEGIN OF ts_type,
         first_data  TYPE string,
         second_data TYPE i,
         third_data  TYPE c,
       END OF ts_type.

DATA : lt_type TYPE STANDARD TABLE OF  ts_type.

LOOP AT lt_type ASSIGNING FIELD-SYMBOL(<fs>).
  <fs>-first_data = 'First_data'.
  <fs>-second_data = 2.
  <fs>-third_data = 'X'.
ENDLOOP.
```

The presented method of using the symbol field is one possible way of doing this. The declaration takes place dynamically in this case. You can also use the previously declared variable. An example of this implementation is as follows:

```
TYPES: BEGIN OF ts_type,
         first_data  TYPE string,
         second_data TYPE i,
         third_data  TYPE c,
       END OF ts_type.
DATA : lt_type TYPE STANDARD TABLE OF ts_type.

FIELD-SYMBOLS: <fs> TYPE ts_type.

LOOP AT lt_type ASSIGNING <fs>.
  <fs>-first_data = 'First_data'.
  <fs>-second_data = 2.
  <fs>-third_data = 'X'.
ENDLOOP.
```

Summary

This chapter described everything you need to know about when you work with the SAP system. It is worth you understanding this chapter because it is the introduction to the modern SAP system. The information in this chapter teaches you about the use of explicit techniques when working with the system dictionary.

The ABAP Dictionary contains information about all the metadata in the SAP system. The ABAP Dictionary is a very important part of the SAP system, and understanding it is necessary for fast and efficient programming. This issue is very extensive and, in most programming cases, you need to use the ABAP Dictionary.

In the next chapter, we will talk about database access in ABAP.

Questions

The following questions will allow you to consolidate the information contained in this chapter:

1. What characters must the names of the objects in the ABAP Dictionary begin with?
2. What is a field symbol?
3. What are the elementary types in the SAP system?

Database Access in ABAP 3

Reading and operating on databases is one of the most frequently used skills for an **Advanced Business Application Programming (ABAP)** developer. A good understanding of the principles of ABAP OpenSQL is an essential skill that is required for operating in databases. To access the database in SAP, we can use two types of SQLs—ABAP OpenSQL and Native SQL. The main difference between these is that OpenSQL can be used in all database platforms to gain access to database tables declared in the ABAP Dictionary, while through Native SQL, you can use a database-specific SQL statement, which allows you to use a table that is not managed by the ABAP Dictionary. One of the biggest issues with Native SQL is the fact that a query written in Native SQL cannot be used in all databases and is specific to each type of database. In this chapter, we will be looking at OpenSQL only.

In this chapter, we will cover the following topics:

- Extracting data from the database in an efficient way
- Using an advanced function of SQL, for example, Subquery
- The ability to change or delete data on databases
- Optimizing queries

Technical requirements

All the code used in this chapter can be downloaded from the following GitHub link: https://github.com/PacktPublishing/Mastering-SAP-ABAP/tree/master/Chapter03.

Starting with OpenSQL

As ABAP was invented as a report language, it has a huge set of statements for accessing tables. ABAP was designed for high-performance database operations, but not for the definition or control of database tables. By definition, it's usually not the mission of the program to create or control database tables. However, those functionalities are included implicitly within the SAP system.

The section of ABAP that accesses the database tables is named OpenSQL and includes similar commands to standard SQL, such as SELECT, INSERT, UPDATE, and DELETE, which are known as **data manipulation language** (**DML**). The differences between standard SQL and OpenSQL include the fact that OpenSQL is platform independent and part of the ABAP language. This enables the syntax check to identify errors within the implementation of the SQL statement. Furthermore, there are several variants of the commands that are only for ABAP programs, which ease or accelerate the database accesses.

The platform-dependent SQL is generated by the database interface of the ABAP interpreter as part of the **application server** (**AS**) ABAP.

The **data definition language** (**DDL**), with all database-dependent commands such as CREATE, ALTER, and DROP, is given implicitly by the SAP Data Dictionary, as explained in Chapter 1, *Creating Custom Code*.

The DCL of standard SQL is not included in ABAP. Data consistency has to be guaranteed through the proper use of the concept of the SAP **Logical Unit of Work** (**LUW**) and the SAP concept of database locks.

In this chapter, we will see how the database tables can be accessed and manipulated, how several tables can be read at one time, and how huge amounts of data can be read with high performance. You will also learn about some obsolete statements, as well as the current recommendations and best practices for accessing data with high performance and optimized SQL statements.

When you access the database tables within an ABAP program, you always have to have an eye on performance. In development or consolidation systems, the amount of accessible data doesn't usually exceed a couple of thousands. The amount of the same data in productive systems can be measured even in millions (this amount can be even higher when it comes to the **Internet of Things** (**IoT**), big data, and the SAP **High-Performance Analytic Appliance** (**HANA**)).

You should think a little about performance while implementing database access, as the costs of implementing high-performance statements are insignificant in comparison to the costs of optimizing programs that are already productive.

Basics

In the first section, I'd like to present the most basic aspects of how to extract data from a database. In this subsection, we will explore how to create a basic *select from* table, as well as look at what components the SELECT statement is creating.

The SELECT statement is built from at least three mandatory parts. The first part in the SELECT statement is the resulting set. The resulting set is a list of fields that state what we want to get from the selected table. For the resulting set, we can use a list of fields directly entered in the statement, or we can use * to get all fields in the table. However, using * is not recommended due to performance issues, as we often do not need all fields in a table – only a few of them. The second part is a FROM statement, used to define which table we want to get the data from. The third part is INTO, which makes it possible to define which internal variable or variables input the data.

All examples presented in this chapter will be presented in SELECT from the sflight table. This SELECT statement will gradually be expanded by new capabilities.

The following is an example of a basic SELECT statement:

```
SELECT *
    FROM sflight
    INTO TABLE gt_sflight.
```

In the preceding code snippet, we can see the most basic SELECT statement. This selects all fields from the sflight table and puts them into a previously prepared table, named gt_sflight.

Data selected in this query is presented in the following screenshot:

Client	Airline	Flight No.	Flight Date	Airfare	Currency	Plane Type	Capacity	Occupied	Total	Capacity	Occupied	Capacity	Occupied
400	AA	17	20.05.2015	422,94	USD	747-400	385	375	193.508,04	31	31	21	19
400	AA	17	17.06.2015	422,94	USD	747-400	385	372	191.490,54	31	30	21	20
400	AA	17	15.07.2015	422,94	USD	747-400	385	374	193.596,86	31	29	21	21
400	AA	17	12.08.2015	422,94	USD	747-400	385	366	190.259,80	31	30	21	20
400	AA	17	09.09.2015	422,94	USD	747-400	385	373	195.246,25	31	31	21	21
400	AA	17	07.10.2015	422,94	USD	747-400	385	373	190.475,54	31	30	21	19
400	AA	17	04.11.2015	422,94	USD	747-400	385	363	186.889,01	31	30	21	19
400	AA	17	02.12.2015	422,94	USD	747-400	385	374	193.190,71	31	29	21	20
400	AA	17	30.12.2015	422,94	USD	747-400	385	371	193.537,46	31	30	21	21
400	AA	17	27.01.2016	422,94	USD	747-400	385	124	64.045,87	31	9	21	7
400	AA	17	24.02.2016	422,94	USD	747-400	385	77	39.904,41	31	6	21	4
400	AA	17	23.03.2016	422,94	USD	747-400	385	143	73.781,98	31	11	21	8
400	AA	17	20.04.2016	422,94	USD	747-400	385	84	44.002,81	31	7	21	5
400	AA	17	18.05.2016	422,94	USD	747-400	385	41	20.423,81	31	3	21	2
400	AA	17	15.06.2016	422,94	USD	747-400	385	0	0,00	31	0	21	0

As we can see, all existing fields in this table were selected.

If we want to select only several fields—for example, `mandt`, `carrid`, and `connid`—from the `sflight` table, we can use the following SELECT statement:

```
SELECT mandt carrid connid
  FROM sflight
  INTO TABLE gt_sflight.
```

The result of the preceding query is as follows:

Client	Airline	Flight No.	Date	Price	Currency	Pl.type	Capacity	Occupied	Total	Capacity	Occupied	Capacity	Occupied
400	AA	17					0	0	0	0	0	0	0
400	AA	17					0	0	0	0	0	0	0
400	AA	17					0	0	0	0	0	0	0
400	AA	17					0	0	0	0	0	0	0
400	AA	17					0	0	0	0	0	0	0
400	AA	17					0	0	0	0	0	0	0
400	AA	17					0	0	0	0	0	0	0
400	AA	17					0	0	0	0	0	0	0
400	AA	17					0	0	0	0	0	0	0
400	AA	17					0	0	0	0	0	0	0
400	AA	17					0	0	0	0	0	0	0
400	AA	17					0	0	0	0	0	0	0
400	AA	17					0	0	0	0	0	0	0
400	AA	17					0	0	0	0	0	0	0
400	AA	17					0	0	0	0	0	0	0

As we only highlighted several fields, only those highlighted in the resulting set are selected from the table.

Possibilities with SELECT - the first part of the SQL statement

In the first part of the SQL statement (SELECT), we can also use the SELECT SINGLE and SELECT DISTINCT options. An example of SELECT SINGLE is as follows:

```
SELECT SINGLE carrid connid
    FROM sflight
    INTO gs_sflight.
```

When we use the SELECT SINGLE statement, we get only one record. The first row that is found is therefore placed in the results set.

The SELECT SINGLE statement should be used with a where condition, which is explained later in this book.

We can only use a work area as a target. When we use a SELECT SINGLE statement, we cannot use the ORDER BY and APPENDING clauses.

The following is an example of SELECT DISTINCT:

```
SELECT DISTINCT carrid connid
    FROM sflight
    INTO TABLE gt_sflight.
```

The result of the preceding query is as follows:

Client	Airline	Flight No.	Date	Price	Currency	Pl.type	Capacity	Occupied	Total	Capacity	Occupied	Capacity	Occupied
400	AA	17					0	0	0	0	0	0	
400	AA	64					0	0	0	0	0	0	
400	AZ	555					0	0	0	0	0	0	
400	AZ	788					0	0	0	0	0	0	
400	AZ	789					0	0	0	0	0	0	
400	AZ	790					0	0	0	0	0	0	
400	DL	106					0	0	0	0	0	0	
400	DL	1699					0	0	0	0	0	0	
400	DL	1984					0	0	0	0	0	0	
400	JL	407					0	0	0	0	0	0	
400	JL	408					0	0	0	0	0	0	
400	LH	400					0	0	0	0	0	0	
400	LH	401					0	0	0	0	0	0	
400	LH	402					0	0	0	0	0	0	
400	LH	2402					0	0	0	0	0	0	
400	LH	2407					0	0	0	0	0	0	

SELECT DISTINCT can be used when we want to exclude duplicate rows. As you can see, the selected values (marked in blue) are not the same in any rows.

Possibilities with INTO - the third part of the SQL statement

In the third part of the SELECT statement, we can also use several possibilities. These possibilities may include the following:

- INTO: When we choose this, we can select fields to structure. An example can be found in the explanation of SELECT SINGLE.
- INTO CORRESPONDING FIELDS OF: We can also use this addition, but, during SELECT, the system tries to select and match fields corresponding to data elements in a result. The differences in the results will be shown in the example.
- INTO [obj1, obj2 ...]: We can select fields in relation to a given variable. For example, if we want to select the carrid and connid fields, we can select these fields directly in relation to a variable instead of a structure or table.
- INTO TABLE: This is the same as INTO, but we can use a table rather than structure and we can also select more than one row.
- INTO CORRESPONDING FIELDS OF TABLE: This is the same as INTO CORRESPONDING FIELDS OF, but we can select more than one row here, and we need to use the table as an internal variable where we can store the result.
- APPENDING: Appending can be used when we want to append new rows instead of replacing them with a new selection, which is the case when using INTO.

What are the main differences between INTO and INTO CORRESPONDING FIELDS OF? Let me explain this by using an example.

When we use INTO, we need to remember to select the fields in the correct order. If we use SELECT, this is presented as follows:

```
SELECT connid carrid
    FROM sflight
    INTO TABLE gt_sflight.
```

We skip one `mandt` field and change the `carrid` and `connid` places and the result is as follows:

Client	Airline	Flight No.	Date	Price	Currency	Pl.type	Capacity	Occupied	Total Capacity	Occupied	Capacity	Occupied
001	AA						0	0	0	0	0	0
001	AA						0	0	0	0	0	0
001	AA						0	0	0	0	0	0
001	AA						0	0	0	0	0	0
001	AA						0	0	0	0	0	0
001	AA						0	0	0	0	0	0
001	AA						0	0	0	0	0	0
001	AA						0	0	0	0	0	0
001	AA						0	0	0	0	0	0
001	AA						0	0	0	0	0	0
001	AA						0	0	0	0	0	0
001	AA						0	0	0	0	0	0
001	AA						0	0	0	0	0	0
001	AA						0	0	0	0	0	0
001	AA						0	0	0	0	0	0
006	AA						0	0	0	0	0	0
006	AA						0	0	0	0	0	0
006	AA						0	0	0	0	0	0

As you can see, the result of this query is different in comparison to if we used the correct order for the fields.

As we can see in the preceding screenshot, the client is switching from **400** to **001** and **006**. The reason for this is that `SELECT` tries to fit data into given fields. Data from the `connid` fields is landing in the `mandt` fields in the following example. This result can be misleading, as data is not stored in the correct field here.

When we use `CORRESPONDING FIELDS OF`, this problem will not exist. However, if we used the following `SELECT`, the result would be quite different:

```
SELECT connid carrid
    FROM sflight
    INTO CORRESPONDING FIELDS OF TABLE gt_sflight.
```

The result of this query with corresponding fields is presented as follows:

Client	Airline	Flight No.	Date	Price	Currency	Pl.type	Capacity	Occupied	Total Capacity	Occupied	Capacity	Occupied
	AA	17					0	0	0	0	0	0
	AA	17					0	0	0	0	0	0
	AA	17					0	0	0	0	0	0
	AA	17					0	0	0	0	0	0
	AA	17					0	0	0	0	0	0
	AA	17					0	0	0	0	0	0
	AA	17					0	0	0	0	0	0
	AA	17					0	0	0	0	0	0
	AA	17					0	0	0	0	0	0
	AA	17					0	0	0	0	0	0
	AA	17					0	0	0	0	0	0
	AA	17					0	0	0	0	0	0
	AA	17					0	0	0	0	0	0
	AA	17					0	0	0	0	0	0
	AA	17					0	0	0	0	0	0
	AA	64					0	0	0	0	0	0
	AA	64					0	0	0	0	0	0
	AA	64					0	0	0	0	0	0

As we can see, all of the fields will be selected in accordance with their corresponding columns.

However, corresponding fields have one issue compared to INTO. The comparison of fields during the execution of SELECT and adding data to the corresponding fields requires more time to execute when using INTO. This increase is especially easy to observe when we select a large amount of data.

Last, but not least, we have APPENDING. We can also use this with corresponding fields. APPENDING can be used when we want to append some rows without clearing the previously selected rows. If we use INTO, all previously selected rows will be deleted and replaced by new ones.

The following is an example of having two SELECT statements in the same table:

```
SELECT connid carrid
   FROM sflight
   INTO CORRESPONDING FIELDS OF TABLE gt_sflight.

SELECT connid carrid fldate price
   FROM sflight
   APPENDING CORRESPONDING FIELDS OF TABLE gt_sflight.
```

When we used this, we selected all rows from the `sflight` table. Initially, we only selected the `connid` and `carrid` fields, but in the next selection, we appended the same rows, but with the `fldate` and `price` fields.

The result of the first `SELECT` statement is the same as in the previous query, but since we have 400 rows in the `sflight` table, in row **401**, we can see the next results but with an additional field.

The following is the result of selecting to same table:

Client	Airline	Flight No.	Flight Date	Airfare	Currency	Pl.type	Capacity	Occupied	Total Capacity	Occupied	Capacity	Occupied
	UA	3517					0	0	0	0	0	0
	UA	3517					0	0	0	0	0	0
	UA	3517					0	0	0	0	0	0
	UA	3517					0	0	0	0	0	0
	UA	3517					0	0	0	0	0	0
	UA	3517					0	0	0	0	0	0
	UA	3517					0	0	0	0	0	0
	UA	3517					0	0	0	0	0	0
	UA	3517					0	0	0	0	0	0
	UA	3517					0	0	0	0	0	0
	UA	3517					0	0	0	0	0	0
	AA	17	20.05.2015	422,94			0	0	0	0	0	0
	AA	17	17.06.2015	422,94			0	0	0	0	0	0
	AA	17	15.07.2015	422,94			0	0	0	0	0	0
	AA	17	12.08.2015	422,94			0	0	0	0	0	0
	AA	17	09.09.2015	422,94			0	0	0	0	0	0
	AA	17	07.10.2015	422,94			0	0	0	0	0	0
	AA	17	04.11.2015	422,94			0	0	0	0	0	0
	AA	17	02.12.2015	422,94			0	0	0	0	0	0

From row **401**, the data will be the same as in row 1, but with new fields.

The WHERE condition

The `WHERE` condition is one of the most commonly used additions to the `SELECT` query. We don't require all the data from the table too often, but, quite often, we do need to get some fields from the table where they have a number of values. In this case, the `WHERE` condition in particular can be used.

The most basic use of WHERE is when we choose a field with only one value. For example, we want to select data from the sflight table, where carrid has a value of LH.

Our SELECT looks like this:

```
SELECT carrid connid
    FROM sflight
    INTO CORRESPONDING FIELDS OF TABLE gt_sflight
    WHERE carrid = 'LH'.
```

The result of this is as follows:

Client	Airline	Flight No.	Date	Price	Currency	Pl.type	Capacity	Occupied	Total Capacity	Occupied	Capacity	Occupied
	LH	400					0	0	0	0	0	0
	LH	400					0	0	0	0	0	0
	LH	400					0	0	0	0	0	0
	LH	400					0	0	0	0	0	0
	LH	400					0	0	0	0	0	0
	LH	400					0	0	0	0	0	0
	LH	400					0	0	0	0	0	0
	LH	400					0	0	0	0	0	0
	LH	400					0	0	0	0	0	0
	LH	400					0	0	0	0	0	0
	LH	400					0	0	0	0	0	0
	LH	400					0	0	0	0	0	0
	LH	400					0	0	0	0	0	0
	LH	400					0	0	0	0	0	0
	LH	400					0	0	0	0	0	0
	LH	400					0	0	0	0	0	0
	LH	400					0	0	0	0	0	0
	LH	401					0	0	0	0	0	0
	LH	401					0	0	0	0	0	0
	LH	401					0	0	0	0	0	0
	LH	401					0	0	0	0	0	0
	LH	401					0	0	0	0	0	0

As you can see, SELECT only returns data when carrid has an LH value.

If we want to select data when using the more condition in WHERE, we can use WHERE with AND. For example, if we only want to select the rows where carrid has a LH value and connid has a 2407 value, we can use the following SELECT statement:

```
SELECT carrid connid
    FROM sflight
    INTO CORRESPONDING FIELDS OF TABLE gt_sflight
```

```
    WHERE carrid = 'LH'
       AND connid = '2407'.
```

The result of that query is as follows:

Client	Airline	Flight No.	Date	Price	Currency	Pl.type	Capacity	Occupied	Total	Capacity	Occupied	Capacity	Occupied
	LH	2407					0	0	0	0	0	0	0
	LH	2407					0	0	0	0	0	0	0
	LH	2407					0	0	0	0	0	0	0
	LH	2407					0	0	0	0	0	0	0
	LH	2407					0	0	0	0	0	0	0
	LH	2407					0	0	0	0	0	0	0
	LH	2407					0	0	0	0	0	0	0
	LH	2407					0	0	0	0	0	0	0
	LH	2407					0	0	0	0	0	0	0
	LH	2407					0	0	0	0	0	0	0
	LH	2407					0	0	0	0	0	0	0
	LH	2407					0	0	0	0	0	0	0
	LH	2407					0	0	0	0	0	0	0
	LH	2407					0	0	0	0	0	0	0
	LH	2407					0	0	0	0	0	0	0
	LH	2407					0	0	0	0	0	0	0

As you can see, only rows with `carrid` LH and `connid` 2407 are selected. Fields with the `WHERE` condition do not necessarily need to be part of the `WHERE` condition.

An example of this is as follows:

```
    SELECT carrid connid
       FROM sflight
       INTO CORRESPONDING FIELDS OF TABLE gt_sflight
       WHERE planetype = '747-400'.
```

In this `SELECT`, only `carrid` and `connid` are selected when the plane is equal to 747-400. These are the basic operations of reading data from databases in ABAP. Before you move onto the next section, try to write some `SELECT` statements with the possibilities discussed in this section. A good understanding of these basics is essential to progressing with ABAP OpenSQL.

How to see data selected from a database

In order to exercise SELECT, we need to know which values were selected from the database. How to show data is covered in Chapter 7, *Building User Interfaces*. For now, I will get you a fragment of code to display data, which is selected from your SELECT statement.

The following is an example of code to show data from an internal table:

```
DATA: gr_alv     TYPE REF TO cl_salv_table,
      gr_columns TYPE REF TO cl_salv_columns_table.

CALL METHOD cl_salv_table=>factory
  IMPORTING
    r_salv_table = gr_alv
  CHANGING
    t_table      = YOUR TABLE.

gr_columns = gr_alv->get_columns( ).
gr_columns->set_optimize( value = 'X' ).
gr_alv->display( ).
```

Do you see YOUR TABLE in this piece of code? This is where you can input the name of your table.

For instance, if you want to see data stored in gt_sflight, you use the following code:

```
DATA: gr_alv     TYPE REF TO cl_salv_table,
      gr_columns TYPE REF TO cl_salv_columns_table.

CALL METHOD cl_salv_table=>factory
  IMPORTING
    r_salv_table = gr_alv
  CHANGING
    t_table      = gt_sflight.

gr_columns = gr_alv->get_columns( ).
gr_columns->set_optimize( value = 'X' ).
gr_alv->display( ).
```

It is important to note that your SELECT statement must be executed first, otherwise you will not be able to see any data.

More advanced possibilities in OpenSQL

In OpenSQL in ABAP, we have more advanced possibilities. In this section, we will cover the following topics:

- The WHERE conditions
- The logical operators in WHERE
- Casting in WHERE
- The IN operator
- Range table
- The dynamic WHERE condition
- SELECT SINGLE FOR UPDATE
- GROUP BY
- ORDER BY
- UP TO N ROWS
- SELECT and ENDSELECT
- FOR ALL ENTRIES
- Subqueries

There are many possibilities here. When we are familiar with them, we can write selects in effective ways while retaining the speed of the executing statement.

WHERE conditions

In the WHERE condition, we can make it a requirement that fields need to have some values. The important thing here is that when we have STRING or RAWSTRING plus LCHR and LRAW, we cannot use this field in WHERE. Creating WHERE with the mandt fields is not possible, as the client automatically handles this, but this automatization can be deactivated using CLIENT SPECIFIED after the FROM clause. However, this is only the most basic possibility of the WHERE condition.

In SELECT, we can use dynamic parameters. When creating the code with the exact values of the WHERE condition, we rarely know exactly what values we need. In such a case, dynamic values would be helpful. They might be found, for example, on some screens:

```
SELECT carrid connid
    FROM sflight
    INTO CORRESPONDING FIELDS OF TABLE gt_sflight
    WHERE carrid EQ gv_carrid.
```

In this example, values in `carrid` are the same as values in the `gv_carrid` variable.

We can also use other operands as follows:

`EQ` or `=`: Select all data where the field is equal to the second operand:

```
SELECT carrid connid
    FROM sflight
    INTO CORRESPONDING FIELDS OF TABLE gt_sflight
    WHERE carrid EQ 'AA'.
```

This code snippet provides an example of code that shows data from the internal table.

The result is the `SELECT` statement's `carrid` and `connid` parameters, where `carrid` is equal to `AA`.

`NE` or `<>`: This operand selects **Get all data** when the field is not equal to the second operand:

```
SELECT carrid connid
    FROM sflight
    INTO CORRESPONDING FIELDS OF TABLE gt_sflight
    WHERE carrid NE 'AA'.
```

As a result, all `carrid` and `connid` fields are selected, except those in which `carrid` is equal to `AA`.

`LT` or `<`: This operand selects **Get all data** when the value of the field is less than the second operand:

```
SELECT carrid connid
    FROM sflight
    INTO CORRESPONDING FIELDS OF TABLE gt_sflight
    WHERE carrid LT 'AA'.
```

As a result, the `carrid` and `connid` fields are selected only if `carrid` is smaller than `AA`.

`GT` or `>`: This operand selects **Get all data** when the field is greater than the second operand:

```
SELECT carrid connid
    FROM sflight
    INTO CORRESPONDING FIELDS OF TABLE gt_sflight
    WHERE carrid GT 'AA'.
```

As a result, the `carrid` and `connid` fields are selected only if `carrid` is greater than `AA`.

LE or <=: SELECT gets all of the data when the field is less than, or equal to, the second operand:

```
SELECT carrid connid
    FROM sflight
    INTO CORRESPONDING FIELDS OF TABLE gt_sflight
    WHERE carrid LE 'AA'.
```

As a result, the `carrid` and `connid` fields are selected only if `carrid` is less than, or equal to, `AA`.

GE or >=: SELECT gets all of the data when the field is greater than, or equal to, the second operand:

```
SELECT carrid connid
    FROM sflight
    INTO CORRESPONDING FIELDS OF TABLE gt_sflight
    WHERE carrid GE 'AA'.
```

As a result, the `carrid` and `connid` fields are selected only if `carrid` is greater than, or equal to, `AA`.

In the `WHERE` condition, we can also use the `BETWEEN` condition:

```
SELECT carrid connid
    FROM sflight
    INTO CORRESPONDING FIELDS OF TABLE gt_sflight
    WHERE carrid BETWEEN 'AA' AND 'DL'.
```

The result of that `SELECT` statement is to get all the `carrid` and `connid` fields where `carrid` is inclusive between `'AA'` and `'DL'`.

We can get the same result if we use `SELECT` like this:

```
SELECT carrid connid
    FROM sflight
    INTO CORRESPONDING FIELDS OF TABLE gt_sflight
    WHERE carrid GE 'AA'
      AND carrid LE 'DL'.
```

We can also use the LIKE operator, which may be helpful for getting data from a table, using only parts of searched words. The operator is built as follows: LIKE 'XXX_', where XXX stands for the part of the word we are looking for, and _ stands for any other set of symbols. XXX and (_) can be used in any order. In the given example in the preceding code snippet, SELECT gets all the carrid values when the values start with AND. In this case, the second character may be any letter.

The following is an example of LIKE in SELECT:

```
SELECT carrid connid
    FROM sflight
    INTO CORRESPONDING FIELDS OF TABLE gt_sflight
    WHERE carrid LIKE 'A_'.
```

In the results, we get two different carrid parameters. The first of these is 'AA' and the second is 'AZ'.

When using LIKE, we must have characters as a value. However, if we want to use a non-character, we can try to use CAST.

In our table, we have CONNID, for example, which does not have character-like values:

```
SELECT carrid, connid
    FROM sflight
    WHERE CAST( connid AS CHAR ) LIKE '00__'
    INTO CORRESPONDING FIELDS OF TABLE @gt_sflight.
```

All of the WHERE conditions can also be used with the NOT addition.

For instance, we can use NOT BETWEEN to select where we get all data from the table, excluding data with selected fields that are not in range.

The next operator in WHERE is IN. The IN operator is used to create ranges in a SELECT query. In this example, we add three values to a range. We add 'AA', 'DL', and 'LH' as values of carrid:

```
SELECT carrid connid
    FROM sflight
    INTO CORRESPONDING FIELDS OF TABLE gt_sflight
      WHERE carrid in ('AA', 'DL', 'LH' ).
```

In the result, we get values where carrid is 'AA', 'DL', or 'LH'.

In the `IN` operator, we can also use a special internal table to describe the conditions. One of the most common uses of these possibilities is when we want to dynamically establish conditions in `WHERE` based on one value, or by using ranges from the selection screen (we will go into more detail about the selection screen in `Chapter 7`, *Building User Interfaces*).

The range table has four fields, and three of them need to be filled. These fields are as follows:

- SIGN
- OPTION
- LOW
- HIGH

In the `SIGN` field we can input `I` or `E`. If we input `I`, values of this row will be included in the selection. If we input `E`, the value will not be included.

In the `OPTION` field, we have the same option as in `WHERE` (which is `EQ` or `GE`) and we can also put `CP` and `BT` here. `CP` is similar to the `LIKE` command, and `BT` is similar to `BETWEEN`.

When we put an `EQ` or `ELSE` option using only one operand, values should be in `LOW`. `HIGH` is used only when using `BETWEEN` in the `OPTION` field.

The range table is really useful for maintaining code, which will be easier to maintain as the `SELECT` statement is shorter, as demonstrated in the following example:

```
SELECT carrid connid
    FROM sflight
    INTO CORRESPONDING FIELDS OF TABLE gt_sflight
      WHERE carrid IN gt_carrid.
```

In the `gt_carrid` table, we have the following values:

SIGN	OPTION	LOW	HIGH
I	EQ	AA	
I	BT	DL	NW
I	GE	SA	
E	EQ	NG	
E	CP	F_	

If we want to make this directly in SELECT, it should look like this:

```
SELECT carrid connid
   FROM sflight
   INTO CORRESPONDING FIELDS OF TABLE gt_sflight
     WHERE carrid EQ 'AA'
       AND carrid BETWEEN 'DL' AND 'NW'
       AND carrid GE 'SA'
       AND carrid NE 'NG'
       AND carrid NOT LIKE 'F_'.
```

This WHERE condition in SELECT is more complicated, and even if we have dynamic values, we cannot use more than five values with operands that have been set up in advance in this example.

Dynamic SELECT in WHERE

If we do not know what field we need in the WHERE condition, we can use the dynamic WHERE condition. We can decide during runtime which field will be added to the WHERE condition.

The dynamic WHERE condition is a variable typed as a string, where we have stored text that is similar to code. Let's take a look at the SELECT statement:

```
SELECT carrid connid
   FROM sflight
   INTO CORRESPONDING FIELDS OF TABLE gt_sflight
     WHERE carrid EQ 'AA'
       AND connid EQ '0017'
       AND fldate GT '01.01.2015'.
```

We can also develop this SELECT statement as the following:

```
SELECT carrid connid
 FROM sflight
 INTO CORRESPONDING FIELDS OF TABLE gt_sflight
 WHERE (lv_dyn_where).
```

lv_dyn_where has the following values: carrid EQ 'AA', connid EQ '0017', and fldate GT '01.01.2015'. The result of both of these SELECT statements is identical.

SINGLE FOR UPDATE

The FOR UPDATE statement can be used to set an exclusive lock for a selected row. However, if we have more than one entry with the same primary key, the result set will be empty. Consequently, it is really important to specify a full key. Furthermore, when our FOR UPDATE statement causes deadlock, an exception will be raised. When we use the FOR UPDATE statement, it is also important for the SELECT statement to bypass SAP buffering.

An example of SELECT SINGLE FOR UPDATE is as follows:

```
SELECT SINGLE FOR UPDATE carrid connid
    FROM sflight
    INTO CORRESPONDING FIELDS OF TABLE gs_sflight
      WHERE carrid EQ 'AA'
        AND connid EQ '0017'
        AND fldate GT '01.01.2015'.
```

GROUP BY

The GROUP BY clause combines identical content in columns specified by a GROUP BY clause, or content that has the same result in a SQL expression for a single row.

The GROUP BY clause combines identical content in columns specified by a GROUP BY clause, or content that has the same result in a SQL expression for a single row:

```
SELECT carrid connid
    FROM sflight
    INTO CORRESPONDING FIELDS OF TABLE gt_sflight
     GROUP BY carrid connid.
```

The result of that query is as follows:

Client	Airline	Flight No.	Date	Price	Currency	Pl.type	Capacity	Occupied	Total Capacity	Occupied	Capacity	Occupied
AA	17						0	0	0	0	0	0
AA	64						0	0	0	0	0	0
AZ	555						0	0	0	0	0	0
AZ	788						0	0	0	0	0	0
AZ	789						0	0	0	0	0	0
AZ	790						0	0	0	0	0	0
DL	106						0	0	0	0	0	0
DL	1699						0	0	0	0	0	0
DL	1984						0	0	0	0	0	0
JL	407						0	0	0	0	0	0
JL	408						0	0	0	0	0	0
LH	400						0	0	0	0	0	0
LH	401						0	0	0	0	0	0
LH	402						0	0	0	0	0	0
LH	2402						0	0	0	0	0	0
LH	2407						0	0	0	0	0	0
QF	5						0	0	0	0	0	0
QF	6						0	0	0	0	0	0
SQ	2						0	0	0	0	0	0
SQ	15						0	0	0	0	0	0
SQ	158						0	0	0	0	0	0
SQ	988						0	0	0	0	0	0
UA	941						0	0	0	0	0	0
UA	3504						0	0	0	0	0	0
UA	3516						0	0	0	0	0	0
UA	3517						0	0	0	0	0	0

As you can see, the result set is pretty much the same in that example as when we use SELECT DISTINCT. However, in GROUP BY, we can also specify a field with an IS NOT key, and SELECT DISTINCT only selects unique values in a selected key.

ORDER BY

ORDER BY clauses are used to sort data directly through the SELECT statement. Sorting can be carried out using a primary key:

```
SELECT carrid connid
    FROM sflight
    INTO CORRESPONDING FIELDS OF TABLE gt_sflight
    ORDER BY PRIMARY KEY.
```

It can also sort other columns in ascending or descending order, or even in a `dynamic` order, which is created on the same principle as `dynamic`, with different values compared with a `dynamic` variable:

```
SELECT carrid connid planetype
    FROM sflight
    INTO CORRESPONDING FIELDS OF TABLE gt_sflight
    ORDER BY planetype ASCENDING.
```

UP TO and ROWS

`UP TO (natural number) ROWS` is used for defining a limit in terms of the number of rows that can be selected in `SELECT`:

```
SELECT carrid connid planetype
    UP TO 10 ROWS
    FROM sflight
    INTO CORRESPONDING FIELDS OF TABLE gt_sflight.
```

In this example, we will get the first 10 rows:

Client	Airline	Flight No.	Date	Price	Currency	Plane Type	Capacity	Occupied	Total Capacity	Occupied	Capacity	Occupied
	AA	17				747-400	0	0	0	0	0	0
	AA	17				747-400	0	0	0	0	0	0
	AA	17				747-400	0	0	0	0	0	0
	AA	17				747-400	0	0	0	0	0	0
	AA	17				747-400	0	0	0	0	0	0
	AA	17				747-400	0	0	0	0	0	0
	AA	17				747-400	0	0	0	0	0	0
	AA	17				747-400	0	0	0	0	0	0
	AA	17				747-400	0	0	0	0	0	0
	AA	17				747-400	0	0	0	0	0	0

SELECT and ENDSELECT

`SELECT` and `ENDSELECT` are used when we want to create a loop on a database:

```
SELECT carrid connid planetype
    FROM sflight
    INTO CORRESPONDING FIELDS OF gs_sflight.
ENDSELECT.
```

This means that this SELECT statement gets one row following a single execution and the loop ends when SELECT cannot get the next rows with the defined key.

This is helpful when we want to make changes directly to data after SELECT. In this example, we delete leading zeros from connid before appending them to the main gt_sflight table:

```
SELECT carrid connid planetype
    FROM sflight
    INTO CORRESPONDING FIELDS OF gs_sflight.
    SHIFT gs_sflight-connid LEFT DELETING LEADING '0'.
    APPEND gs_sflight TO gt_sflight.
  ENDSELECT.
```

We can also get data in a loop on a database, sent directly to a table with a PACKAGE SIZE addition. PACKAGE SIZE is responsible for establishing how many entries need to be selected in one execution of a loop:

```
SELECT carrid connid planetype PACKAGE SIZE 100
    FROM sflight
    INTO CORRESPONDING FIELDS OF gt_sflight.
ENDSELECT.
```

In this case, we get 100 rows in 1 loop.

FOR ALL ENTRIES

FOR ALL ENTRIES can be used when we have two tables and we want get data from the second table based on a field in the first table:

```
SELECT carrid connid
    FROM sflight
    INTO CORRESPONDING FIELDS OF gt_sflight
    WHERE planetype = '747-400'.

    IF gt_sflight IS NOT INITIAL.
      SELECT carrid connid counryfr cityfr
             airpfrom countryto
        FROM spfli
        INTO CORRESPONDING FIELDS OF TABLE gt_spfli
        FOR ALL ENTRIES IN gt_sflight
        WHERE carrid = gt_sflight-carrid
          AND carrid = gt_sflight-connid.
    ENDIF.
```

In the first SELECT statement, we get data about carrid and connid, but only if planetype is '747-400'. In the second table, as we do not have planetype, we can only get rows where we want them.

One thing that we need to remember when using FOR ALL ENTRIES is that we need to check before executing SELECT with FOR ALL ENTRIES, if the table using this is not empty. If the table is empty, all records will be obtained from the spfli table in this example.

Subqueries

Subqueries can be used in the WHERE condition to get maximum values directly from another table. For example, SUBQUERY can be used with the following additions:

- **ALL|ANY|SOME**

If using ALL, the expression is true if the comparison is true for all rows in the results set of the scalar subquery. Consequently, if the ANY or SOME addition is used, the expression is true if it is true for at least one of the rows in the results set of the subquery:

- **EXIST**

If using the EXIST subquery, the expression is true if the table with a subquery contains at least one row:

- **IN**

The IN operator is working in the same way as in the WHERE condition, but the result will be taken dynamically from the database.

For instance, if we want to book a flight with the highest price, we can make the following subquery:

```
SELECT *
   FROM sflight
   INTO CORRESPONDING FIELDS OF gt_sflight
   WHERE price = ( SELECT MAX( price )
                          FROM sflight ).
```

Reading data from several tables

We have several possibilities for reading data from several tables in SQL and merging that data in one internal table. I will present three possibilities for getting the data from several tables into one internal table. Here, we can use FOR ALL ENTRIES, SELECT...ENDSELECT, and JOIN. As the mechanism and principle of the FOR ALL ENTRIES operation has been discussed previously, I have only shown how to get data from several tables.

We need to split a query into two SELECT statements. However, first of all, I will prepare the structure and table when we have fields from two tables—sflight and spfli:

```
TYPES:
  BEGIN OF s_for_all_entries,
    mandt     TYPE mandt,
    carrid    TYPE s_carr_id,
    connid    TYPE s_conn_id,
    fldate    TYPE s_date,
    countryfr TYPE land1,
    cityfrom  TYPE s_from_cit,
    airpfrom  TYPE s_fromairp,
    countryto TYPE land1,
    cityto    TYPE s_to_city,
    airpto    TYPE s_toairp,
  END OF s_for_all_entries.

  DATA: gt_for_all_enties      TYPE TABLE OF s_for_all_entries,
        gt_for_all_enties_spfli TYPE TABLE OF spfli.
```

I have fields from sflight mandt, carrid, connid, and fldate, as well as spfli countryfr, cityfrom, airpfrom, countryto, cityto, and airpto. In the preceding code snippet, I have used a local definition of structure and I have defined the structure and table as a variable.

The first SELECT statement is to be used to get data from the sflight table. This might look as follows:

```
SELECT mandt carrid connid fldate
  INTO CORRESPONDING FIELDS OF TABLE gt_for_all_entries
  FROM sflight.
```

The result of SELECT from `sflight` is as follows:

Client	Airline	Flight No.	Flight Date	Country	Depart.cit	Depart	Country	Dest.	Target
400	AA	17	20.05.2015						
400	AA	17	17.06.2015						
400	AA	17	15.07.2015						
400	AA	17	12.08.2015						
400	AA	17	09.09.2015						
400	AA	17	07.10.2015						
400	AA	17	04.11.2015						
400	AA	17	02.12.2015						
400	AA	17	30.12.2015						
400	AA	17	27.01.2016						
400	AA	17	24.02.2016						
400	AA	17	23.03.2016						
400	AA	17	20.04.2016						
400	AA	17	18.05.2016						
400	AA	17	15.06.2016						
400	AA	64	22.05.2015						
400	AA	64	19.06.2015						
400	AA	64	17.07.2015						
400	AA	64	14.08.2015						

When I use data from the `spfli` table, the code should look as follows:

```
IF gt_for_all_entries IS NOT INITIAL.

   SELECT mandt carrid conid cityfrom
          airpfrom countryto cityto airpto
     INTO CORRESPONDING FIELDS OF TABLE gt_for_all_entries_spfli
     FROM spfli
     FOR ALL ENTRIES IN gt_for_all_entries
     WHERE carrid = gt_for_all_entries-carrid
       AND connid = gt_for_all_entries-connid.

ENDIF.
```

The result of SELECT from spfli is as follows:

Client	Airline	Flight No.	Date Country	Depart. city	Depart	Country	Arrival city	Target
400	AA	17	US	NEW YORK	JFK	US	SAN FRANCISCO	SFO
400	AA	64	US	SAN FRANCISCO	SFO	US	NEW YORK	JFK
400	AZ	555	IT	ROME	FCO	DE	FRANKFURT	FRA
400	AZ	788	IT	ROME	FCO	JP	TOKYO	TYO
400	AZ	789	JP	TOKYO	TYO	IT	ROME	FCO
400	AZ	790	IT	ROME	FCO	JP	OSAKA	KIX
400	DL	106	US	NEW YORK	JFK	DE	FRANKFURT	FRA
400	DL	1699	US	NEW YORK	JFK	US	SAN FRANCISCO	SFO
400	DL	1984	US	SAN FRANCISCO	SFO	US	NEW YORK	JFK
400	JL	407	JP	TOKYO	NRT	DE	FRANKFURT	FRA
400	JL	408	DE	FRANKFURT	FRA	JP	TOKYO	NRT
400	LH	400	DE	FRANKFURT	FRA	US	NEW YORK	JFK
400	LH	401	US	NEW YORK	JFK	DE	FRANKFURT	FRA
400	LH	402	DE	FRANKFURT	FRA	US	NEW YORK	JFK
400	LH	2402	DE	FRANKFURT	FRA	DE	BERLIN	SXF
400	LH	2407	DE	BERLIN	TXL	DE	FRANKFURT	FRA
400	QF	5	SG	SINGAPORE	SIN	DE	FRANKFURT	FRA
400	QF	6	DE	FRANKFURT	FRA	SG	SINGAPORE	SIN
400	SQ	2	SG	SINGAPORE	SIN	US	SAN FRANCISCO	SFO
400	SQ	15	US	SAN FRANCISCO	SFO	SG	SINGAPORE	SIN
400	SQ	158	SG	SINGAPORE	SIN	ID	JAKARTA	JKT
400	SQ	988	SG	SINGAPORE	SIN	JP	TOKYO	TYO
400	UA	941	DE	FRANKFURT	FRA	US	SAN FRANCISCO	SFO
400	UA	3504	US	SAN FRANCISCO	SFO	DE	FRANKFURT	FRA
400	UA	3516	US	NEW YORK	JFK	DE	FRANKFURT	FRA
400	UA	3517	DE	FRANKFURT	FRA	US	NEW YORK	JFK

We then need to merge the table:

```
LOOP AT gt_for_all_entries ASSIGNING FIELD-SYMBOL(<gs_for_all_entires>).

   READ TABLE gt_for_all_entries-spfli ASSIGNING field-
symbol(<gs_for_all_entires_spfli>)
     WITH KEY carrid = <gs_for_all_entires>-carrid connid =
<gs_for_all_entires>-connid.

   MOVE-CORRESPONDING <gs_for_all_entires_spfli> TO <gs_for_all_entires>.
ENDLOOP.
```

The result of this piece of code is presented in the following screenshot. All fields will be filled with data from two tables:

Client	Airline	Flight No.	Flight Date	Country	Depart. city	Depart	Country	Arrival city	Target
400	AA	17	20.05.2015	US	NEW YORK	JFK	US	SAN FRANCISCO	SFO
400	AA	17	17.06.2015	US	NEW YORK	JFK	US	SAN FRANCISCO	SFO
400	AA	17	15.07.2015	US	NEW YORK	JFK	US	SAN FRANCISCO	SFO
400	AA	17	12.08.2015	US	NEW YORK	JFK	US	SAN FRANCISCO	SFO
400	AA	17	09.09.2015	US	NEW YORK	JFK	US	SAN FRANCISCO	SFO
400	AA	17	07.10.2015	US	NEW YORK	JFK	US	SAN FRANCISCO	SFO
400	AA	17	04.11.2015	US	NEW YORK	JFK	US	SAN FRANCISCO	SFO
400	AA	17	02.12.2015	US	NEW YORK	JFK	US	SAN FRANCISCO	SFO
400	AA	17	30.12.2015	US	NEW YORK	JFK	US	SAN FRANCISCO	SFO
400	AA	17	27.01.2016	US	NEW YORK	JFK	US	SAN FRANCISCO	SFO
400	AA	17	24.02.2016	US	NEW YORK	JFK	US	SAN FRANCISCO	SFO
400	AA	17	23.03.2016	US	NEW YORK	JFK	US	SAN FRANCISCO	SFO
400	AA	17	20.04.2016	US	NEW YORK	JFK	US	SAN FRANCISCO	SFO
400	AA	17	18.05.2016	US	NEW YORK	JFK	US	SAN FRANCISCO	SFO
400	AA	17	15.06.2016	US	NEW YORK	JFK	US	SAN FRANCISCO	SFO
400	AA	64	22.05.2015	US	SAN FRANCISCO	SFO	US	NEW YORK	JFK
400	AA	64	19.06.2015	US	SAN FRANCISCO	SFO	US	NEW YORK	JFK
400	AA	64	17.07.2015	US	SAN FRANCISCO	SFO	US	NEW YORK	JFK
400	AA	64	14.08.2015	US	SAN FRANCISCO	SFO	US	NEW YORK	JFK

The next possibilities include using the SELECT...ENDSELECT statements.

For this method, we need to create two more variables, as we know that SELECT...ENDSELECT needs structure, and we need the next structure to select 'single' inside the SELECT...ENDSELECT loop. It is also worth noting that I renamed the table:

```
DATA: gt_loop  TYPE TABLE OF s_2_tables,
      gs_loop  TYPE s_2_tables,
      gs_spfli TYPE spfli.
```

SELECT...ENDSELECT is presented in the following code snippet. In this loop, we are using two SELECT queries. First of all, to get data from sflight, we must get corresponding data from spfli, and then move all data to where it is needed from the spfli structure to our target structure. As a final step, we will append our result to the table, as shown in the following code snippet:

```
SELECT mandt carrid connid fldate
   INTO CORRESPONDING FIELDS OF gs_loop
   FROM sflight.
```

```
    SELECT SINGLE mandt carrid connid cityfrom
                  airpfrom countryto cityto airpto
      INTO CORRESPONDING FIELDS OF gs_spfli
      FROM spfli
      WHERE carrid = gs_loop-carrid
        AND connid = gs_loop-connid.

    MOVE-CORRESPONDING gs_spfli TO gs_loop.
    APPEND gs_loop TO gt_loop.

  ENDSELECT.
```

Of course, the result of this query is identical to FOR ALL ENTRIES.

The main difference between them is that, in FOR ALL ENTRIES, we make two SELECT statements and merge tables directly on the application server, as we have all of the required data. In contrast, in SELECT...ENDSELECT, we have to enter the database every time we need data. Let's assume that in the sflight table, we have 400 rows. In FOR ALL ENTRIES, we always have two independent SELECT statements, regardless of how many rows are in the table. In the case of SELECT...ENDSELECT, there are 800 separate SELECT statements to include on the database, which increases the database workload.

The third option for getting data from more than one table is JOIN. For this option, I have renamed the main table and deleted the rest of the table and structure, as we do not need them:

```
    DATA: gt_join TYPE TABLE OF s_2_tables.
```

The SELECT statements used for JOIN are shown as follows:

```
    SELECT sf~mandt sf~carrid sf~connid sf~fldate
           sp~countryfrom sp~cityfrom sp~airpfrom
           sp~countryto sp~cityto sp~airpto
      INTO CORRESPONDING FIELDS OF TABLE gt_join
      FROM sflight AS sf
      JOIN spfli AS sp
        ON sf~carrid = sp~carrid
       AND sf~connid = sp~connid.
```

In the preceding code snippet, you may see pieces of code that were not previously used; for example, sf~mandt and sflight as sf.

Using this statement, every field in a resulting set needs to have an alias corresponding to a table. Every field on a resulting set needs to be with an alias. This is because the SQL engine needs to define the table that each field is to be selected from.

Furthermore, ON can be a new statement. This uses joins to indicate the JOIN condition. It is worth noting that inner and outer joins require a JOIN condition. In JOIN, we can use three types of join, which are listed as follows:

- JOIN or INNER JOIN: In this type of JOIN, the INNER JOIN joins a column of rows in the result set of the left-hand side and right-hand side only if the rows meet the JOIN condition and the statement creates all combinations of keys. If some rows do not have their equivalent on the first and second table, rows are not created.

- LEFT/RIGHT JOIN or LEFT/RIGHT OUTER JOIN: OUTER JOIN is pretty much the same as INNER JOIN, but with a number of differences. The difference between them is the following. In the case of LEFT OUTER JOIN, the function selects all rows from the left-hand side and all the matching rows from the right-hand side and includes them in the result set. The RIGHT OUTER JOIN function works identically, but selects rows from the right-hand side and matches them from the left-hand side. This is even the case if no corresponding rows are on the other side.

- CROSS JOIN: CROSS JOIN creates every possible combination from the rows on both tables, without any special conditions.

We can also create JOIN from more than two tables. For this example, I have created a new type with three tables:

```
TYPES:
  BEGIN OF s_3_tables,
    mandt      TYPE mandt,
    carrid     TYPE s_carr_id,
    connid     TYPE s_conn_id,
    fldate     TYPE s_date,
    countryfr  TYPE land1,
    cityfrom   TYPE s_from_cit,
    airpfrom   TYPE s_fromairp,
    countryto  TYPE land1,
    cityto     TYPE s_to_city,
    airpto     TYPE s_toairp,
    bookid     TYPE s_book_id,
    customid   TYPE s_customer,
  END OF s_3_tables.

DATA: gt_3join TYPE TABLE OF s_3_tables.
```

The code to join three tables looks like this:

```
SELECT sf~mandt sf~carrid sf~connid sf~fldate
       sp~countryfr sp~cityfrom sp~airpfrom
       sp~countryto sp~cityto sp~airpto
       sb~bookid sb~customid
  INTO CORRESPONDING FIELDS OF TABLE gt_3join
  FROM sflight AS sf
  JOIN spfli AS sp
    ON sf~carrid = sp~carrid
   AND sf~connid = sp~connid
  JOIN sbook AS sb
    ON sb~carrid = sf~carrid
   AND sb~connid = sf~connid
   AND sb~fldate = sf~fldate .
```

To create a JOIN condition from three tables, we just need to expand the result set and the next table to join with the JOIN condition.

If we want to select from three tables in the previous two ways (FOR ALL ENTRIES and SELECT...ENDSELECT), we need to make three separate SELECT statements in FOR ALL ENTRIES. However, for SELECT...ENDSELECT, as seen in the sbook table, we can have more than one combination of carrid and connid. As a result of that, the number of SELECT statements will increase significantly.

A comparison of the efficiency and execute time methods will be made in the explanation of the SQL TRACE tool.

Identifying and saving the changes

Before you save the data from an application, you should reflect on which data needs to be stored. In most cases, you don't need to save all the data you've read. Some actions can be executed to identify whether it's an insertion, an update, or a deletion of data.

Let's have a short look on the different meanings of these terms:

- INSERT: A new database table entry is created
- UPDATE: Existing data is changed
- DELETE: Existing data is deleted from the database table

In the case of implementing any logic for reading and maintaining data, you should follow the performance rules from the beginning. As a best practice, you can compare the data changed by the application with the unchanged data read in the beginning of your **logical unit of work** (**LUW**).

For this, you can hold a copy of the original data within a data object that is similar to your workspace. In comparison, you can identify all actions, such as `INSERT`, `UPDATE`, or `DELETE`. Depending on the amount of accessed data (single row or multiple rows), this is a simple comparison of structures, or a slightly more complex comparison of tables and their entries. When it comes to having multiple rows, you should compare each row of your workspace table with the corresponding row of original data. This logic is a bit more complex due to the situation in which some entries can be added, removed, or changed.

You have two possibilities for identifying the action taken by the user. The first option is to give a sign for the database action with the entry within your program. You can achieve this by extending the data structure with a database action flag and by setting this to `I`, `U`, or `D` for the `INSERT`, `UPDATE`, or `DELETE` actions, for example. You have to take care of this flag in any action you might undertake with the data and some dependencies have to be used.

The second option is to make the comparison just before saving the data and making just the required changes to the methods of saving. This is a bit more convenient and gives you more flexibility within the program, as well as reducing the complexity of the program.

In the next sections, we will have a deeper look at the different actions on the database.

Creating datasets

Datasets are created by using the `INSERT` statement. You can either create a single row or multiple rows with this statement.

To add a single row, you can use one of the following variants, which acts in an equal manner on the database:

```
INSERT INTO dbtab VALUES wa
```

Alternatively, you can use one of the following:

```
INSERT dbtab FROM wa.
```

The structure of `wa` should be identical to the structure of `dbtab`. This operation will only be executed if there is no entry with the same primary key. If there is an entry with the same key, `SY-SUBRC` will be set to 4 instead of 0.

To add multiple datasets, you can use the following statement:

```
INSERT dbtab FROM TABLE itab [ACCEPTING DUPLICATE KEYS]
```

All entries from `itab` are inserted into the `dbtab` table. If at least one entry with the same key exists on the database, an exception will be raised and no data will be inserted.

You can avoid this exception by using the `ACCEPT DUPLICATE KEYS` addition. In this case, the duplicated datasets are ignored and `SY-SUBRC` will be set to 4. All datasets without a duplicate will be inserted in the database. The `SY-DBCNT` field contains the number of inserted entries.

Following the five golden performance rules, you should execute the operation with internal tables whenever possible instead of executing loops and single rows.

Updating datasets

To change existing database entries, you can use the `UPDATE` statement. Three different options are available for the `UPDATE` statement.

To change specific columns, you can use the following syntax:

```
UPDATE dbtab
    SET [col1 = f1 col2 = f2 ...]
        [col1 = col1 + f2 col2 = col2 + f2 ...]
        [col1 = col1 - f1 col2 = col2 - f2 ...]
    WHERE ...
```

With this statement, you change the columns named at the `SET` clause for all rows within the `dbtab` table for which the conditions of the `WHERE` clause take effect. Without the `WHERE` clause, all rows of the table are changed.

You can either override the existing value or add to or subtract from those values.

To change the entire row, you can use the following statement:

```
UPDATE dbtab FROM wa
```

To change multiple entries, the syntax is as follows:

```
UPDATE dbtab FROM TABLE itab
```

As usual, the work area should be the same type as the database table.

Deleting datasets

Use the `DELETE` statement to remove one or more rows. Deletion can be done in two variants:

- The `DELETE FROM` target: When the `DELETE FROM` target is used, data will be deleted from the table. To avoid situations like this, the `WHERE` condition needs to be filled in or you should add additions, such as `ORDER BY`, `OFFSET`, and `UP TO`.
- The `DELETE` target from the source: When we use the `DELETE` target from the source, we can only delete rows specific to a work area or multiple rows specified in a table.

The optimization of reading big datasets

The performance of a program is often determined by the efficiency of a database and how its operations are used on it.

The efficiency of using a database and downloading only necessary data to the application server can be critical to the general speed of a program, so operations on a database should be as low as possible.

We need to follow a rule that helps us to maintain an operation on a database in good performance.

In order to ensure correct performance, we must ensure that we follow these steps:

- **Get only the required rows from a table**: For example, if we need to get a flight from America Airlines from the `sflight` table, we must use the proper conditions in `WHERE`. When it comes to the effective use of all data, what we can get to specify the condition is really important.
- **Get only the required columns from a table**: In every `SELECT` statement, the result set should only contain a column that you really need. If we need to get data with regard to the flight, country, and airport we will fly from, we cannot use `*`, because we do not need all columns.
- **Do not use more reads than necessary**: To keep a low number of database reads, use a mass operation instead of a single one. For example, we should not use any reads in a loop. Instead of this, use `JOIN`, `SELECT VIEW`, or `SUBQUERY`.
- **Using local buffers and indexes**: In all cases when the secondary index can improve selection performance, these indexes should be used. When the same data is read more than once, we can save this data to a local SAP buffer. This operation can significantly save time, since reading data from a local buffer is faster than getting data from a database.

Even if we performed all of these actions, the load of data may sometimes be too big and can cause dumps, resulting in getting a notification that the connection to the database took too long.

In this case, we need to enter the `CURSOR` statement. `CURSOR` is the way to split `SELECT` into smaller partitions. If we want to use `CURSOR`, we need to declare them as a variable. A `CURSOR` statement consists of three pieces. The first of these is `OPEN CURSOR`, where we can define which `SELECT` statement will be executed in this cursor.

When we used `OPEN CURSOR`, we created a database cursor, which is pointed to the result set of a database selection. A database `CURSOR` is always assigned to a line in the result set. `CURSOR` handling is usually implicit, but when we use `CURSOR`, we can control the database cursor.

We then need to use `FETCH` to fetch the next rows, where we can decide how many rows `FETCH` should select.

After all, we need to use CLOSE CURSOR to close the database cursor. An example of using the CURSOR statement is as follows:

```
DATA: c_cursor TYPE cursor,
      gt_cursor TYPE TABLE OF sflight.

 OPEN CURSOR c_cursor FOR
 SELECT carrid connid
   FROM sflight.

 DO.
   FETCH NEXT CURSOR c_cursor APPENDING TABLE gt_cursor PACKAGE SIZE 100.
   IF sy-subrc <> 0.
     EXIT.
   ENDIF.
 ENDDO.

 CLOSE CURSOR c_cursor.
```

In this example, we get data from the sflight table with a package of at least 100 rows in 1 call.

We need to use the DO loop to get all of these records. Of course, the SELECT statement of the CURSOR can be more extensive, and in the DO loop, we executed an operation. It is also really important to create an EXIT statement, otherwise we can create an infinite loop.

The new SQL syntax

From version 7.40, SP08 SAP introduced a few important changes in SQL:

- Inline declaration
- SQL expression

There are more changes, but here is the focus on the most important and most helpful in daily work.

Inline declaration

The main changes compared to the old SQL is data declaration, where we needed to declare all the necessary fields that will be selected. By using inline declaration, this is no longer needed. During select from database, a structure or table will be created. This is really helpful, as when you need to select a new field or fields, just add them to the field list.

The following are three SELECT statements. The first of these is created in the *old* SQL, while the second and third are created with the inline declaration. All the SELECT statement results are identical.

The first SELECT statement is also presented with the declaration of the table:

```
TYPES:
  BEGIN OF t_spfli,
    mandt     TYPE s_mandt,
    carrid    TYPE s_carr_id,
    connid    TYPE s_conn_id,
    countryfr TYPE land1,
    countryto TYPE land1,
  END OF t_spfli.

DATA: lt_spfli TYPE TABLE OF t_spfli.

SELECT mandt carrid connid countryfr countryto
  FROM spfli
  INTO TABLE lt_spfli.
```

In the following code snippet, the fragment is presented as an inline declaration (a declaration of a variable is not needed):

```
SELECT mandt, carrid, connid, countryfr, countryto
  FROM spfli
  INTO TABLE @data(lt_spfli).
```

The following is the second version of the new SQL:

```
SELECT FROM spfli
  FIELDS mandt, carrid, connid, countryfr, countryto
  INTO TABLE @DATA(lt_splfi).
```

The declaration can also contain fields that are not selected, and the inline declaration was created with only the fields that were selected.

In the new SQL, it is possible to add a field that is not selected from the database.

To add this field, we need to add a TYPE variable to the list of the SELECT fields. The following example shows the first SELECT statement from the inline declaration with an added field named flag, which is of the Boolean type:

```
SELECT mandt, carrid, connid,
       countryfr, countryto, lv_flag AS flag
    FROM spfli
    INTO TABLE @data(lt_spfli).
```

In this case, only one field is added, but it is also possible to add more fields, structure, tables, and so on.

If the new SQL is used, it is also necessary to make all variables a host variable, for example, if WHERE is used in SELECT. In the following SELECT statement, use the variable named lv_carrid in WHERE, and this variable needs to be escaped by @:

```
DATA: lv_carrid TYPE s_carr_id VALUE 'AA'.

SELECT mandt, carrid, connid
    FROM sflight
    INTO TABLE @DATA(lt_spfli)
    WHERE carrid = @lv_carrid.
```

SQL expression

SQL expression introduced the ability to add, for example, arithmetic calculations or case to SELECT.

The first example involves creating the case. In code, you need to add the case after the list of fields, the list of conditions, and the name of the field where the result is shown.

In the following example, use a case in the carrid field. When a field in the entry is equal to AA, a field named flag will be X; if carrid is not equal to AA, the flag field is empty:

```
SELECT mandt, carrid, connid, countryfr, countryto,
    CASE carrid
      WHEN 'AA' THEN 'X'
      ELSE ' '
    END AS flag
    FROM spfli
    INTO TABLE @DATA(lt_spfli).
```

To create the calculation, you need to create the new field with the result of the calculation. In the following example, we have created the result of an addition of two fields, `seatsocc_b` and `seatsocc_f`:

```
SELECT mandt, carrid, connid,
    ( seatsocc_b + seatsocc_f ) AS occupy
    FROM sflight
    INTO TABLE @DATA(lt_spfli).
```

The addition of fields in brackets results in the `occupy` field.

Using the SQL Trace tool for performance analysis

We discussed how to exercise care in relation to the performance of database reads, but how can we measure that? For this, we can use the `SQL Trace` tool and the `RUNTIME` analysis tool.

To start the SQL trace, we can open the `ST05` transaction and `RUNTIME` analysis in the SAT transaction.

The main window of the SQL trace looks like this:

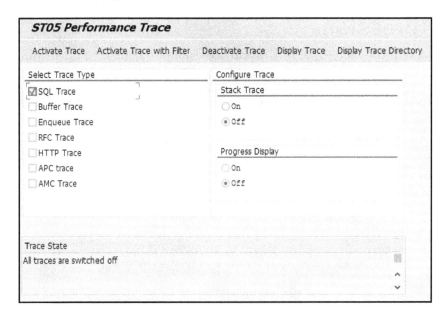

Here, we have several options to analyze the tracing, but right now, we will focus on **SQL Trace**. To start tracing, we need to click on the **Activate Trace** button. Right after clicking on that button, tracing begins. Now, we can execute our program.

After ending a program, click on **Deactivate Trace**. When we want to see the trace, click on **Display Trace**.

After doing this, we get the window where we can select which **Trace Types** will be shown, or the time period of the trace. When we select our values, click on **RUN**. At this point, we will get the values of the selected trace:

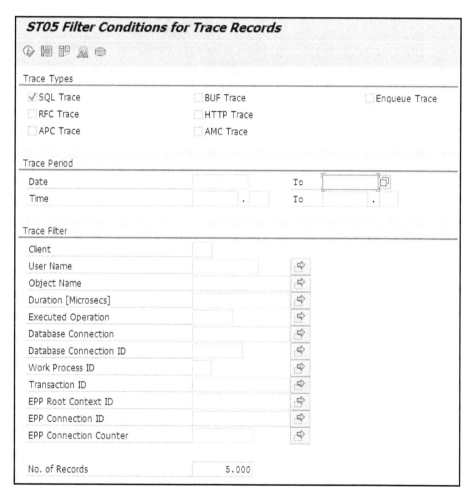

Let's check how time-consuming it is to join two tables. To do this, we will follow these steps:

1. Run the ST05 transaction
2. Activate the trace
3. Execute our program with JOIN SELECT
4. Deactivate the trace
5. Display the trace

We now need to locate interesting rows. In the following window, we can see trace information about this call:

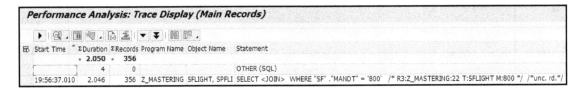

From this window, we can get values such as the following:

- The duration of SQL
- The number of selected records
- The object name that is used for this call
- The program
- The SELECT statement that is used for this call

To measure performance, we can also use **Runtime Analysis**. **Runtime Analysis** can be called by the SAT transaction.

The main window of this transaction appears as follows:

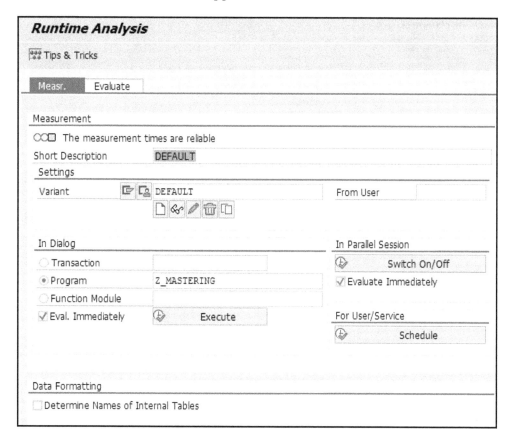

In this transaction, we can run the chosen program in a similar manner to running the program in the SQL Trace tool. The remaining values can also be useful, such as the time to execute the loop in entries.

To run the program/transaction/function module, we mark the corresponding radio button, enter the name, and click on **Execute**.

The window that lists the values looks like this:

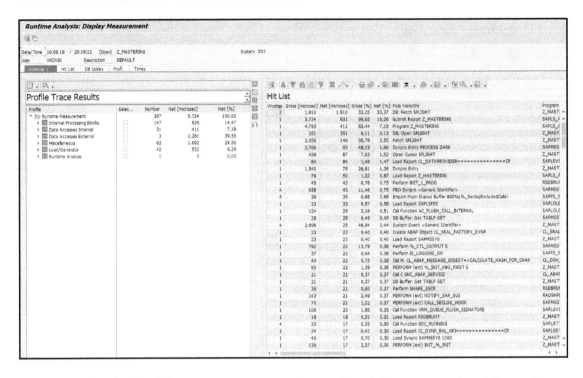

On the left-hand side of the screen, we can see the profile of the trace result, while on the **Hit List** on the right-hand side of the screen, we can see the time of the execution statement, as well as how long the entire statement needs.

We can now run an experiment to determine which method of selecting data from more than one table is the most efficient. The SAT transaction is the best option for this, as the join option only gets data directly in SELECT; other options also need other statements. The rules for the experiment are as follows:

- Use the same result (same data and number of entries) of execution in the internal table
- Run only SELECT and the requisite statements in all versions of the code
- Using the same code as is to be found in the *Reading data from several tables* section
- All versions will run three times
- All time will be presented in microseconds

The first version used in this comparison is the version with FOR ALL ENTRIES.

The whole program takes the following amount of time:

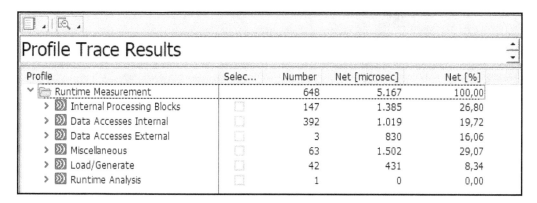

The following is the execution timetable of FOR ALL ENTRIES:

First run	Second run	Third run	Average
5,167	5,525	5,814	5,502

Now, we will look at the time required to execute SELECT...ENDSELECT:

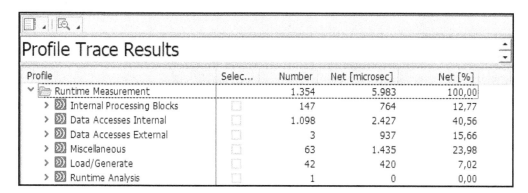

The following is the execution timetable of SELECT...ENDSELECT:

First run	Second run	Third run	Average
5,983	6,647	6,700	6,443.3

Finally, the time required to execute the JOIN version is displayed as follows:

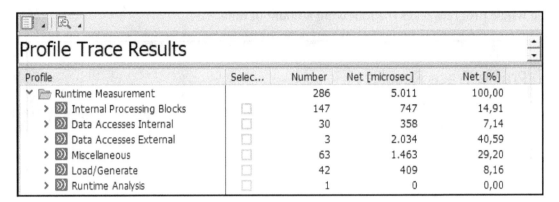

The following is the execution time table of JOIN:

First run	Second run	Third run	Average
5011	5039	5081	5043

As you can see, JOIN is more efficient in this case. Small differences here are caused by small numbers of rows in tables.

Summary

OpenSQL is one of the most important parts of the daily work of an ABAP programmer. To do it right, practice is necessary, and so I encourage you to do this in order to improve your understanding of SQL.

In this chapter, we discussed the basics of ABAP OpenSQL and the advanced functions of SQL. You were also shown how to change data in databases, how to optimize big datasets, and how to measure the efficiency of SQL statements and tracing database operations.

In the next chapter, this knowledge will prove really useful. We will look at how to import and export a documents format, which will be important in scenarios such as ensuring that mass importing or exporting will be executed with efficiency.

Questions

The following questions will allow you to consolidate the information contained in this chapter:

1. What are the mandatory elements of the SELECT statement?
2. Name three ways to read data from multiple tables.
3. What can we do to optimize reading a dataset from a database?

4
Import and Export to Document Formats

Each reasonable algorithm has some input data in addition to the specific processing steps. Input data is processed by a program to generate the expected output. It is no different in the case of algorithms written in the ABAP language. Our input will usually be some business data used in a client-specific process. In this chapter, we will go through some of the possibilities of reading and saving data from and to the application server. We will also go through the steps needed to read and write data from local PC. The chapter will show you typical problems for this type of task and how to deal with the multitude of file formats each developer must deal with on a daily basis. We will be covering the following topics:

- Reading files from the local PC using `gui_upload`
- Writing files to the local PC using `gui_download`
- Basic transactions related to server-side files
- Writing files to the application server
- Reading files from the application server
- Reading data from a Microsoft Excel file
- Saving data into a Microsoft Excel file
- Saving data into a Microsoft Word file
- Creating **Desktop Office Integration** (**DOI**) in an ABAP report

Technical requirements

The following requirements need to be met so that all examples from this chapter will work: **Desktop Office Integration** (**DOI**) and **Object Linking and Embedding** (**OLE**): Most of the examples shown in this chapter will require the Microsoft Office package to be installed.

All the code used in this chapter can be downloaded from the following GitHub link: `https://github.com/PacktPublishing/Mastering-SAP-ABAP/tree/master/Chapter04`.

Client-side file processing

In a NetWeaver environment, we always need to remember the differences between the application server layer and the presentation layer. The application server layer is, as you may already know, a runtime environment for ABAP code. At a lower technical level, the application server is a remote server on which the NetWeaver platform is installed. The presentation layer instead can be understood as your local PC.

This difference is very important in the case of reading and writing files because SAP provides separate sets of tools in each case—one for processing files on the presentation layer and a second for processing files on the application server. Both are commonly used in SAP projects and will be fully covered in this chapter.

Reading files from the local PC using gui_upload

Imagine a situation where a client asks you to develop an ABAP program that reads the content of files stored on the end user's local PC. This section will tell you exactly how to deal with such a situation.

The following steps show how to develop ABAP program that reads the content of files:

1. Go to the ABAP Workbench (transaction `SE80`) and create a new report from the local class-based report template (look at `Appendix A`, *Assessments* for help). You can give it any name, but I suggest sticking to the name given in this book (`ZMSA_R_CHAPTER4_1`). The code will look like this:

   ```
   REPORT ZMSA_R_CHAPTER4_1.

   CLASS lcl_demo DEFINITION.
   ```

```
    PUBLIC SECTION.
      CLASS-METHODS main.
  ENDCLASS.

  CLASS lcl_demo IMPLEMENTATION.
    METHOD main.

    ENDMETHOD.
  ENDCLASS.

  START-OF-SELECTION.
    lcl_demo=>main( ).
```

2. We will put the entire code in the `main` method. Create two variables—one to store the filename and file path on our local system and one to store the contents of our file. The code will look as follows:

```
DATA: lv_filepath TYPE string VALUE 'C:\temp\testfile4_1.txt'.
DATA: lt_data TYPE TABLE OF string.
```

3. We will assume just for now that our filename and file path will always be the same (`C:\temp\testfile4_1.txt`). Later, we will change it and allow the user to choose what he or she needs. Create a text file in `C:\temp` with the name `testfile4_1.txt` and insert the following content:

```
This is first line of testfile4_1.txt.
This is second line of testfile4_1.txt.
This is third line of testfile4_1.txt.
```

4. The best way to read a file from the local PC is to use the `gui_upload` static method from the standard SAP class `cl_gui_frontend_services`. Some people will use the old function module `gui_upload`, but a better approach is to use the `gui_upload` method. It's an object-oriented wrapper for `gui_upload` function which means the only purpose of this method is to call another function module. To save yourself a bit of time, you can always choose **Pattern** from the **ABAP Workbench** menu bar:

5. In the popup that appears, choose **ABAP Objects Patterns** and click on the green checkmark:

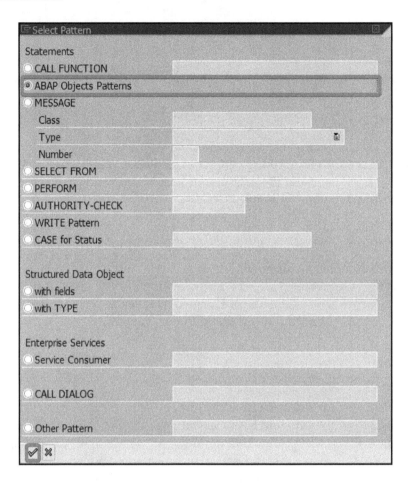

6. Another popup will appear. Fill it in as follows and click the green check mark again:

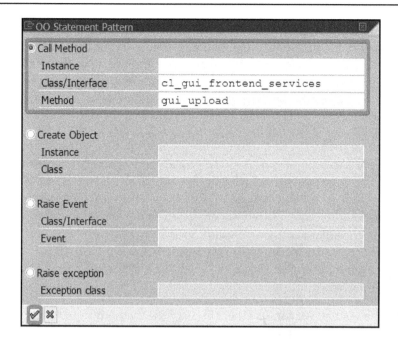

7. Thanks to this, the method call pattern will be pasted into the source code of your program. You should see something similar to the following:

```
CALL METHOD cl_gui_frontend_services=>gui_upload
* EXPORTING
*      filename = SPACE
*      filetype = 'ASC'
*      has_field_separator = SPACE
*      header_length = 0
*      read_by_line = 'X'
*      dat_mode = SPACE
*      codepage = SPACE
*      ignore_cerr = ABAP_TRUE
*      replacement = '#'
*    virus_scan_profile =
* IMPORTING
   * filelength =
   * header =
CHANGING
   data_tab =
   * isscanperformed = SPACE
* EXCEPTIONS
   * [...]
```

We need to provide variables for the `filename` and `data_tab` parameters. It's important to notice that the `filename` parameter also includes a path. In our case, it's a full path so it's an absolute address. It can accept relative addressing and the default root directory is `c:\Users\%USER%\Documents\SAP\SAP GUI\` (in a Windows environment). The parameter `filename` is commented out by default, so you have to remove the asterisk from the parameter name and from the `EXPORTING` section.

If you look closely at the `gui_upload` method call pattern, you will see that there are a bunch of additional parameters that can help you archive specific business requirements. There is the `filetype` parameter, which can take one of three values: `ASC` (if data will be transferred as ASCII text), `BIN` (if data should be transferred unconverted in binary format), and `DAT` (if data should be transported unconverted as an ASCII text table, where the different columns are separated by a tabulator). You can also define code-page if you have different character encoding by`codepage` parameters, the date format using `dat_mode`, or even run a virus scan by filling `virus_scan_profile`. For more information, you can read the class documentation.

For displaying the results, we can use the `display_data` method from the `cl_demo_output` class. It's a very simple way to display something using just a single line of code. Please put the following method call at the end of the main method:

```
cl_demo_output=>display_data( lt_data ).
```

Now you can execute your program. Most likely, a SAP GUI security popup will appear. You need to click the **Allow** button to make this example work. This is standard SAP protection for unauthorized access to your local files. You can also mark the **Remember My Decision** checkbox to avoid being noticed next time you execute this program. You can always change these settings in the **SAP GUI | Options | Security | Security Settings** menu:

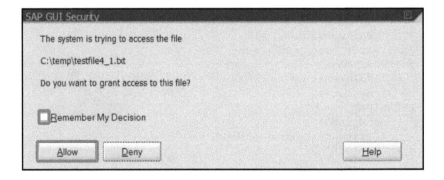

If everything went well, you should see a popup with the following content:

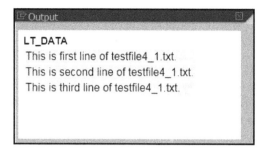

This code is far from perfect. First of all, the user has the possibility to choose a file he or she desires and not get a hardcoded one all the time. Let's be realistic; two user environments are never the same, so the hardcoded approach will never work in real life. To set up a dynamic file location, we need to use the method `file_open_dialog` from `cl_gui_frontend_services`. But first, we need to declare two additional variables—one to store the filename and file path and another to get user operation return code. Your new code should look like this:

```
DATA: lt_filetable TYPE filetable.
DATA: lt_filetable TYPE file_table.
DATA: lv_rc TYPE i.
```

Generate the method call pattern using the **Pattern** button for `file_open_dialog`, exactly like we did for the `gui_upload` method. This time it will produce the following code:

```
CALL METHOD cl_gui_frontend_services=>file_open_dialog
* EXPORTING
    * window_title =
    * default_extension =
    * default_filename =
    * file_filter =
    * with_encoding =
    * initial_directory =
    * multiselection =
  CHANGING
    file_table =
    rc =
    * user_action =
    * file_encoding =
    * EXCEPTIONS
    * file_open_dialog_failed = 1
    * cntl_error = 2
    * error_no_gui = 3
    * not_supported_by_gui = 4
```

```
        * others = 5
                .
IF sy-subrc <> 0.
* Implement suitable error handling here
ENDIF.
```

Provide variables for `file_table` and `rc` parameters. It should be noted that the parameter `file_table` is of `table` type and can include more entries. This can be useful if you want to read multiple files, but can be also annoying if you have only one file in every scenario, because you have to implement additional logic to read the first (and only) file path in the table. The parameter `rc` gives you information on how many files were selected. It will be set to −1 if something went wrong. Use the READ TABLE keyword to read the first file path:

```
READ TABLE lt_filetable INTO lv_filepath INDEX 1.
```

Now if you run your program, you will get an additional popup where you can choose the desired file:

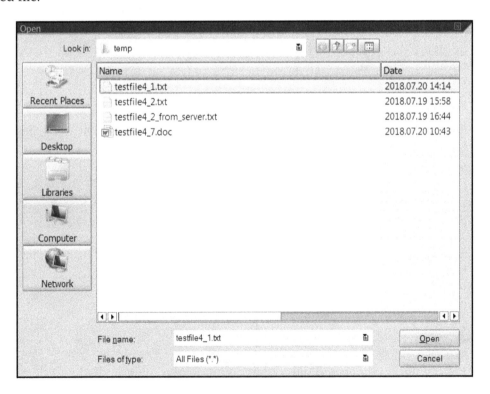

There are many additional useful parameters in the `file_open_dialog` method. You can block multiple file selection options (but you will still have to read the first entry from `lt_filetable`). You can also make your dialog more business oriented and suitable by choosing the default directory path, default filetype, default extension, and additional filters. If you want to improve the user experience, you can make this popup a bit prettier by choosing the text for the title.

There is still one last part missing. We wrote down a nice piece of code but we didn't handle an expected situation we may come across. What will happen when the user does not choose any file at all? What will happen if the file can't be accessed? As a good programmer, you should always take care of such situations. Murphy's law is applicable in computer science more than anywhere else, so if something can go wrong, certainly sooner or later it will. The most obvious way is to tell the user what went wrong, put understandable information on the screen, and terminate processing. You can solve this in the following way (place it just after the `file_open_dialog` call):

```
IF sy-subrc <> 0.
    MESSAGE ID sy-msgid TYPE sy-msgty
      NUMBER sy-msgno
          WITH sy-msgv1 sy-msgv2 sy-msgv3 sy-msgv4.
    RETURN.
ELSEIF lv_rc < 1.
    MESSAGE 'No File choosen' TYPE 'W'.
    RETURN.
ENDIF.
```

Something similar can be also applied to the `gui_upload` call:

```
IF sy-subrc <> 0.
   MESSAGE ID sy-msgid TYPE sy-msgty
       NUMBER sy-msgno
           WITH sy-msgv1 sy-msgv2 sy-msgv3 sy-msgv4.
   RETURN.
ENDIF.
```

Make sure you have uncommented all the exceptions in the method call, otherwise catching an exception will not work and you will end up with a short dump.

Writing files to the local PC using gui_download

Now let's imagine the situation that the client needs a report which will generate a result in the form of a text file saved on the user's local computer. This chapter will expand your skills with this knowledge. It's very similar to the previous example; the only difference is that we write the file to the PC and not read from the PC. To save files and choose a suitable file path, we will be using new methods from the previously used class, `cl_gui_frontend_services`.

First, create new report, `ZMSA_R_CHAPTER4_2`, and include a report template from `Appendix A`, *Assessments*. We need to declare variables. We need three of them to make the method `file_save_dialog` work. `lv_filename` is the name of the file, `lv_path` is for the path-to-file directory where the file will be saved, and `lv_fullpath` is the path plus the filename. The code equivalent to this step looks like this:

```
DATA: lv_filename TYPE string.
DATA: lv_path TYPE string.
DATA: lv_fullpath TYPE string.
```

We will not hardcode the path in this example and will go straight into the method `file_save_dialog`. This is an analogous method to `file_open_dialog` but for choosing a path for where to store the file. Use the `pattern` option on the `file_save_dialog` method to produce a call (if you don't know how, please go back to the *Reading files from the local PC using gui_upload* section). If you did everything according to the instructions, you should see something like this:

```
CALL METHOD cl_gui_frontend_services=>file_save_dialog
* EXPORTING
    * window_title =
    * default_extension =
    * default_file_name =
    * with_encoding =
    * file_filter =
    * initial_directory =
    * prompt_on_overwrite = 'X'
  CHANGING
    filename =
    path =
    fullpath =
    * user_action =
    * file_encoding =
    * EXCEPTIONS
    * cntl_error = 1
    * error_no_gui = 2
    * not_supported_by_gui = 3
```

```
    * invalid_default_file_name = 4
    * others = 5
          .
IF sy-subrc <> 0.
    * Implement suitable error handling here
ENDIF.
```

Now, use the `code pattern` tool to insert the `gui_download` method call structure:

```
    CALL METHOD cl_gui_frontend_services=>gui_download
        EXPORTING
*           bin_filesize            =
            filename                =
*           filetype                = 'ASC'
*           append                  = SPACE
*           write_field_separator   = SPACE
*           header                  = '00'
*           trunc_trailing_blanks    = SPACE
*           write_lf                = 'X'
*           col_select              = SPACE
*           col_select_mask         = SPACE
*           dat_mode                = SPACE
*           confirm_overwrite       = SPACE
*           no_auth_check           = SPACE
*           codepage                = SPACE
*           ignore_cerr             = ABAP_TRUE
*           replacement             = '#'
*           write_bom               = SPACE
*           trunc_trailing_blanks_eol = 'X'
*           wk1_n_format            = SPACE
*           wk1_n_size              = SPACE
*           wk1_t_format            = SPACE
*           wk1_t_size              = SPACE
*           show_transfer_status    = 'X'
*           fieldnames              =
*           write_lf_after_last_line = 'X'
*           virus_scan_profile      = '/SCET/GUI_DOWNLOAD'
*       IMPORTING
*           filelength              =
        changing
            data_tab                =
*       EXCEPTIONS
*           file_write_error        = 1
*           no_batch                = 2
*           gui_refuse_filetransfer = 3
*           invalid_type            = 4
*           no_authority            = 5
*           unknown_error           = 6
```

```
*          header_not_allowed          = 7
*          separator_not_allowed       = 8
*          filesize_not_allowed        = 9
*          header_too_long             = 10
*          dp_error_create             = 11
*          dp_error_send               = 12
*          dp_error_write              = 13
*          unknown_dp_error            = 14
*          access_denied               = 15
*          dp_out_of_memory            = 16
*          disk_full                   = 17
*          dp_timeout                  = 18
*          file_not_found              = 19
*          dataprovider_exception      = 20
*          control_flush_error         = 21
*          not_supported_by_gui        = 22
*          error_no_gui                = 23
*          others                      = 24
            .
    IF sy-subrc <> 0.
*     Implement suitable error handling here
    ENDIF.
```

Two parameters are obligatory—one to tell the method where to store the file and another that contains actual data to be stored. For the first parameter, we will use the `lv_fullpath` variable. For the second parameter, we need to declare a new variable:

```
DATA: lt_data_tab TYPE TABLE OF string.
```

In real life, some business data can be stored in a local file. In this example, we will just add a few dummy lines:

```
APPEND '1st dummy line' TO lt_data_tab.
APPEND '2nd dummy line' TO lt_data_tab.
APPEND '3rd dummy line' TO lt_data_tab.
```

If you execute your program, you will see save the file dialog:

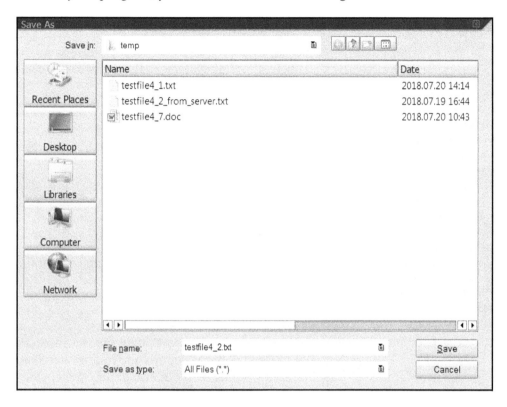

You can choose whatever directory or filename you want, but you have to remember to be consistent in other parts of this example—we will refer to this value. If a file already exists, you will be asked to confirm overwriting:

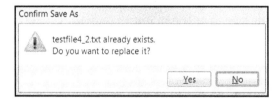

After clicking **Yes**, go to the chosen path and open your file:

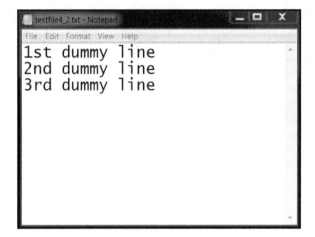

Remember to use the mechanisms from the previous example to handle errors and inform the user what went wrong.

I highly recommend playing around with all the other parameters of the `gui_download` method. It allows you to overwrite files without prompt popups and manipulate file content by using separators or date modifier options. You can also define the writing mode (data may be overwritten or appended at the end of the file).

Also, it's really worthwhile to check other methods from the `cl_gui_frontend_services` class as it can give you a variety of different possibilities. You can copy and delete a file or even read a file's attributes. This gives you a full spectrum of functionalities for working with directories. Apart from operations on files and folders, this class also offers a vast amount of other possibilities, such as the manipulation of registers and the reading of environment variables or other information about the user's system.

Server-side file processing

In this section, we will cover the basic transactions related to server-side files and writing and reading files to an application server. Those examples used in the loop and in the background job may be used for mass import and mass export.

Basic transactions related to server-side files

Before we start going into the ABAP code, we need to get familiar with a few useful transactions. In local environments and common operating systems, every user knows how to explore folders and view file contents. But in the case of server-side files, things are different. Of course, we talk here about a typical situation where the programmer does not have access to the server from the level of the operating system and can view files only by using the SAP GUI. The first transaction, AL11, is very important and useful. It's a SAP equivalent to Windows Explorer. Run AL11 from the **Command Field** in the SAP GUI. This will open the following:

In AL11, you can display server-side SAP directories, files, and file contents. We will use transaction AL11 to check if the files from the following example are really uploaded on the server. The full directory structure depends on the server operating system, but some of them are generic and should be quite similar in every SAP installation.

We will not discuss every single item in this list, but you should definitely know the most useful ones:

- DIR_PROFILE is a central configuration directory of a SAP system. An instance is configured using a profile file stored in the DIR_PROFILE directory.
- DIR_SAPUSERS is a default catalog for user files.
- DIR_TRANS is a transport request directory. Basically, every released transport request is stored here as a file. You can copy such files and move into another system. It may be a good idea to back up your work for future use.
- DIR_TEMP is a directory for temporary data.

Another two applications need to be mentioned before we jump into ABAP. The first one, CG3Z, is used to upload files to the server. The second, CG3Y, is to read files from the server. We will go through a simple example for each transaction, just for better visualization of how this really works. Run CG3Z first and fill everything in as follows:

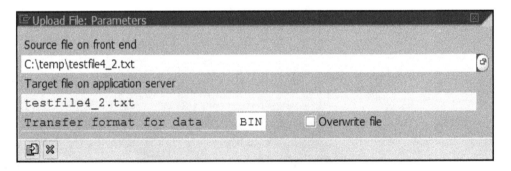

Now you can verify the whole process by going to AL11 and exploring the used directory. If the path is not specified, the default folder will be DIR_SAPUSERS. For easy searching of the file, you can use a filter option on the menu bar:

Just put your filename in the popup:

This will remove all other files from the listing:

When you have located your file, you can open it by double-clicking it:

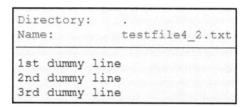

The second transaction, CG3Y, is used to download files from SAP server directories. Open CG3Y (it looks almost the same as CG3Z) and fill it in as follows:

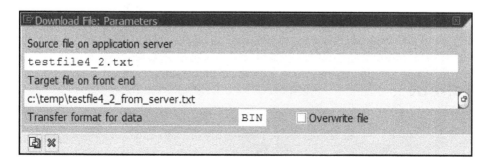

Write the source file path and filename into the **Source file on application server** field (analogously to the previous example in the CG3Z), and then choose to save your file anywhere you want by filling the **Target file on front end** field. Go to a temp directory to verify the new testfile4_2_from_server.txt file. It should have the same content as the original testfile4_2.txt:

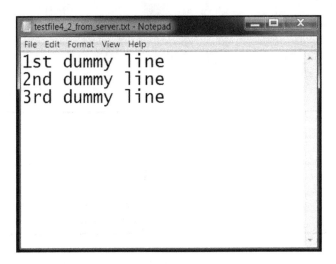

In both transactions, we have two options we haven't covered yet. The **Overwrite file** option will overwrite the file if it exists in the destination directory and the **Transfer format to data** option that defines the method of file transfer as BIN for binary transfer and ASC for ASCII-like transfer. During both operations, a popup with an authorization permission question can appear. To make these examples work, you have to allow for read and write access.

Writing files to the application server

Working with a file on a local PC gives you many capabilities; however, it has important limitations. For example, files are only available to us and if we close the current transaction, data will be lost. This means we can't use this data in a job or later in another transaction. The solution for these two problems can be storing files on the application server. We can't use cl_gui_frontend_services for that because it works only with the frontend layer. For application server-based file operations, we have a special keyword, OPEN DATASET.

Let's check how exactly this works. Please create a new report, ZMSA_R_CHAPTER4_3, from Appendix A, *Assessments* report template and declare the following variables in the main method:

```
DATA: lv_file TYPE string VALUE 'testfile4_3.txt'.
```

To open a file, you need to use the following syntax:

```
OPEN DATASET lv_file FOR OUTPUT IN TEXT MODE ENCODING DEFAULT.
```

This actually opens something that may be considered stream to file. To write data into the file, you have to use the TRANSFER keyword:

```
TRANSFER '1st line on application server' TO lv_file.
TRANSFER '2nd line on application server' TO lv_file.
TRANSFER '3rd line on application server' TO lv_file.
```

After this operation, we have to close the file. To do so, we need to use the CLOSE DATASET statement:

```
CLOSE DATASET lv_file.
```

CLOSE DATASET will also save the current buffer to the file if there is some buffer on the operating system. An opened file that was not explicitly closed will be automatically closed when the program is exited. We can check our new file in an AL11 transaction. Keep in mind that we didn't provide a directory, so the file will be saved in the default root folder, DIR_SAPUSERS.

Reading files from the application server

Reading files from the application server is very easy; even easier than writing a file. But to be sure that this example works, we first need to store something in the application server. Copy a report pattern from Appendix A, *Assessments* into the newly created ZMSA_R_CHAPTER4_4. We need an additional variable to store file content lt_data and lv_line to temporarily store each line of a file. The variable lv_file is used to store the filename:

```
DATA: lv_file TYPE string VALUE 'testfile4_3.txt'.
DATA: lv_line TYPE string.
DATA: lt_data TYPE TABLE OF string.
```

The first statement is almost the same as in the last exercise; we just need to change direction from OUTPUT to INPUT:

```
OPEN DATASET lv_file FOR INPUT IN TEXT MODE ENCODING DEFAULT.
```

Now, to read file content, we have to loop through every single line and put line content to our table variable lt_data:

```
DO.
  READ DATASET lv_file INTO lv_line.
  IF sy-subrc = 0.
    APPEND lv_line TO lt_data.
  ELSE.
    EXIT.
  ENDIF.
ENDDO.
```

If a READ DATASET statement encounters the end of the file, sy-subrc will return a value of 4 and the DO loop will be stopped. Of course, you have to close the file:

```
CLOSE DATASET lv_file.
```

To check the results, we will use the display_data method from the cl_demo_output class again:

```
cl_demo_output=>display_data( lt_data ).
```

If you did everything right after the execution of ZMSA_R_CHAPTER4_4, you should see the following:

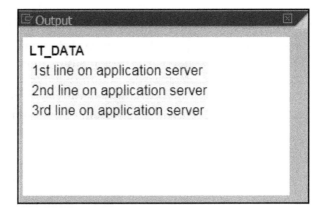

Now you know how to do two basic operations with files on the application server. To learn more, you should check the SAP documentation for the `OPEN DATASET` statement. The last thing worth mentioning is two function modules, `archivfile_client_to_server` and `eps2_get_directory_listing`. The first function allows you to connect two operations—read a file from the client and upload it to the server. You can achieve this by mixing examples from this chapter, but this function can save you some time. The second function allows you to list all files and folders on the application server.

Working with Microsoft Office files

Every Windows system user has heard of the Microsoft Office package. Microsoft Word or Microsoft Excel formats are the most recognizable and characteristic extensions for Windows operating systems. The Office package is also very well integrated with SAP. We have the possibility to export the result to an Excel spreadsheet in many standard transactions. Exporting to Excel is also part of standard **ABAP List Viewer** (**ALV**) functionality. In this section, we dive deeper into SAP and Microsoft integration. Reading, writing, and editing examples will be covered.

Reading data from Microsoft Excel

Let's assume some external system created a report in Excel format. We need to create an ABAP program that is capable of reading this file. Create a new program, `ZMSA_R_CHAPTER4_5`, and copy the report pattern from Appendix A, *Assessments*.

We need to declare variables. The `lv_filename` will be used to store the filename and file path on our local PC. The variable `lt_excel` stores values in a special cell-addressing format:

```
DATA: lv_filename TYPE localfile VALUE 'c:/temp/testfile4_5.xlsx'.
DATA: lt_excel TYPE TABLE OF alsmex_tabline.
```

For reading Excel files, we have to use the function module `alsm_excel_to_internal_table`. You can get a sample Excel file from GitHub or create a file yourself in the temp folder. Use a pattern framework to get a function call structure. The call will look like this:

```
CALL FUNCTION 'ALSM_EXCEL_TO_INTERNAL_TABLE'
    EXPORTING
        filename =
        i_begin_col =
```

```
            i_begin_row =
            i_end_col =
            i_end_row =
        TABLES
            intern =
 *  EXCEPTIONS
 *  INCONSISTENT_PARAMETERS = 1
 *  UPLOAD_OLE = 2
 *  OTHERS = 3

     IF sy-subrc <> 0.
 *  Implement suitable error handling here
     ENDIF.
```

Set `i_end_col` and `i_end_row` to `1000`. These two parameters have a limitation, which can vary depending on your local system and server configuration. Also remember that indexation starts from 1, so the parameters `i_begin_col` and `i_begin_row` have to be set at least to 1. If you open `alms_excel_to_internal_table` and analyze the code behind it, you will find two important things. This function is just wrapper to an **Object Linking and Embedding** (**OLE**) mechanism, which we will use in all other examples. It's also interesting that this function uses some strange tricks. The Excel file is opened in the background and all cells are selected. Then we use the **Copy to clipboard** mechanism, and the algorithm reads values from the clipboard and assigns the values of individual cells to the ABAP table. This has some limitations, for example, a cell will be copied with its display value and not the real value.

Add the `display_data` method from `cl_demo_output`:

```
cl_demo_output=>display_data( lt_excel ).
```

Saving a table to a Microsoft Excel file

The common business case for using OLE is to generate custom-format Excel files generated in an ABAP report. Please create a new ABAP program, `ZMSA_R_CHAPTER4_6`, and copy the report pattern from Appendix A, *Assessments*. If you checked the `alms_excel_to_internal_table` function module, you should know how OLE works. It's important to include just before our class definition OLE type information:

```
INCLUDE ole2incl.
```

We need to declare the following variables:

```
DATA: lv_filename TYPE localfile VALUE 'c:\temp\testfile4_6.xls'.
DATA: lo_excel TYPE ole2_object.
DATA: lo_workbook TYPE ole2_object.
DATA: lo_sheet TYPE ole2_object.
DATA: lo_cell TYPE ole2_object.
```

For some systems, to make this example work, instead of using (/) in the path name, you have to use (\). This is only a problem if a path is hardcoded. Now we need to do some basic setup:

```
CREATE OBJECT lo_excel 'EXCEL.APPLICATION'.
SET PROPERTY OF lo_excel 'visible' = 1.

CALL METHOD OF lo_excel 'Workbooks' = lo_workbook.
CALL METHOD OF lo_workbook 'Add'.

CALL METHOD OF lo_excel 'Worksheets' = lo_sheet
                                EXPORTING #1 = 1.
CALL METHOD OF lo_sheet 'Activate'.
SET PROPERTY OF lo_sheet 'Name' = 'TestSheet'.
```

This will initialize both `lo_workbook` and `lo_sheet`. `lo_workbook` represents our entire workbook and `lo_sheet` is the equivalent of our single spreadsheet. You can also change the name using the `'NAME'` property on the sheet object. If you run this program, Excel will be opened on your local desktop. If you change the `'visible'` parameter to 0, the process will be run in the background.

Now we want to put some information into Excel. To do this, we will get a `lo_cell` object from `lo_sheet` and set the `'Value'` property:

```
DO 10 TIMES.
    CALL METHOD OF lo_sheet 'Cells' = lo_cell EXPORTING #1 = sy-index  #2 =
1.
    SET PROPERTY OF lo_cell 'Value' = sy-index.
ENDDO.
```

We have two exporting parameters here; the first is for the row and the second is for a column. We will put the value of the current index in individual cells. The last thing to do is save the file and close the Excel OLE objects:

```
CALL METHOD OF lo_sheet 'SaveAs'
  EXPORTING
    #1 = lv_filename
    #2 = 1.
```

```
SET PROPERTY OF lo_excel 'visible' = 0.

CALL METHOD OF lo_sheet 'CLOSE'
  EXPORTING
    #1 = 'YES'.

CALL METHOD OF lo_excel 'QUIT'.

FREE OBJECT: lo_excel,
             lo_sheet.
```

If everything went okay, you should have a new Excel file in the `C:/temp` directory. Go there and verify that the content is correct:

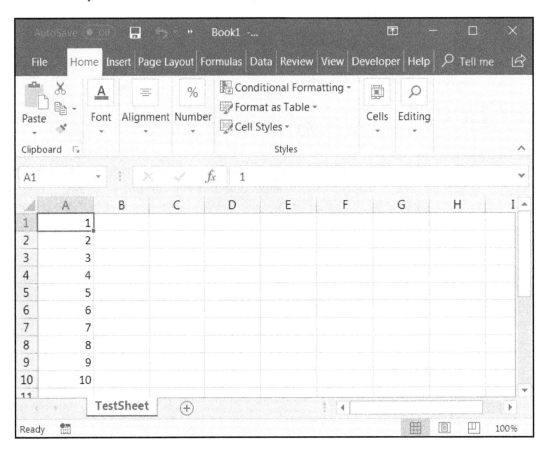

Working with Microsoft Word

In the case of Microsoft Word, we will focus only on writing values to the file due to the fact that reading from a Microsoft Word document is not especially interesting or useful. Word documents can have infinite numbers of layouts. It's much easier to work with structured Excel, where we always expect rows and columns, than with Word, where the table can have any format.

Create a new program, ZMSA_R_CHAPTER4_7, and copy the report pattern from Appendix A, *Assessments*. Add an obligatory INCLUDE statement to the OLE type-pool just before the class definition:

```
INCLUDE ole2incl.
```

Declare a few variables in the main method:

```
DATA: lo_word TYPE ole2_object.
DATA: lo_doc TYPE ole2_object.

DATA: lo_selection TYPE ole2_object.
DATA: lo_font TYPE ole2_object.
DATA: lo_paragraph TYPE ole2_object.
```

In the next step, we will initialize and get the handler of all needed objects:

```
CREATE OBJECT lo_word 'Word.Application'.

CALL METHOD OF lo_word 'Documents' = lo_doc.
CALL METHOD OF lo_doc 'Add'.

GET PROPERTY OF lo_word 'Selection' = lo_selection.
GET PROPERTY OF lo_selection 'ParagraphFormat' = lo_paragraph.
GET PROPERTY OF lo_selection 'Font' = lo_font.
```

You can also prepare your font and paragraph format, and therefore specify the final layout of the document's content:

```
SET PROPERTY OF lo_word 'Visible' = 1.
SET PROPERTY OF lo_font 'Size' = 22.
SET PROPERTY OF lo_font 'Bold' = 1.
SET PROPERTY OF lo_paragraph 'Alignment' = 1. " Centered
```

To write something, you will use the 'TypeText' method on the lo_selecton object. The exporting parameters represent the text you want to put into Word document:

```
CALL METHOD OF lo_selection 'TypeText'
    EXPORTING
        #1 = 'First Word Report of Airlines with OLE'.

CALL METHOD OF lo_selection 'TypeParagraph'.
```

To make this example more reasonable, we will select data from a SAP IDES standard data flight model. Let's say we'd like to list every single airline from the current system. We need an additional variable and a new select statement:

```
DATA: lt_carrname TYPE TABLE OF s_carrname.
DATA: lv_carrname TYPE s_carrname.
SELECT carrname FROM scarr INTO TABLE lt_carrname.
```

The list of the airlines should be written with a smaller font than the header; because of that, we will change a few properties:

```
SET PROPERTY OF lo_font 'Size' = 10.
SET PROPERTY OF lo_font 'Bold' = 0.
SET PROPERTY OF lo_paragraph 'Alignment' = 0.
```

To write the airline list into Word, we will again use the 'TypeText' method of the lo_selection class:

```
LOOP AT lt_carrname INTO lv_carrname.

    CALL METHOD OF lo_selection 'TypeText'
        EXPORTING
            #1 = lv_carrname.

    CALL METHOD OF lo_selection 'TypeParagraph'.
ENDLOOP.
```

If everything went well, you should be able to see the Word document with the airlines report in it:

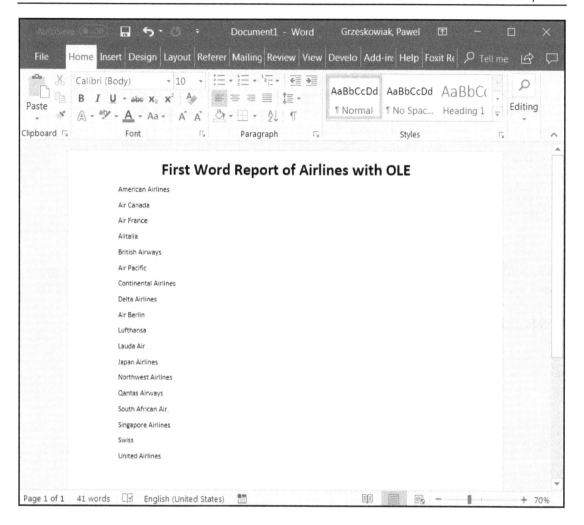

Using DOI to integrate Microsoft Office applications into ABAP reports

DOI is an ABAP object interface that can be used to work with Office applications using the OLE2 interface. You can use it to edit the Office format, but it can also be used to integrate Office applications into ABAP reports. This could be bi-directional integration, meaning the ABAP report can react to Office events and Office can react based on ABAP logic. DOI significantly extends the possibilities presented in previous chapters carried out using OLE classes.

Using DOI is also much more complicated than using OLE objects, so we will focus on only one example of integrating a Word document into the ABAP program. Forget for a moment about our standard program template and create an empty new program, ZMSA_R_CHAPTER4_8. ABAP and the structure of ABAP programs are not flexible when it comes to programs based on classic Dynpro. Using the object, in this case, is not so easy, and in the end, some fragments would have to be made non-objected anyway. First, create a few variables. We also need to include the soi as a TYPE-POOLS:

```
TYPE-POOLS: soi.

DATA: lo_container TYPE REF TO cl_gui_custom_container.
DATA: lo_control TYPE REF TO i_oi_container_control.
DATA: lo_proxy TYPE REF TO i_oi_document_proxy.

DATA: lv_okcode TYPE syst_ucomm.
```

In the next step, we need to create a new screen. This screen will encapsulate our integrated Word application and ABAP-based buttons for interacting with our Word document. To create the screen, right-click on your report name in the navigation bar and choose **Create | Screen**:

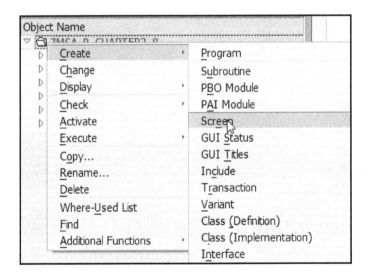

A small popup will appear where you can set a new screen number. You can choose whatever four-digit number you like. When you extend standard SAP reports, it should be in the range of 9000+, but in the case of custom development, it can be anything, such as 0100. Be aware that if you change this number you will also have to remember to change it in other parts of this example:

After clicking the green check mark, you will jump to a new screen where all basic configurations can be set. For this example, only a short description is obligatory:

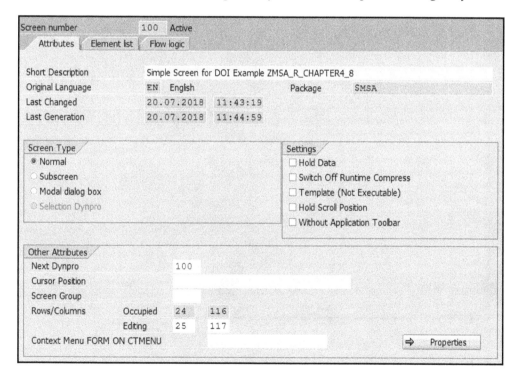

In the next step, we will create a layout for our screen. To jump into the **Screen Editor**, you can hit *Ctrl + F7* on the keyboard or click on the **Layout** button on the toolbar. On your new screen, create three objects (one custom container and two buttons). Use the icons on the left to create everything:

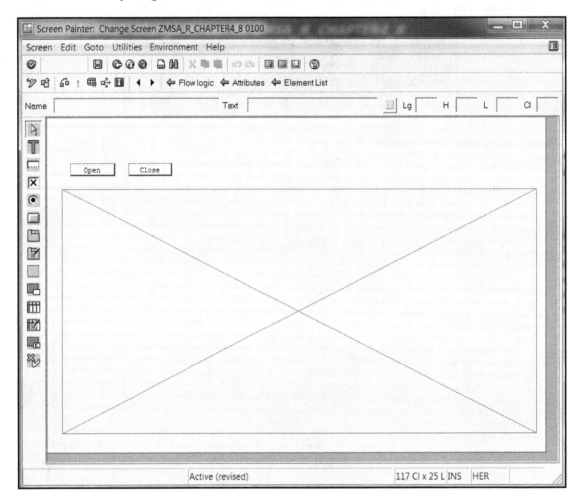

It's very important to include the names and function codes (**FctCode**) as in this example. For BTN_OPEN, use OPEN and for BTN_CLOSE use CLOSE:

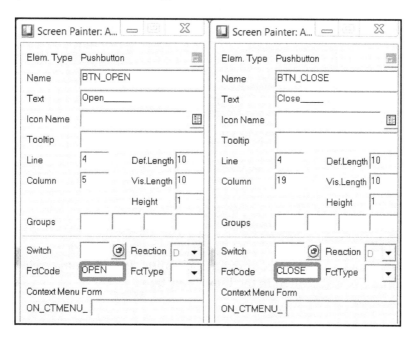

Custom containers also need to have reference names, but **FctCode** is not needed. You can verify names either in the layout object preferences panel or in the **Element list** tab when you close the **Screen Editor**. You should also enter an element name for the **OK** command object:

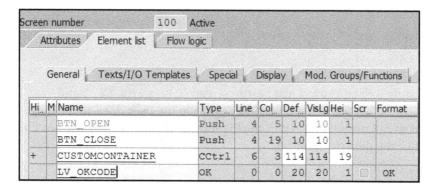

Go to the **Flow logic** tab and remove everything:

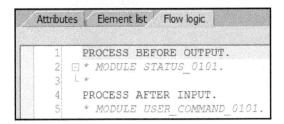

Put the following code there. It will be needed later to handle screen-processing events:

```
PROCESS BEFORE OUTPUT.
 MODULE INIT.

PROCESS AFTER INPUT.
 MODULE EXIT AT EXIT-COMMAND.
 MODULE USER_COMMAND_0100.
```

Activate the screen and go back to your main application. Include some code to handle the three new modules we just created in the **Flow logic** tab:

```
MODULE INIT OUTPUT.

ENDMODULE.


MODULE EXIT INPUT.

ENDMODULE.


MODULE user_command_0100 INPUT.

ENDMODULE.
```

The `INIT` module will be started just before screen `0100` starts. `EXIT` and `user_command_0100` modules are called every time the user does something on the screen. Now we need to call our screen just at the beginning of program execution. This should be placed just after the data declaration:

```
SET SCREEN 100.
```

If you run your program, you should already be able to see your screen:

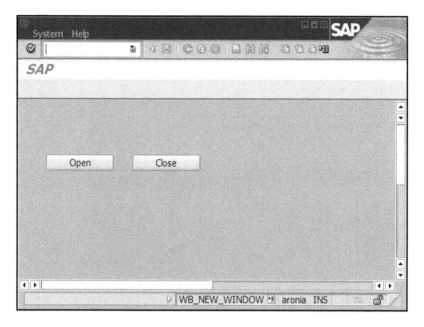

Nothing will work yet, and two very important parts are missing. We need to create a GUI status or **GUI Titles**. Right-click on the report name and select **Create | Gui Titles**:

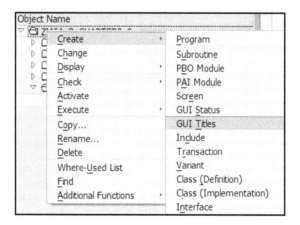

Choose a custom name and select **Title Code**:

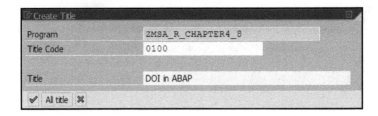

Create **GUI Status**:

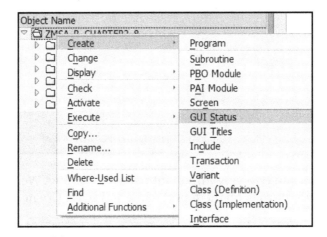

In the **GUI Status** popup, fill in a description and number for **GUI Status**:

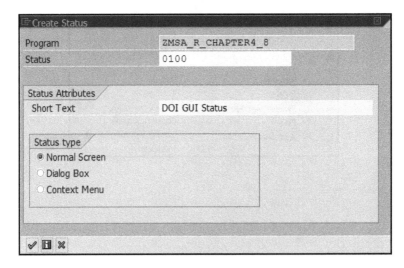

After clicking the green check mark, you will be forwarded to a **GUI Status** setup window. In our case, we need to set up only the **STOP** code:

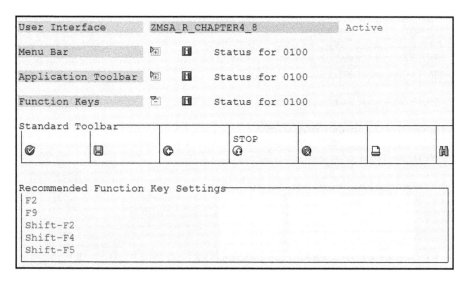

Activate this and go back to the main program code. First, we will start by handling the INIT function code. Put the following source code in the INIT module:

```
SET PF-STATUS '0100'.
SET TITLEBAR '0100'.
```

This will set the earlier-created GUI Status and GUI Titlebar. Move one and add the following calls:

```
CALL METHOD c_oi_container_control_creator=>get_container_control
    IMPORTING
        control = lo_control.

CALL METHOD c_oi_errors=>show_message EXPORTING type = 'E'.
```

This will initialize the lo_control object. The method show_message can help you in case of any troubleshooting. Now add the following code:

```
CREATE OBJECT lo_container
    EXPORTING
        container_name = 'CUSTOMCONTAINER'.
CALL METHOD lo_container->set_visible EXPORTING visible = abap_false.


CALL METHOD lo_control->init_control
```

```
      EXPORTING
        r3_application_name = 'R/3 Basis'
        inplace_enabled = abap_true
        inplace_scroll_documents = abap_true
        parent = lo_container
        register_on_close_event = abap_true
        register_on_custom_event = abap_true
        no_flush = abap_false.

    CALL METHOD c_oi_errors=>show_message EXPORTING type = 'E'.
```

Finally, initialize the document proxy object:

```
    CALL METHOD lo_control->get_document_proxy
      EXPORTING
        document_type = 'Word.Document.8'
        no_flush = abap_false
      IMPORTING
        document_proxy = lo_proxy.

    CALL METHOD c_oi_errors=>show_message EXPORTING type = 'E'.
```

One last thing is missing in the INIT module. We need to create mechanisms that will avoid creating and initializing objects after every user action. For this, we will create a global variable. We can also create a second global variable that will be useful for us later:

```
    DATA: lv_init TYPE boolean.
    DATA: lv_closed TYPE i.
```

Use this variable in the INIT module. The first line of the following coding should be put at the beginning of the module and the second at the end:

```
    CHECK lv_init = abap_false.
    lv_init = abap_true.
```

So far, so good. Now we need to add buttons logic. We have two actions, OPEN and CLOSE. CLOSE will also save a document into a database table. Put the following code in the USER_COMMAND_0100 module:

```
    CASE lv_okcode.

    WHEN 'OPEN'.
      CALL METHOD lo_proxy->is_destroyed
        IMPORTING
          ret_value = lv_closed.
      CHECK NOT lv_closed IS INITIAL.
      CALL METHOD lo_container->set_visible
        EXPORTING
```

```
          visible = abap_true.
      CALL METHOD lo_proxy->create_document
        EXPORTING
          open_inplace = abap_true
          document_title = 'DOI Test Document'
          no_flush = abap_false.
      CALL METHOD c_oi_errors=>show_message EXPORTING type = 'E'.

    WHEN 'CLOSE'.

  ENDCASE.
  CLEAR: lv_okcode.
```

The first method checks if a document proxy exists; we don't want to create it again in such a case. We will also make our container visible. The final step, the `create_document` method, creates an actual document. The parameter `open_inplace` determines whether the Word application should be opened embedded in the GUI or as a new window. If you execute your program now and click on the **Open** button, you will see the Word application:

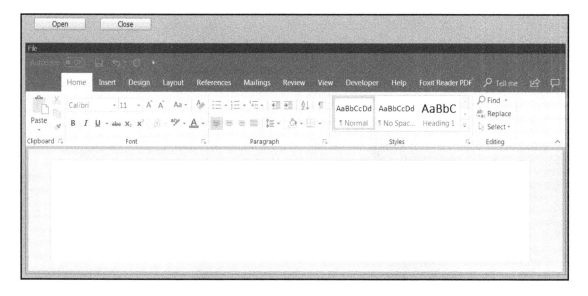

From a functional perspective, our program is still missing two things—saving and reopening the document. First, create three additional variables:

```
DATA: lv_changed TYPE i.

TYPES: ty_row TYPE x LENGTH 2048.
DATA: lt_doc_table TYPE STANDARD TABLE OF ty_row.
DATA: lv_doc_size TYPE i.
```

Now add the following code into the USER_COMMAND_0100 module; this module concerns the CLOSE command in the CASE statement:

```
CALL METHOD lo_proxy->is_destroyed
  IMPORTING
    ret_value = lv_closed.

IF lv_closed IS INITIAL.
  CALL METHOD lo_proxy->close_document
    EXPORTING
      do_save = abap_true
    IMPORTING
      has_changed = lv_changed.

  CALL METHOD c_oi_errors=>show_message EXPORTING type = 'E'.

  IF NOT lv_changed IS INITIAL.
    CALL METHOD lo_proxy->save_document_to_table
      CHANGING
        document_table = lt_doc_table
        document_size = lv_doc_size.
    CALL METHOD c_oi_errors=>show_message EXPORTING type = 'E'.
  ENDIF.

  CALL METHOD lo_proxy->release_document.
  CALL METHOD c_oi_errors=>show_message EXPORTING type = 'E'.
ENDIF.

CALL METHOD lo_container->set_visible EXPORTING visible = abap_false.
```

The `is_destoryed` method checks whether our document exists or not. We cannot save or release a document if it doesn't exist. `save_document_to_table` saves document contents into a local ABAP table. The call of the method `set_visible` hides the container. We can already open and close the document, but now we need to take care of reopening it. We need to delete everything from the *open* part of the USER_COMMAND_0100 module and paste the following:

```
CALL METHOD lo_proxy->is_destroyed
  IMPORTING
    ret_value = lv_closed.

CHECK NOT lv_closed IS INITIAL.
CALL METHOD lo_container->set_visible
  EXPORTING
    visible = abap_true.

IF lv_doc_size > 0.

  CALL METHOD lo_proxy->open_document_from_table
    EXPORTING
      document_table = lt_doc_table
      document_size = lv_doc_size
      document_title = 'DOI Test Document'
      open_inplace = abap_true.
ELSE.


  CALL METHOD lo_proxy->create_document
    EXPORTING
      open_inplace = abap_true
      document_title = 'DOI Test Document'
      no_flush = abap_false.

ENDIF.
CALL METHOD c_oi_errors=>show_message EXPORTING type = 'E'.
```

Some parts of the code are the same as earlier. The new part concerns a condition statement, where we check whether the size of a closed document is not initial. If not, we will open the previously—saved document. Please test it by clicking **Open**, writing something, closing the document, and clicking **Open** again:

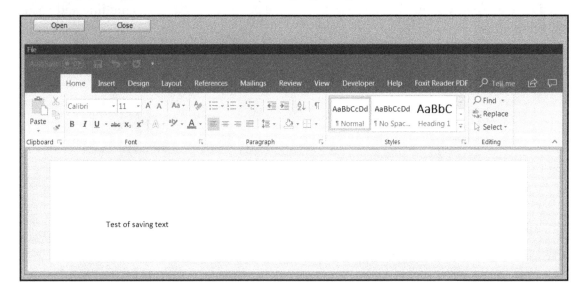

The last formality is to create a mechanism to turn off the program. Copy and paste the following code into the EXIT module. This will release all memory, close all objects, and exit the program:

```
CASE lv_okcode.
  WHEN 'STOP'.
    IF NOT lo_proxy IS INITIAL.
      CALL METHOD lo_proxy->close_document.
      FREE lo_proxy.
    ENDIF.
    IF NOT lo_control IS INITIAL.
      CALL METHOD lo_control->destroy_control.
      FREE lo_control.
    ENDIF.
    LEAVE PROGRAM.
ENDCASE.
```

In this section, we looked at the basic possibilities of DOI. The examples presented here should give you a basic idea of how to work with DOI. Of course, this mechanism opens up a wide range of different possibilities and it can handle a lot more sophisticated business requirements.

Summary

In this chapter, we went through the most common cases of working with files in SAP projects. After reading this chapter, you should understand the differences between working on files from the presentation server and the application server. You should also be able to perform all basic operations on these files such as reading, writing, and modification. You learned some basic transactions for file management on the application—serverside, such as `AL11` and `CG3Z` or `CG3Y`. It will not be a problem for you to work with Microsoft Excel and Microsoft Word files. You will also be able to integrate any application from Microsoft Office into your ABAP program. In the next chapter, you will learn about exposing data to print the form and about all available print form technology in SAP.

Questions

The following questions allow you to consolidate the information contained in this chapter:

1. What class should you use for uploading files from the presentation layer into the application layer?
2. Which parameter of the `file_open_dialog` method controls how many files can be selected?
3. What function module can be used to upload files from the presentation layer into the application layer in only one function call?
4. What is the purpose of the different settings of the `filetypes` parameter (`ASC`, `BIN`, `DAT`) in the `gui_upload` method?
5. What transaction can be used to upload a file into the SAP application server?
6. What will happen if you don't specify a directory path in the `OPEN_DATASET` statement?
7. What is the name of the library that works with Microsoft Office applications in ABAP?
8. What requirements must be met by the application so that it can be integrated into the ABAP report using DOI?

Further reading

You may want to check out the following:

- **OPEN DATASET**: https://help.sap.com/doc/abapdocu_750_index_htm/7.50/en-US/abapopen_dataset_mode.htm
- **Desktop Office Integration**: https://help.sap.com/saphelp_nw70ehp2/helpdata/en/49/173404a2e314d3e10000000a42189b/frameset.htm

5
Exposing Data to Print Forms

Forms are used for the representation of business data in a clear and structured way. They can be understood as everything that's printed from the SAP system. These forms can be printed on paper, but also as PDF documents or emails. There are three technologies that are used to generate forms. By default, two of them are integrated into the SAP ERP core, that is, SAPScript and SAP Smart Forms, while the other is external and requires an additional server and software, that is, Adobe Interactive Forms. All three have their advantages and disadvantages. Most new forms are created in SAP Smart Forms or by using Adobe Interactive Forms. We will discuss all three technologies within this chapter and use two of them to create a real-life printout example.

The following topics will be covered in this chapter:

- SAPScript and SmartForm as native forms of technology in SAP
- Adobe PDF forms as an agile and flexible tool
- Interactive Adobe PDF forms
- JavaScript scripting in Adobe Forms

Technical requirements

The following requirements need to be met to get all of the examples in this chapter to work:

- **Adobe Form**:
  - **Server**: SAP Web AS 6.40 Java (for all scenarios), SAP Web AS 6.40 ABAP (if you are looking at high-volume print scenarios), Adobe document services (a runtime component), and Adobe credential management (for creating interactive PDF forms)
  - **Frontend**: SAP NetWeaver Developer Studio with Adobe LiveCycle Designer (for Web Dynpro for Java development) and/or SAP GUI 6.40 with Adobe LiveCycle Designer (or 6.20, for developing in SAP Web AS 6.40 ABAP), the Active Component Framework (for filling interactive forms in a Web Dynpro application), and Adobe Reader 6.0.2 or higher (on the frontend PC)

- **SAP Smart Forms**: SAP R/3 4.6C

All the code used in this chapter can be downloaded from the following GitHub link: `https://github.com/PacktPublishing/Mastering-SAP-ABAP/tree/master/Chapter05`.

Introduction to printouts in SAP

When discussing the topic of print forms, apart from the programming aspect, we can't omit the subject of aesthetics. For the company, forms are a method of communication with the client. And a poorly designed form, both in terms of programming and appearance, can be a straightforward way to offend contractors. During the design phase, you can't forget about form readability, leaving enough space between elements to avoid individual parts overlapping each other, and other such concerns.

All of the examples in this chapter will be using the following form template:

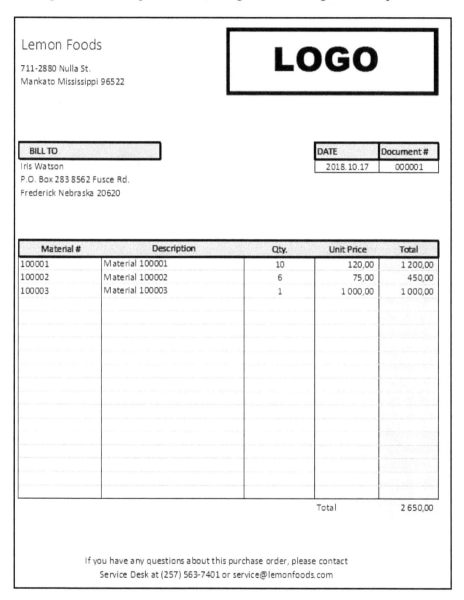

This is a standard sales document. You have two address blocks, a logo, document information, document positions, and a footer. We will discuss all of these elements and how to create them in the next chapter.

SAPScript - the great-grandfather of all printouts

SAPScript is the first and oldest technology available in SAP. Many projects still use SAPScript due to legacy reasons, but almost all new printouts are already in SmartForm or Adobe. SAP even provides a set of tools that allow you to migrate from SAPScript if you still have one in your current process. We will not cover SAPScripts in detail here, but every self-respecting developer should know at least the basics and understand the main differences between each technology.

SAPScript can be created entirely in transaction SE71:

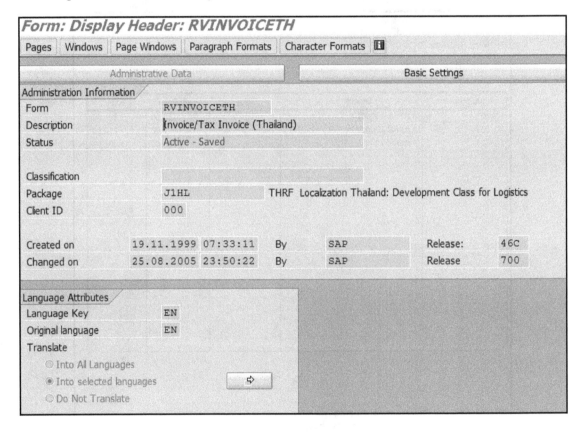

In this transaction, you have access to functionality related to SAPScript object instances, but there are some other transactions related to global SAPScript settings that you need to be aware of:

- **SE72** SAPScript Styles Basis
- **SE73** SAPScript Font Maintenance Basis
- **SE75** SAPScript Settings Basis
- **SE76** SAPScript Form Translation Basis

The following table compares two native SAP printout technologies:

Features	SAP Script	Smart Forms
Tables	Can't create real tables; can only simulate such a layout using tabulations	Can have true tables, along with borders
Main window	Can have several main windows	Can have only one main window
XML/HTML	Not possible to generate	Generates XML that you can move from one system to another
Color	Only possible by using a work around; not possible in an easy way	Can use multiple colors
Client	Client dependent	Client independent

If you are working in version 4.6 or higher, you should consider using Smart Forms and try and use version 6.40. This is due to the general principle of using the latest technology available, but if the customer has already designed a solution in SAPScript or Smartform, then a better solution may be to maintain consistency and stay with the previously selected option.

Creating our first SmartForm

In this example, based on our `Sales Document` template, we will create a printout in SAP SmartForm. When working with printouts, we need to consider two separate tasks—a printout program with data selection and a printout object with layout configuration. Go to **SAP Smart Forms** editor (transaction SmartFormS).

In the main window, put a name in the **Form** input field (in this case, ZMSA_05_SMARTFORM) and hit **Create**:

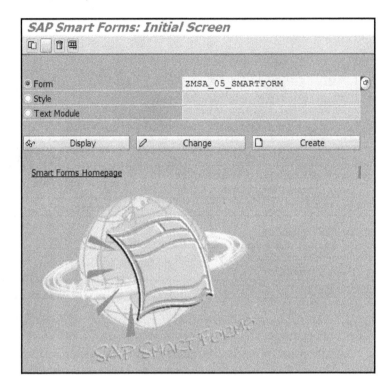

You will be switched to the main window of **SmartForm Editor**. It's very easy to use and has a nice appearance. You can put a description just below the **Form name** field:

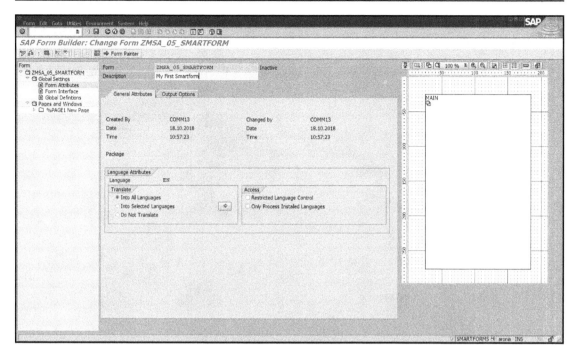

This editor has three main sections. On the left-hand side, you have a hierarchy view of form parts and the **Global Setting** section. In **Global Settings**, you can set basic form attributes, global definitions, and form interface. In the middle, the attributes of the individual objects are displayed, and on the right-hand side is a graphical view of the current configuration. First of all, we have to create placeholders for each element – by default, we have only one main window and one page. To create an element, simply click on the page node and choose **Create | Window** from the context menu. We need four additional **Window** elements and one **Graphic** element (for the logo):

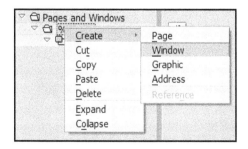

To manipulate the size and position of elements, you can use the graphics editor on the right or change each parameter in the **Output Options** tab:

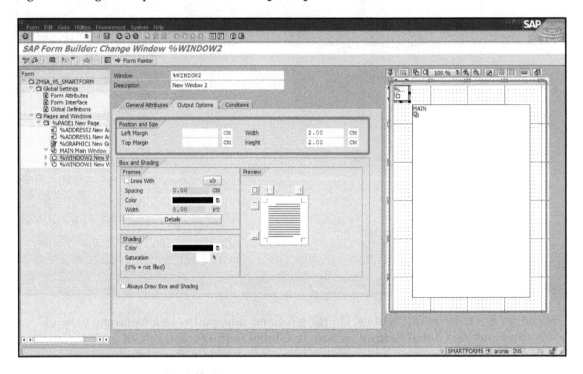

You should get something that looks like the following, which suits our template:

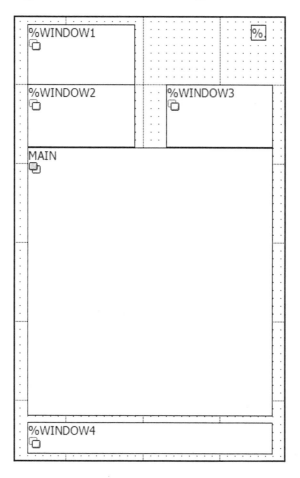

For the **Graphics** object, you can only set the top and left margin. The width and height is set based on an image file that's assigned to object. Click on the **Graphic** object and in **General Attributes**, open the context menu (by pressing *F4*) for the image name:

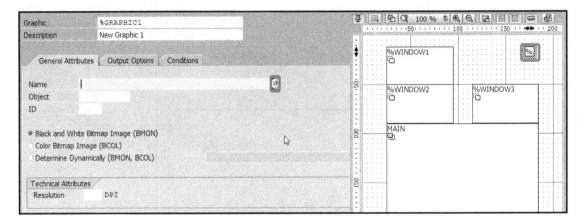

In the window that appears, click on the **Execute** button:

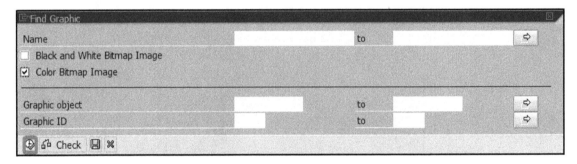

This will give you a full list of images on the server:

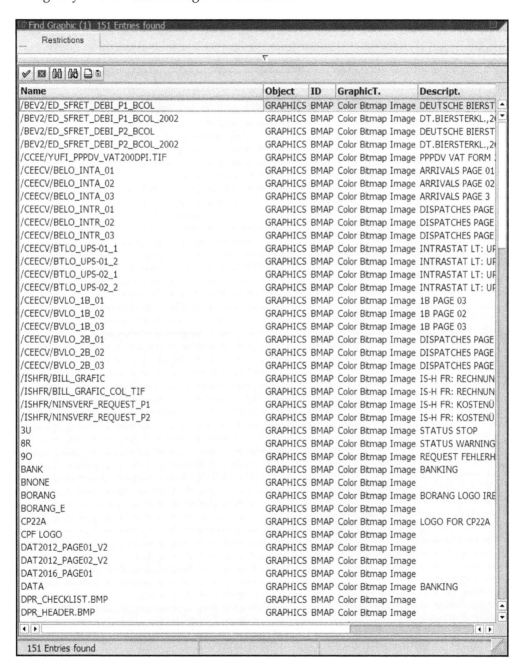

You can choose whatever you like, but to get the exact same result as in the template, you need to follow the instructions in regards to the uploaded image using transaction SE78 in `Appendix A`, *Assessments*. You can get a sample image from GitHub. When the image size is retrieved, you can make some final margin adjustments to make everything align:

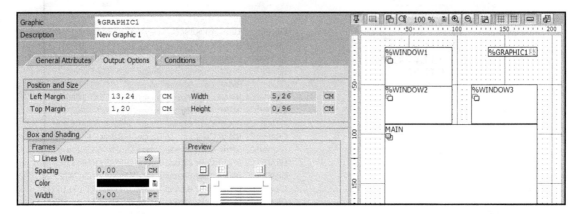

In the next step, we will define form interface, which allows a print program to communicate with the printout. Go to the **Form Interface** tab and add the following lines:

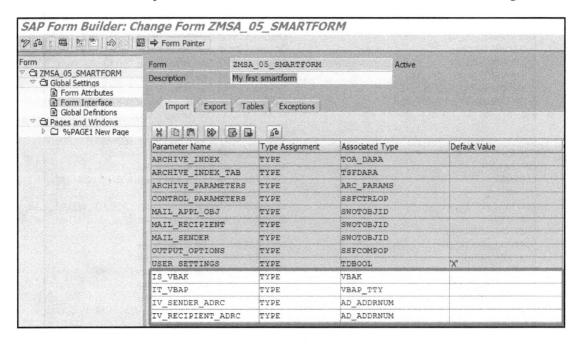

Inside **%WINDOW1**, we will create an **Address** object. This object automatically creates the address layout. This is very helpful because in certain cases, we will have a different address structure. For example, you could have a PO box or street without a number or country name, which should be included when going abroad. Manually handling such cases would be a nightmare. To create an **Address** element, right-click on the **%WINDOW1** object and choose **Create | Address**:

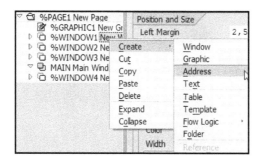

In the **General Attributes** tab of the **%ADDRESS1** object, allow the address number to be read from the &IV_SENDER_ADRC& global variable (we will create all global variables later on). The hierarchy may be collapsed or expanded. Click on the small white arrow beside the box to do this:

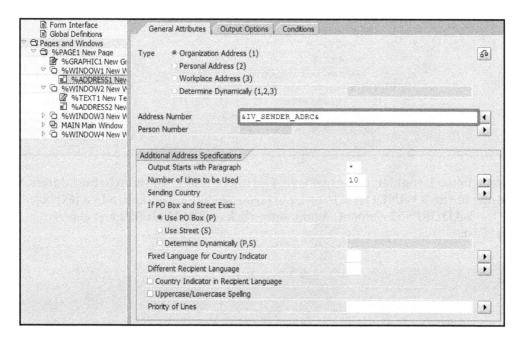

Note the small black arrow to the right of the variable name. If it is not set to the same page that's shown in the following screenshot, click on it. Only this setting allows you to use dynamic variables. Create another address object inside %WINDOW2. For the second address, we will use the &IV_RECIPIENT_ADRC& variable:

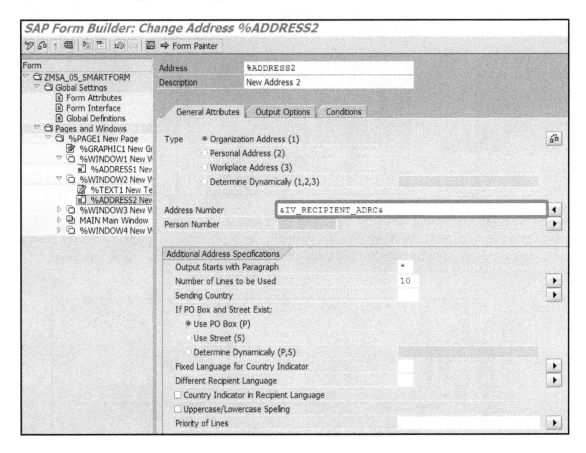

If we refer to the layout template again, we will notice that in addition to the address, there is a header inside **%WINDOW2**. In order to create something similar, add a text object just above the **%ADDRESS2** element. Again, right-click on **%WINDOW2** and choose **Create | Text**:

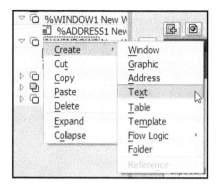

Now, we need input some **Bill To** text:

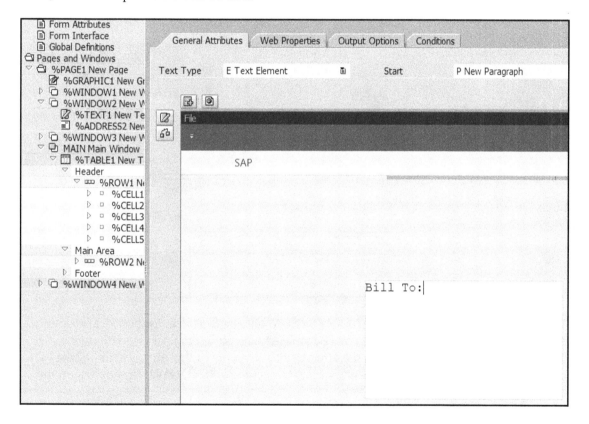

You should also take care of the appearance of the element. In **Output Options**, you can set a background and borders. It should look like this:

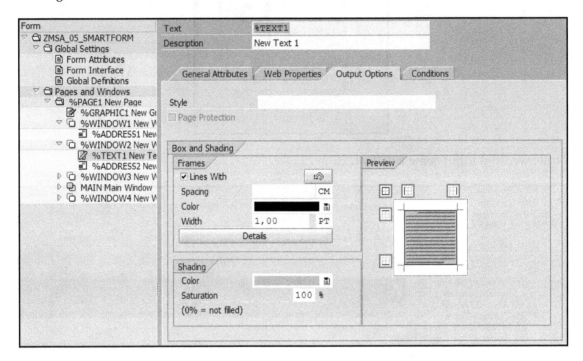

Such settings will produce the following output:

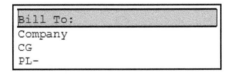

You could also play around with **SMARTSYLE** to change font size, font style, appearance, and paragraph alignment. We will create a smartstyle a bit later. Now, we will deal with **%WINDOW3**. In order to achieve the effect of being visible in this area, it will be best to use the template object. Create a new template object in **%WINDOW3**. Right-click on the element and choose **Create | Template**:

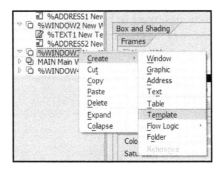

In the **Template** tab, set up some borders using the **Box** option and then click on the **Details** button:

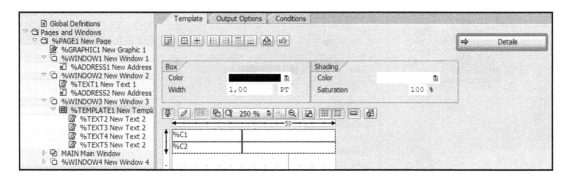

In the **Details** window, create lines `%C1` and `%C2` with the values that are shown in the following screenshot, and then add four **Text** elements inside **Template**:

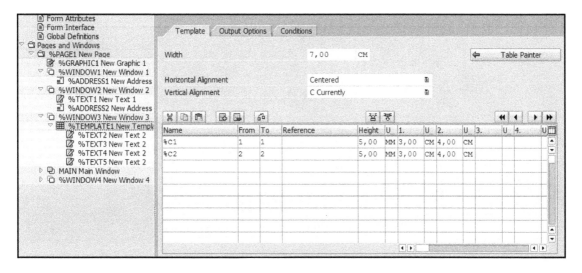

Keep in mind that template elements need to be same size or smaller than that windows that contain them. In every **Text** element, we have to set **Output structure** values in the **Output Options** tab:

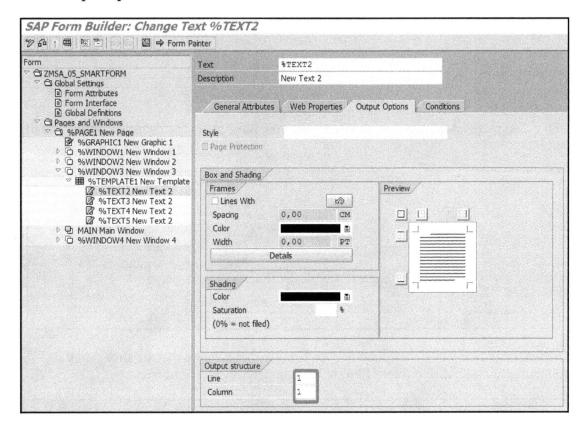

This will define the order of the **Text** element inside **Template**. For the top-left element, set **Line** to 1 and **Column** to 1, and for the top right element, set **Line** to 1 and **Column** to 2. In the **%TEXT2** element, put the **Static Text** Date in **%TEXT3** and put Document #, as shown in the following screenshot:

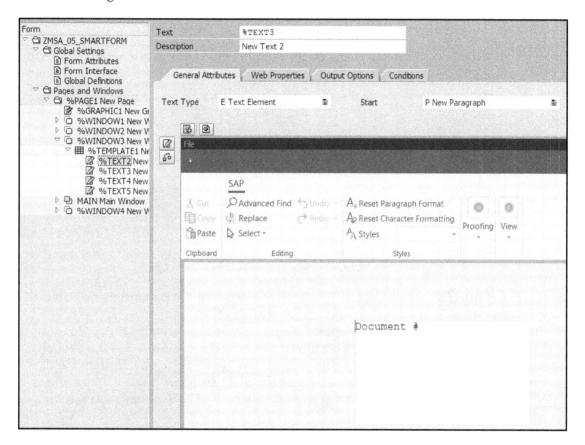

For **%TEXT4** and **%TEXT5**, we need to set dynamic values that will we retrieve from the SmartForm interface. Open **Field List** by clicking on the following icon:

This will give you access to a new menu on the bottom left:

In the **Import Interface** section, you will have all the default input parameters available, such as the printout archive, emails, and output settings. These values are typically populated in the printing program. **Export Interface** are values that our printout sends back to the printing program. **Global Data** are global variables that we defined in the **Global Definitions** windows in the **Global Settings** directory. The last category, **System Fields**, shows some of the variables that are available in the **SFSY** structure. In this category, you can find the current time, date, or current page. Go to the **%TEXT4** element. Click on the insert field icon:

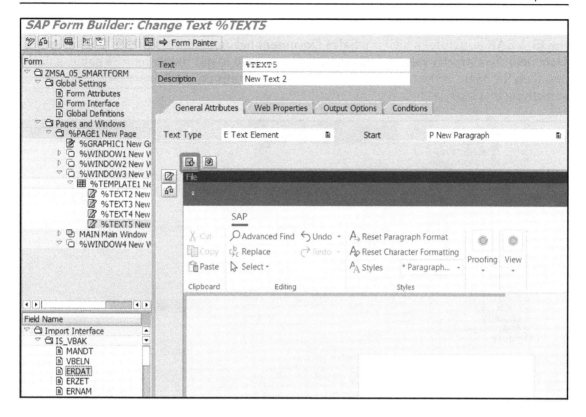

In the **Insert Fields** popup, add `&IS_VBAK-AUDAT&` as text, as shown in the following screenshot:

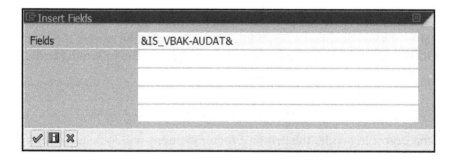

You can get the name of a field from the **Field Name** area. In this example, we are using the **IS_VBAK** structure, which is a **Sales Document** header and an **AUDAT Document Date** field. To extract a value from a structure, you have to put the structure's name, a dash, and then the name of the field. After clicking on the **Continue** check mark, you will get something that looks as follows:

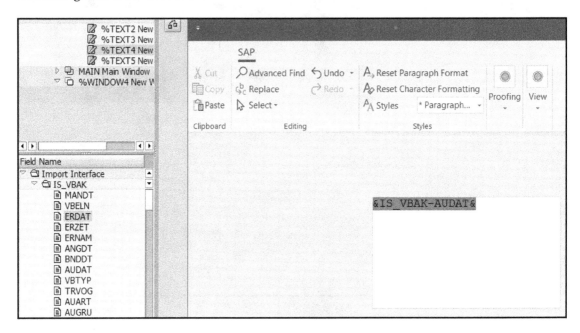

A gray color means that the text has been recognized as a dynamic variable. Follow the same procedure that you did for **%TEXT5**. The document number is in the **VBELN** field of the **IS_VBAK** structure. There are two last elements missing: the footer and main window, along with table of sales document positions. Now, we will take care of the footer. Go to the **%WINDOW4** element, add a new text object, and insert the following text:

```
If you have any questions about this purchase order, please contact

Service Desk at (257) 563-7401 or service@lemonfoods.com
```

By running the preceding code, the printout footer element will look as follows:

```
If you have any questions about this purchase order, please
contact
Service Desk at (257) 563-7401 or service@lemonfoods.com
```

It's not quite the same as in the original template. In order to achieve the same effect (the size and style of the font and the alignment of the paragraph), we have to use Smart Styles. To create new style, go to the **SMARTSYLES** transaction and create a new object:

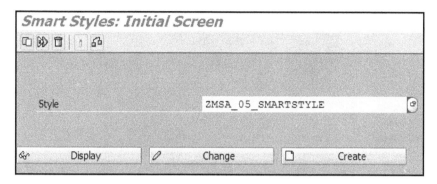

Click on the create node icon:

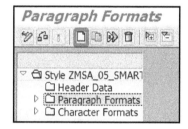

Then, choose **Paragraph Format**:

Set the **Alignment** to **CENTER**:

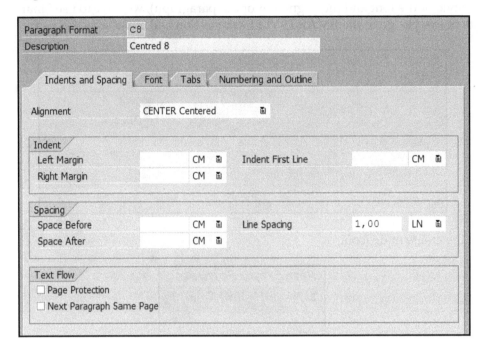

In the **Font** tab, set **Font Family** and **Font Size**:

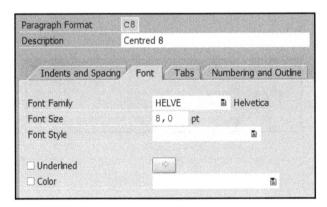

Create another paragraph format, **L0**, and leave it with its default values. The last missing settings are in the **Header Data** window. You need to set **L0** as the standard paragraph:

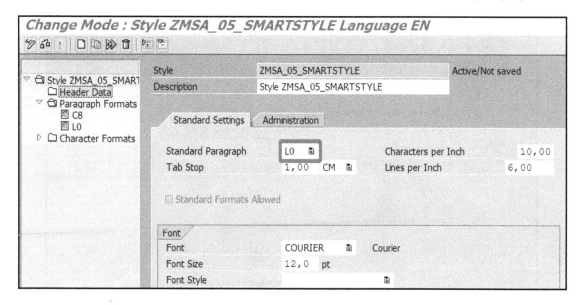

Make everything **Active** and go back to **%TEXT6** in the **SmartForm** object. Set **Style** in the **Output Options** table:

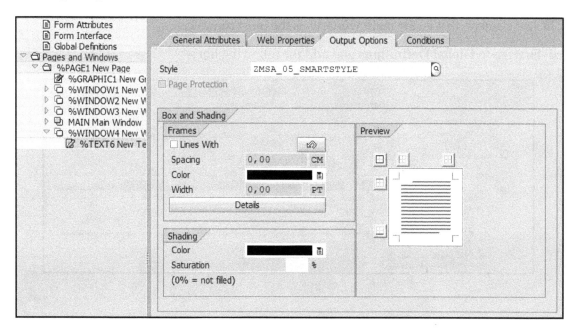

In the **General Attributes** tab, set **Styles** to **C8**. The text style in the footer should change immediately:

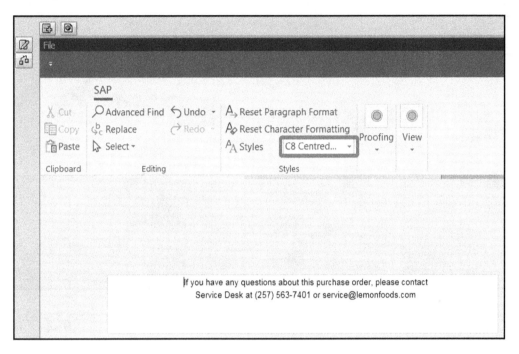

The last element, that is, the main window, is the most complicated.

ed. First, go to **Global Definitions** and add the following lines:

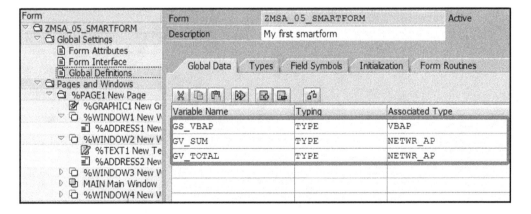

Then, **Create** a **Table** object:

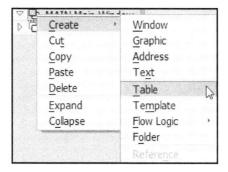

Every **Table** object has three sections. The **Header** section is where we put information that has to be displayed at the start of the table and/or in the page break. In the **Main Area**, you insert the list of elements that you want to display in the table. This section will include our individual sales document items. The content of the **Footer** section is displayed at the end of the table and/or in the page break:

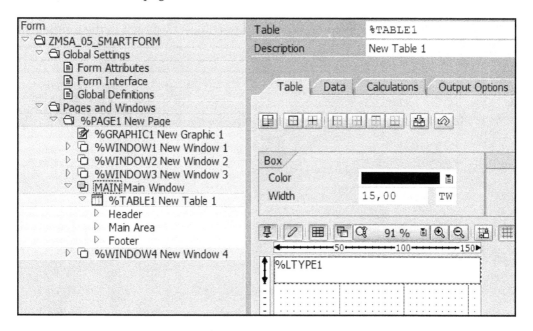

First of all, we have to create three types of lines: one for the header of our table, one for the list, and one with only two columns for the footer, where the total value is displayed. Lines define the layout of the row. Click on the **%TABLE1** object and in the **Table** tab, click on **Details**:

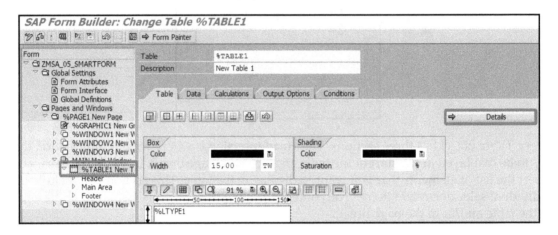

In the **Details** section, create the aforementioned three lines, as shown in the following screenshot:

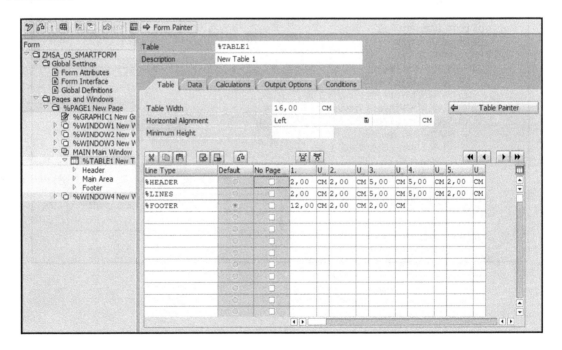

Go back to **Table Painter** and set all the styles according to the template. We need to add a new line to each section of **%TABLE1**. Do this for the **Header**, **Main Area**, and **Footer**:

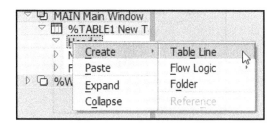

After creating the line, you need to define the **Line Type** for every newly created line. Set **%HEADER** in **Header**, **%LINES** in **Main Area**, and **%FOOTER** in **Footer**. Keep in mind that you may have different values here if you created lines differently than in the previous steps:

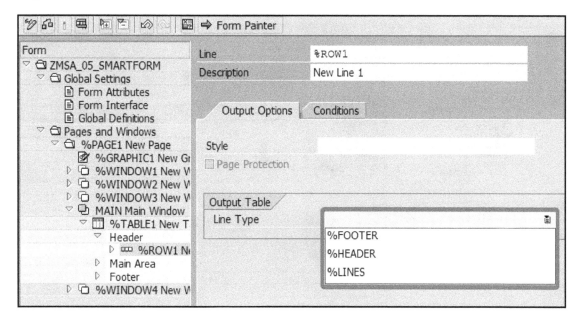

After choosing a **Line Type**, multiple cell objects will be generated:

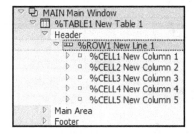

In every cell, create a text object and place a dynamic or static value, according to the template. In the **Data** tab of the **%TABLE1** object, you need to add a reference to the IT_VBAP table and the GS_VBAP structure:

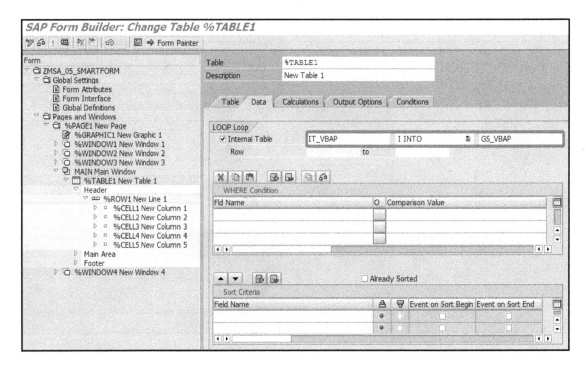

In the GS_VBAP structure, you will find all the necessary fields. The material number is in the **MATNR** field, the description is in **MATKL**, the ordered quantity is in **KWMENG**, and the unit price is in **NETWR**. For the total item price, you need to multiply the amount by the number of pieces. For such operations, we need a command object. Right-click on **%CELL6** (the first cell of the **Main Area** row) and choose to **Create | Flow Logic | Program Lines**:

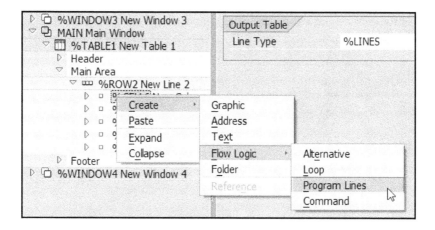

Program Lines allows you to add almost any ABAP code to SAP SmartForm. Put the following code inside the new object:

```
CLEAR: GV_SUM.
GV_SUM = GS_VBAP-KWMENG * GS_VBAP-NETWR.
GV_TOTAL = GV_TOTAL + GV_SUM.
```

It's important to define all three variables in the input/output section. If you did everything according to our instructions, you should have something similar to this:

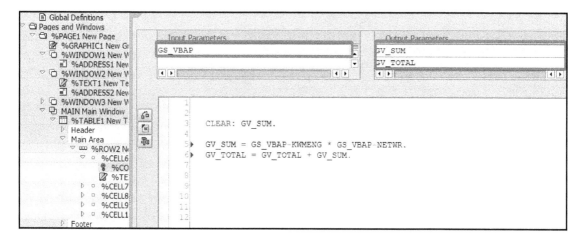

You don't need to activate the **Program Lines** object. It will be activated during the activation of SAP SmartForm. Now, use &GV_SUM& in **%CELL10** as dynamic fields:

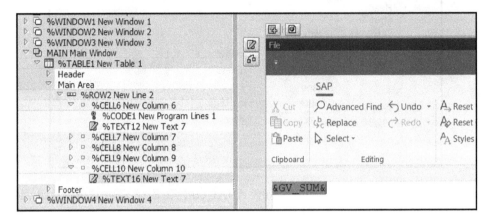

The only thing that's missing is the total sum of the sales document. Create a dynamic reference to GV_TOTAL. You can test the printout manually, but I recommend using a dedicated print program. Create a new report called ZMSA_R_CHAPTER5_1 and put the following code into it:

```
REPORT zmsa_r_chapter5_1.
TABLES: vbak.

PARAMETERS: p_vbeln LIKE vbak-vbeln.
PARAMETERS: p_sf RADIOBUTTON GROUP rb1 DEFAULT 'X'.
PARAMETERS: p_af RADIOBUTTON GROUP rb1.

CLASS lcl_demo DEFINITION.
  PUBLIC SECTION.
    CLASS-METHODS main IMPORTING iv_vbeln TYPE vbeln iv_smart TYPE boolean.

  PRIVATE SECTION.
    CLASS-METHODS factory IMPORTING iv_vbeln TYPE vbeln RETURNING
                          VALUE(ro_demo) TYPE REF TO lcl_demo.
    METHODS print_SmartForm.
    METHODS print_adobe.
    METHODS load_data IMPORTING iv_vbeln TYPE vbeln.

    DATA: mt_vbap TYPE vbap_tty.
    DATA: ms_vbak TYPE vbak.
    DATA: mv_sender_adrc TYPE adrnr.
    DATA: mv_recipient_adrc TYPE adrnr.

ENDCLASS.
```

We also need CLASS implementation:

```
CLASS lcl_demo IMPLEMENTATION.
  METHOD main.
    IF p_sf = abap_true.
      lcl_demo=>factory( p_vbeln )->print_SmartForm( ).
    ELSE.
      lcl_demo=>factory( p_vbeln )->print_adobe( ).
    ENDIF.
  ENDMETHOD.

  METHOD factory.
    CREATE OBJECT ro_demo.
    ro_demo->load_data( iv_vbeln ).
  ENDMETHOD.
ENDCLASS.

START-OF-SELECTION.
  lcl_demo=>main( EXPORTING iv_vbeln = p_vbeln iv_smart = p_sf ).
```

Add the load_data method to the implementation section. It will load data from the database or generate one if needed. First, add the following SELECT logic:

```
METHOD load_data.

    SELECT SINGLE kunnr vkorg audat vbeln FROM vbak INTO CORRESPONDING
FIELDS OF ms_vbak WHERE vbeln = iv_vbeln.

    IF ms_vbak-vbeln IS NOT INITIAL.
    ELSE.
    ENDIF.

ENDMETHOD.
```

Inside the IF statement, put the following code for cases where vbeln is supplied:

```
      SELECT netwr matnr kwmeng matkl FROM vbap APPENDING CORRESPONDING
FIELDS OF TABLE mt_vbap.

      SELECT SINGLE vkorg FROM tvko INTO ms_vbak-bukrs_vf WHERE vkorg =
ms_vbak-vkorg.

      SELECT SINGLE adrnr FROM t001 INTO mv_sender_adrc WHERE bukrs =
ms_vbak-bukrs_vf.

      SELECT SINGLE adrnr FROM kna1 INTO mv_recipient_adrc WHERE kunnr =
ms_vbak-kunnr.
```

For the ELSE statement, put the following logic, which will generate fake data for you:

```
ms_vbak-vbeln = '100001'.
ms_vbak-audat = '20180101'.

SELECT SINGLE addrnumber INTO mv_recipient_adrc FROM adrc.
mv_sender_adrc = mv_recipient_adrc.

DATA: ls_vbap TYPE vbap.
CLEAR: ls_vbap.
ls_vbap-matnr = '101'.
ls_vbap-matkl = 'Test1'.
ls_vbap-netwr = '13.5'.
ls_vbap-kwmeng = '10'.
APPEND ls_vbap TO mt_vbap.

CLEAR: ls_vbap.
ls_vbap-matnr = '102'.
ls_vbap-matkl = 'Test2'.
ls_vbap-netwr = '25'.
ls_vbap-kwmeng = '5'.
APPEND ls_vbap TO mt_vbap.

CLEAR: ls_vbap.
ls_vbap-matnr = '103'.
ls_vbap-matkl = 'Test3'.
ls_vbap-netwr = '100'.
ls_vbap-kwmeng = '2'.
APPEND ls_vbap TO mt_vbap.
```

To test SmartForm, add the print_SmartForm method by using the following code:

```
METHOD print_SmartForm.
  DATA: lv_fname TYPE rs38l_fnam.

  CALL FUNCTION 'SSF_FUNCTION_MODULE_NAME'
    EXPORTING
      formname = 'ZMSA_05_SmartForm'
    IMPORTING
      fm_name = lv_fname
    EXCEPTIONS
      no_form = 1
      no_function_module = 2
      OTHERS = 3.

ENDMETHOD.
```

This will retrieve a function module for the ZMSA_05_SmartForm SmartForm object. After the SSF_FUNCTION_MODULE_NAME function call, add the following logic to the call form object:

```
CALL FUNCTION lv_fname
      EXPORTING
        is_vbak = ms_vbak
        it_vbap = mt_vbap
        iv_sender_adrc = mv_sender_adrc
        iv_recipient_adrc = mv_recipient_adrc
      EXCEPTIONS
        formatting_error = 1
        internal_error = 2
        send_error = 3
        user_canceled = 4
        OTHERS = 5.
```

To test Adobe, we need something similar. First, add a new method, print_adobe:

```
METHOD print_adobe.
    DATA: ie_outputparams TYPE sfpoutputparams.
    DATA: lv_funcname TYPE funcname.

    CALL FUNCTION 'FP_JOB_OPEN'
      CHANGING
        ie_outputparams = ie_outputparams.

    TRY.
        CALL FUNCTION 'FP_FUNCTION_MODULE_NAME'
          EXPORTING
            i_name = 'ZMSA_05_AF_ADOBE'
          IMPORTING
            e_funcname = lv_funcname.
      CATCH cx_fp_api_repository.
      CATCH cx_fp_api_usage.
      CATCH cx_fp_api_internal.
    ENDTRY.

  ENDMETHOD.
```

This will open a form generation JOB and retrieve the function's module name. We also need to add the following coding, just after ENDTRY, to invoke Adobe object logic:

```
DATA: ls_docparams TYPE sfpdocparams.
DATA: ls_formoutput TYPE fpformoutput.

    CALL FUNCTION lv_funcname
      EXPORTING
```

```
    /1bcdwb/docparams = ls_docparams
    is_vbak = ms_vbak
    it_vbap = mt_vbap
    iv_sender_adrc = mv_sender_adrc
    iv_recipient_adrc = mv_recipient_adrc
IMPORTING
    /1bcdwb/formoutput = ls_formoutput
EXCEPTIONS
    usage_error = 1
    system_error = 2
    internal_error = 3.
```

Adobe jobs have to be closed after the form is generated. To do that, you need to add he following call to the end of the method:

```
CALL FUNCTION 'FP_JOB_CLOSE'
    EXCEPTIONS
        usage_error = 1
        system_error = 2
        internal_error = 3
        OTHERS = 4.
```

If you run the report, you should be able to see something that looks similar to the original template:

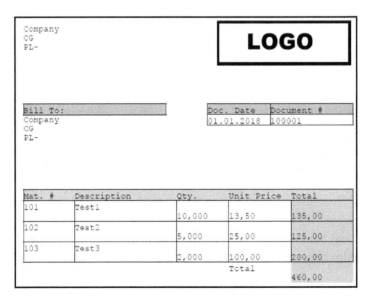

A PDF file of this document can be found in this book's GitHub repository.

Adobe Forms

SAP Interactive Forms by Adobe is the latest approach to creating printouts. The Adobe package has been an integral part of NetWeaver since its 2004 version, but it is also a separate product and can be successfully used in enterprises that do not use SAP software. It consists of a LifeCycle Designer with a form editor and the Adobe Document Service, a server that interprets calls and generates printouts.

Adobe Document Service works on Java stacks, which means you need to have Java Stack SAP Web Application Server installed. This is not the only difference between native print technologies and Adobe. A large advantage of Adobe is the ability to implement interactive solutions, which, for example, allow users to enter information into the system. Adobe uses two languages for programming FormCalc logic and classic JavaScript. Examples of the use of both technologies will be available in the next section.

Creating our first Adobe Form

In this example, we will try to create our sales document using Adobe technology. You need to install Adobe LifeCycle Designer (available on the SAP Marketplace) on your frontend machine before taking any further actions. A link to instructions on how to do this are available in the *Further reading* section of this chapter. The creation of Adobe Forms takes place in the SFP transaction:

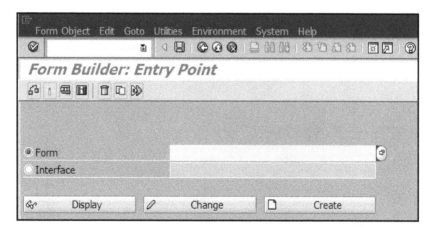

On the main screen, you will see two options: **Form** is an Adobe Form object, while **Interface** is an object that connects two worlds, that is, SAP and Adobe. We will start by creating a new interface called ZMSA_05_AI_ADOBE. Put a name into the **Interface** field and click on the **Create** button. In the new popup, choose a description and **Interface Type**, and then click **Save**:

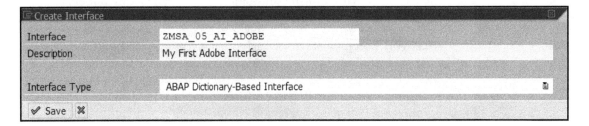

On the next screen, you will see some similarities to the SmartForm transaction. There is the **Code Initialization** section, the **Import** and **Export** parameters, and **Global Data**:

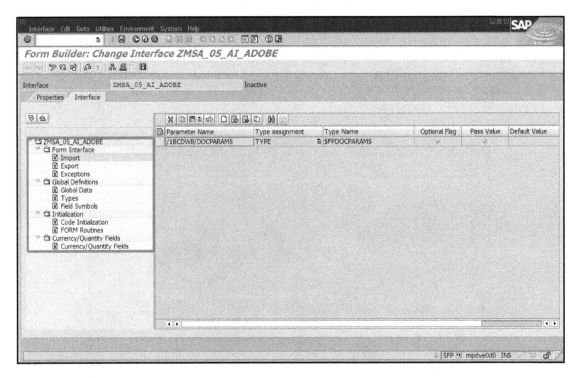

Based on the SmartForm example, we know what import parameters we will need here. Click on the add button and add the following rows:

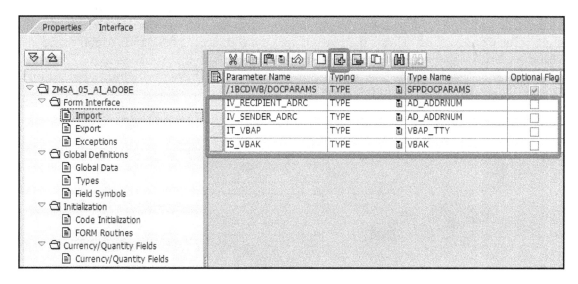

Activate the interface object and go back to the main menu. Now, create a new Adobe Form object:

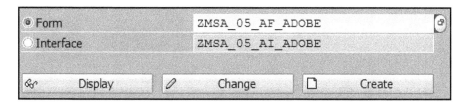

In the popup window, set a **Description** and choose the **Interface** we just created. Then, click on the **Save** button:

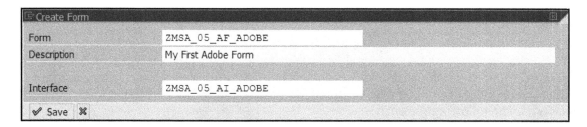

On the next screen, you will see three tabs. Properties are just basic information and settings related to the form—date of creation, author user, and form interface. In the **Context** menu, you will see two main sections. On the left-hand side, you have the **Interface** section, where all import parameters are available. On the right-hand side, there is the **Context** form. This is the place where we connect the SAP and Adobe worlds. You can grab any parameters from ABAP and drop them into the Adobe section. This will allow you to access the value inside the printout. We need to have pretty much everything. Drag and drop **IS_VBAK** and **IT_VBAP**:

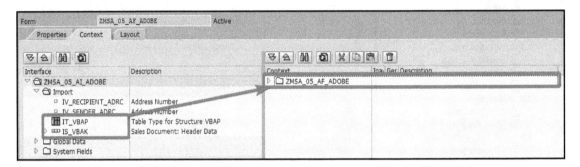

For the address, we need to create two address objects (similar to what we did in SmartForm). Click on the main folder of the **Context** section and choose **Create | Address**:

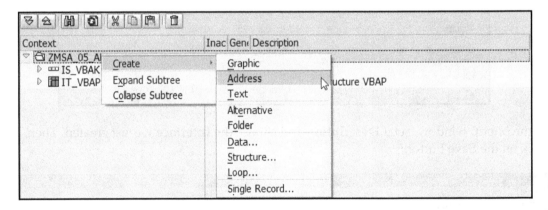

If you click on the address object, you will see the new option, just below the context section. We need to connect the **Address** object with our import parameter. You can input the name of the import parameter manually (**IV_SENDER_ADRC**) or drag and drop, as shown in the following screenshot:

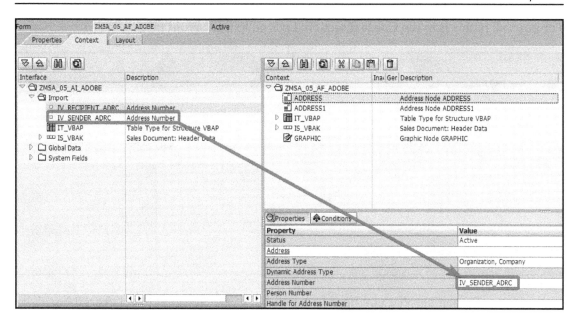

Repeat the procedure of adding the address for the **IV_RECIPIENT_ADRC** parameter. At this stage, it is also required that you enter the country in the **Country** field. It can be made dynamic by using a variable or static if the company works on the territory of one country. We also need to deactivate all of the fields that aren't needed in the **IT_VBAP** and **IS_VBAK** tables:

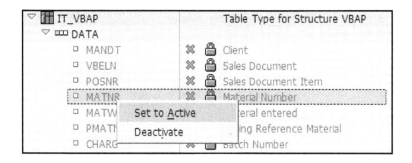

For now, all of this is in the **Context** section. Let's go to the **Layout** tab:

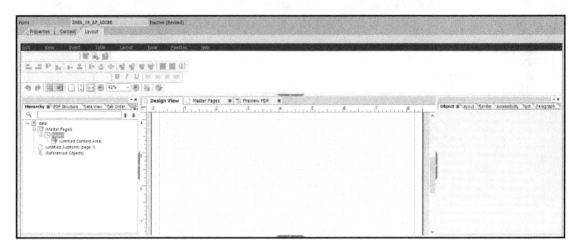

 Remember that you need to install LifeCycle Designer to get everything working.

By default, on the left-hand side, you have a hierarchy panel with all the available data. In the middle, you have the form's layout, and on the right-hand side, you have multiple tabs with specific parameters set for the Adobe model. If a panel or tab is missing, you can turn them on by using the **Palettes** menu in the top bar. Let's go to the **Data View** tab on the left-hand panel. Drag and drop the **ADDRESS** object:

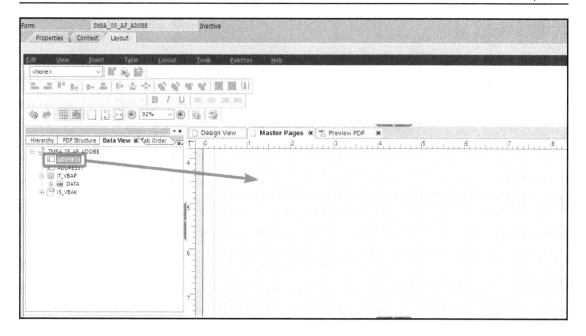

Set all of the necessary settings in **Object | Field**, as follows:

Do the same for **Layout**:

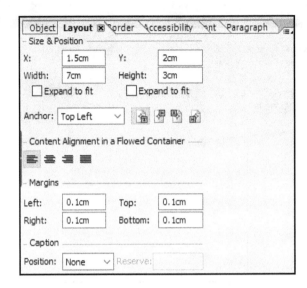

Repeat this for **ADDRESS1**. Adjust the positions to make them look like they do on our template. After all of these steps, you should have something similar to the following:

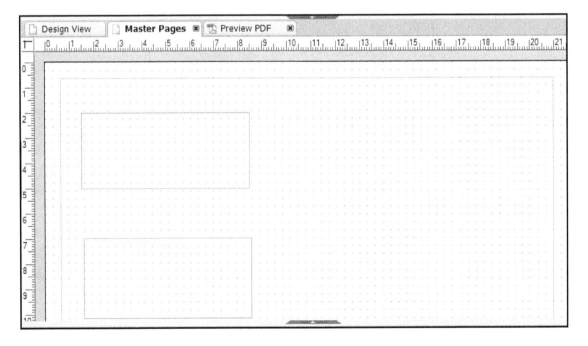

Now, we can take care of the main table with document positions. Drag and drop the table, like we did with **ADDRESS**:

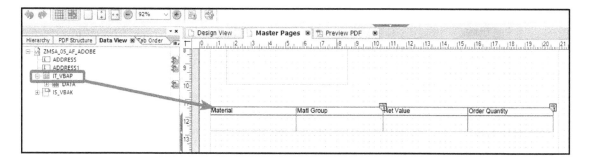

We need to add an additional column for the total sum, but to do this, we need to shrink the current columns to make some space:

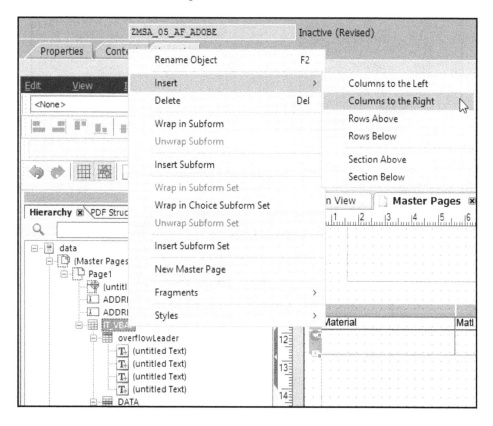

An additional row has to be added to the bottom of the table to make space for the total sum of all positions. Don't forget to add a **Description**:

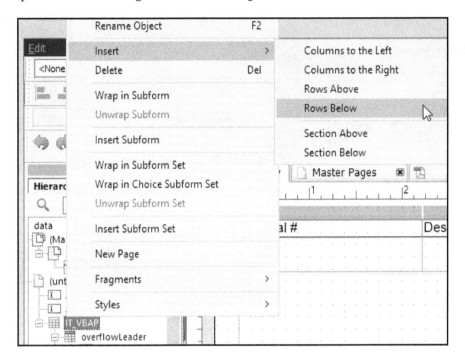

You have to play around with the layout, add a background color, and change the border's layout. These settings can be found in the **Borders** tab:

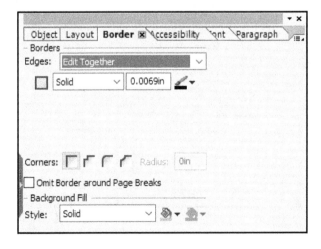

You may need to change fonts in the **Font** tab:

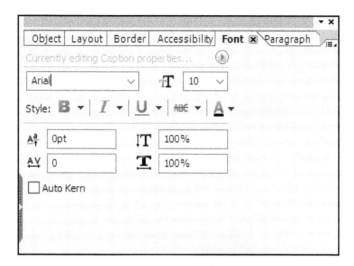

The paragraph settings can be found in the **Paragraph** tab:

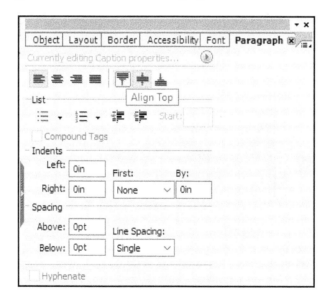

We will use the same technique to populate the **Sum** and **totalSum** fields. In Adobe Forms, you can use two script languages – FormCalc and JavaScript. FormCalc has higher performance and may be easier for non-programmers, but JavaScript is more useful for creating sophisticated interactive and dynamic forms. It's also a very popular programming language, so it will be quite easy for a programmer to jump into scripting. This script can be assigned to form a layout object as follows:

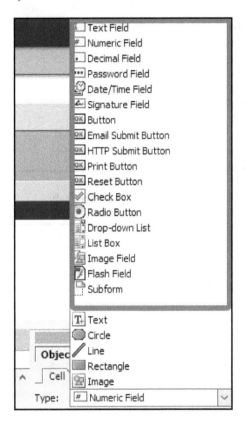

It's very important to understand when scripts are executed. In each object, the script is divided into multiple sections, and each section represents different events of the form's life cycle. In our case, we will only focus on the calculate event from the process events category. First, we will create two scripts. One will calculate the total of each position, while the other will calculate the total value of the document. To create a script, open the **Script Editor**:

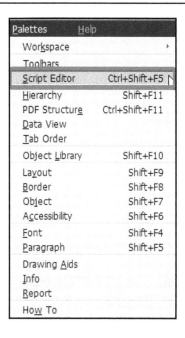

It will be above **Design View** by default:

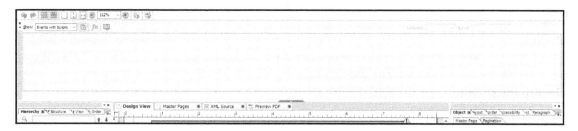

To start working with the script, you need to choose an object that allows you to write scripts. In our case, this will be the **posSum** field or **totalSum**. You can set the name of the field by right-clicking on it and choosing **Rename Object**. You can either choose an object from the **Hierarchy** tab or from the **Design view**:

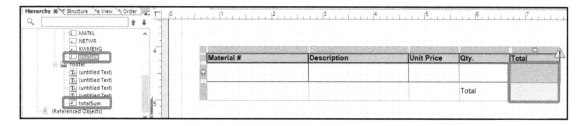

Then, choose an event where you want to put the script (`calculate`) and the scripting language (`JavaScript`):

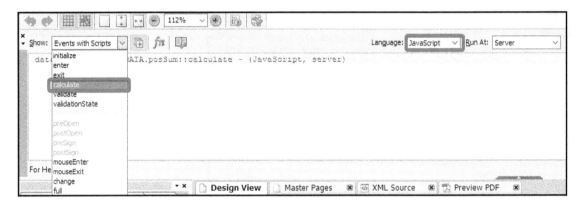

Inside **posSum**, calculate the event by using the following code:

```
this.rawValue = xfa.resolveNode("Main.IT_VBAP.DATA[" + this.parent.index +
"].NETWR").rawValue * xfa.resolveNode("Main.IT_VBAP.DATA[" +
this.parent.index + "].KWMENG").rawValue;
```

This refers to an object where you placed the script. `rawValue` is an attribute where raw object values are stored. The `resolveNode` method from the `xfa` object can return a reference to any node of a form. In our case, we need to get the value of the quantity field and net price. We will calculate the necessary data using multiplication. This script will run once for every item element. For the `totalSum` value, we will put following script in the **totalSum** field:

```
var num = 0, rowList = xfa.resolveNodes("Main.IT_VBAP.DATA[*]");

for (var i = 0; i < rowList.length; i++){
if (!rowList.item(i).posSum.isNull &&
parseFloat(rowList.item(i).posSum.rawValue) != 0) {
num += parseFloat(rowList.item(i).posSum.rawValue);
}
}

this.rawValue = num;
```

This is pretty similar to what we did for posSum. First, we define variables and resolve nodes. We will refer to every item in our tables. Basically, we take the entire posSum column and add each value to the num variable. We also check that the value in posSum is not null and can be parsed to a float, just to make sure that no exceptions will appear. Finally, we will insert the rawValue attribute of the totalSum node. So far, so good. Next, we will take care of the graphic element. Go back to the Interface object and create **Global Data**:

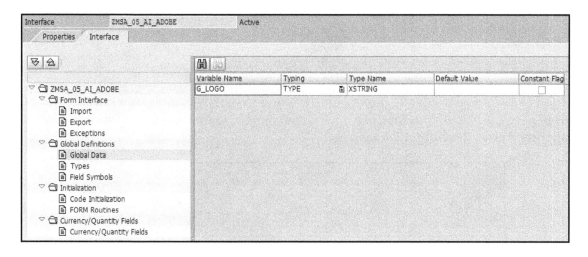

Go to the **Code Initialization** section:

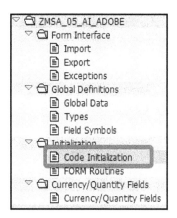

We need to add the following ABAP code:

```
CALL METHOD cl_ssf_xsf_utilities=>get_bds_graphic_as_bmp
EXPORTING
p_object = 'GRAPHICS' "Name of object
p_name = 'ZLOGO' "Name of the SE78 logo inside Quotes
p_id = 'BMAP' "BMAP
p_btype = 'BCOL' "'BCOL' for color, 'BMON' for Black & White
RECEIVING
p_bmp = g_logo "v_field and g_logo must be typed xstring
EXCEPTIONS
not_found = 1
internal_error = 2
OTHERS = 3.
```

This code will read the ZLOGO object from SE78 and store it in G_LOGO. You can check this in Appendix A, *Assessments* for more information on how to upload custom images. It's also important to set the **Output Parameters**:

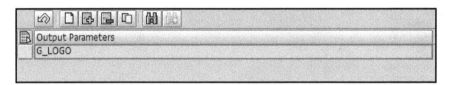

Save and active everything and head back to the **Context** tab in the Adobe Form object. Right-click in the right-hand section and choose to **Create|Graphic**:

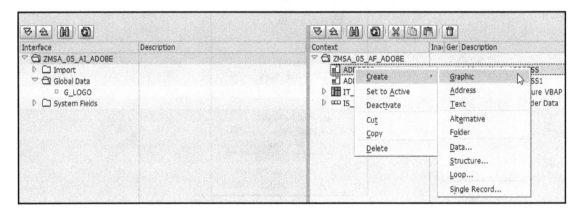

In the graphics object attribute, set G_LOGO as the source and **MIME Type** as 'IMAGE/BMP':

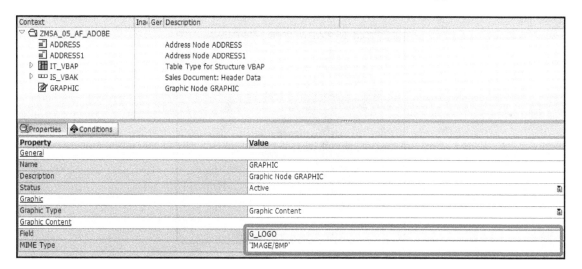

Now, we can go back to the **Layout** tab and use a new graphic. You can simply grab a graphics object from **Data View** and drag it into the **Design View**:

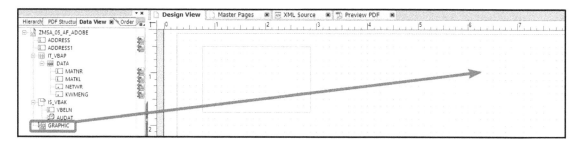

The **Graphic** is ready, so now we need to take care of the footer. Create another subform in **Page1** and inside the new subform, create a text object:

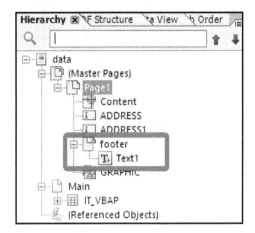

Pass the following text into the text object:

```
If you have any questions about this purchase order, please contact
Service Desk at (257) 563-7401 or service@lemonfoods.com
```

You will see something that looks similar to the following screenshot:

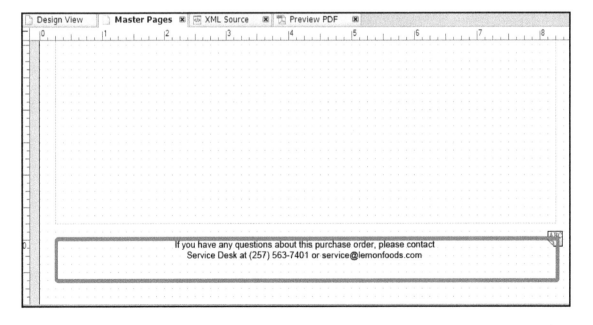

Now, we will create a box that holds the main information of the document (date and document number). Drag and drop the following fields from **DataView**:

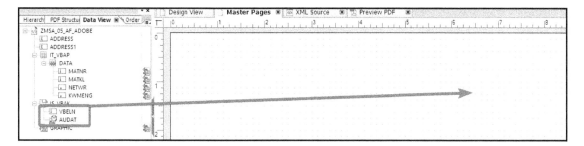

You will need to remove **Caption**:

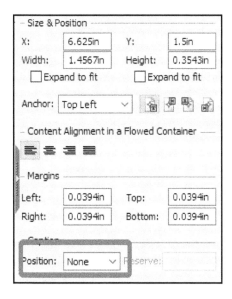

Then, add two text objects. By now, you should have four objects:

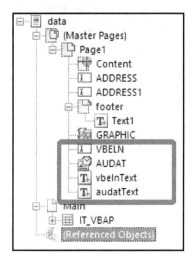

Play around with the style and position to get the layout close to the template's:

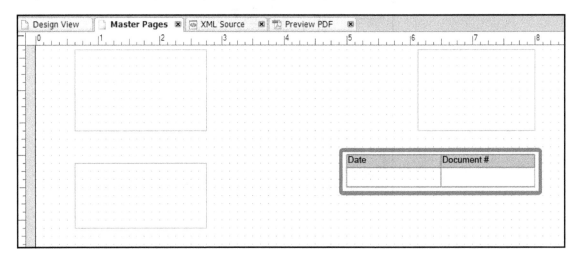

By the way, we can also add a description to the window with the address. Simply create another test element:

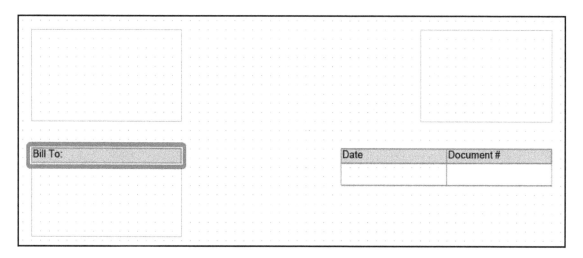

To test the form, you can simply use the ZMSA_R_CHAPTER5_1 report and run an Adobe example. Try and play around with the layout to make this form look exactly like the template.

Summary

I'm glad to inform you that you are ready to make a commercial printout project. In this chapter, you've come across two technologies that are widely used in the SAP ecosystem–SAP Smart Form and Interactive Forms by Adobe. Now you know the advantages and disadvantages of both solutions and you are able to pre-form the form according to the requirements of the clients. You should also have a basic understanding of SAPScript technology and its historical meaning. You also know that printouts are not only for technical knowledge but also for aesthetics and accuracy.

In the next chapter, we will discuss how we can handle XML files in ABAP.

Questions

The following questions will allow you to consolidate the information contained in this chapter:

1. What object is used in SmartForm as an ABAP code container?
2. On the printout template, there are multiple empty rows in the position table. How can we achieve this effect in SAP SmartForm/Adobe Forms?
3. What two languages can you use in an Adobe Form for scripting?
4. What transaction should you use if you want to upload additional graphics to the server?
5. What's the difference between positioned and flowed object location?
6. What mean by **events** in the context of Adobe Form and when happen in each of event?
7. What is the meaning of the word *interactive* in Interactive Forms?

Further reading

You may want to check out the following links for more information regarding what was covered in this chapter:

- **Adobe**: `https://help.adobe.com/en_US/livecycle/10.0/DesignerScriptingBasics/index.html`
- **SmartForm**: `https://help.sap.com/saphelp_nw70ehp1/helpdata/en/a5/de6838abce021ae10000009b38f842/frameset.htm`
- **SAPScript**: `https://help.sap.com/saphelp_nw70/helpdata/en/d6/0db8bb494511d182b70000e829fbfe/frameset.htm`

6
ABAP and XML

Working with XML files is a common task in any SAP project, especially where we have multiple systems (SAP or non-SAP) and we need to integrate them with the interface. In a NetWeaver environment, there are multiple approaches to handling the XML format. You can use one of the standard classes prepared by SAP, or create your own transformation using an SAP declarative language called **Simple Transformation** (**ST**). On the basis of examples prepared in this chapter, you will learn how to apply each method and learn about their advantages and disadvantages.

The following topics will be covered in this chapter:

- Parsing and displaying XML files into the `CL_XML_DOCUMENT` class
- Changing the content of an XML using the `CL_XML_DOCUMENT` class
- Introduction to ST
- XML serialization and deserialization using ST
- JSON-XML format in ABAP
- Converting XML to JSON with the sXML Library

Technical requirements

The following requirements need to be met for all examples from this chapter to work:

- **JSON-XML**: NetWeaver system of at least version releases 7.02 and 7.03/7.31 (Kernel patch 116)

All the code used in this chapter can be downloaded from the following GitHub link: `https://github.com/PacktPublishing/Mastering-SAP-ABAP/tree/master/Chapter06`.

Using the CL_XML_DOCUMENT class for XML

The class described in this chapter is based on the very well known and frequently used iXML library. The *integrated* XML provides a full spectrum of useful tools and methods to read, parse, and edit the XML format. We will use the following XML file in all examples in this chapter:

```
<?xml version="1.0" encoding="UTF-8"?>
<AIRLINES>
 <SCARR>
 <CARRID>A2</CARRID>
 <CARRNAME>Antarctica Airlines</CARRNAME>
 <CURRCODE>AQD</CURRCODE>
 <URL>http://antarcticaairlines.aq</URL>
 </SCARR>
</AIRLINES>
```

The following XML is an airline and booking data model system available in most SAP system IDES versions. We will start every example with a standard, local class—based report. You can find this template in `Appendix A`, *Assessments*.

Reading and parsing XML files to ABAP

This example shows how to resolve a situation where we have an external system, *Y*, which exports airline data to an XML file and uploads it onto the FTP server. The ABAP report needs to read those files and store them in a database table in SAP ERP.

Create a new report: `ZMSA_R_CHAPTER6_01`. Delete everything, and copy and paste the sample report template. We will put the entire logic in the main method from our `lcl_demo` class. In real life, we should always follow SOC design principles and create a separate method for each function, but this is just for demonstrative purposes and creating an additional method may cause unnecessary confusion.

Add the following code to your report:

```
CONSTANTS: lv_filepath   TYPE localfile VALUE 'C:\temp\carr.xml'.
DATA: lo_xml      TYPE REF TO cl_xml_document.

CREATE OBJECT lo_xml.

lo_xml->import_from_file( filename = lv_filepath ).

lo_xml->display( ).
```

The file path is hardcoded in the `lv_filepath` constant, but, in a real project, you'll use an additional method, for example, the one from the `cl_gui_frontend_services` class called `file_open_dialog`, to choose a file from any directory. This class is already used in the `import_from_file` method to handle file reading requests. Keep in mind that this is a frontend scenario, so the XML will be uploaded from your local PC—after running your code, you will be asked for authorization, and you have to grant it. Be sure to have the `carr.xml` file in the `C:\temp\` directory or, if needed, change the path in the constant to align it with your system. Reading the file from the local PC is done less frequently in an interface scenario than reading files from the server, but is perfect as a starting point in terms of becoming familiar with the generic ideas behind XML. Remember to test your code every time you do make changes.

There is nothing complex in this code. We create a constant and variable and initialize both. After that final step, you call the `import_from_file` method and load the XML file into the `lo_xml` class. The last line is required to display XML in a pop-up window. If everything went well, after execution, you should see the following content of the XML file we just created:

Changing XML data

This example shows you how to change XML data when it turns out that System Y uses different currency code than the SAP customization. After reading the XML file, we need to map external currency codes to SAP ERP internal ones. Airlines from the XML file, *Antarctica Airline,* use Antarctica dollars as currency and CURRCODE in external system use AQD acronym in context of Antarctica dollars and in SAP system we use AQQ. This will not differ from our previous example, so you can simply copy the ZMSA_R_CHAPTER6_01 report into a new ZMSA_R_CHAPTER6_02 file.

We need to access a currency code value from our XML structure and from the CURRCODE node. To handle such requests, we have to use the find_simple_element method which can read element value:

```
CONSTANTS: cv_currname TYPE string VALUE 'CURRCODE'.
CONSTANTS: cv_currcode_old TYPE string VALUE 'AQD'.
CONSTANTS: cv_currcode_new TYPE string VALUE 'AQQ'.

DATA(lo_node) = lo_xml->find_node( EXPORTING name = cv_currname ).

WRITE: lo_node->get_value( ).
```

We have three constants. cv_currname is the name of the node we would like to find, cv_currcode_old is the currency code, and we need to map to our new currency using cv_currcode_new. In the preceding code, we call the find_node method and put the result in the lo_node variable. The find_node method returns an implementation of the if_ixml_node interface. This gives us access to a very nice method called get_value. If we invoke it, we will be able to read values from our current node. The last line is just for testing purposes, but, if you like to test code, remember to comment on the last line of the report to avoid the XML popup displaying the following:

```
*  lo_xml->display( ).
```

The final step is to change the value in our node. It's very simple. We just need to call the set_value method on the node object. Of course, we first need to check whether that is the currency we want to map, so an additional IF condition is required.

Use the following code as a reference for what you should have at this stage:

```
IF lo_node->get_value( ) = cv_currcode_old.
    lo_node->set_value( value = cv_currcode_new ).
ENDIF.

lo_xml->display( ).
```

Remember to remove the line with the `write` command and uncomment the display method to check your code. You should see new values in the XML display window:

```
Display XML document

<?xml version="1.0" encoding="UTF-8"?>
- <AIRLINES>
  - <SCARR>
       <CARRID>A2</CARRID>
       <CARRNAME>Antarctica Airlines</CARRNAME>
       <CURRCODE>AQD</CURRCODE>
       <URL>http://antarcticaairlines.aq</URL>
    </SCARR>
</AIRLINES>
```

At this point, we did three basic operations—**XML read**, **XML display**, and **XML change**. Those are, of course, only basic change operations and, in real life, we will have to do something more sophisticated. Cutting, adding the whole node, changing the attribute, or even transforming entire XML structures are very common challenges to deal with. The previous examples should be treated as a starting point for learning more about the `cl_xml_document` class.

Simple transformations in ABAP

ST was created by an SAP declarative language that allows serialization and deserialization between XML formats and ABAP data. Most SAP developers have heard about ST at least once, but only a few have chance to use it in a real project. This is probably due to a lack of working examples on the internet and some additional difficulties described in this chapter. Before using ST, you should take into consideration the following constraints:

- It's only allowed to transform between two formats of ABAP data and XML but not between XML, and XML, or ABAP and ABAP.
- To find a problem in ST, you have to use an ST debugger. This is much more limiting compared with an ABAP debugger.
- You can only transform value-based data, such as fields, structures, or internal tables. You are not able to work with references.

From another point of view, using ST also has a lot of advantages:

- It's a declarative language, but still very simple to use and understand.
- Transformations work both ways, which means you can write one transformation program and use it for serialization and deserialization.
- It offers nice performance due to serial restriction access and direct addressing of the ABAP data.

You can create an ST in the ABAP Workbench (Transaction SE80) and the Transformation Editor (Transaction XSLT_TOOL), which is a common tool used to create simple transformation and extensible stylesheet language transformations.

Serialization using ST

This example shows you how to deal with a situation where we have an external System X, which requires airline data from SAP ERP. System X is old and very limited. The only possible way to exchange data between System X and SAP ERP is to export the table into an XML file format and then import it into System X's database.

We will start with a standard class-based executable report and put the program logic in the main method. The first part of our program is data selection:

```
DATA: lt_carr TYPE TABLE OF scarr.
DATA: lv_xml TYPE xstring.

SELECT *
        FROM scarr
        INTO CORRESPONDING FIELDS OF TABLE @lt_carr.
```

The next step is to create an ST. We will use a dedicated tool for that—the Transformation Editor (Transaction XSLT_TOOL). On the main screen, fill everything in, as shown in the following screenshot:

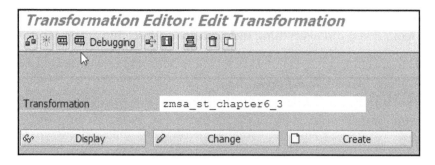

Choose a name and click on **Create**. Call this transformation ZMSA_ST_CHAPTER6_3:

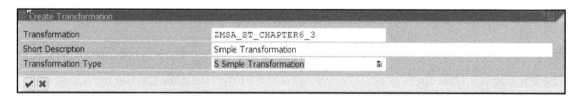

Fill in the description and transformation type. Choose S Simple Transformation. We will discuss XSLT in further chapters. An ST can be created using a text-based editor or graphically. Both approaches will be covered here. Initially, we always get the following transformation template:

```
<?sap.transform simple?>
<tt:transform xmlns:tt="http://www.sap.com/transformation-templates">

<tt:root name="ROOT"/>

<tt:template>
</tt:template>

</tt:transform>
```

The first line is just to identify the type of transformation. The second and last are root elements, where we include everything else. The "ROOT" element is an interface between the ABAP program and the ST. One root element is obligatory for every transformation. The last two tags are template tags. Every transformation needs to have at least one template, but, if necessary, you can have a few of them. Every template must have a unique name in the name attribute. You can always check the descriptions of tags in the tag library; it can be invoked by using the keyboard shortcut *Ctrl + F9*.

To switch to graphical mode, you can use the keyboard shortcut *Ctrl + Shift + F11*, or click on the wand icon. If you did everything right, you should see the graphical editor as follows:

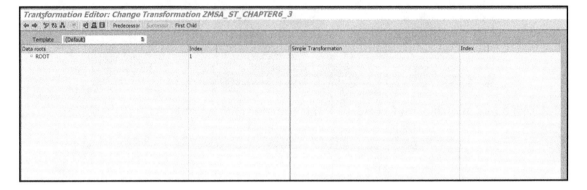

The left side is a **Data roots** panel where you have ST interface data. On the right side is a graphical representation of an ST. Click the right mouse button in the left editor panel and choose the **Insert new root** option from the context menu:

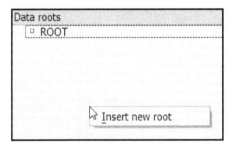

Root-Name is the name of the transformation input/output parameter, and **Type-Name** is an ABAP dictionary type used with this parameter. SCARR_TAB is the table type of the SCARR structure:

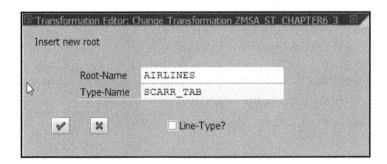

Drag and drop the AIRLINES table from the left side and bring it over to the right side. The transformation will be created automatically. We can now clean it up a bit. Delete the MANDT field from the transformation side and the ROOT element from the data roots side. Save and activate the project and go back to the **Source Code Editor**; you should see something along the lines of the following:

```
<?sap.transform simple?>
<tt:transform xmlns:tt="http://www.sap.com/transformation-templates"
xmlns:ddic="http://www.sap.com/abapxml/types/dictionary"
xmlns:def="http://www.sap.com/abapxml/types/defined">
  <tt:root name="AIRLINES" type="ddic:SCARR_TAB"/>
  <tt:template>
    <AIRLINES>
      <tt:loop ref=".AIRLINES">
        <SCARR>
          <CARRID tt:value-ref="CARRID"/>
          <CARRNAME tt:value-ref="CARRNAME"/>
          <CURRCODE tt:value-ref="CURRCODE"/>
          <URL tt:value-ref="URL"/>
        </SCARR>
      </tt:loop>
    </AIRLINES>
  </tt:template>
</tt:transform>
```

Let's go back to our ABAP report. Put in the CALL TRASFORMATION keyword and fill in the parameters:

```
CALL TRANSFORMATION zmsa_st_chapter6_3
                    SOURCE airlines = lt_carr
                    RESULT XML lv_xml.
```

The last part of our report is to check whether everything works as expected. We will use cl_demo_output and the following method:

```
cl_demo_output=>write_xml( lv_xml ).

cl_demo_output=>display( ).
```

If everything goes well, you will see the following popup, which is in XML format:

```
Output
<AIRLINES>
 <SCARR>
  <MANDT>100</MANDT>
  <CARRID>AA</CARRID>
  <CARRNAME>American Airlines</CARRNAME>
  <CURRCODE>USD</CURRCODE>
  <URL>http://www.aa.com</URL>
 </SCARR>
 <SCARR>
  <MANDT>100</MANDT>
  <CARRID>AC</CARRID>
  <CARRNAME>Air Canada</CARRNAME>
  <CURRCODE>CAD</CURRCODE>
  <URL>http://www.aircanada.ca</URL>
 </SCARR>
 <SCARR>
  <MANDT>100</MANDT>
  <CARRID>AF</CARRID>
  <CARRNAME>Air France</CARRNAME>
  <CURRCODE>EUR</CURRCODE>
  <URL>http://www.airfrance.fr</URL>
 </SCARR>
 <SCARR>
  <MANDT>100</MANDT>
  <CARRID>AZ</CARRID>
  <CARRNAME>Alitalia</CARRNAME>
  <CURRCODE>EUR</CURRCODE>
  <URL>http://www.alitalia.it</URL>
 </SCARR>
```

Deserialization using ST

This example shows you how to read XML files using ST. If you did the serialization example, you are halfway done, at least from an ST perspective. ST works both ways, so it can be used both for serialization and deserialization. Copy the previous example into the ZMSA_R_CHAPTER6_04 report and delete everything you had in the main method.

First, we need to read a file. We will again use our local PC as a starting point. We will use the cl_gui_frontend_services and gui_upload methods. Put everything in the main method, as we did in every previous example:

```
CONSTANTS: lv_filepath   TYPE string VALUE 'C:\temp\carr.xml'.

DATA: lt_carr TYPE TABLE OF scarr.
DATA: lt_filetable    TYPE STANDARD TABLE OF string.
DATA: lv_filecontent  TYPE string.

    CALL METHOD cl_gui_frontend_services=>gui_upload
      EXPORTING
        filename                = lv_filepath
      CHANGING
        data_tab                = lt_filetable
```

```
    EXCEPTIONS
      file_open_error          = 1
      file_read_error          = 2
      no_batch                 = 3
      gui_refuse_filetransfer  = 4
      invalid_type             = 5
      no_authority             = 6
      unknown_error            = 7
      bad_data_format          = 8
      header_not_allowed        = 9
      separator_not_allowed    = 10
      header_too_long          = 11
      unknown_dp_error         = 12
      access_denied            = 13
      dp_out_of_memory         = 14
      disk_full                = 15
      dp_timeout               = 16
      not_supported_by_gui     = 17
      error_no_gui             = 18
      OTHERS                   = 19.

  IF sy-subrc <> 0.
    MESSAGE ID sy-msgid TYPE sy-msgty NUMBER sy-msgno WITH sy-msgv1 sy-
msgv2 sy-msgv3 sy-msgv4.
    RETURN.
  ENDIF.
```

This method has limitations, and file content is imported into an internal table. ST requires the XML content to be stored in a single string. You can use the following code to concatenate internal table lines into a single string:

```
CONCATENATE LINES OF lt_filetable INTO lv_filecontent.
```

Call the simple transformation we created in example *6_3*. Note that we changed the order of XML SOURCE and the airline result in an `lt_carr` table. The transformation calls should look like the following code snippet:

```
CALL TRANSFORMATION zmsa_st_chapter6_3
                SOURCE XML lv_filecontent
                RESULT airlines = lt_carr.
```

The final step is to check out the code and test the results:

```
cl_demo_output=>display( lt_carr ).
```

If you did everything according to the instructions, you should be able to see the following popup:

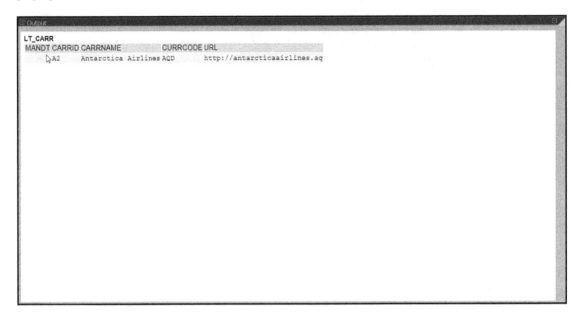

As you can see, there is an additional column, **MANDT**. This is because we used the SCARR structure as a reference to our table. You can change it by creating a new local type that includes only necessary columns.

sXML library for XML and JSON

In this chapter, we will handle conversion of the XML format to JSON format. It's become much easier since releases 7.02 and 7.03/7.31 (Kernelpatch 116), as JSON is now natively supported. To handle JSON format, we will use the sXML library.

Before we start, there are a few important things to mention:

- In SAP, we will be dealing with so-called JSON-XML. It's a special XML format that enables JSON data to be described using an XML representation.
- In sXML, JSON is handled by a new format stored behind the constant value of the sXML interface, IF_SXML=>CO_XT_JSON.

- For serialization and deserialization we will be using transformation with identity ID.

JSON-XML format is required because ST can't interpret JSON; it can use only XML. So, the trick is to get the temporary format and then use the JSON writer class to convert it into the final format. So as to have a better understanding of what the JSON format is, analyze the following example:

```
//JSON
{
 "CARRID":"A2",
 "CARRNAME":"Antarctica Airlines,
 "CURRCODE":"AQD",
 "URL":"http://antarcticaairlines.aq"
}
```

When we convert it into JSON-XML format, we see something similar to this:

```
//JSON-XML
  <object>
      <str name="CARRID">A2</str>
      <str name="CARRNAME">Antarctica Airlines</str>
      <str name="CURRCODE">AQD</str>
      <str name="URL">http://antarcticaairlines.aq</str>
  </object>
```

Here are some basic conversion rules for JSON and JSON-XML formats:

Type	JSON	JSON-XML
Character data	"example"	`<str>abcde</str>`
Numeric data	1410	`<num>1410</num>`
Boolean value	true	`<bool>true</bool>`
Null value	null ["example" 1410 true]	`<null/>`
Array	["example" 1410 true]	`<array> <str>abcde</str> <num>1.234e+5</num> <bool>true</bool> </array>`

Empty array	[]	`<array/>`

Object	{
	"example"
	1410
	true
	}
		`<object>`
		`<str name="text">example</str>`
		`<str name="num">1410</str>`
		`<str name="bool">true</str>`
		`</object>`

Converting XML to JSON

In this section, we will be focusing on how to export SAP ERP database records into a JSON file. Such a file can be used as an SAPUI5 mockup.

We will start with our report template. You can copy any of the previous examples into a new report and delete the content of the main method. To be consistent, name your report ZMSA_R_CHAPTER6_5.

We will start by creating the ty_carr type so that the details in the client field will be invisible. Also, we need to create variables and select data from the SCARR table:

```
TYPES: BEGIN OF ty_carr,
        carrid TYPE s_carr_id,
        carrname TYPE s_carrname,
        currcode TYPE s_currcode,
        url TYPE s_carrurl,
      END OF ty_carr.

DATA: lt_carr TYPE TABLE OF ty_carr.
DATA: lv_result TYPE string.

SELECT *
      FROM scarr
      INTO CORRESPONDING FIELDS OF TABLE @lt_carr.
```

The second step is to create a JSON writer. From a technical perspective, this is the cl_sxml_string_writer class and we will use it in transformations. Note that we use the ID standard transformation:

```
DATA(lo_json_writer_t) = cl_sxml_string_writer=>create( type =
if_sxml=>co_xt_json ).

CALL TRANSFORMATION id SOURCE values = lt_carr
RESULT XML lo_json_writer_t.
```

Now we need to use the code page and endian conversion classes. This will result in getting JSON format from the JSON `writer` class:

```
cl_abap_conv_in_ce=>create( )->convert(
    EXPORTING
      input = lo_json_writer_t->get_output( )
    IMPORTING
      data = lv_result ).
```

The final step is to test our code. We will use the `write_json` method and then the `display()` method from the `cl_demo_output` class:

```
cl_demo_output=>write_json( lv_result ).

cl_demo_output=>display( ).
```

If you did everything right, you should see the following results:

```
Output
{
 "VALUES":
 [
  {
   "CARRID":"AA",
   "CARRNAME":"American Airlines",
   "CURRCODE":"USD",
   "URL":"http://www.aa.com"
  },
  {
   "CARRID":"AC",
   "CARRNAME":"Air Canada",
   "CURRCODE":"CAD",
   "URL":"http://www.aircanada.ca"
  },
  {
   "CARRID":"AF",
   "CARRNAME":"Air France",
   "CURRCODE":"EUR",
   "URL":"http://www.airfrance.fr"
  },
  {
   "CARRID":"AZ",
   "CARRNAME":"Alitalia",
   "CURRCODE":"EUR",
   "URL":"http://www.alitalia.it"
  },
  {
   "CARRID":"BA",
```

Summary

Complex landscapes with multiple systems aren't rare. To get the most out of such landscapes, systems have to communicate with each other smoothly. There are many different technologies available to achieve such a goal. We can use, for example, RFC, ALE, oData, or simple text files as an interface. In order to avoid problems with file interfaces, we should use common, standardized, and well-described data formats. One such format is XML.

In the next chapter, the primary focus will be on building further user interfaces.

Questions

The following questions will allow you to consolidate the information contained in this chapter:

1. What method is used to parse an XML stream using the CL_XML_DOCUMENT class?
2. What does the DISPLAY method from the CL_XML_DOCUMENT class do?
3. What constant describes JSON format in the sXML library?
4. Are you allowed to use regular expressions or an xPath in ST?
5. What are the advantages of using XSLT over ST?
6. Are you able to change XML structures using single ST?
7. How do we define the version and encoding of the file in XML format?

Further reading

You may want to refer to the following for additional information:

- XML standard: `https://www.w3.org/standards/xml/`
- XSLT standard: `https://www.w3.org/TR/xslt/all/`
- JSON standard: `https://www.json.org/`
- xPath standard: `https://www.w3.org/TR/1999/REC-xpath-19991116/`
- SAP ST documentation: `https://help.sap.com/doc/abapdocu_752_index_htm/7.52/en-US/abenabap_st.htm`
- SAP XML documentation: `https://help.sap.com/doc/abapdocu_752_index_htm/7.52/en-US/abenabap_xml.htm`
- *JS Regular Expression*, by *Loiane Groner* and *Gabriel Manricks*, published by *Packt Publishing*: `https://www.packtpub.com/web-development/javascript-regular-expressions`

Building User Interfaces 7

In **Systems, Applications, Products** (**SAP**), we have various technologies for presenting user interfaces. We can use classic DynPro, which we will focus on in this chapter. This is based on the SAP GUI and is almost completely integrated with ABAP and web-based technologies such as SAPUI5.

Classic DynPro is divided into two categories:

- Classic DynPro
- Selection screens

Despite the fact that these two categories use the same technology, the methods for programming them are different.

Classic DynPro (named **screen**) needs to be created in Screen Painter in the ABAP Workbench, as well as being called in `CALL SCREEN` statement. The selection screen can be defined purely in ABAP and it is a specific classic DynPro.

We will cover the following topics:

- Creating a selection screen
- Advanced options of the selection screen
- Creating user interfaces based on DynPro
- Creating an **ABAP List Viewer** (**ALV**) based on `CL_GUI_ALV_GRID` with a few additions
- Creating and using advanced options in classic DynPro

Technical requirements

All the code used in this chapter can be downloaded from the following GitHub link: `https://github.com/PacktPublishing/Mastering-SAP-ABAP/tree/master/Chapter07`.

Classic DynPro

As some may not know the basics of classics DynPro, I will start with a short introduction explaining how we can call screens or types of screens. If you have some knowledge of screens, you can skip this part.

Firstly, we need to know what types of screens exist. The classic DynPro screen is divided into four different types, as follows:

- Normal
- Subscreen
- Modal dialog box
- Selection DynPro (also known as the **selection screen**)

Normal is a regular screen, which is mostly used to create a screen. Subscreen is used when we want to embed another one. The modal dialog box is a screen that does not take up the whole screen, like a popup.

As previously stated, classic DynPro is called using the `CALL SCREEN`. All screens are numbered with up to four digits. We can use a number from `1` to `9999`. The number `0` is not allowed.

When we click on **CALL SCREEN**, we can create a screen using a number of our choice.

For example, when we use `CALL SCREEN 100`, we are asked whether we want to create a screen; if we click **YES**, we will see the following window:

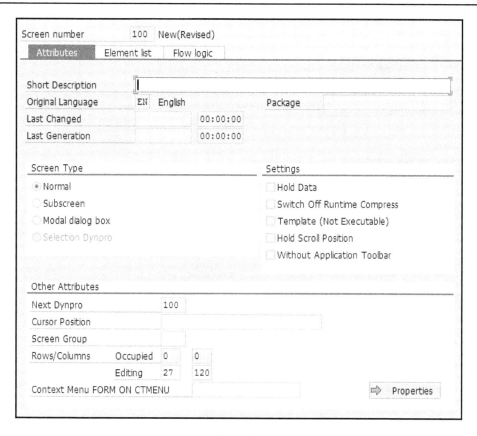

Screen options

In this window, we can define values such as a short description (mandatory field) or how many rows and columns will be used.

In the next tab, we can see all elements in a given screen, such as custom containers and text.

The third tab is crucial for the whole process of screen creation. In the **Flow logic** tab, we can define **Process Before Output** (**PBO**), **Process After Input** (**PAI**), chains and field behavior. Field behavior serves to, for example, check the value of a single field, while chain checks look at the values of multiple fields. Chains are used to set the order when checking fields and modules.

PBO is a process that happens before output in which we can have all
actions defined between the call screen and output screen. For example, here we can use the
SELECT statement to get data before the screens are shown.

PAI is a process that occurs after input. In PAI, we can define what happens when we take
actions on the screen, such as clicking a button.

Screen painter

To open a screen painter, you need to click on the **Layout** button in the main screen
window. After clicking, a window appears:

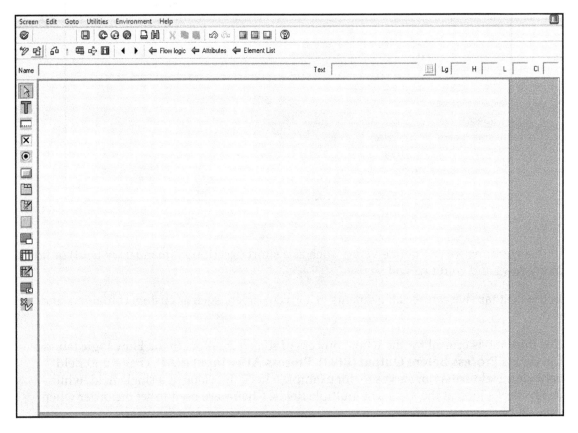

Screen painter

At the top of the window, there are several icons. Some of these are standard icons such as activate or test. Here, we also have three buttons specific to DynPro: **Flow logic**, **Attributes**, and **Element List**. These buttons are used to move us to corresponding functionalities. For example, when we click **Element List,** we get a list of all elements on the screen. At the top, we also have the **Name** and **Text** input fields. All of the UI components need to have a unique name and, for some components, we also need to put some text on them.

On the left side of the window, we can see all of the UI components of which our DynPro can be composed.

The components that can be used are as follows:

- **Text field**: This is a non-dynamic text field where we can put some text.
- **Output/Input field**: This is a dynamic text field where we can input some text. We can also get this field as an output field.
    - Checkbox
    - Radiobutton
    - Pushbutton
    - Tabstrip
    - Tabstrip (with the wizard).
    - Box.
- **Subscreen arena**: This is an arena where we can embed a subscreen.
    - Table control.
    - Table control (with the wizard).
- **Custom control**: We can embed custom containers, which are used to embed ALVs, for example (more information on that later in the chapter).
- **Status icon**: This describes a specific output/input field with icons.

Selection screens

A selection screen is a specific type of screen used to create selections, such as parameters, and to select queries or ranges. To create a selection screen, we can use the parameters or the selection option.

If we use PARAMETERS, we can create a single input field to put values in, in contrast to the select-option, where we get two input fields; the first is a lower value and the second is a high value of a range. Parameters and the select-option inherit values from search-help if it was created for using data elements.

To create parameters, we can use the following statement:

```
PARAMETERS: p_car TYPE s_carr_id.
```

To create select-option, we can use the following statement:

```
SELECT-OPTIONS s_con FOR lv_connid.
```

Lv_connid in the preceding example needs to be declared before select-option is called.

The following example shows shortcode in which we can see how to use parameters and the select-option in the SELECT statement. In this example, we use a parameter to select the values of carrid and select-options to select connid:

```
DATA: lv_connid TYPE s_conn_id.

PARAMETERS: p_car TYPE s_carr_id.
SELECT-OPTIONS: s_con FOR lv_connid.

SELECT *
  FROM spfli
  INTO TABLE @DATA(lt_spfli)
  WHERE carrid = @p_car
    AND connid IN @s_con.
```

More advanced options of the selection screen

In the selection screen, we also have some more advanced options. For example, we can group elements of a screen or add elements such as a checkbox or radio button.

Checkbox

To create a checkbox in the selection screen, we can use the AS CHECKBOX statement. The field with AS CHECKBOX needs to have a maximum length of 1:

```
PARAMETERS: p_car TYPE c AS CHECKBOX.
```

When a checkbox is selected, the value of the p_car field is X, otherwise, values of the field are required.

Radiobutton

To create a list of radiobuttons, we can use the RADIOBUTTON GROUP statement, as follows:

```
PARAMETERS: p_car TYPE c RADIOBUTTON GROUP rb1,
            p_con TYPE c RADIOBUTTON GROUP rb1.
```

The name of the radiobutton group is very important as this needs to be the same in one group, otherwise, these parameters will be presented like radiobuttons, but without the main radiobuttons specifics, which makes it possible to select only one at a time.

In parameters, we also have the following capabilities:

- **Obligatory**: After this addition, parameters will be obligatory to fill.
- **No-display**: This means that the parameter is not displayed on the selection screen. We can use this if we need to have this parameter in the interface, but this will only be used when we SUBMIT a program.
- **Visible length**: This describes a parameter where we can define the length of the input field.

As well as the preceding capabilities, in select-option, we also have a few more:

- **No-intervals**: When we use this addition, the select-option will be created without a second input field. Intervals can still be selected in the dialog box for multiple selections.
- **No-extension**: When this addition is used, a pushbutton will not be created for multiple selections.
- **Default**: The selected option will be started with some initial values.
- **Lower case**: This addition prevents the content of character-like fields from being converted into uppercase if data is moved from **Selection Screen** (**SS**) to screen and vice versa.
- **Matchcode objects**: This creates the association with search-help defined in the ABAP dictionary.
- **Memory ID**: After inputting any value to the field with this addition, values from the field will be moved to user memory.

Blocks in selection screens

We can also create a block in selection screens, for example, if we want to create the screen presented here:

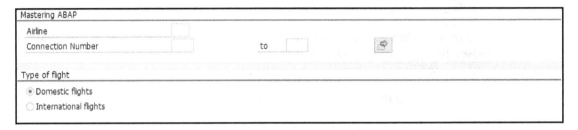

Selection screen

We can use the following code to display the screen:

```
DATA: lv_connid TYPE s_conn_id.

SELECTION-SCREEN BEGIN OF BLOCK b1 WITH FRAME TITLE text-000.
PARAMETERS: p_car TYPE s_carr_id.
SELECT-OPTIONS: s_con FOR lv_connid.
SELECTION-SCREEN END OF BLOCK b1.

SELECTION-SCREEN BEGIN OF BLOCK b2 WITH FRAME TITLE text-001.

PARAMETERS: p_dom TYPE c RADIOBUTTON GROUP rb1,
            p_int TYPE c RADIOBUTTON GROUP rb1.

SELECTION-SCREEN END OF BLOCK b2.
```

When we need to create text for a field, we can define it in **GOTO | TEXT ELEMENTS**. After clicking on this, we get the following screen:

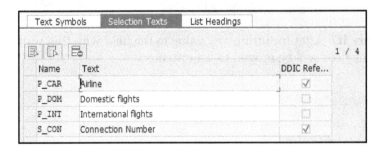

Selection text

If we want to create text, we can put our text in the input field or we can use the reference from the **Data Dictionary** (**DDIC**).

Selection screen event model

On the selection screen, we can define several events. These events are processed during the processing of the selection screen.

A list of selection screen events is provided as follows:

- OUTPUT: This is an event raised during the PBO of the selection screen. This is used to prepare data in the selection screen or dynamic modifications of a screen.
- ON: This is an event raised during the PAI of the selection screen.
- ON END OF: This is an event raised after the selection table is passed to the program and after user action in the dialog box for multiple selections has taken place. In this event, entire selections can be checked.
- ON BLOCK: This is an event raised when all fields in a block are filled and passed to the ABAP program.
- ON RADIOBUTTON GROUP: This is an event raised when data from radio buttons are passed to an ABAP program.
- ON (HELP REQUEST | VALUE REQUEST) FOR: This event is raised in a **Process On Help Request** (**POH**) and **Process of Values Request** (**POV**), when *F1* (help) or *F4* (values) is called. It can be used to create custom help and overrides the help from the ABAP dictionary.
- ON EXIT COMMAND: This event is raised when a user has called one of the Back, Exit, or Cancel functions. Any cleanup actions can be executed in this event block.

One of the most common uses of events in the selection screen is using the dynamic modification of the selection screen.

First of all, we need to add USER_COMMAND and MODIF ID to the corresponding fields:

```
DATA: lv_connid TYPE s_conn_id.

SELECTION-SCREEN BEGIN OF BLOCK b1 WITH FRAME TITLE text-000.
PARAMETERS: p_car TYPE s_carr_id.
SELECT-OPTIONS: s_con FOR lv_connid.
PARAMETERS: p_type TYPE c AS CHECKBOX USER-COMMAND uc1.
SELECTION-SCREEN END OF BLOCK b1.
```

```
SELECTION-SCREEN BEGIN OF BLOCK b2 WITH FRAME TITLE text-001.

PARAMETERS: p_dom TYPE c RADIOBUTTON GROUP rb1 MODIF ID b2,
            p_int TYPE c RADIOBUTTON GROUP rb1 MODIF ID b2.

SELECTION-SCREEN END OF BLOCK b2.
```

We can mark the p_type parameter here, and the second block will be shown.

In order to create this action, we need to assign a user command to the checkbox and create a corresponding PAI action. Pressing the button will call the PAI action with the user command UC1 (this action will do nothing, as it was not created) and then the PBO will be launched. In the PBO, the code under AT SELECTION-SCREEN OUTPUT will be executed. We need to make it this way because we want to initially get the screen without this component and turn it on only when the special condition is fulfilled.

For changing the selection screen, we also need to assign the p_dom and p_int parameters to a modification group named in the b2 example. We need to create this addition to indicate which field should be changed:

```
AT SELECTION-SCREEN OUTPUT.

  LOOP AT SCREEN.

    IF p_type = abap_true AND screen-group1 = 'B2'.
      screen-active = 1.
    ELSEIF p_type = abap_false AND screen-group1 = 'B2'.
      screen-active = 0.
    ENDIF.

    MODIFY SCREEN.
  ENDLOOP.
```

Right after defining a selection screen, we can add the preceding piece of code. In this code, we can see the event definition (in our example, this is the output). We make a loop at the screen to check every field and check whether or not our condition was fulfilled.

We also need to remember to add the MODIFY SCREEN statement. Without this, any change to the screen will not be visible.

ALV

In this section, I will present an example of how to create ALVs in two ways. In the same example, I will show you the possibilities of ALVs, also using the selection screen created before.

ALV is an integrated element of the ABAP objects environment. This makes it possible to implement the display of structured datasets. We can display simple and two-dimensional tables, hierarchical-sequential lists, and tree structures.

The possibilities of these two methods are similar, so I will present all examples based on the CL_GUI_ALV_GRID class and then I will present code where I created a basic ALV by using SALV classes.

Basics

If we want to create an ALV first, we need to declare a local variable of type references to the cl_gui_alv_grid class, a variable of type references to the cl_gui_custom_container class, and a local constant with the name of the container and the table where we store data that will be shown on screen:

```
DATA: lt_spfli       TYPE TABLE OF spfli,
      lr_alv         TYPE REF TO cl_gui_alv_grid,
      lr_ccontainer  TYPE REF TO cl_gui_custome_container.

CONSTANTS: lc_container_name TYPE scrfname VALUE 'ALV'.
```

Then, we need to create a screen and two modules—one for the PBO and one for the PAI. In this example, we use screen 100.

In the **Flow Logic** tab, create the PBO and PAI modules as follows:

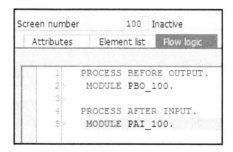

Flow logic on screen

It is really important to create a module right after PROCESS BEFORE OUTPUT in the case of the PBO module, and after PROCESS AFTER INPUT for the PAI. If this module is created in a different way, for example, with the PBO module after PROCESS AFTER INPUT, this module will be considered a PAI module and it will not work properly.

After creating a screen, we get two new modules:

```
*&---------------------------------------------------------------------*
*&      Module  PBO_100   OUTPUT
*&---------------------------------------------------------------------*
*       text
*----------------------------------------------------------------------*
MODULE pbo_100 OUTPUT.
* SET PF-STATUS 'xxxxxxxx'
* SET TITLEBAR ' xxx'.
ENDMODULE.                  " PBO_100  OUTPUT
*&---------------------------------------------------------------------*
*&      Module  PAI_100   INPUT
*&---------------------------------------------------------------------*
*       text
*----------------------------------------------------------------------*
MODULE pai_100 INPUT.

ENDMODULE.                  " PAI_100  INPUT
```

In pbo_100, we see the two commented rows. In the first of them is PF_STATUS and in the second is TITLEBAR.

In the TITLEBAR, we can establish the title being shown on the screen.

Using ON PF-Status, we can embed an action to an icon on the screen. If we do not do this, any icon (including back or cancel) will not work. Here is an example of how to create PF-STATUS and the TITLEBAR:

```
MODULE pbo_100 OUTPUT.
  SET PF-STATUS 'STATUS_100'.
  SET TITLEBAR 'TITLEBAR_100'.
ENDMODULE.
```

PF-STATUS and TITLEBAR can have any name. In our example, we have 'STATUS_100' as PF-STATUS and 'TITILEBAR_100' as the titlebar.

Right after clicking on the title, a window is shown. In the title input field, we can insert text, which will be shown on the screen:

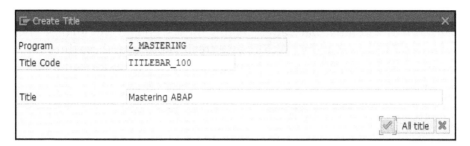

Creating a title

After clicking on **OK**, a title will be created. Next, click on **PF-STATUS** and a popup will appear:

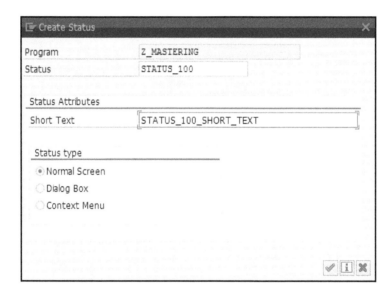

Creating a status

When this pops up, input some short text and choose a type of status. We mostly use **Normal Screen** here. **Dialog Box** is a status type for screens without a menu bar and **Context Menu** is a status used for the context menu only.

After creating PF_STATUS, we will see a screen where we can define buttons in the menu bar, application toolbar, and function keys.

In the beginning, we should define at least three buttons (BACK, CANCEL, and EXIT). If we do not do this, we cannot move back after creating the screen and we can only create a new session and turn off the present one. We can also create more than these three buttons. In order to create these actions on screen, we can fill the input field as an example and then click on **Activate**:

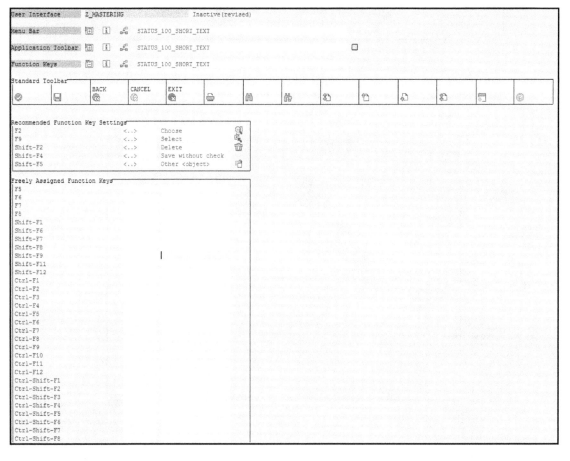

Screen status option

Next, in the PAI module action, we should determine what this button needs to do and code what will be executed.

To do this, create a global field named, for example, OK_CODE, to keep the name of action assigned to the button. Then, we need to assign this field to a variable on screen in the element list:

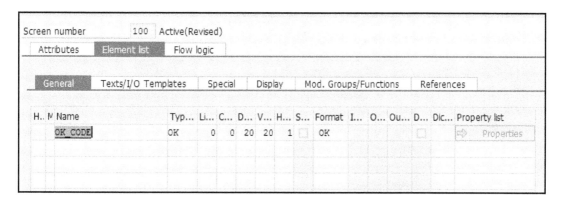

Element list on the screen

After this, we need to insert the code to the PAI in order to handle these actions:

```
MODULE pai_100 INPUT.

    CASE ok_code.
      WHEN 'BACK'.
        LEAVE TO SCREEN 0.
      WHEN 'CANCEL'.
        LEAVE TO SCREEN 0.
        LEAVE PROGRAM.
      WHEN 'EXIT'.
        LEAVE PROGRAM.
    ENDCASE.

  ENDMODULE.
```

Every action on the PAI can be handled in this way. Just add a new case and code to execute it.

After creating basic things on the screen, we can create a container for our ALV. To do this, enter **Screen Painter** and click on **Layout** to enter the **Screen Painter|Layout editor**:

Screen painter

Your screen should look the same as the preceding screenshot.

To add the element to the screen, we can just click on an interesting element in the left-hand list and drag and drop it onto the screen. In our case, we need the **Custom control** element, so search for **Custom control** and drag and drop this onto the screen. After doing this, you should see an element with crossed lines, like this:

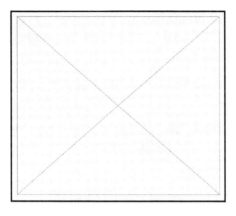

Custom control

This is the **Custom control**. To move objects on screen, we can drag and drop them. If we want to change the size of elements, we can double-click on the element and change the variables named **Height** and `Vis.Length`. Alternatively, we can simply enlarge or decrease elements on the screen:

ID	No.	Ctr	Depart. city	De	Ctr	Arrival city	Apt	FlightT	Departure	Arrival	Distance	Dis.	C	Da
A	17	US	NEW YORK	JFK	US	SAN FRANCISCO	SFO	6:01	11:00:00	14:01:00	2.572	MI		0
AA	64	US	SAN FRANCISCO	SFO	US	NEW YORK	JFK	5:21	09:00:00	17:21:00	2.572	MI		0
AZ	555	IT	ROME	FCO	DE	FRANKFURT	FRA	2:05	19:00:00	21:05:00	845	MI		0
AZ	788	IT	ROME	FCO	JP	TOKYO	TY	12:55	12:00:00	08:55:00	6.130	MI		1
AZ	789	JP	TOKYO	TY	IT	ROME	FCO	15:40	11:45:00	19:25:00	6.130	MI		0
AZ	790	IT	ROME	FCO	JP	OSAKA	KIX	13:35	10:35:00	08:10:00	6.030	MI	X	1
DL	106	US	NEW YORK	JFK	DE	FRANKFURT	FRA	7:55	19:35:00	09:30:00	3.851	MI		1
DL	1699	US	NEW YORK	JFK	US	SAN FRANCISCO	SFO	6:22	17:15:00	20:37:00	2.572	MI		0
DL	1984	US	SAN FRANCISCO	SFO	US	NEW YORK	JFK	5:25	10:00:00	18:25:00	2.572	MI		0
JL	407	JP	TOKYO	NRT	DE	FRANKFURT	FRA	12:05	13:30:00	17:35:00	9.100	KM		0
JL	408	DE	FRANKFURT	FRA	JP	TOKYO	NRT	11:15	20:25:00	15:40:00	9.100	KM	X	1
LH	400	DE	FRANKFURT	FRA	US	NEW YORK	JFK	7:24	10:10:00	11:34:00	6.162	KM		0
LH	401	US	NEW YORK	JFK	DE	FRANKFURT	FRA	7:15	18:30:00	07:45:00	6.162	KM		1
LH	402	DE	FRANKFURT	FRA	US	NEW YORK	JFK	7:35	13:30:00	15:05:00	6.162	KM	X	0
LH	2402	DE	FRANKFURT	FRA	DE	BERLIN	SXF	1:05	10:30:00	11:35:00	555	KM		0
LH	2407	DE	BERLIN	TXL	DE	FRANKFURT	FRA	1:05	07:10:00	08:15:00	555	KM		0
QF	5	SG	SINGAPORE	SIN	DE	FRANKFURT	FRA	13:45	22:50:00	05:35:00	10.000	KM		1
QF	6	DE	FRANKFURT	FRA	SG	SINGAPORE	SIN	11:10	20:55:00	15:05:00	10.000	KM		1
SQ	2	SG	SINGAPORE	SIN	US	SAN FRANCISCO	SFO	18:25	17:00:00	19:25:00	8.452	MI		0
SQ	15	US	SAN FRANCISCO	SFO	SG	SINGAPORE	SIN	18:45	16:00:00	02:45:00	8.452	MI		2
SQ	158	SG	SINGAPORE	SIN	ID	JAKARTA	JKT	1:35	15:25:00	16:00:00	560	MI		0
SQ	988	SG	SINGAPORE	SIN	JP	TOKYO	TY	6:40	16:35:00	00:15:00	3.125	MI		1
UA	941	DE	FRANKFURT	FRA	US	SAN FRANCISCO	SFO	11:36	14:30:00	17:06:00	5.685	MI		0
UA	3504	US	SAN FRANCISCO	SFO	DE	FRANKFURT	FRA	10:30	15:00:00	10:30:00	5.685	MI		1
UA	3516	US	NEW YORK	JFK	DE	FRANKFURT	FRA	7:25	16:20:00	05:45:00	6.162	KM		1
UA	3517	DE	FRANKFURT	FRA	US	NEW YORK	JFK	8:15	10:40:00	12:55:00	6.162	KM		0

Screen painter—element option

The next field we must fill in is **Name** (for all of the elements on the screen). **Custom control** has been named ALV. We need to remember this name because we need to use it in the code.

As we have created a **Custom control** box in the screen, we can create an ALV and display it in the **Custom control** box.

As the first step, we need to create the lr_ccontainer object with the container name and lr_alv, which is defined in our global variable:

```
CREATE OBJECT lr_ccontainer
   EXPORTING
     container_name = lc_container_name.

 CREATE OBJECT lr_alv
   EXPORTING
     i_parent = lr_ccontainer.
```

The name of the container needs to be declared in Capital Letters, otherwise, it will not work, as all of the letters will be changed to capital letters.

To create a field catalog, we can use two methods—we can use the **Data Dictionary** (**DDIC**) structure or create a custom field catalog. In the first example of an ALV, we can use this version.

If we want to create a custom field, add them to the field catalog, which is a table where we store all names of the field and we can define the parameter of the ALV in many ways, including by the following:

- Displayed name
- Size of the column—width counted in chars
- Conversion exit
- Number of displayed decimals

To create a field catalog, we need to use a variable table of LVC_T_FCAT type and a structure of LVC_S_FCAT type.

An example of one field in a custom field catalog is as follows:

```
ls_fcat-fieldname = 'CARRID'.
ls_fcat-scrtext_s = 'Airline Code'.
ls_fcat-outputlen = 4.
APPEND ls_fcat TO lt_fcat.
CLEAR ls_fcat.
```

To display the field in the ALV grid, we need to add it to the field catalog first. In our preceding example, we add a field with the name CARRID (fieldname). In the ALV, we see the short text 'Airline code' (scrtext). We also add a parameter specifying the length of the field (outputlen).

To display the table on the screen, use the set_table_for_first_display method. In the following code, we have the most basic version of the code to see the ALV:

```
CALL METHOD lr_alv->set_table_for_first_display
    EXPORTING
      i_structure_name = 'SPFLI'
    CHANGING
      it_outtab        = lt_spfli.
```

The use of our custom field catalog is depicted in the following example:

```
CALL METHOD lr_alv->set_table_for_first_display
    CHANGING
      it_outtab       = lt_spfli
      it_fieldcatalog = lt_fcat.
```

Now, we can see the differences between those two ALVs.

Here, we can see an example of the ALV created with the field catalog created by the DDIC:

ID	No.	Ctr	Depart. city	De...	Ctr	Arrival city	Apt	FlghtT...	Departure	Arrival	Distance	Dis.	C	Da...
A	17	US	NEW YORK	JFK	US	SAN FRANCISCO	SFO	6:01	11:00:00	14:01:00	2.572	MI		0
AA	64	US	SAN FRANCISCO	SFO	US	NEW YORK	JFK	5:21	09:00:00	17:21:00	2.572	MI		0
AZ	555	IT	ROME	FCO	DE	FRANKFURT	FRA	2:05	19:00:00	21:05:00	845	MI		0
AZ	788	IT	ROME	FCO	JP	TOKYO	TY...	12:55	12:00:00	08:55:00	6.130	MI		1
AZ	789	JP	TOKYO	TY...	IT	ROME	FCO	15:40	11:45:00	19:25:00	6.130	MI		0
AZ	790	IT	ROME	FCO	JP	OSAKA	KIX	13:35	10:35:00	08:10:00	6.030	MI	X	1
DL	106	US	NEW YORK	JFK	DE	FRANKFURT	FRA	7:55	19:35:00	09:30:00	3.851	MI		1
DL	1699	US	NEW YORK	JFK	US	SAN FRANCISCO	SFO	6:22	17:15:00	20:37:00	2.572	MI		0
DL	1984	US	SAN FRANCISCO	SFO	US	NEW YORK	JFK	5:25	10:00:00	18:25:00	2.572	MI		0
JL	407	JP	TOKYO	NRT	DE	FRANKFURT	FRA	12:05	13:30:00	17:35:00	9.100	KM		0
JL	408	DE	FRANKFURT	FRA	JP	TOKYO	NRT	11:15	20:25:00	15:40:00	9.100	KM	X	1
LH	400	DE	FRANKFURT	FRA	US	NEW YORK	JFK	7:24	10:10:00	11:34:00	6.162	KM		0
LH	401	US	NEW YORK	JFK	DE	FRANKFURT	FRA	7:15	18:30:00	07:45:00	6.162	KM		1
LH	402	DE	FRANKFURT	FRA	US	NEW YORK	JFK	7:35	13:30:00	15:05:00	6.162	KM	X	0
LH	2402	DE	FRANKFURT	FRA	DE	BERLIN	SXF	1:05	10:30:00	11:35:00	555	KM		0
LH	2407	DE	BERLIN	TXL	DE	FRANKFURT	FRA	1:05	07:10:00	08:15:00	555	KM		0
QF	5	SG	SINGAPORE	SIN	DE	FRANKFURT	FRA	13:45	22:50:00	05:35:00	10.000	KM		1
QF	6	DE	FRANKFURT	FRA	SG	SINGAPORE	SIN	11:10	20:55:00	15:05:00	10.000	KM		1
SQ	2	SG	SINGAPORE	SIN	US	SAN FRANCISCO	SFO	18:25	17:00:00	19:25:00	8.452	MI		0
SQ	15	US	SAN FRANCISCO	SFO	SG	SINGAPORE	SIN	18:45	16:00:00	02:45:00	8.452	MI		2
SQ	158	SG	SINGAPORE	SIN	ID	JAKARTA	JKT	1:35	15:25:00	16:00:00	560	MI		0
SQ	988	SG	SINGAPORE	SIN	JP	TOKYO	TY...	6:40	16:35:00	00:15:00	3.125	MI		1
UA	941	DE	FRANKFURT	FRA	US	SAN FRANCISCO	SFO	11:36	14:30:00	17:06:00	5.685	MI		0
UA	3504	US	SAN FRANCISCO	SFO	DE	FRANKFURT	FRA	10:30	15:00:00	10:30:00	5.685	MI		1
UA	3516	US	NEW YORK	JFK	DE	FRANKFURT	FRA	7:25	16:20:00	05:45:00	6.162	KM		1
UA	3517	DE	FRANKFURT	FRA	US	NEW YORK	JFK	8:15	10:40:00	12:55:00	6.162	KM		0

Results of the DDIC field catalog

An example of a field catalog is in the following screenshot:

Airli..	Flig..	Cou..	Departure	De..	Co..	Arrival ci	Destinatio	Flight tim	Depart..	Arrival ti	Distance	UN..	F	Ar..
AA	17	US	NEW YORK	JFK	US	SAN FRANCISCO	SFO	6:01	11:00:..	14:01:..	2.572,00..	MI		0
AA	64	US	SAN FRANCISCO	SFO	US	NEW YORK	JFK	5:21	09:00:..	17:21:..	2.572,00..	MI		0
AZ	555	IT	ROME	FCO	DE	FRANKFURT	FRA	2:05	19:00:..	21:05:..	845,0000	MI		0
AZ	788	IT	ROME	FCO	JP	TOKYO	TYO	12:55	12:00:..	08:55:..	6.130,00..	MI		1
AZ	789	JP	TOKYO	TY..	IT	ROME	FCO	15:40	11:45:..	19:25:..	6.130,00..	MI		0
AZ	790	IT	ROME	FCO	JP	OSAKA	KIX	13:35	10:35:..	08:10:..	6.030,00..	MI	X	1
DL	106	US	NEW YORK	JFK	DE	FRANKFURT	FRA	7:55	19:35:..	09:30:..	3.851,00..	MI		1
DL	1699	US	NEW YORK	JFK	US	SAN FRANCISCO	SFO	6:22	17:15:..	20:37:..	2.572,00..	MI		0
DL	1984	US	SAN FRANCISCO	SFO	US	NEW YORK	JFK	5:25	10:00:..	18:25:..	2.572,00..	MI		0
JL	407	JP	TOKYO	NRT	DE	FRANKFURT	FRA	12:05	13:30:..	17:35:..	9.100,00..	KM		0
JL	408	DE	FRANKFURT	FRA	JP	TOKYO	NRT	11:15	20:25:..	15:40:..	9.100,00..	KM	X	1
LH	400	DE	FRANKFURT	FRA	US	NEW YORK	JFK	7:24	10:10:..	11:34:..	6.162,00..	KM		0
LH	401	US	NEW YORK	JFK	DE	FRANKFURT	FRA	7:15	18:30:..	07:45:..	6.162,00..	KM		1
LH	402	DE	FRANKFURT	FRA	US	NEW YORK	JFK	7:35	13:30:..	15:05:..	6.162,00..	KM	X	0
LH	2402	DE	FRANKFURT	FRA	DE	BERLIN	SXF	1:05	10:30:..	11:35:..	555,0000	KM		0
LH	2407	DE	BERLIN	TXL	DE	FRANKFURT	FRA	1:05	07:10:..	08:15:..	555,0000	KM		0
QF	5	SG	SINGAPORE	SIN	DE	FRANKFURT	FRA	13:45	22:50:..	05:35:..	10.000,0..	KM		1
QF	6	DE	FRANKFURT	FRA	SG	SINGAPORE	SIN	11:10	20:55:..	15:05:..	10.000,0..	KM		1
SQ	2	SG	SINGAPORE	SIN	US	SAN FRANCISCO	SFO	18:25	17:00:..	19:25:..	8.452,00..	MI		0
SQ	15	US	SAN FRANCISCO	SFO	SG	SINGAPORE	SIN	18:45	16:00:..	02:45:..	8.452,00..	MI		2
SQ	158	SG	SINGAPORE	SIN	ID	JAKARTA	JKT	1:35	15:25:..	16:00:..	560,0000	MI		0
SQ	988	SG	SINGAPORE	SIN	JP	TOKYO	TYO	6:40	16:35:..	00:15:..	3.125,00..	MI		1
UA	941	DE	FRANKFURT	FRA	US	SAN FRANCISCO	SFO	11:36	14:30:..	17:06:..	5.685,00..	MI		0
UA	3504	US	SAN FRANCISCO	SFO	DE	FRANKFURT	FRA	10:30	15:00:..	10:30:..	5.685,00..	MI		1
UA	3516	US	NEW YORK	JFK	DE	FRANKFURT	FRA	7:25	16:20:..	05:45:..	6.162,00..	KM		1
UA	3517	DE	FRANKFURT	FRA	US	NEW YORK	JFK	8:15	10:40:..	12:55:..	6.162,00..	KM		0

Results of a custom field catalog

As we can see, the example of the DDIC is *prettier*. the ALV automatically transports the names of fields, adjust the length of the fields, and highlight key columns. However, if we create a field catalog on our own, we would have many more possibilities. For example, if we create a field catalog on our own, we can change the order of the field.

Every time we make changes on screen or perform a PAI action, PBO is automatically called right before the output screen. But as we create a container, ALV instance, and field catalog and initialize ALV, those methods need some time to complete. If we do not need to create this again, for example, when we only need to change displayed data, we should use the `refresh_table_display` method. Consequently, we can check whether the container was created. If so, we can only use the method mentioned previously.

Advanced capabilities of ALV sand screens

ALVs and screens also have many more advanced possibilities. We will look at the most commonly used in this section, as follows:

- Zebra
- Coloring
- Events on the ALV in an example of a button click
- ALV icons

Following are the advanced possibilities of screens:

- Text field and translations
- Input/output field
- Radiobuttons
- Buttons
- Addition of dynamic display possibilities for individual elements and groups, and examples of using all of the discussed possibilities

Zebra

To create zebra coloring where the background of one row is white and the next is gray and so on, we just need to add one more structure to the ALV called a layout structure.

At the beginning of creating a zebra pattern, we need to declare a variable of `lvc_s_layo` type, as follows:

```
DATA: ls_layout TYPE lvc_s_layo.
```

Of course, a layout structure has many more fields, for instance, a field named `edit`. If we add `abap_true` to this, then we can change data in rows. After this, we just need to fill in one field of this structure:

```
ls_layout-zebra = abap_true.
```

Add this structure to `set_table_to_first_display` as an export parameter:

```
CALL METHOD lr_alv->st_table_for_first_display
    EXPORTING
      is_layout        = ls_layout
    CHANGING
      it_outtab        = lt_spfli
      it_fieldcatalog  = lt_fcat.
```

Coloring

To color an entire column, we can use the **Emphasize** option of the field catalog. To add a value, we need to follow the pattern, C123, where the following applies:

- C: Constant
- 1: Color numbers
- 2: Inverse yes/no
- 3: Intensified on/off

A list of possible colors of columns or rows is provided here:

Value of the first variable	Color
1	Gray or Blue
2	Light gray
3	Yellow
4	Blue or Green
5	Green
6	Red
7	Orange

You need to add the following piece of code to the field catalog field to obtain the yellow color of the column:

```
ls_fcat-emphasize = 'C300'.
```

Coloring a row is a bit more complicated. To enable coloring rows, you should add an additional field to your data table.

First, we need to declare the structure in the same way as spfli, with an additional rowcolor field and table based on this structure:

```
DATA:
    BEGIN OF ls_colouring_rows.
          INCLUDE STRUCTURE splfi.
    DATA: rowcolor(4) TYPE c.
    DATA END OF ls_colouring_rows.

    DATA: lt_color LIKE TABLE OF ls_colouring_rows.
```

Now we need to add the information about the name of the column where the information about the color is stored. To do this, we need to add the layout structure name of this field. For example, look at the following code snippet:

```
ls_layout-info_fname = 'ROWCOLOR'.
```

We just need to add data about the color into the table and the color will be defined, as in the preceding method. In our example, we color all rows where `carrid = 'AA'` to green:

```
LOOP AT lt_color ASSIGNING FIELD-SYMBOL(<fs_color>) WHERE carrid = 'AA'.
   <fs_color>-rowcolor = 'C500'.
 ENDLOOP.
```

For coloring purposes, I changed the results table to `lt_color`. Of course, the table in the `set_table_for_first_display` method also needs to be changed.

If we want to, we can color only one cell in the ALV. In the example shown in an image named *Results of coloring*, I colored the destination cell orange only for flights to JFK.

First, we need to declare the structure with colors in a table. Right now, our declaration of the table type will look as follows:

```
DATA:
   BEGIN OF ls_colouring_rows.
        INCLUDE STRUCTURE splfi.
 DATA rowcolor(4) TYPE c.
 DATA cellcolors TYPE lvc_s_scol.
 DATA END OF ls_colouring_rows.
```

We also need to declare structure consistently in accordance with the type of row added to the master table:

```
DATA: ls_ccolor TYPE lvc_s_scol.
```

We also need to inform the runtime, that we will pass the coloring information. This can be done by providing the table name in the `ctab_fname` attribute, similar to the following screenshot:

```
ls_ccolor-ctab_fname = 'CELLCOLORS'.
```

The user needs to make a loop in the result table in order to add the needed value and change the colors:

```
LOOP AT lt_color ASSIGNING FIELD-SYMBOL(<fs_cellcolor>) WHERE airpto =
'JFK'.
    ls_coolor-fname = 'AIRPTO'.
    ls_ccolor-col = '7'.
    ls_ccolor-int = '1'.
    APPEND ls_ccolor TO <fs_cellcolor>-cellcolors.
ENDLOOP.
```

Let's have a look at the following screenshot:

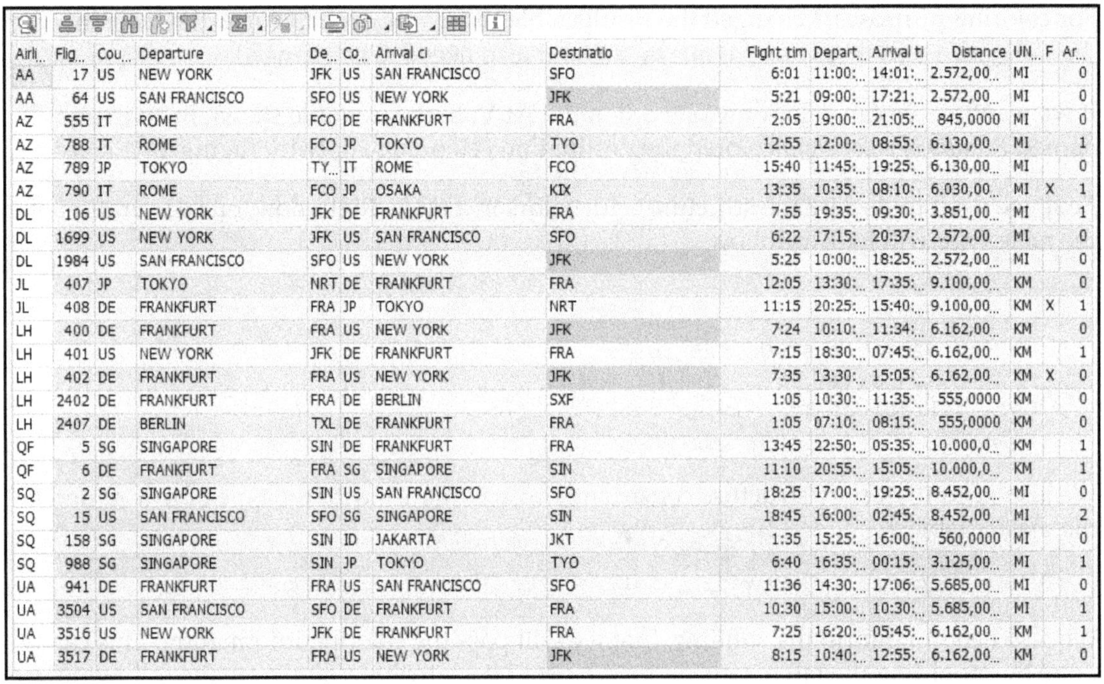

Airli	Flig	Cou	Departure	De	Co	Arrival ci	Destinatio	Flight tim	Depart	Arrival ti	Distance	UN	F	Ar
AA	17	US	NEW YORK	JFK	US	SAN FRANCISCO	SFO	6:01	11:00:	14:01:	2.572,00	MI		0
AA	64	US	SAN FRANCISCO	SFO	US	NEW YORK	JFK	5:21	09:00:	17:21:	2.572,00	MI		0
AZ	555	IT	ROME	FCO	DE	FRANKFURT	FRA	2:05	19:00:	21:05:	845,0000	MI		0
AZ	788	IT	ROME	FCO	JP	TOKYO	TYO	12:55	12:00:	08:55:	6.130,00	MI		1
AZ	789	JP	TOKYO	TY	IT	ROME	FCO	15:40	11:45:	19:25:	6.130,00	MI		0
AZ	790	IT	ROME	FCO	JP	OSAKA	KIX	13:35	10:35:	08:10:	6.030,00	MI	X	1
DL	106	US	NEW YORK	JFK	DE	FRANKFURT	FRA	7:55	19:35:	09:30:	3.851,00	MI		1
DL	1699	US	NEW YORK	JFK	US	SAN FRANCISCO	SFO	6:22	17:15:	20:37:	2.572,00	MI		0
DL	1984	US	SAN FRANCISCO	SFO	US	NEW YORK	JFK	5:25	10:00:	18:25:	2.572,00	MI		0
JL	407	JP	TOKYO	NRT	DE	FRANKFURT	FRA	12:05	13:30:	17:35:	9.100,00	KM		0
JL	408	DE	FRANKFURT	FRA	JP	TOKYO	NRT	11:15	20:25:	15:40:	9.100,00	KM	X	1
LH	400	DE	FRANKFURT	FRA	US	NEW YORK	JFK	7:24	10:10:	11:34:	6.162,00	KM		0
LH	401	US	NEW YORK	JFK	DE	FRANKFURT	FRA	7:15	18:30:	07:45:	6.162,00	KM		1
LH	402	DE	FRANKFURT	FRA	US	NEW YORK	JFK	7:35	13:30:	15:05:	6.162,00	KM	X	0
LH	2402	DE	FRANKFURT	FRA	DE	BERLIN	SXF	1:05	10:30:	11:35:	555,0000	KM		0
LH	2407	DE	BERLIN	TXL	DE	FRANKFURT	FRA	1:05	07:10:	08:15:	555,0000	KM		0
QF	5	SG	SINGAPORE	SIN	DE	FRANKFURT	FRA	13:45	22:50:	05:35:	10.000,0	KM		1
QF	6	DE	FRANKFURT	FRA	SG	SINGAPORE	SIN	11:10	20:55:	15:05:	10.000,0	KM		1
SQ	2	SG	SINGAPORE	SIN	US	SAN FRANCISCO	SFO	18:25	17:00:	19:25:	8.452,00	MI		0
SQ	15	US	SAN FRANCISCO	SFO	SG	SINGAPORE	SIN	18:45	16:00:	02:45:	8.452,00	MI		2
SQ	158	SG	SINGAPORE	SIN	ID	JAKARTA	JKT	1:35	15:25:	16:00:	560,0000	MI		0
SQ	988	SG	SINGAPORE	SIN	JP	TOKYO	TYO	6:40	16:35:	00:15:	3.125,00	MI		1
UA	941	DE	FRANKFURT	FRA	US	SAN FRANCISCO	SFO	11:36	14:30:	17:06:	5.685,00	MI		0
UA	3504	US	SAN FRANCISCO	SFO	DE	FRANKFURT	FRA	10:30	15:00:	10:30:	5.685,00	MI		1
UA	3516	US	NEW YORK	JFK	DE	FRANKFURT	FRA	7:25	16:20:	05:45:	6.162,00	KM		1
UA	3517	DE	FRANKFURT	FRA	US	NEW YORK	JFK	8:15	10:40:	12:55:	6.162,00	KM		0

Results of coloring

If all of the colors were added at the same time, the result of this would be the preceding screenshot.

Event of an ALV, exemplified by a button click

To create an event, we need to declare a method of handling events. The method in the example presented in the following code block is declared as a local class but can be declared as a global class too (more about the global and local class, can be found in Chapter 13, *Advanced Techniques in ABAP Objects*).

The button we want to create in this example will provide a popup with **Mastering ABAP** as text.

To create class, we first need to create a definition and implementation of a method to handle the button click:

```
CLASS lcl_event_handler DEFINITION.
  PUBLIC SECTION.
    METHODS: handle_button_click FOR EVENT button_click OF cl_gui_alv_grid
      IMPORTING
        es_col_id es_row_no.
ENDCLASS.
CLASS lcl_event_handler IMPLEMENTATION.
  METHOD handle_button_click.

    CALL FUNCTION 'POPUP_TO_DISPLAY_TEXT'
      EXPORTING
        textline1 = 'MASTERING ABAP'.

  ENDMETHOD.
ENDCLASS.
```

It is also required to declare a variable with reference to the type of class declared in the preceding code snippet:

```
DATA: lr_event_handler TYPE REF TO lcl_event_handler.
```

To handle the method and register an event on the ALV, we need to create the object defined previously and register an event in the ALV instance, as follows:

```
CREATE OBJECT lr_event_handler.

SET HANDLER lr_event_handler->handle_button_click FOR lr_alv.
```

The mechanism for creating an event is pretty much the same for all events; the only difference is the creation of appropriate methods for different events.

We need to create a button on the ALV. To do this, we create the following field on the table structure:

```
DATA button(5) TYPE c.
```

We then add a button field to the ALV field catalog:

```
ls_fcat-fieldname = 'BUTTON'.
ls_fcat-scrtext_s = 'Button'.
ls_fcat-outputlen = 6.
APPEND ls_fcat TO lt_fcat.
CLEAR ls_fcat.
```

As in the previous example (the details are on GitHub at `https://github.com/PacktPublishing/Mastering-SAP-ABAP`), to change the cell to a button, we need to add cell style to the layout structure:

```
ls_layout-stylefname = 'CELLSTYLES'.
```

In our ALV, the push button has been created in the second position:

Airl	Button	Flig	Cou	Departure	De	Co	Arrival ci	Destinatio	Flight tim	Depart	Arrival ti	Distance	UN	F	Ar
AA	Click	17	US	NEW YORK	JFK	US	SAN FRANCISCO	SFO	6:01	11:00:	14:01:	2.572,00	MI		0
AA	Click	64	US	SAN FRANCISCO	SFO	US	NEW YORK	JFK	5:21	09:00:	17:21:	2.572,00	MI		0
AZ	Click	555	IT	ROME	FCO	DE	FRANKFURT	FRA	2:05	19:00:	21:05:	845,0000	MI		0
AZ	Click	788	IT	ROME	FCO	JP	TOKYO	TYO	12:55	12:00:	08:55:	6.130,00	MI		1
AZ	Click	789	JP	TOKYO	TY	IT	ROME	FCO	15:40	11:45:	19:25:	6.130,00	MI		0
AZ	Click	790	IT	ROME	FCO	JP	OSAKA	KIX	13:35	10:35:	08:10:	6.030,00	MI	X	1
DL	Click	106	US	NEW YORK	JFK	DE	FRANKFURT	FRA	7:55	19:35:	09:30:	3.851,00	MI		1
DL	Click	1699	US	NEW YORK	JFK	US	SAN FRANCISCO	SFO	6:22	17:15:	20:37:	2.572,00	MI		0
DL	Click	1984	US	SAN FRANCISCO	SFO	US	NEW YORK	JFK	5:25	10:00:	18:25:	2.572,00	MI		0
JL	Click	407	JP	TOKYO	NRT	DE	FRANKFURT	FRA	12:05	13:30:	17:35:	9.100,00	KM		0
JL	Click	408	DE	FRANKFURT	FRA	JP	TOKYO	NRT	11:15	20:25:	15:40:	9.100,00	KM	X	1
LH	Click	400	DE	FRANKFURT	FRA	US	NEW YORK	JFK	7:24	10:10:	11:34:	6.162,00	KM		0
LH	Click	401	US	NEW YORK	JFK	DE	FRANKFURT	FRA	7:15	18:30:	07:45:	6.162,00	KM		1
LH	Click	402	DE	FRANKFURT	FRA	US	NEW YORK	JFK	7:35	13:30:	15:05:	6.162,00	KM	X	0
LH	Click	2402	DE	FRANKFURT	FRA	DE	BERLIN	SXF	1:05	10:30:	11:35:	555,0000	KM		0
LH	Click	2407	DE	BERLIN	TXL	DE	FRANKFURT	FRA	1:05	07:10:	08:15:	555,0000	KM		0
QF	Click	5	SG	SINGAPORE	SIN	DE	FRANKFURT	FRA	13:45	22:50:	05:35:	10.000,0	KM		1
QF	Click	6	DE	FRANKFURT	FRA	SG	SINGAPORE	SIN	11:10	20:55:	15:05:	10.000,0	KM		1
SQ	Click	2	SG	SINGAPORE	SIN	US	SAN FRANCISCO	SFO	18:25	17:00:	19:25:	8.452,00	MI		0
SQ	Click	15	US	SAN FRANCISCO	SFO	SG	SINGAPORE	SIN	18:45	16:00:	02:45:	8.452,00	MI		2
SQ	Click	158	SG	SINGAPORE	SIN	ID	JAKARTA	JKT	1:35	15:25:	16:00:	560,0000	MI		0
SQ	Click	988	SG	SINGAPORE	SIN	JP	TOKYO	TYO	6:40	16:35:	00:15:	3.125,00	MI		1
UA	Click	941	DE	FRANKFURT	FRA	US	SAN FRANCISCO	SFO	11:36	14:30:	17:06:	5.685,00	MI		0
UA	Click	3504	US	SAN FRANCISCO	SFO	DE	FRANKFURT	FRA	10:30	15:00:	10:30:	5.685,00	MI		1
UA	Click	3516	US	NEW YORK	JFK	DE	FRANKFURT	FRA	7:25	16:20:	05:45:	6.162,00	KM		1
UA	Click	3517	DE	FRANKFURT	FRA	US	NEW YORK	JFK	8:15	10:40:	12:55:	6.162,00	KM		0

The button on ALV

After clicking on the button, a popup will appear, as follows:

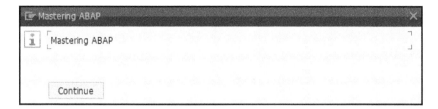

Popup

Let's move on to our next topic about icons in the ALV.

Icons in the ALV

To show an icon, we need to add one parameter to the field catalog and the values of this field need to be the values assigned to the icon. All icons can be seen in the ICON table.

For example, we can show an icon based on the values in the charter. When ✓ appears, a flight will be in the charter, and this will not be the case when ✗ appears.

At the beginning of the icon-creation process, we need to add a field to the resulting table structure:

```
DATA icon TYPE icon_int.
```

Next, we need to make changes to the field catalog. This parameter indicates that this field is an icon and will be shown as one. It will also change the name of the field from FLTYPE to ICON:

```
ls_fcat-fieldname = 'ICON'.
ls_fcat-scrtext_s = 'Charter?'.
ls_fcat-auto_value = 'X'.
ls_fcat-icon = 'X'.
APPEND ls_fcat TO lt_fcat.
CLEAR ls_fcat.
```

As the last step of creating an icon, we need to add an icon value to the corresponding field, as follows:

```
LOOP AT lt_color ASSIGNING FIELD-SYMBOL(<ls_icon>).
    IF <ls_icon>-fltype = 'X'.
        <ls_icon>-icon = '@B_OKAY@'.
    ELSEIF <ls_icon>-fltype IS INITIAL.
        <ls_icon>-icon = '@B_CANC@'.
    ENDIF.
ENDLOOP.
```

The result of this operation is demonstrated in the following screenshot:

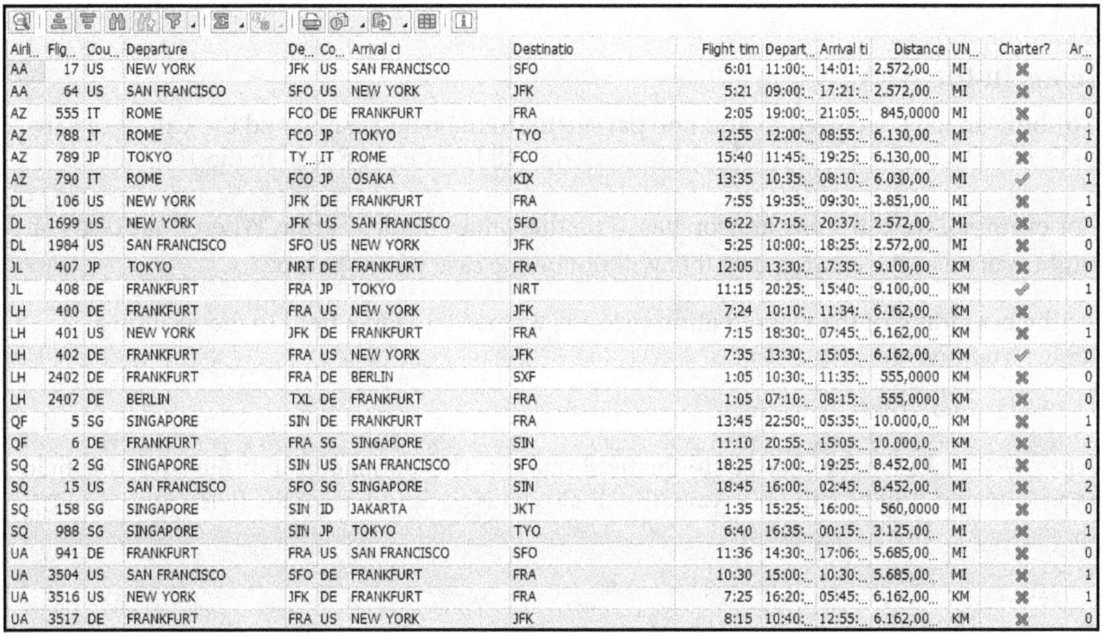

Airl	Flig	Cou	Departure	De	Co	Arrival ci	Destinatio	Flight tim	Depart	Arrival ti	Distance	UN	Charter?	Ar
AA	17	US	NEW YORK	JFK	US	SAN FRANCISCO	SFO	6:01	11:00:	14:01:	2.572,00	MI	✖	0
AA	64	US	SAN FRANCISCO	SFO	US	NEW YORK	JFK	5:21	09:00:	17:21:	2.572,00	MI	✖	0
AZ	555	IT	ROME	FCO	DE	FRANKFURT	FRA	2:05	19:00:	21:05:	845,0000	MI	✖	0
AZ	788	IT	ROME	FCO	JP	TOKYO	TYO	12:55	12:00:	08:55:	6.130,00	MI	✖	1
AZ	789	JP	TOKYO	TY	IT	ROME	FCO	15:40	11:45:	19:25:	6.130,00	MI	✖	0
AZ	790	IT	ROME	FCO	JP	OSAKA	KIX	13:35	10:35:	08:10:	6.030,00	MI	✓	1
DL	106	US	NEW YORK	JFK	DE	FRANKFURT	FRA	7:55	19:35:	09:30:	3.851,00	MI	✖	1
DL	1699	US	NEW YORK	JFK	US	SAN FRANCISCO	SFO	6:22	17:15:	20:37:	2.572,00	MI	✖	0
DL	1984	US	SAN FRANCISCO	SFO	US	NEW YORK	JFK	5:25	10:00:	18:25:	2.572,00	MI	✖	0
JL	407	JP	TOKYO	NRT	DE	FRANKFURT	FRA	12:05	13:30:	17:35:	9.100,00	KM	✖	0
JL	408	DE	FRANKFURT	FRA	JP	TOKYO	NRT	11:15	20:25:	15:40:	9.100,00	KM	✓	1
LH	400	DE	FRANKFURT	FRA	US	NEW YORK	JFK	7:24	10:10:	11:34:	6.162,00	KM	✖	0
LH	401	US	NEW YORK	JFK	DE	FRANKFURT	FRA	7:15	18:30:	07:45:	6.162,00	KM	✖	1
LH	402	DE	FRANKFURT	FRA	US	NEW YORK	JFK	7:35	13:30:	15:05:	6.162,00	KM	✓	0
LH	2402	DE	FRANKFURT	FRA	DE	BERLIN	SXF	1:05	10:30:	11:35:	555,0000	KM	✖	0
LH	2407	DE	BERLIN	TXL	DE	FRANKFURT	FRA	1:05	07:10:	08:15:	555,0000	KM	✖	0
QF	5	SG	SINGAPORE	SIN	DE	FRANKFURT	FRA	13:45	22:50:	05:35:	10.000,0	KM	✖	1
QF	6	DE	FRANKFURT	FRA	SG	SINGAPORE	SIN	11:10	20:55:	15:05:	10.000,0	KM	✖	1
SQ	2	SG	SINGAPORE	SIN	US	SAN FRANCISCO	SFO	18:25	17:00:	19:25:	8.452,00	MI	✖	0
SQ	15	US	SAN FRANCISCO	SFO	SG	SINGAPORE	SIN	18:45	16:00:	02:45:	8.452,00	MI	✖	2
SQ	158	SG	SINGAPORE	SIN	ID	JAKARTA	JKT	1:35	15:25:	16:00:	560,0000	MI	✖	0
SQ	988	SG	SINGAPORE	SIN	JP	TOKYO	TYO	6:40	16:35:	00:15:	3.125,00	MI	✖	1
UA	941	DE	FRANKFURT	FRA	US	SAN FRANCISCO	SFO	11:36	14:30:	17:06:	5.685,00	MI	✖	0
UA	3504	US	SAN FRANCISCO	SFO	DE	FRANKFURT	FRA	10:30	15:00:	10:30:	5.685,00	MI	✖	1
UA	3516	US	NEW YORK	JFK	DE	FRANKFURT	FRA	7:25	16:20:	05:45:	6.162,00	KM	✖	1
UA	3517	DE	FRANKFURT	FRA	US	NEW YORK	JFK	8:15	10:40:	12:55:	6.162,00	KM	✖	0

Icons in the ALV

Let's have a look at another such example in the following screenshot:

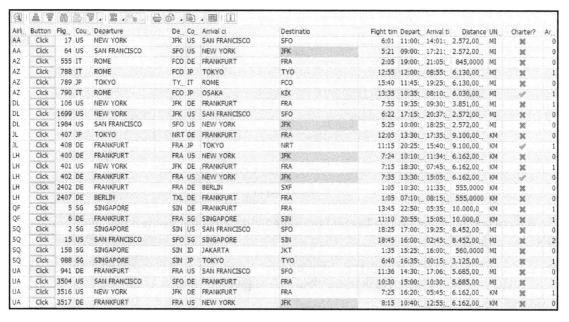

Airli..	Button	Flig..	Cou..	Departure	De..	Co..	Arrival ci	Destinatio	Flight tim	Depart..	Arrival ti	Distance	UN..	Charter?	Ar..
AA	Click	17	US	NEW YORK	JFK	US	SAN FRANCISCO	SFO	6:01	11:00:	14:01:	2.572,00	MI	✕	0
AA	Click	64	US	SAN FRANCISCO	SFO	US	NEW YORK	JFK	5:21	09:00:	17:21:	2.572,00	MI	✕	0
AZ	Click	555	IT	ROME	FCO	DE	FRANKFURT	FRA	2:05	19:00:	21:05:	845,0000	MI	✕	0
AZ	Click	788	IT	ROME	FCO	JP	TOKYO	TYO	12:55	12:00:	08:55:	6.130,00	MI	✕	1
AZ	Click	789	JP	TOKYO	TY..	IT	ROME	FCO	15:40	11:45:	19:25:	6.130,00	MI	✕	0
AZ	Click	790	IT	ROME	FCO	JP	OSAKA	KIX	13:35	10:35:	08:10:	6.030,00	MI	✓	1
DL	Click	106	US	NEW YORK	JFK	DE	FRANKFURT	FRA	7:55	19:35:	09:30:	3.851,00	MI	✕	1
DL	Click	1699	US	NEW YORK	JFK	US	SAN FRANCISCO	SFO	6:22	17:15:	20:37:	2.572,00	MI	✕	0
DL	Click	1984	US	SAN FRANCISCO	SFO	US	NEW YORK	JFK	5:25	10:00:	18:25:	2.572,00	MI	✕	0
JL	Click	407	JP	TOKYO	NRT	DE	FRANKFURT	FRA	12:05	13:30:	17:35:	9.100,00	KM	✕	0
JL	Click	408	DE	FRANKFURT	FRA	JP	TOKYO	NRT	11:15	20:25:	15:40:	9.100,00	KM	✓	1
LH	Click	400	DE	FRANKFURT	FRA	US	NEW YORK	JFK	7:24	10:10:	11:34:	6.162,00	KM	✕	0
LH	Click	401	US	NEW YORK	JFK	DE	FRANKFURT	FRA	7:15	18:30:	07:45:	6.162,00	KM	✕	1
LH	Click	402	DE	FRANKFURT	FRA	US	NEW YORK	JFK	7:35	13:30:	15:05:	6.162,00	KM	✓	0
LH	Click	2402	DE	FRANKFURT	FRA	DE	BERLIN	SXF	1:05	10:30:	11:35:	555,0000	KM	✕	0
LH	Click	2407	DE	BERLIN	TXL	DE	FRANKFURT	FRA	1:05	07:10:	08:15:	555,0000	KM	✕	0
QF	Click	5	SG	SINGAPORE	SIN	DE	FRANKFURT	FRA	13:45	22:50:	05:35:	10.000,0	KM	✕	1
QF	Click	6	DE	FRANKFURT	FRA	SG	SINGAPORE	SIN	11:10	20:55:	15:05:	10.000,0	KM	✕	1
SQ	Click	2	SG	SINGAPORE	SIN	US	SAN FRANCISCO	SFO	18:25	17:00:	19:25:	8.452,00	MI	✕	0
SQ	Click	15	US	SAN FRANCISCO	SFO	SG	SINGAPORE	SIN	18:45	16:00:	02:45:	8.452,00	MI	✕	2
SQ	Click	158	SG	SINGAPORE	SIN	ID	JAKARTA	JKT	1:35	15:25:	16:00:	560,0000	MI	✕	0
SQ	Click	988	SG	SINGAPORE	SIN	JP	TOKYO	TYO	6:40	16:35:	00:15:	3.125,00	MI	✕	1
UA	Click	941	DE	FRANKFURT	FRA	US	SAN FRANCISCO	SFO	11:36	14:30:	17:06:	5.685,00	MI	✕	0
UA	Click	3504	US	SAN FRANCISCO	SFO	DE	FRANKFURT	FRA	10:30	15:00:	10:30:	5.685,00	MI	✕	1
UA	Click	3516	US	NEW YORK	JFK	DE	FRANKFURT	FRA	7:25	16:20:	05:45:	6.162,00	KM	✕	1
UA	Click	3517	DE	FRANKFURT	FRA	US	NEW YORK	JFK	8:15	10:40:	12:55:	6.162,00	KM	✕	0

Result of all changes made in the ALV

Of course, we can mix all of the previous changes and the result of doing so is presented in the preceding screenshot.

Text fields and translations

To create text, we need to select the text field (🔲) from the elements on the left in Screen Painter and drag and drop it onto the screen.

We need to add a name and some text. The name is the name of the field and the text is the text shown on the screen. We do not need to manually adjust the size of the text field as this will be adjusted automatically:

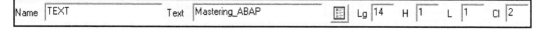

Name	TEXT		Text	Mastering_ABAP		Lg	14	H	1	L	1	Cl	2

Text in Screen Painter

To create a translation of a field, we need to click on **Goto** and select **Translation** from the list. After locking on to the target language for which there are translations, the text will automatically be displayed in the selected language:

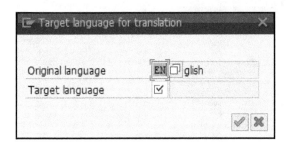

Selecting a language

On the pop-up window, in the **Target language** field, select the desired language and click **OK**.

On the next window, we can add translations and select text-to-translation. In this case, the text will be divided into two categories. The first is text on the screen and the second is for headers:

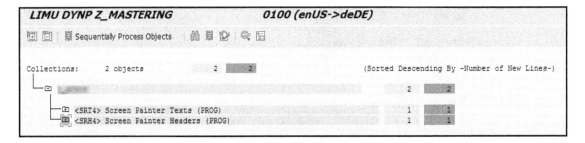

Translation screen

To create text for the Screen Painter, for example, expand the list **<SRT4> Screen Painter Texts (PROG)** and double-click on selected rows.

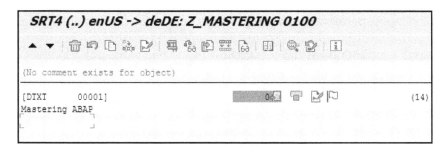

Translation

Click on and check whether any proposals exist. If not, you can accept this translation as system-wide after clicking ⊙A . Next, go back to the previous screen and save the translations.

Input/output field

To create an input field/output field, we need to click on the ⌷ icon and select an area for it. After creating a field, we need to add a name. The naming of fields is really important. This is because if we create a field with the same name as something else in a program, values from the program will automatically be transmitted to screen and vice versa.

In the input/output field, we can also specify some parameters. The most important fields are listed here:

- On the **Dict** tab, there's the following:
    - **Format drop-down menu**: The user can select the field format from the list. They can select from many possibilities such as CHAR or DEC.
    - **From dict checkbox**: If the **dict** checkbox is checked, data (such as format, conversion exit, and more from the DDIC) will be automatically recovered.
    - Conv.Exit: This is a conversion exit which is automatically applied for values in a given field.
    - Search help.
    - **Case-sensitive checkbox**: If checked, this field will be case sensitive. By default, fields are converted into capital letters.
- On the **Program** tab, there's the following:
    - **Checkbox input field**: If this checkbox is checked, we can put some data into this field. If not, the field only consists of output.

- **Input dropdown**: We can select this if filling out this field is possible, recommended, or even required.
- **Output field checkbox**: If this checkbox is checked, we can show some data from the program in this field. If not, the field is only an input field:

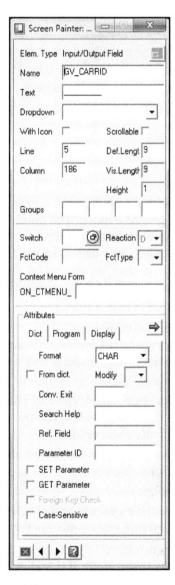

Options of the input/output field

We need to double-click on the elements of the list shown in the preceding screenshot in order to get a window in which these values can be put in order.

Radiobuttons and checkbox

Radiobuttons and checkboxes are created by clicking the ⊠ button for a checkbox or ⦿ for a radiobutton and selecting an area for a field. Next, we need to input a name for this field. In the same way as in the input/output field, if we name this field identically as in the program, data will be transferred.

On radiobuttons and checkboxes, we cannot select field formats, for example. This is specific to the input/output field.

To create a group of radio buttons, we need to mark the radio buttons that are to be in one group and right-click them, selecting **Radio button group** followed by **define**.

Button

The button is created by clicking the ⬛ button in the list and selecting an area for this field.

We need to create a name for the button, but in this case, this is not crucial. In the button attribute, we need to specify the function code. This is specified after clicking a button on the PAI module. The user command is then moved, at which point we can make programming actions.

In our example, the button function code will be RES:

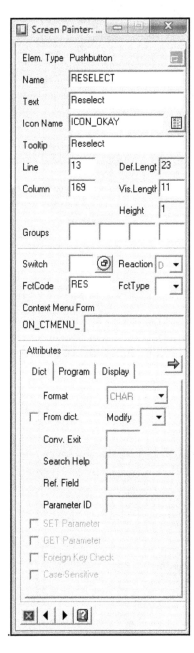

Options in the button

All of the fields necessary for button creation are shown in the preceding screenshot.

Dynamic display possibilities for individual elements and groups

To create a dynamic display, we need to add the name of a group to the attributes of a field.

In our example, we can hide or display two radiobuttons based on a checkbox. By default, these two radiobuttons are not present, but if we check the checkbox, this makes them appear. We also need to add a dummy action to the checkbox to process the PBO and change the screen.

After doing this, the screen should look as follows:

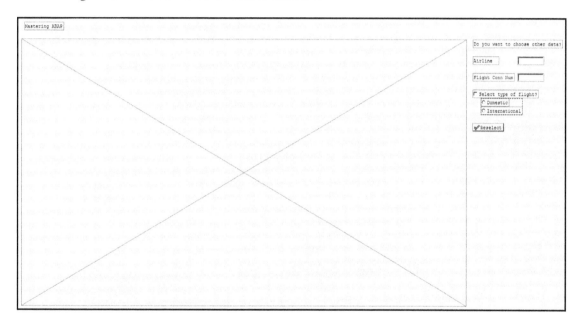

Screen after making changes

We need to create global fields with the same name as the screen:

```
gv_carrid          TYPE s_carr_id,
gv_connid          TYPE s_conn_id,
gv_type            TYPE c,
gv_domestic        TYPE c,
gv_international   TYPE c,
gv_dyn_where       TYPE string VALUE '1 = 1'.
```

Now, all values from fields are available in the program. Next, we need to write a piece of code:

```
WHEN 'RES'.

 IF lv_dyn_where IS INITIAL.
   lv_dyn_where = '1 = 1'.
 ENDIF.
 IF gv_carrid IS NOT INITIAL.
 lv_dyn_where = |{ lv_dyn_where } and carrid = '{ gv_carrid }'|.
 ENDIF.

 IF gv_connid IS NOT INITIAL.
 lv_dyn_where = |{ lv_dyn_where } and connid = '{ gv_connid }'|.
 ENDIF.

 IF gv_domestic IS NOT INITIAL.
 lv_dyn_where = |{ lv_dyn_where } and countryfr EQ s~countryto|.
 ENDIF.

 IF gv_international IS NOT INITIAL.
 lv_dyn_where = |{ lv_dyn_where } and countryfr NE s~countryto|.
 ENDIF.

 SELECT carrid, connid,
        countryfr, cityfrom, airpfrom,
        countryto, cityto, airpto,
        fltime, deptime, arrtime, distance,
        distid, fltype, period
   FROM spfli AS s
   WHERE (lv_dyn_where)
   INTO CORRESPONDING FIELDS OF TABLE @lt_color.

 CLEAR lv_dyn_where.
```

After clicking on **reselect**, data is reselected based on the value input to the fields on the screen.

Summary

Classics DynPro and the ALV are essential to an ABAP programmer's work on a daily basis. Classic DynPro is mostly used for creating reports and custom transactions, so having a good understanding of this topic is crucial. This portion of ABAP knowledge is one of the first things that we need to understand.

In the next chapter, we will focus on further options for creating screens, namely SAPUI5.

Questions

The following questions will allow you to consolidate the information contained in this chapter:

1. Which two categories have Classic Dynpro been divided into?
2. What is the main difference between `Parameters` and `Select-options` on the **Selection** screen?
3. What do you need to remember when creating the custom container for ALV?

8
Creating Stunning UI5 Interfaces

When the SAP environment was created, its main focus was on delivering the most reliable and efficient functionalities. As a result, it may have been observed that the **user interface (UI)** was somehow neglected when considering SAP products. There were some efforts to improve the overall visual reception, from new skins (themes) to SAP **Graphical User Interface (GUI)**, WebDynPros, SAP Personas, and so on, but these were rather small and insufficient steps.

Things changed significantly once a completely new approach arose—*to think Fiori*. SAP Fiori had its origin in very straightforward ideas—make the interface as simple as possible and only as complicated as is necessary, make it responsive, and, most importantly, make it delightful. This approach turns away from overwhelming transaction screens, with plenty of options, buttons, popups, tables, and lists, and tailors the application to fulfill the goal of a single process without any distractions. Furthermore, this application should only be offered to the group who will use it. Don't make a single multi-purpose application with the functionalities designed for employees, managers, and administrators—give each of them only what they really need.

This idea, although very simple and noble in its goals, couldn't be brought quickly and efficiently to life without one radical step—to abandon cumbersome SAP GUI, which was a little archaic, and go completely mobile. The most flexible way to achieve this was to focus on web technologies (as they are available for both mobile and stationary users) and to incorporate them into reliable business processes using the well-tested and publicly-available libraries. All these efforts led to the first foundations of what we now call the SAPUI5 libraries.

SAPUI5, and its sister, OpenUI5, are built on top of several solid technologies, such as HTML5, CSS3, and JavaScript, and some pretty convenient and mature tools and libraries, for example jQuery, `d3.js`, `Crossroads.js`, and many, many more. The SAPUI5 libraries are designed and considered to be a one-stop-shop framework and, by design, don't require any additional configurations and installations once they are delivered. There is, however, one thing to consider—only the OpenUI5 libraries are open source. SAPUI5, in contrast, is a part of several SAP products, such as SAP HANA, SAP Cloud Platform, and SAP NetWeaver, but is delivered without any additional license. Aside from the licensing difference, in OpenUI5 there are some elements missing, which are designed specifically to integrate with SAP systems and products, so it has very little or no impact on the core functionalities of the library.

The following topics will be covered in this chapter:

- Development tools
- Layouts and floorplans
- The SAPUI5 library
- Creating your first mobile app
- Testing SAPUI5 apps

Technical requirements

It is recommended that you use one of the following integrated development environments (IDEs):

- Eclipse JEE (http://www.eclipse.org/downloads/eclipse-packages/) with SAPUI5 Tools (https://tools.hana.ondemand.com/#sapui5).
- WebIDE Personal Edition (https://tools.hana.ondemand.com/#sapui5).
- WebIDE Cloud Edition—this requires a trial account at SAP Cloud Platform as a minimum (https://cloudplatform.sap.com/index.html).

All the code used in this chapter can be downloaded from the following GitHub link: `https://github.com/PacktPublishing/Mastering-SAP-ABAP/tree/master/Chapter08`.

Development tools

Together with the new way of thinking, new design rules, and new libraries, SAP has started to develop tools that allow the programmers to easily develop the applications in the new technology, but also to integrate them with the existing systems. As the overall policy was to make the libraries as open and as available as possible, the tool should be made publicly available as well. At first, the choice was to use the Eclipse environment, as the IDE, which is available publicly, has a great community and is being constantly improved. The SAP team has developed several plugins for the Eclipse IDE, which are responsible for managing the SAPUI5 projects, automating the applications enhancing process, and integrating Eclipse with the on-premise SAP systems, its repositories, and its transport management system.

The Eclipse IDE with all its SAP plugins was more than enough to create, maintain, and deploy the SAPUI5 applications. Although the plugins are still available, even for the Neon and Oxygen releases, they are no longer improved and, at present, they don't offer all the possibilities that are delivered with other tools.

Once SAP acknowledged the need to go mobile, it was expected that, sooner or later, this idea will be found in more and more aspects of the whole environment. And, eventually, this happened to the development tool itself. SAP introduced the Web IDE in two editions, Personal and Cloud, and it is now the recommended tool to develop the SAPUI5 applications.

The Web IDE Personal Edition is a standalone, offline tool, yet it is running on the local server delivered as a bundle, and so it is accessed through web browsers. It offers all the tools that are necessary to build a SAPUI5 application either from scratch, from the template, or as an extension project to any standard Fiori application. Starting from the graphical layout editor, code completion, and internationalization maintenance, through built-in Git integration, support for testing frameworks and tools (such as OPA or Sinon.JS), and easy data mocking, even to integration with on-premise systems available in local networks. All these functionalities are available without any license or fee for non-productive scenarios.

Although the Web IDE Personal Edition seems to be a complete tool for a SAPUI5 developer, it can still be considered as a limited version of what is available in the Web IDE Cloud version. Due to the biggest advantage of the Web IDE Cloud version, its constant improvement, it is hard to list all of the functionalities that make this variant superior compared to any other tool. Among the others, the most important one is the **Hybrid Application Toolkit** (**HAT**) plugin that enables the possibility to pack the SAPUI5 web apps into native applications for mobile devices running Android or iOS. Another useful functionality is cloud-based, community-driven internationalization automation, which utilizes the fact that, during the development of lots of applications, some texts, labels, or headers are used repeatedly in different languages, therefore it automatically offers translations for internationalization files. The full-blown cloud version for productive scenarios requires a paid license; however, the trial access (unlimited in terms of functionalities available and without an expiration date) is available for everyone.

Another very convenient tool, which, in fact, should be used as the first one in the development process, is SAP Build, also known as **Build.me**. It is a very easy-to-use prototyping application for **User Experience** (**UX**) experts, which allows you to create interactive models of the SAPUI5-based UI without a single line of code. The outcome of this is that it can be easily used to deliver several prototypes of the application in no time, and can adjust them in the low-cost iterative approach before getting the developers involved. The final model can be then exported to the Web IDE (either Personal or Cloud), and the actual application logic can be programmed as for any other SAPUI5 application.

Layouts and floorplans

Keeping in mind the philosophy of making simple, responsive, and task-oriented applications, while keeping them visually consistent and appealing, the SAP team delivered a bundle of several predefined and preconfigured templates and frameworks with SAP Fiori. Depending on the use case and complexity level, the bundle can be described in three categories—SAP Fiori elements, layouts, and floorplans. The first of these is a purpose-oriented set of ready-to-use templates, whereas layouts and floorplans are simple designs that comply with the Fiori guidelines, simultaneously allowing freedom of development.

SAP Fiori elements

The increased need for more and more SAPUI5 applications, which accompanied the introduction of the S/4 HANA suite, eventually led to the conclusion that most of them share some similar parts and concepts. Thus, it seemed inevitable that a set of predefined templates should be developed, which can be used almost without any major changes, to speed up the application build process. At present, there are already five of these:

- The analytical list page
- The list report
- The object page
- The overview page
- The worklist

Each one is designed to serve a specific purpose.

 The SAP Fiori elements can be used only with OData services that support annotations, as they are one of the layout building blocks.

The analytical list page

This is meant to be used for analytical tasks, data comparison, and root cause investigations. The analytical list page is recommended whenever there is a need to present aggregated data in a specific way, to investigate through drill-down, dynamically apply filters, or to interact with both tables and charts.

The analytical list page consists of three main sections—the title, header, and content. Although the title section seems to be self-explanatory, it serves a greater purpose than just showing the title. It is the main entry point to save and manage page variants (that is, applied filters, grouping, and so on), it shows global KPIs and allows users to apply some global visual filters. The header section's main feature is to show filtered data representation, mainly in the form of several charts. The content section can display a chart, a table, or both, and is designed to operate on raw data.

The list report

The list report can be used whenever the user needs to work on large datasets, but there is no need to work on charts and tables simultaneously, or if drill-down reporting is not necessary, but it is crucial to work on multiple items at once. Similarly to the analytical list page, there are also three main sections, but with quite different meanings. The first one, the header title, is meant to display the page title, a summary of filter information, and some global action buttons. The header content should contain all necessary filtering options, whereas the content supports simple content with multiple views.

The object page

The object page is designed as a simple information sheet and should be used for single-item managing tasks (create, display, or edit). The three main building blocks are the snapping header, navigation bar, and content area. The header contains all key information about the object and global actions, such as copying or deleting the object. The navigation bar is used to navigate within the object page, either through anchors or tabs. The content area arranges sections and subsections in a responsive column layout. While subsections can contain any control and any data, the sections are only meant to be simple containers for subsections, giving them a meaningful title.

The overview page

This application type serves as a hub gathering data from several other applications and showing them in one place in forms of cards, based on the user's role. It allows the user to react to information from more than one application shown in various formats. The cards are entry points to the applications, but, what is more important, is that they display the most relevant data to the user in a more detailed way than tiles on the launch-pad page—they support most major data representations, such as lists, charts, images, tables, or information sheets.

The worklist

As the name suggests, the worklist is intended to show the list of items that the user has to work on. It supports multiple views of the same content and acts as a single entry point to all actions on the work items.

Layouts

Whenever the designer decides that neither of the SAP Fiori elements can fulfill the requirements, or there are some technical limitations of using them out of the box, there are still several recommendations and templates that can be used. There are two basic layout types for the SAP Fiori applications recommended in the Fiori design guidelines—the dynamic page layout and the flexible column layout. The former is a full-screen application with a header title and a single content area with a footer, whereas the latter splits the content area into a master-detail or master-detail-detail scenario. Each of them supports various floorplans that can be embedded in the content area.

Floorplans

The floorplan is a general term to describe the structure of the controls on the page, or, to be precise, within the content area of the layout. The predefined layouts are as follows:

- The analytical list page floorplan
- The initial page floorplan
- The list report floorplan
- The multi-instance floorplan
- The object page floorplan
- The overview page floorplan
- The wizard floorplan
- The worklist floorplan

The analytical list page, list report, object page, overview page, and worklist floorplans are the same as those in the SAP Fiori elements; however, due to free development, they support more different options and controls. The remaining ones are described in the following subsections.

The initial page floorplan

This is the most simple application floorplan, which consists only of a single input field to search with, and the result area. It is useful to work with a single object when the object list is not necessary.

The multi-instance floorplan

The multi-instance floorplan is a natural extension to the object page, as it supports working with multiple objects at a time, using convenient tabs.

The wizard floorplan

This floorplan is designed to be used in multi-step tasks. This helps us to organize all data inputs and user interactions into subsequent views, with the indicator of steps completed and remaining.

The detailed description and examples of each layout and floorplan can be found in the SAP Fiori design guidelines, available at `https://experience.sap.com/fiori-design-web/floorplan-overview/`.

Basic templates

Apart from the templates recommended by the SAP Fiori design guidelines, the SAPUI5 library suggests the use of three simple templates—Worklist, Master-Detail, and Basic, which are more or less simplified versions of the floorplans already covered and there is no need to give a more detailed description.

The SAPUI5 library

Once the top-level view of the application is already designed, it is time to get familiar with the actual building blocks of the UI. SAPUI5 is already a mature library with a plethora of controls and elements. In order to get a quick overview of most of them, it is recommended that you visit `https://sapui5.hana.ondemand.com/#/controls`, which contains various samples and use cases of the most common ones.

The samples are ready to download and run in the developer's chosen IDE, or simply to check all the source codes.

During the actual development, it is more convenient to use the API reference than to check sample codes. The whole documentation of every single control is available at `https://sapui5.hana.ondemand.com/#/api` and is divided into several libraries. Although from the technical perspective, all the libraries are written in the same language and should be compatible, there are few strong recommendations regarding using them together, and violating them may cause the application to crash. There are three groups, as follows:

- `sap.ui.comp`, `sap.m`, `sap.f`, `sap.tnt`, `sap.ea` (deprecated), `sap.me` (deprecated), `sap.suite.ui`, `sap.ushell`, `sap.uxap`, and `sap.gantt`
- `sap.ui.commons` (deprecated), `sap.ui.richtexteditor`, `sap.ui.suite`, and `sap.ui.ux3` (deprecated)
- `sap.ui.core`, `sap.ui.layout`, `sap.ui.unified`, `sap.ui.table`, and `sap.viz`

Groups one and two are mutually exclusive and cannot be used together. Group three can be used both with one and two. This division is valid for SAPUI5 version 1.54.4, and it may vary if older or more recent versions are used.

Control documentation page and inheritance

The documentation page for each control is divided into several sections—contextual info, overview, constructor, properties, associations, aggregations, events, and methods.

Contextual info

This is placed on the top of the page and contains basic information about the control's visibility (thus whether it is possible to use it directly within the application, or it is used only by other controls), the library version from which the control is available, in what module the control is implemented, what object it extends, or what other controls are dependent.

Overview

This presents a short summary of the control's purpose, where it should and where it should not be used, and what the most common settings and methods are. In case the control is deprecated, there is also information about possible replacements.

Constructor

In case the control has to be instantiated programmatically instead of statically, the constructor section contains the sample JavaScript code to create the new instance, alongside the description of its arguments.

Properties

The properties section contains all parameters that can be set in this specific control using standard APIs. Although due to the non-restrictive nature of the JavaScript language, it is possible to set manually any single property of the control that is not listed here, there is no guarantee that such a change won't break the control or even the application. It is also important to note that all the controls are inheriting the properties from their superclasses as well (look at the *Contextual info* section), so their properties are also considered as a part of the API. For all the properties, there is a corresponding `get` and `set` (if the property is changeable) method. These methods should be used to `set`/`get` the properties values every time, except for the object instantiation.

Associations

This section contains the information about the controls that are associated with the one in question but are not connected to its life cycle, therefore, there is no guarantee that they exist when the control is created.

Aggregations

If the control is designed as a container, the aggregations sections list all possible controls (or types) that can be assigned as children of the one in question. In many cases, the type listed here is a generic one, or it is control from which lots of others inherit and can be used as well.

Events

User actions or data updates cause the control to interact with the JavaScript code through events and handlers. During the control instantiation (or later through the appropriate methods) the developer is supposed to attach handlers (functions) to the specified events and perform the necessary steps.

The handler function receives the first argument of the `sap.ui.base.Event` type, with the information about the parameters dependent on the event type and about the event source, thus allowing the usage of one handler method for several controls or events. The events from the controls superclasses (objects) can be handled as well.

Methods

This section contains all the information about the methods defined for the object in question. Among the ones related to properties (getters and setters), there are also a lot of control-specific methods together with their arguments and results. It should be noted that, similar to properties and events, methods are also inherited from the superclasses, and, therefore, all of them are perfectly valid.

Inheritance

As it was previously mentioned, the UI controls are not completely separated objects and the library is based on the inheritance. For example, the button control from the `sap.m` library (`sap.m.Button`) has its own properties, methods, and events listed on the documentation page, but it extends `sap.ui.core.Control`, which, in turn, extends `sap.ui.core.Element`, and then `sap.ui.base.ManagedObject`, `sap.ui.base.EventProvider`, and, eventually, `sap.ui.base.Object`. All the properties, methods, and events of these objects, in general, can be used with `sap.m.Button` objects.

Main controls

The SAPUI5 library contains several hundred controls. Some of them are the UI controls and can be shown on the screen as the HTML objects, the others are responsible for communication with the data providers. To simplify the building of the application, the `sap.m` library was introduced. At first, it was designed to handle the interface of the mobile device, but eventually, it replaced `sap.ui.commons` on the desktop devices as well as making it deprecated. The `sap.m` library is now considered as a main library for the UI and should be used as a first choice in every application. Some of the most common building blocks from the `sap.m` library are as follows:

- `sap.m.App`/`sap.m.SplitApp`: These are the roots of the SAPUI5 applications, one for the one-container scenario and the other for master-detail applications.

- `sap.m.List`/`sap.m.Table`: These are the most common mass-data-displaying controls, which are able to generate several repeatable rows. These can be used either for the sole purpose of displaying data or to perform navigation and drill-down scenarios.
- `sap.m.Button`, `sap.m.Text`, `sap.m.Label`, and `sap.m.Input`: These are basic input/output controls for interaction with the user.
- `sap.m.Page` and `sap.m.Panel`: These are basic grouping containers; `sap.m.Page` is required as a top-most node in `sap.m.App`/`sap.m.SplitApp`.
- `sap.m.Dialog`, `sap.m.SelectDialog`, and `sap.m.Popover`: These are simple controls for overlaying information and dialog.

It is crucial for the developer to be able to swiftly navigate through the documentation in order to get familiar with the most commonly-used controls and at least get a glimpse of the less common ones. This will result in better choices when building the application and less custom coding.

Custom controls

Even though the SAPUI5 library is vast and contains various controls, sometimes it is impossible to find the control that really fits the requirements. In this case, the developer can leverage the inheritance model and the elasticity introduced in the library. Depending on the actual needs, you can gather the few existing controls into a new one implementing some additional logic and automation, or extend one of the classes (for example `sap.ui.core.Control`) manually, providing appropriate control interface properties, rendering methods, events, and so on. Once the new control is instantiated, the core processor will take care of its life cycle and event processing the same way that it does with the standard ones.

Creating our first mobile app

Once the top-level design of the application is determined, the data flow is designed, and the interface between the app and the backend system is confirmed, it is time to start the development.

A simple example of a flight searching application will be covered in the next sections.

Application and project structure

The SAPUI5 applications are supposed to follow the **Model-View-Controller** (**MVC**) paradigm when the build and the libraries are designed to support it. The top-level architecture of the application should consist of JavaScript controllers responsible for any application logic, data services to provide and store information (either as `.json` files, **Simple Object Access Protocol** (**SOAP**) services, or OData Services) attached through models, and views defining the UI. Although there is a technical possibility of creating views using JavaScript files or JSON objects, it is highly recommended that you use XML files instead. The MVC paradigm forces the separation of the concerns policy and makes the applications easier to maintain and debug.

The views and controllers files should be accompanied with internationalization (i18n) files to store all the text values of the UI. This approach allows for quick and easy translations of the interface, without the need to scroll through all other files.

Regardless of the development tool (Eclipse with plugins, the WebIDE Personal Edition, or the WebIDE Cloud Edition), once the new project is created, there should be a particular structure of files and catalogs in it. To be precise, in the top-most (usually named WebContent) catalog, you should find the `index.html` file (if the app is supposed to be standalone), `Component.js`, and `manifest.json`. If the application is meant to be accessed through the Fiori launchpad, the `index.html` file is not mandatory in the deployment process. The lower-level structure of the project is free to choose from.

index.html

The index file is the default entry point to every web page on the internet. Keeping in mind that the SAPUI5 applications are, in fact, web applications, they also use the index file if accessed directly. The basic structure of an index file should provide references both to the SAPUI5 core library and to the application structure itself. The example file is listed as follows:

```
<!DOCTYPE HTML>
<html>
    <head>
        <meta http-equiv="X-UA-Compatible" content="IE=edge">
        <meta http-equiv='Content-Type' content='text/html;charset=UTF-8'/>
        <!-- SAPUI5 library bootstrap -->
            <script src='[sap-ui-core.js URL]'
                    id="sap-ui-bootstrap"
                    data-sap-ui-libs="sap.m"
                    data-sap-ui-theme="sap_belize"
                    data-sap-ui-bindingSyntax="complex"
```

```
                data-sap-ui-resourceroots='{
                    "my.namespace":"./"
                }'>
        </script>

        <script>
            sap.ui.getCore().attachInit(function(){
                sap.ui.require([
                    "sap/m/Shell","sap/ui/core/ComponentContainer"
                ], function(Shell, ComponentContainer){
                    new Shell({
                        id: "shellId",
                        app: new ComponentContainer({
                            id:"componentId",
                            name:"componenName",
                            height:"100%"
                        })
                    }).placeAt("content");
                });
            });
        </script>
    </head>
    <body class="sapUiBody" role="application" id="content"></body>
</html>
```

A similar file is automatically generated when creating a new project in any of the development tools mentioned. There are several parts of this file with different functionalities and responsibilities, and these will be explained step by step.

Due to the fact that the libraries are based on modern web technologies, we need to ensure that some older browsers are also supported. In this particular case, the following line ensures that Internet Explorer runs the application with the most recent standards:

```
<meta http-equiv="X-UA-Compatible" content="IE=edge">
```

The next part, the SAPUI5 library bootstrap, is responsible for loading the whole SAPUI5 framework and libraries as necessary. There are several ways of loading the library core, and the most common are are mentioned in the following sections.

The standard variant

This is the most common way of bootstrapping and is the recommended way. The `src` value should point directly to the `sap-ui-core.js` file. This loads all the libraries listed in `data-sap-ui-libs` synchronously.

The `src` value is as follows:

```
<script
    id="sap-ui-bootstrap"
    src="resources/sap-ui-core.js"
    data-sap-ui-libs="sap.m"
    data-sap-ui-theme="sap_belize">
</script>
```

The content delivery network

The **content delivery network** (**CDN**) variant leverages the availability of several web servers with the SAPUI5 libraries, therefore increasing the overall performance of loading the application. When using this variant, it is possible to choose the exact version of the SAPUI5 library that should be used by the application. For the OpenUI5 libraries, you should use the `openui5.hana.ondemand.com` host instead. The `src` value is shown as follows:

```
<script
    id="sap-ui-bootstrap"
src="https://sapui5.hana.ondemand.com/[version]/resources/sap-ui-core.js"
    data-sap-ui-libs="sap.m"
    data-sap-ui-theme="sap_belize">
</script>
```

The miscellaneous variants

If the SAPUI5 application is a part of some other web application, and jQuery is already loaded, you can use the special non-jQuery version of the libraries by using `resources/sap-ui-core-nojQuery.js`. If, due to performance requirements, there are some specific needs regarding libraries preloading, you can also use the preload variant, which is described in detail in the SAPUI5 documentation. Let's have a look at the following code snippet:

```
data-sap-ui-bindingSyntaxt="complex"
data-sap-ui-resourceroots='{ "my.namespace":"./" }'
```

The two remaining lines are responsible for enabling the advanced binding syntax in views and specifies the naming convention in the application structure respectively.

The JavaScript coding within the next `<script></script>` tags is launched once the SAPUI5 core is loaded and initialized. The function creates a new `sap.ui.core.ComponentContainer` with `sap.m.Shell` as a direct child node and places it inside the HTML tag with `id` as `content`—in this case, the following `<body>` tag.

Component.js

The `Component.js` file is the main entry point to the application. It is called either by the `index.html` file or the Fiori launchpad tile and contains the most important reference—to the application manifest—and the initial logic for the application. The sample file is listed here:

```
sap.ui.define([ "sap/ui/core/UIComponent"], function(UIComponent){
   "use strict";
   return UIComponent.extend("my.namespace.Component",{
     metadata:{
       manifest: "json"
     },
     init: function(){
       UIComponent.prototype.init.apply(this,arguments);
       this.getRouter().initialize();
     }
   });
});
```

The first line is a simple statement defining what the content of the file is in a form that the SAPUI5 core understands. Have a look at the following code snippet:

```
return UIComponent.extend("my.namespace.Component",{  ...
```

Then, the preceding line builds a custom `Component` object, which extends the standard `sap.ui.core.UIComponent` class with the data defined in the following JSON object:

```
{
  metadata:{
    manifest: "json"
  },
  init: function(){
    UIComponent.prototype.init.apply(this,arguments);
    this.getRouter().initialize();
  }
}
```

`metadata`, in this case, only points to the `manifest` file, telling the parser that it can be found in the `manifest.json` file. The `init` section performs the `init` function from the superclass, and additionally initializes the router to handle navigation within the application.

manifest.json

The manifest.json file is the main descriptor file of the application. Due to a large number of possible settings, only the most relevant parts will be covered here. A more detailed description is available in the SAPUI5 reference.

Going section by section, as it is a large JSON object, the file configures the application in several ways. The "sap.app" section contains basic information about the sources to which the application refers—the internationalization (i18n) files' locations, OData services, and static data sources (JSON files). The application name, title, id, version, and others can also be listed. The sample "sap.app" part with a basic configuration is shown as follows:

```
"sap.app":{
  "_version":"1.0.0",
  "id":"appId",
  "type":"application",
  "i18n":"i18n/i18n.properties",
  "dataSources":{
    "staticJSONSource":{
      "uri":"staticData/data.json",
      "type":"JSON"
    },
    "mainService": {
      "uri": "/sap/opu/odata/sap/ZODATA_SERVICE",
      "type": "OData",
      "settings": {
        "odataVersion": "2.0"
      }
    }
  }
},
```

The "sap.ui" section contains information about the UI: the technology, which device types are supported, which themes, and so on. The simple snippet for the "sap.ui" section can be created as follows:

```
"sap.ui":{
    "_version":"1.0.0",
    "technology":"UI5",
    "deviceTypes":{
      "desktop": true,
      "tablet": true,
      "phone": true
    }
},
```

The last section, `"sap.ui5"`, configures the application itself. `"rootView"` points to the view file, which acts as a top-most and will be considered as a base for the router. The `"models"` section initializes specific models, based on the `"dataSources"` defined in `"sap.app"`. It is important to note a few differences between them. The `"i18n"` model is a special type of model, designed particularly to contain text values of the UI and should not be used for any other purposes. The `""` model (without a name) is considered a root model. It is possible to have an unlimited number of models with names, but only one can be nameless. An example of the `"sap.ui5"` section with the initialization of models and application root controls is shown as follows:

```
"sap.ui5":{
    "_version": "1.0.0",
    "rootView":"my.namespace.view.MainView",
    "controlId":"app",
    "controlAggregation":"pages",
    "models":{
      "i18n":{
        "type":"sap.ui.model.resource.ResourceModel",
        "settings":{
          "bundleName": "my.namespace.i18n.i18n"
        }
      },
      "staticModel":{
        "type":"sap.ui.model.json.JSONModel",
        "dataSource":"staticJSONSource"
      },
      "": {
        "dataSource": "mainService"
      }
    },
    "routing": { . . . }
}
```

Finally, there is the `"routing"` section. It contains all information for the router (pointed in `"config"` > `"routerClass"`) to handle the navigation between views in the application. The special `"bypassed"` property is used whenever the router doesn't know what view should be displayed. In the `"routes"` subsection, you can define the URL patterns and bind them with the targets. It is important to know that the patterns are checked in the order of declaration and the first matching one is applied. That means that more general patterns should be placed after specific ones. The targets, in turn, point to specific views in the project structure, along with `"viewLevel"`, which decides whether the navigation animation should be `"to"` the view or `"back"`.

"viewNames" of "targets" are resolved against "viewPath" in "routing" > "config", therefore there is no need to write the full, absolute path to them.

The simple "routing" section with one route and two targets is shown as follows:

```
"routing":{
    "config":{
      "routerClass":"sap.m.routing.Router",
      "viewType":"XML",
      "viewPath":"my.namespace.views",
      "controlId":"app",
      "controlAggregation":"pages",
      "clearTarget":false,
      "transition":"show",
      "bypassed":{
        "target":["invalid"]
      }
    },
    "routes":[
      {
        "pattern":"search",
        "name":"search",
        "target":"search"
      }
    ],
    "targets":{
      "search":{
        "viewName":"SearchView",
        "viewLevel":1
      },
      "invalid":{
        "viewName":"NotFound",
        "viewLevel":1
      }
    }
  }
```

Views and controllers

In the very simple application that this book is going through, the files structure is as follows:

Two views are created in the `views` folder, with corresponding controllers in the controller's catalog. Additionally, the `data.json` file is created inside `staticData` to store some static information, which can be used by the application and is loaded at the application start into the `staticModel` model (as shown in the `manifest.json` file).

`NotFound.view.xml` is a fallback for the router when it doesn't reach any specific target, therefore the focus will be on the remaining two views.

MainView.view.xml

This view is relatively small and is a good example to show the logic and the notation:

```
<mvc:View
    controllerName="my.namespace.controllers.MainView"
    xmlns="sap.m"
    xmlns:mvc="sap.ui.core.mvc"
    displayBlock="true">
    <App id="app"
        backgroundColor="#fff"
/>
</mvc:View>
```

The top-most XML node of each view file is the `View` node. As for every other XML object or file, the first node must define all the namespaces used in the XML tree. In this case, there are two namespaces declared—`"sap.m"` for tags without a prefix, and `"sap.ui.core.mvc"` with `mvc` prefixes. The built-in XML parser resolves these names into the SAPUI5 libraries and gets the appropriate definitions of the corresponding objects. The obligatory `controllerName` parameter points to the controller file, which has to be loaded alongside the view to handle its life cycle and events. Each view has to point to one controller, but it is possible to use the same controller file for more than one view (keeping in mind that two separate instances will be created in runtime).

This particular view has only one child node—app (`sap.m.App`). This node is referred to in the router description as the main control of the application, and all the navigation will take place within this control.

As `MainView` is just a container for the application, there is no specific logic implemented in its controller, just its simple declaration:

```
sap.ui.define(["sap/ui/core/mvc/Controller"],function(Controller){
    return Controller.extend("my.namespace.controllers.MainView",{})
});
```

SearchView.view.xml

This simple application's sole functionality will be searching for a flight from a specific location. The location should be entered by the user and then confirmed by pressing the **Search** button.

The code for the appropriate view is listed as follows:

```
<mvc:View
  controllerName="my.namespace.controllers.SearchView"
  xmlns="sap.m"
  xmlns:mvc="sap.ui.core.mvc"
  xmlns:l="sap.ui.layout">
  <Page
    id="searchPage"
    title="{i18n>TTL_SearchPage}">
    <Panel
      expandable="false"
      expanded="true"
      headerText="{i18n>HDR_SearchPanel}">
      <l:Grid defaultSpan="XL2 L3 M6 S12">
        <l:content>
          <Label text="{i18n>LBL_Search}"/>
```

```
                <Input id="searchInput"/>
                <Button
                   text="{i18n>BTN_Search}"
                   press="searchButtonPressed"/>
            </l:content>
          </l:Grid>
        </Panel>
        <List
          id="flightsList"
          items="{filteredFlights>/FlightsSet/}">
          <items>
            <StandardListItem
              title="{filteredFlights>DestinationAirport}"
              description="{filteredFlights>FlightDate}"
              info="{filteredFlights>FlightTime}"
              />
          </items>
        </List>
      </Page>
    </mvc:View>
```

The `View` node is similar to the previous one—it contains information about the controller assigned to the view and declares all namespaces used within the file. The first child node of the view is `Page`, the default container used in navigation. Its property title refers to the specific entry in the internationalization file through the `i18n` model instantiated by `manifest.json`. The page consists of two major parts—the panel with `Label`, `Input`, and `Button` arranged in `Grid` and `List`. Using the `Grid` control allows us to control the child's control dimensions on various screen sizes. If not defined otherwise in the control, `defaultSpan` determines how many columns are used. The size of `Grid` is divided into 12 equal columns.

The `"press"` property of the button is declared to fire the `"searchButtonPressed"` method of the controller. Once the user presses it, the controller will handle all the necessary logic.

The `"items"` property of the list is bound to the `"filteredFlights"` model and to the `FlightsSet` collection. Once there are any contents in this model, the template used inside the `<items>` tag will be copied to display all the items. The template itself, `StandardListItem,` binds its own properties to specific properties of the items from the `FlightsSet` collection. `DestinationAirport` will be displayed as a title of `StandardListItem`, `FlightDate` as a description, and `FlightTime` as information. Any control that inherits from `sap.m.ListItemBase` can be used instead if there is a need for this.

SearchView.controller.js

This time there is some logic behind the screen—the user can press the button and then the values on the list should be displayed. The sample file is described as follows.

The first lines, similar to `MainView.controller.js`, are a simple definition of the controller.

```
sap.ui.define(["sap/ui/core/mvc/Controller"],function(Controller){
    return Controller.extend("my.namespace.controllers.SearchView",{
```

Then, within the JSON object that extends the standard controller, the `onInit` function is defined. It is triggered right after the same function from the superclass. Here, due to the fact that `View` is bound to the non-existent `"filteredFlights"` model, the model is created and set on `View`. The model's sole property is `"FlightsSet"`, and, so far, it is an empty array:

```
onInit:function(){
  this.getView()
    .byId('flightsList')
    .setModel(
      new sap.ui.model.json.JSONModel(
        {
          'FlightsSet':[]
        }
      ),
      'filteredFlights'
    );
},
```

Later on, there is a logic for handling the user's interaction with the button. Once it is pressed, the value is read from the `"searchInput"` control and the call to the OData service (assigned to the nameless model) is triggered. The call consists of two arguments—first, the OData entity collection name, `"FlightsSet"`, then a JSON object with several properties:

```
searchButtonPressed:function(oEvent){
    var sValue = this.getView().byId('searchInput').getValue();
    this.getView().getModel().read('/FlightsSet',{
      filters:[new sap.ui.model.Filter({
        path: 'DepartureAirport',
        operator: sap.ui.model.FilterOperator.EQ,
        value1: sValue
      })],
      success:jQuery.proxy(this.handleValuesFetched,this),
```

```
        error:jQuery.proxy(this.handleError,this)
    });
}
```

The properties passed to the call are as follows:

- Filter with the value taken from `"searchInput"`
- Success handler—the controller's method fired when the call is completed successfully
- Error handler—called when there is any error during the call

 Note that the success and error handler is wrapped with a `jQuery.proxy` statement. Due to the asynchronous nature of the Ajax calls, sometimes the reference to a `this` object can be lost causing the application to crash. Using this proxy statement ensures that the callbacks are triggered within the proper `this` context.

The success handler puts all the fetched results into the JSON model instantiated in the `onInit` function. The exact coding of this handler is shown as follows:

```
handleValuesFetched: function(data){
    this.getView()
        .getModel('filteredFlights')
            .setProperty('/FlightsSet',data.results);
},
```

The simple error handling—for developing purposes only—writes the whole error object into the browser's console. This way of showing errors is very convenient during development; however, it should not be used in productive scenarios. The code used is as follows:

```
handleError: function(error){
    console.error(error);
    }
  })
});
```

i18n.properties

The one thing that left is the internationalization file. By default, the library core looks for the i18n_xx.properties file, where xx contains the user's language code. When there is no specific i18n file for this language, the default i18n.properties file is used, and, therefore, it is the only one that is actually required. This simple application doesn't have many text fields, so the file is rather short:

```
TTL_SearchPage=Flights search engine
HDR_SearchPanel=Enter filter
LBL_Search=Departure Airport
BTN_Search=Search flights!
```

Once the application grows bigger and bigger it is wise to stick to one naming convention and group the text properties. This is automatically handled when using the SAP Web IDE as a development tool but has to be maintained manually in the Eclipse environment.

Testing SAPUI5 apps

Every SAPUI5 application—either small and simple or very complex—should be considered a software project. The nature of software projects is that, sometimes, they can cause problems or errors, especially when changes are introduced quickly, the developing team changes, or simply due to typos or non-straightforward logic. In order to avoid or at least minimize the risk, all projects should be tested. The SAPUI5 supports several ways of testing, but the most general is mocking data with Mock Servers, unit tests, and integration tests. These three techniques will be covered in the following sections. It is recommended to write a separate index-like file in the test folder, to separate testing area from development.

Mock Server

The Mock Server is used to perform simple testing with dummy data, when the backend service is not yet implemented or simply not reachable. As the SAPUI5 applications are data-driven rather than completely standalone, it is crucial to have at least fake data to test their behavior. In order to implement the Mock Server functionality, several changes are necessary to the .html file.

Let's assume that the testing area is created in the project structure and the launching page, mockServer.html, is placed in the test catalog:

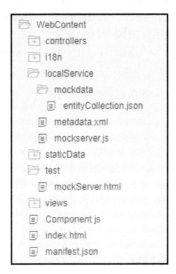

Then, the initial .html file must be enhanced as follows:

```
. . .
sap.ui.getCore().attachInit(function(){
  sap.ui.require([
    "my/namespace/localService/mockServer",
    "sap/m/Shell",
    "sap/ui/core/ComponentContainer"], function(mockserver, Shell,
ComponentContainer){
  mockserver.init()
  new Shell({
    . . .
```

Then, the actual server must be created in the mockserver.js file:

```
sap.ui.define(["sap/ui/core/util/MockServer"], function(MockServer){
  "use strict";
  return {
    init: function(){
      var oMockServer = new MockServer({
        rootUri: "/sap/opu/odata/sap/ZODATA_SERVICE/"
      });
      oMockServer.simulate("../localService/metadata.xml", {
        sMockdataBaseUrl: "../localService/mockdata",
        bGenerateMissingMockData: true
      });
```

```
        oMockServer.start();
    }
  }
}
```

This simple snippet creates a virtual server that servers the data according to its definition in the `metadata.xml` file. It uses the `.json` files stored in `localService/mockdata`, or, thanks to `bGenerateMissingMockData` flag, generates missing values if there are no appropriate `.json` files. As a rule, the `.json` files should be named as the entity collections in OData service, and their structure should reflect the entity properties.

The `metadata.xml` file is a simple OData metadata file available in an OData service. Provided that this file describes the same structure as the target service, the application will work with both the mock server and the real one.

The server, although already working, has some limitations if kept in the current form. It will not handle any custom parameter in the request call and does not recognize function imports. To achieve this, more advanced configuration and coding is required. Details can be found in the SAPUI5 documentation.

Unit tests

When the project grows and new functionalities are added, it will be necessary to be able to quickly check whether each and every part still works as expected. For this purpose, the SAPUI5 libraries support unit tests with the use of the QUnit framework. To set up a simple unit testing module, first, it is necessary to create the test launcher site, `unitTests.qunit.html`. The file should be placed in the `test/unit` catalog:

A short snippet of the launcher file is shown as follows:

```html
<!DOCTYPE html>
<html>
  <head>
    ...
    <script id="sap-ui-bootstrap"
      <!-- SAPUI5 core bootstrap -->
      ... >
    </script>
    <script>
      jQuery.sap.require("sap.ui.qunit.qunit-css");
      jQuery.sap.require("sap.ui.thirdparty.qunit");
      jQuery.sap.require("sap.ui.qunit.qunit-junit");
      jQuery.sap.require("sap.ui.qunit.qunit-coverage");
      QUnit.config.autostart = false;
      sap.ui.require(
        ["test/unit/testModules"],
        function(){
          QUnit.start();
        }
      );
    </script>
  </head>
  <body>
    <ol id="qunit-tests"></ol>
    <div id="qunit-fixture"></div>
  </body>
</html>
```

At first, the SAPUI5 core library is loaded by standard bootstrap. Then, through `jQuery.sap.require`, QUnit modules and the `QUnit.start` fires test that is declared in the `test/unit/testModules` file are loaded:

```
sap.ui.define([
    "test/unit/simpleTest",
    "test/unit/simpleTest2"], function(){
    "use strict";
});
```

All test files defined through `sap.ui.define` will be loaded and executed once they are called through the launcher site.

The test files themselves are written in the following structure (this time, some pseudo-code is used):

```
sap.ui.require([
    "path/to/file/tested1",
    "path/to/file/tested2",
    . . .
  ],
  function(file1, file2, ... ){
  "use strict";
  QUnit.module("Simple module");
  function testCase(assert, argument, expected){
    var result = file1.method1(argument);
    assert.stricEqual(result, expected, "Correct result");
  }
  QUnit.test("Name of the test case", function(assert){
    testCase.call(this, assert, "testArgument1", "expectedValue");
  });
  . . .
});
```

The algorithm is as follows—load the JavaScript files with the code to be tested by the `sap.ui.require` command, define a function with a call to the method in question with at least one assertion, and finally, write the test cases with appropriate arguments and expected values.

Once the tests are created, there is no need to check all possible values and outcomes manually.

Integration tests

The integration tests are used to efficiently check whether or not the new functionalities interfere with the existing ones. In SAPUI5, the integration tests are executed with the **One Page Acceptance 5 (OPA5)** tool, which is suitable for any SAPUI5 application that works in a single HTML page. The OPA tests scenarios are called journeys and are automated executions of the user's interaction with the application. The core of this tool simply mimics pushing buttons, entering values, navigating through views, and so on, following the programmed scenarios.

Similar to unit tests, integration tests also need a launching page, `integrationTests.qunit.html`, and it should be placed in the `test/integration` catalog:

The launching page structure is as follows:

```
<!DOCTYPE html>
<html>
  <head>
    . . .
    <script id="sap-ui-bootstrap"
      <!-- SAPUI5 core bootstrap -->
      . . .>
    </script>
    <script>
      jQuery.sap.require("my.namespace.test.integration.Journeys");
    </script>
  </head>
  <body>
    <div id="qunit"></div>
    <div id="qunit-fixture"></div>
  </body>
</html>
```

Similar to unit tests, this launching page also refers to a single file that stores all testing scenarios. The `Journeys.js` file is built in the following way:

```
jQuery.sap.require("sap.ui.qunit-css");
jQUery.sap.require("sap.ui.thirdparty.qunit");
jQuery.sap.require("sap.ui.qunit.qunit-junit");
Qunit.config.autostart = false;

sap.ui.require([
  "sap/ui/test/Opa5",
  "my/namespace/test/integration/pages/BasicArrangements",
  "my/namespace/test/integration/pages/SearchView
  ...], function(Opa5, Arrangements){
    "use strict";
    Opa5.extendConfig({
      arrangements: new Arrangements(),
      viewNamespaece: "my.namespace.views",
      autoWait: true
    });
    sap.ui.require([
      "my/namespace/test/integration/SearchViewJourney"
    ], function(){
      QUnit.start();
    });
});
```

The script loads the standard testing module (OPA5) together with a common arrangements file—it is useful to move the arrangements that are used in many scenarios to a separate file. The `BasicArrangement` file is explained as follows:

1. Firstly, the main testing module is loaded:

   ```
   sap.ui.define(["sap/ui/test/Opa5"],
     function(Opa5){
       "use strict";
   ```

2. Then, the helper method to create a valid URL from a hash and parameters are defined as follows:

   ```
   function getFrameUrl(sHash, sUrlParameters){
       sHash = sHash || "";
       var sUrl =
   jQuery.sap.getResourcePath("my/namespace/test/mockServer",".html");
       if(sUrlParameters){
         sUrlParameters = "?" + sUrlParameters;
       }
       return sUrl + sUrlParameters + "#" + sHash;
   ```

```
        }
```

3. Then, the OPA5 object is extended to define BasicArrangements, with several additional simple methods:

```
return
Opa5.extend("my/namespace/test/integration/pages/BasicArrangements"
, {
        constructor: function(oConfig){
          Opa5.apply(this,arguments);
          this._oConfig = oConfig;
        },
        iStartMyApp: function(oOptions){
          var sUrlParameters;
          oOptions = oOptions || { delay: 0 };
          sUrlParameters = "serverDelay=" + oOptions.delay;
this.iStartMyAppInAFrame(getFrameUrl(oOptions.hash,sUrlParamters));
        },
        iLookAtTheScreen: function(){
          return this;
        },
    }
  });
```

4. Once the common file is created, the view-specific one is required with all its arrangements. SearchView.js is as follows:

```
sap.ui.require([
    'sap/ui/test/Opa5',
    'sap/ui/test/actions/EnterText',
    'my/namespace/test/integration/pages/BasicArrangements'
  ],
  function (Opa5, EnterText, BasicArrangements) {
    "use strict";
```

5. Then, all needed modules are loaded and the new page object is created within Opa5, named onTheFlightsPage. This page object extends BasicArrangements, and therefore inherits all the methods defined in its body:

```
Opa5.createPageObjects({
    onTheFlightsPage: {
      baseClass: BasicArrangements,
```

6. For this simple case, the only requirement is to check whether it is possible to enter a value into the `"searchInput"` field, therefore, the `EnterText` action is triggered, and, if successful, the assertion is evaluated to `true`:

```
assertions: {
    theTextShouldBeEntered: function () {
        return this.waitFor({
            id: "searchInput",
            viewName: "SearchView",
            actions: new EnterText({
                clearTextFirst: true,
                text: "New York"
            }),
            success: function () {
                Opa5.assert.ok(true, "Text is entered");
            },
            errorMessage: "Failed to enter text"
        });
    }
});
});
```

7. Once the page object is defined, it is possible to define the steps in the `SearchViewJourney.js` file:

```
sap.ui.require(["sap/ui/test/opaQunit"],
    function(opaTest){}
        "use strict";
        QUnit.module("Simple test");
        opaTest("Should be able to enter value", function(Given, When,
Then){
            Given.iStartMyApp();
            When.onTheFlightsPage.iLookAtScreen();
            Then.onTheFlightsPage.theTextShouldBeEntered();
        });
    );
```

It is easy to see why the scenarios are called journeys—the whole interaction is written in the form of a story, or a journey, that the user is participating in.

Summary

The introduction of the SAPUI5 libraries finally separated the powerful and efficient backend logic of the SAP systems from the UI. This decision allowed greater flexibility in creating new applications with the use of modern technologies. Thanks to the fact that the libraries are based on well-known and well-tested modules, they are compatible with all major modern browsers and have mature development and testing tools. Together with samples and templates, SAPUI5 authors created several guidelines, recommendations, and project structures, which were introduced in the previous sections. The SAPUI5-based applications are currently the most recent UI technology in the SAP environment; therefore, this chapter is the last one covering the topic of UIs. In the next chapter, the main focus will be placed on more business-oriented logic and possibilities available in the Business Object Processing Framework.

Questions

The following questions will allow you to consolidate the information contained in this chapter:

1. What tools are recommended for use in UI5 app development?
2. How can the SAPUI5 application be translated?
3. What is MVC and why should it be used?
4. What tools are provided for testing UI5 applications?

Further reading

More detailed examples of testing and more samples and cases are available in the official documentation of the SAPUI5 library: `https://sapui5.hana.ondemand.com/#/topic`

Business Object Processing Framework

9

Every ABAP programmer during their carrier will have to (sooner or later) create a fully customized solution from scratch. In a large development environment, we will have to work with a database, create appropriate structures for our business objects, separate individual development fragments into layers, implement a lock mechanism, and handle error logs. We can create all of these things manually, but this will require a lot of work and will only be understood by developers who create this solution. The **Business Object Processing Framework** (**BOPF**) allows you to speed up development and increase its quality.

In this chapter, we will cover the following topics:

- An introduction to BOPF
- The components of BOPF
- The elements of the BOPF programming model
- BOPF developer tools
- Using BOPF

Technical requirements

In order to get this chapter's examples working, you need to meet the following requirements:

- **BOPF:** SAP Business Suite EHP5 SP11, SAP Business Suite EHP6 SP05, and SAP Business Suite EHP7, starting with the SAP NetWeaver 7.50 release as the SAP BASIS layer

All the code used in this chapter can be downloaded from the following GitHub link: `https://github.com/PacktPublishing/Mastering-SAP-ABAP/tree/master/Chapter09`.

An introduction to BOPF

BOPF is widely used in SAP standard modules (that is, transportation management, environment, and health and safety). As we mentioned in this chapter's introduction, we can also use this framework in our custom development. BOPF handles the most common development features, such as authorization control, low-level transaction handling, buffer management, provisioning of the consumer API, and business logic orchestration. It's well-integrated with a wide range of SAP components. From an interface and consumption perspective, it is integrated with SAPUI5, Classic DynPro, Web DynPro, and Gateway and **Business Object Layer** (BOL). From an infrastructure perspective, it is integrated with **Archive Development Kit** (ADK), Change Document, Application Log, BRF+, and Enterprise Search. This makes BOPF a powerful solution that every ABAP developer should know about.

Transaction

Working with BOPF can take different forms. We can expand existing objects, use standard objects in our transactions, or create completely new things from scratch. Regardless of what we do, our work is limited to just a few transactions that have been presented in this chapter. The following list provides basic information on this topic:

- BOPF is an internal SAP transaction where you can see all standard **Business Objects (BOs)**:

- **Business Object Builder** (**BOB**) is a transaction where you can create a custom BO from scratch:

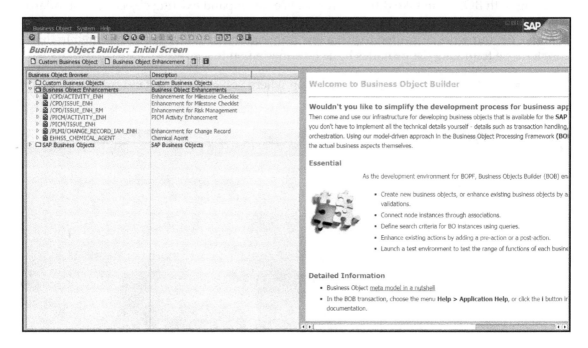

- **Business Object Builder eXpert** (**BOBX**) is the recommended transaction for standard business object enhancement:

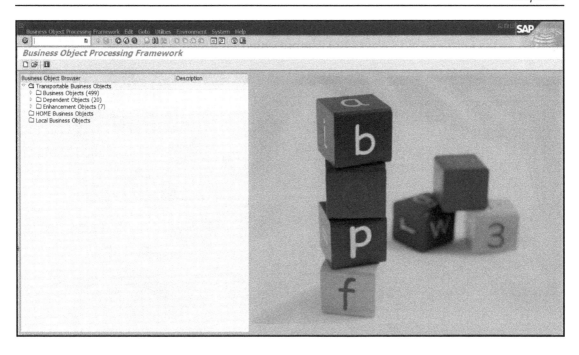

The logic and development are encapsulated in **Business Objects**. You can open any BO by choosing it from the hierarchy on the left-hand side and double-clicking on its name. Let's check out /BOBF/DEMO_SALES_ORDER:

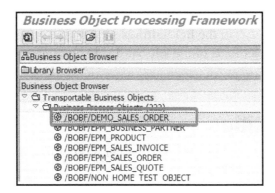

On the next screen, you will see a hierarchy panel on the right-hand side and node-specific options on the left-hand side. Every BO is represented with such a hierarchy:

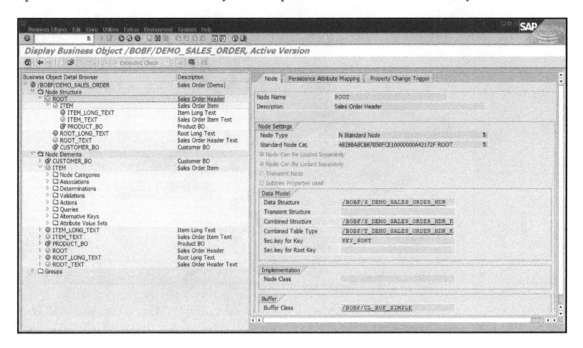

If you choose the main element, you will see basic information, business object settings, transactional behaviors, test data, and so on. There is a very important constant interface called /BOBF/IF_PRODUCT_C in the **BO Settings** section that we will use in the following example. The individual elements of the left-hand side hierarchy are described in the next chapter.

Nodes and entities

Every BO contains multiple entities. There are several types of entity that can be used. The following list describes each of them:

- **Nodes**: These are basic entity types that are used for the data models of our business objects. Nodes are attributes that describe the features of a business object. They can be divided into two types: a persistent node, to keep data taken from a database, and a transient node, to keep data loaded on demand.

- **Actions**: These are operations that are performed on a node. An action is always triggered by the user through the user interface. It can be anything your user wants to do with an object, such as save or archive it, or even something a bit closer to business, such as deliver a sales order or post an invoice. Actions are an implementation of the `/BOPF/IF_FRW_ACTION` interface.

- **Determinations**: These are close to actions, but happen deeper inside development. Determinations are triggered when certain conditions are fulfilled; therefore, a determination can be compared to database triggers. From a technical perspective, it's just the implementation of the `/BOBF/IF_FRW_DETERMINATOIN` interface.

- **Associations**: It's not easy to imagine a situation where one business object is just a totally hermetic standalone component and doesn't have any relation with other business parts. The association entity allows you to create a relation between your BO and another BO.

- **Validations**: These give you the opportunity to check whether something is right. There are two types of validation: the first is related to the action entity, where you can implement and check whatever action can be carried out. The second checks the consistency of the object. In order to create a validation, you need to implement the `/BOBF/IF_BR_VALIDATION` interface.

- **Queries**: These are nothing more than searches for specific BO instances. You can have node attribute queries (for example, searching for a sales order with its number) or custom queries that can be implemented using `/BOPF/IF_FRW_QUERY`. There is one last thing that has to be explained before jumping into programming. When working with BOPF, we will use a number of classes that form the BOPF API:

  - `/BOBF/IF_TRA_TRANSACTION_MGR`: This is a class that takes care of all the transactions on the object. It can be either a single modification of the nodes or a bundle of changes that are generated in multiple steps.
  - `/BOBF/IF_TRA_SERVICE_MANAGER`: This class is dedicated to handling validation and performing actions on our business object. It's also where queries and retrieve actions are taken.
  - `/BOBF/IF_FRW_CONFIGURATION`: This class provides information pertaining to the basic metadata of business objects.

All of these classes have separate factory classes, all of the which will be shown in the upcoming example. This is caused by the generic nature of the BOPF framework.

First BOPF example

In this section, we will try to play around with one of standard BOs to get a better understanding of how individual elements interact with each other. This example uses a standard object called /BOBF/DEMO_PRODUCT, which represents the product.

Creating the object

Create a new report called ZMSA_R_CHAPTER9_1 in the ABAP Workbench and pass the report template from the Appendix. We will start by adding class attributes, that is, the three main BOPF API classes I mentioned previously. Put the following code into a private section of the lcl_demo class definition:

```
DATA: mo_transaction_mgr TYPE REF TO /bobf/if_tra_transaction_mgr.
DATA: mo_service_manager TYPE REF TO /bobf/if_tra_service_manager.
DATA: mo_configuration TYPE REF TO /bobf/if_frw_configuration.
```

We also need a specific constructor definition:

```
METHODS:
constructor RAISING /bobf/cx_frw.
```

The custom constructor initializes all of the variables. For this, we will use factory classes and their corresponding factory methods. Put the following code into the constructor:

```
mo_transaction_mgr =
/bobf/cl_tra_trans_mgr_factory=>get_transaction_manager( ).
mo_service_manager = /bobf/cl_tra_serv_mgr_factory=>get_service_manager(
    /bobf/if_demo_product_c=>sc_bo_key ).
mo_configuration = /bobf/cl_frw_factory=>get_configuration(
/bobf/if_demo_product_c=>sc_bo_key ).
```

As you can see, we are using the constant interface that we mentioned previously to get the BO key. In our example, we will try to create, query, and display the product object. Let's start by creating the function. Add a new method definition:

```
create_product.
```

Inside the `CREATE_PRODUCT` method, insert the following code:

```
"Modification variables used to make change on object
DATA: lt_modification TYPE /bobf/t_frw_modification.
FIELD-SYMBOLS: <ls_modification> TYPE /bobf/s_frw_modification.
DATA: lo_change TYPE REF TO /bobf/if_tra_change.

"This part is related to errors and success message handling
DATA: lo_message TYPE REF TO /bobf/if_frw_message.
DATA: lv_issue TYPE boolean.
DATA: lo_exception TYPE REF TO /bobf/cx_frw.
DATA: lv_err_return TYPE string.
DATA: lv_rejected TYPE boolean.

"Combined data model structure, fields of product BO
DATA: lr_product_hdr TYPE REF TO /bobf/s_demo_product_hdr_k.
DATA: lr_short_text TYPE REF TO /bobf/s_demo_short_text_k.
```

This is everything we need from a data declaration perspective. Next, we will need to fill in all the necessary fields and add a modification request to the modification table, first for the product header data:

```
"Create product header data
CREATE DATA lr_product_hdr.
lr_product_hdr->key = /bobf/cl_frw_factory=>get_new_key( ).
lr_product_hdr->product_id = '101'.
lr_product_hdr->product_type = 'FOOD'.
lr_product_hdr->base_uom = 'KG'.
lr_product_hdr->buy_price = 1.
lr_product_hdr->buy_price_curr = 'USD'.
lr_product_hdr->sell_price = 2.
lr_product_hdr->sell_price_curr = 'USD'.

"Add product header to modification table
APPEND INITIAL LINE TO lt_modification ASSIGNING <ls_modification>.
<ls_modification>-node = /bobf/if_demo_product_c=>sc_node-root.
<ls_modification>-change_mode = /bobf/if_frw_c=>sc_modify_create.
<ls_modification>-key = lr_product_hdr->key.
<ls_modification>-data = lr_product_hdr.
```

Now, we will do the same for the short text data:

```
"Create short text data
CREATE DATA lr_short_text.
lr_short_text->key = /bobf/cl_frw_factory=>get_new_key( ).
lr_short_text->language = sy-langu.
lr_short_text->text = 'Banana'.
```

```
"Add short text data to modification table
APPEND INITIAL LINE TO lt_modification ASSIGNING <ls_modification>.
<ls_modification>-node = /bobf/if_demo_product_c=>sc_node-root_text.
<ls_modification>-change_mode = /bobf/if_frw_c=>sc_modify_create.
<ls_modification>-source_node = /bobf/if_demo_product_c=>sc_node-root.
<ls_modification>-association = /bobf/if_demo_product_c=>sc_association-
root-root_text.
<ls_modification>-key = lr_short_text->key.
<ls_modification>-source_key = lr_product_hdr->key.
<ls_modification>-data = lr_short_text.
```

Now, you need to call the `modify` method from the service manager. This will put the data into the stage area. It hasn't yet been saved into the database. Place the following code after the table's modification:

```
me->mo_service_manager->modify(
EXPORTING
it_modification = lt_modification
IMPORTING
eo_change = lo_change " Interface of Change Object
eo_message = lo_message " Interface of Message Object
).
```

Before we make any commits to the database, we will display a message that's returned by the service manager. All of this information is stored in the `lo_change` and `lo_message` objects. We will need another method to display these messages. Put the following code into the class definition section:

```
display_message IMPORTING io_message TYPE REF TO /bobf/if_frw_message.
```

In the `display_message` method's implementation, we will get messages from the `io_message` object, which we will put on screen using the simple `WRITE` keyword. Every `io_message` can have multiple messages, so we have to make a loop for that:

```
METHOD display_message.
DATA: lt_messages TYPE /bobf/t_frw_message_k.
FIELD-SYMBOLS: <ls_message> TYPE /bobf/s_frw_message_k.

IF io_message IS BOUND.
io_message->get_messages( importing et_message = lt_messages ).

LOOP AT lt_messages ASSIGNING <ls_message>.
    WRITE: <ls_message>-message->get_text( ).
ENDLOOP.
ENDIF.
ENDMETHOD.
```

Then, we will call the `display_message` method inside the `create_product` method:

```
IF lo_message IS BOUND.
  IF lo_message->check( ) EQ abap_true.
    me->display_message( lo_message ).
    RETURN.
  ENDIF.
ENDIF.
```

These changes aren't in the database yet, so you will need to call the `save` method from the `transaction manager`. After that, we will call the `display` method once more:

```
CALL METHOD me->mo_transaction_mgr->save
    IMPORTING
        ev_rejected = lv_rejected
        eo_message = lo_message.

IF lv_rejected EQ abap_true.
   me->display_message( lo_message ).
   RETURN.
ENDIF.
```

The final step to take to get this example working is just to put the following code in the main method:

```
DATA: lo_demo TYPE REF TO lcl_demo.
DATA: lo_cx TYPE REF TO /bobf/cx_frw.

TRY.
CREATE OBJECT lo_demo.

lo_demo->create_product( ).

CATCH /bobf/cx_frw INTO lo_cx.
    WRITE lo_cx->get_text( ).
ENDTRY.
```

After running your program, you can go to transaction **se16n** and check the content of the `/BOBF/DM_PRD_HDR` table:

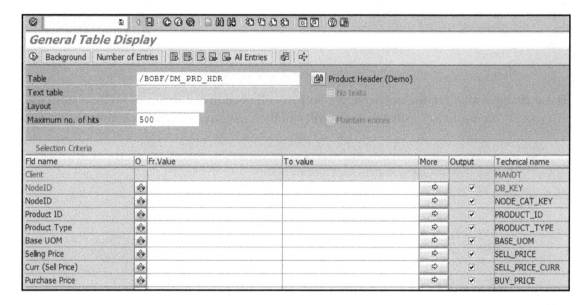

You should be able to see the following values after hitting *F8*:

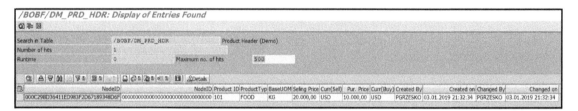

There is also a check `/BOBF/DM_PRD_HDT` table for the text node:

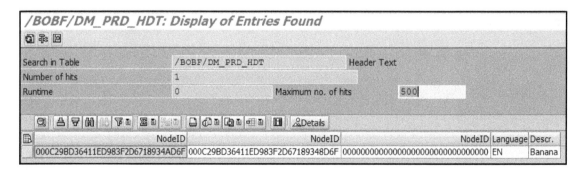

Of course, we hardcoded every value for our product. After running the program again, you will get the following exception:

To prevent this, we will create an additional select screen that allows the user to fill every value by hand. Incorporate the following code before the `lcl_demo` definition:

```
PARAMETERS: p_prd_id TYPE /bobf/demo_product_id OBLIGATORY.
PARAMETERS: p_price TYPE /bobf/demo_buying_price.
PARAMETERS: p_text TYPE /bobf/demo_product_id.
```

Put in some new class attributes:

```
DATA: mv_price TYPE /bobf/demo_buying_price.
DATA: mv_prd_id TYPE /bobf/demo_product_id.
DATA: mv_text TYPE /bobf/demo_description.
```

You will also need to change the following lines in the `create_product` method:

```
lr_product_hdr->product_id = '101'.
lr_product_hdr->buy_price = '1'.
lr_product_hdr->sell_price = 2.
lr_short_text->text = 'Banana'.
```

The following code snippet shows how we do this:

```
lr_product_hdr->product_id = mv_prd_id.
lr_product_hdr->buy_price = mv_price.
lr_short_text->text = mv_text.
lr_product_hdr->sell_price = lr_product_hdr->buy_price * '1.2'.
```

Change the main method definition to accept selection screen parameters:

```
CLASS-METHODS
main IMPORTING
        iv_prd_id TYPE /bobf/demo_product_id
        iv_price TYPE /bobf/demo_buying_price
        iv_text TYPE /bobf/demo_description
```

Do the same for the constructor:

```
constructor IMPORTING
            iv_prod_id TYPE /bobf/demo_product_id
            iv_price TYPE /bobf/demo_buying_price
            iv_text TYPE /bobf/demo_description
                 RAISING /bobf/cx_frw.
```

In the constructor, we need to populate new attributes:

```
    mv_price = iv_price.
    mv_prod_id = iv_prod_id.
    mv_text = iv_text.
```

The main method call in START-OF-SELECTION needs to be adjusted:

```
    lcl_demo=>main(
      iv_prd_id = p_prd_id
      iv_price = p_price
      iv_text = p_text
    ).
```

The final step is to change the main method implementation. Only CREATE OBJECT has to be changed:

```
    CREATE OBJECT lo_demo EXPORTING iv_price = iv_price iv_prod_id = iv_prd_id
    iv_text = iv_text.
```

Take care of the selection screen text by choosing **Goto | Text Elements**. If you run this report, you will be able to set those three main parameters.

Displaying an object

This example is a continuation of the previous example, so please complete that if you haven't already. We will add some functionality that enables the user to choose whatever they want to display in relation to the product. You need an extend selection screen with the following parameters:

```
    SELECTION-SCREEN BEGIN OF BLOCK bl1 WITH FRAME.
    PARAMETERS: p_crt RADIOBUTTON GROUP gr1 DEFAULT 'X'.
    PARAMETERS: p_dsp RADIOBUTTON GROUP gr1.
    SELECTION-SCREEN END OF BLOCK bl1.
```

Add the following to the main method definition. We can only take one radio button since those parameters work in a group:

```
CLASS-METHODS
main IMPORTING
          iv_prd_id TYPE /bobf/demo_product_id
          iv_price TYPE /bobf/demo_buying_price
          iv_text TYPE /bobf/demo_description
          iv_disp TYPE boolean.
```

Enhance the main method call with a new parameter, `p_dsp`:

```
lcl_demo=>main(
  iv_prd_id = p_prd_id
  iv_price = p_price
  iv_text = p_text
  iv_disp = p_dsp
).
```

All the BOPF data is stored in typical database tables so, in theory, you could use the `select` statement against the `product` table to get all the data that you require. However, this isn't recommended and against BOPF standards. To select data, we will be using the query function. Create a new method called `get_product_node` and incorporate the following code into its implementation:

```
DATA: lr_t_data TYPE REF TO data.
DATA: lt_parameters TYPE /bobf/t_frw_query_selparam.
DATA: lt_product_keys TYPE /bobf/t_frw_key.
DATA: ls_node_conf TYPE /bobf/s_confro_node.
DATA: lo_change TYPE REF TO /bobf/if_tra_change.
DATA: lo_message TYPE REF TO /bobf/if_frw_message.

FIELD-SYMBOLS <lt_data> TYPE INDEX TABLE.
FIELD-SYMBOLS <ls_parameter> LIKE LINE OF lt_parameters.
FIELD-SYMBOLS <ls_product_key> LIKE LINE OF lt_product_keys.
FIELD-SYMBOLS <ls_row> TYPE any.

APPEND INITIAL LINE TO lt_parameters ASSIGNING <ls_parameter>.
<ls_parameter>-attribute_name =
/bobf/if_demo_product_c=>sc_query_attribute-root-select_by_elements-
product_id.
<ls_parameter>-sign = 'I'.
<ls_parameter>-option = 'EQ'.
<ls_parameter>-low = mv_prod_id.


CALL METHOD me->mo_service_manager->query
```

```
EXPORTING
iv_query_key = /bobf/if_demo_product_c=>sc_query-root-select_by_elements
it_selection_parameters = lt_parameters
IMPORTING
et_key = lt_product_keys.

CALL METHOD me->mo_configuration->get_node
EXPORTING
iv_node_key = /bobf/if_demo_product_c=>sc_node-root
IMPORTING
es_node = ls_node_conf.

CREATE DATA lr_t_data TYPE (ls_node_conf-data_table_type).
ASSIGN lr_t_data->* TO <lt_data>.

CALL METHOD me->mo_service_manager->retrieve
EXPORTING
iv_node_key = /bobf/if_demo_product_c=>sc_node-root
it_key = lt_product_keys
IMPORTING
eo_message = lo_message
eo_change = lo_change
et_data = <lt_data>.

READ TABLE <lt_data> INDEX 1 ASSIGNING <ls_row>.
IF sy-subrc EQ 0.
GET REFERENCE OF <ls_row> INTO ro_data.
ENDIF.
```

This is a lot of code, but it's actually quite easy. We use the product ID with the `query` method to get the object key. Then, we need to use this key with the retrieve method to get data. What makes this code a bit complicated is that we need to create dynamic data using `get_node` and a configuration structure that we get from this call. We also need a `get_text_node` method, which will take care of data that is stored in the text node:

```
DATA lr_t_data TYPE REF TO data.
DATA lt_key TYPE /bobf/t_frw_key.
DATA ls_node_conf TYPE /bobf/s_confro_node.
DATA ls_association TYPE /bobf/s_confro_assoc.
DATA lo_change TYPE REF TO /bobf/if_tra_change.
DATA lo_message TYPE REF TO /bobf/if_frw_message.

FIELD-SYMBOLS <lt_data> TYPE INDEX TABLE.
FIELD-SYMBOLS <ls_row> TYPE any.
FIELD-SYMBOLS <ls_key> LIKE LINE OF lt_key.

CALL METHOD me->mo_configuration->get_assoc
```

```
      EXPORTING
      iv_assoc_key = /bobf/if_demo_product_c=>sc_association-root-root_text
      iv_node_key = /bobf/if_demo_product_c=>sc_node-root
       IMPORTING
         es_assoc = ls_association.

ls_node_conf = ls_association-target_node->*.

CREATE DATA lr_t_data TYPE (ls_node_conf-data_table_type).
ASSIGN lr_t_data->* TO <lt_data>.

APPEND INITIAL LINE TO lt_key ASSIGNING <ls_key>.
<ls_key>-key = iv_key.

CALL METHOD me->mo_service_manager->retrieve_by_association
      EXPORTING
        iv_node_key =
           /bobf/if_demo_product_c=>sc_node-root
        it_key = lt_key
        iv_association = /bobf/if_demo_product_c=>sc_association-root-
root_text
        iv_fill_data = abap_true
      IMPORTING
        eo_message = lo_message
        eo_change = lo_change
        et_data = <lt_data>.


    IF lo_message IS BOUND.
      IF lo_message->check( ) EQ abap_true.
        display_message( lo_message ).
      ENDIF.
    ENDIF.

    ASSIGN lr_t_data->* TO <lt_data>.
    READ TABLE <lt_data> INDEX 1 ASSIGNING <ls_row>.
    IF sy-subrc EQ 0.
      GET REFERENCE OF <ls_row> INTO ro_data.
    ENDIF.
```

To display actual information, we will create a `display_product` method and insert the following code there:

```
DATA lx_bopf_ex TYPE REF TO /bobf/cx_frw.
DATA lx_bopf_dac TYPE REF TO /bobf/cx_dac.
DATA lv_err_msg TYPE string.

DATA lr_s_root TYPE REF TO /bobf/s_demo_product_hdr_k.
```

```
DATA lr_s_text TYPE REF TO /bobf/s_demo_short_text_k.

TRY.
lr_s_root ?= me->get_product_node( ).
lr_s_text ?= me->get_text_node( lr_s_root->key ).

WRITE: / 'Product #', lr_s_root->product_id.
WRITE: / 'Product', lr_s_text->text.
WRITE: / 'Buy Price', lr_s_root->buy_price LEFT-JUSTIFIED.
WRITE: / 'Sell Price', lr_s_root->sell_price LEFT-JUSTIFIED.
CATCH /bobf/cx_frw INTO lx_bopf_ex.
lv_err_msg = lx_bopf_ex->get_text( ).
WRITE: / lv_err_msg.
ENDTRY.
```

All of these methods require new definitions:

```
METHODS:
get_product_node
RETURNING VALUE(ro_data) TYPE REF TO data,
get_text_node
IMPORTING iv_key TYPE /bobf/conf_key RETURNING VALUE(ro_data) TYPE REF TO
data,
display_product.
```

Also, remember to make the following adjustment in the main method:

```
DATA: lo_demo TYPE REF TO lcl_demo.
DATA: lo_cx TYPE REF TO /bobf/cx_frw.
TRY.
CREATE OBJECT lo_demo EXPORTING iv_price = iv_price iv_prod_id = iv_prd_id
iv_text = iv_text.
IF iv_disp = abap_true.
lo_demo->display_product( ).
ELSE.
lo_demo->create_product( ).
ENDIF.
CATCH /bobf/cx_frw INTO lo_cx.
WRITE lo_cx->get_text( ).
ENDTRY.
```

Now, if you run your program with product ID **101**, you will receive the following output:

```
Program ZMSA_R_CHAPTER9_1

Program ZMSA_R_CHAPTER9_1

Product # 101
Product Banana
Buy Price 1,000000
Sell Price 2,000000
```

Summary

By completing this chapter, you can proudly say that you know how to use BOPF and how to create big standardized ABAP solutions from scratch. You don't have to bother with creating tables, structures, implementing locking mechanisms, or application log wrappers. It's all there, just waiting for you to use it. I highly recommended checking all the other functionality that BOPF gives you for free. Try to implement validation or a change object method. You can even try to create your own BOPF object from scratch and play around with the entire complex business process.

In the following chapters, the primary focus will be on modification and customization of different techniques.

Questions

The following questions will allow you to consolidate the information contained in this chapter:

1. What BOPF transaction is used to enhance standard BO?
2. What BOPF transaction is used only for SAP internal use?
3. What type of entity is used to create a relation with two BOPF objects?
4. What type of association exists in BOPF?
5. What BOPF technical object is used to save data in a database?
6. What main exception is thrown from BOPF methods?
7. What technical object can you use to get BO metadata?

Further reading

You may also want to check out BOPF at `https://help.sap.com/viewer/`
`aa7fc5c3c1524844b811735b9373252a/7.5.3/en-US/e5ea9085cfe2494faacae415ff8131da.`
`html`.

10
Modification and Customization Techniques

SAP software is a so-called out-of-the-box type of product. This means that companies should be able to use every functionality immediately after installation. Of course, you need to customize some basic information about your business, but accounting and logistic processes are part of the system from the very outset. For many years, SAP has been developing its software in cooperation with its clients and partners. Most transactions are prepared in such a way that they can be adapted to business without the need for programming or installing anything extra. However, every enterprise is unique, and not everything can be provided from the offset. To solve this problem, SAP gives every customer a rich number of abilities to modify processes using various extension technologies. This is the place where ABAP developers are needed. It's impossible to be an ABAP developer without knowing about what's included in this chapter.

The following topics will be covered in this chapter:

- Legacy ways of changing the standard
- The Enhancement Framework and its components

Technical requirements

Some of the techniques that are presented in this chapter require NetWeaver version 7.0. Strong integration of the individual examples in this chapter with business logic may require additional customization in **Sap Project Reference Object** (SPRO).

All the code used in this chapter can be downloaded from the following GitHub link: `https://github.com/PacktPublishing/Mastering-SAP-ABAP/tree/master/Chapter10`.

Legacy ways of changing the standard

The idea of enhancements is to give SAP consultants the ability to use the SAP system in every business scenario without exception and to guarantee the stability of the system's operation. Enhancements are given result of a gap between SAP standard functionality and the customer business model. Given this, almost every example in this chapter is closely related to a business process. This is something far more complicated than the technical level example we provided in previous chapters. Here, we added an additional business layer that we need to understand. Let's provide some examples of where enhancements may be needed. We have customer master data stored in the SAP system (from a technical perspective, this means that we have records in a few database tables, for example, KNA1). SAP gives us lots of standard fields, such as names, addresses, tax details, payment information, and so on. Those fields cover a large part of a business, but you also have a unique field that hasn't been implemented in the standard, or you have a custom **Single Euro Payments Area** (**SEPA**) reference structure that can't be achieved by customizing. For all such cases, we can use enhancement. There are many possibilities that can be realized by using an enhancement technique. It's very important to understand the difference between enhancements, modification, and customizing. Customizing is everything that we can do in an SPRO transaction, that is, the configuration of the available options and parameters. The term *customizing* is also used in the context of standalone z-development from scratch, where we build a customized solution that fits our model. Enhancements are techniques that can be used to extend standard SAP functionality that's been created by SAP itself. These include customer exits, **Business Add-In** (**BAdI**), **Business Data Toolset** (**BDT**), **Business Transaction Event** (**BTE**), FQEVENTS, and implicit and explicit enhancements. The final category of SAP functionality adjustment is modifications. Modifications change SAP standard code. You need to use an object key to modify any standard object. Modifications are not recommended because they are overwritten during system upgrades.

SAP has been changing its approach to enhancements over the years. Separate solutions were implemented for different modules at different times. Due to backward compatibility, all of these extensions still exist and can be used to achieve client business goals. In this chapter, we will go through the most important techniques that can be useful for a daily ABAP developer. Descriptions of BAdIs and the Enhancement Framework will be provided in brief due to the fact that these are comprehensive topics that will be talked about in separate chapters. Some extension techniques, such as Web Dynpro, BSP, or Fiori enhancement, are not part of this book. To read about those, please go to the *Further reading* section at the end of this chapter.

Customer Exits

Customer Exits are a type of enhancement that can extend the programs, screens, and menus of standard applications. From a technical perspective, Customer Exits are just hooks and do not contain any functionality in themselves. You can attach your own function modules to a Customer Exit. The entire functionality is stored in the attached function module. Customer Exits refer to most SAP modules (MM, SD, PP, FICO, and many other modules), but can only be used in predefined places – not on every screen or with every program. The main advantages of Customer Exits is that they don't affect standard code and software updates. There are four types of customer exits, as follows:

- **Function Exits** are used to extend standard functionality on data (that is, add a default value, validate a field, and so on).
- **Screen Exits** are used to extend standard screen functionality (to display additional data, for example).
- **Menu Exits** are used to extend menu options.
- **Table Exits** are used to extend a standard table by a new field; they are always connected to a Function Exit.

In this example, we will extend customer transaction functionality (XD01/XD02/XD03). Customer Exits implementation is stored in a container called Enhancement Projects. You can store lots of Customer Exits in one enhancement project. To start, we have to create Enhancement Projects. Go to the **Customer Exits (CMOD)** transaction and create a new project called ZMSA0001:

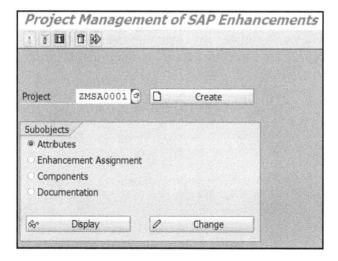

The following screenshot shows an overview of this project. Save your work by clicking on the **Disk** button on the toolbar:

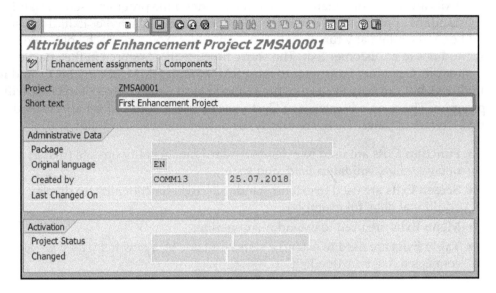

You need to know exactly which process and which enhancement you want to change. You can find this by searching the report source code for CALL CUSTOMER, or by debugging your transaction and setting the CALL CUSTOMER keyword breakpoint. If you don't know the name of the report, you can find it based on the transaction code in SE93. If you have an enhancement name but you don't know the exit name, you can find it in the MODSAP table. As we stated previously, we will be extending the customer object. Here, we need to verify additional fields based on the customer's country. Customer data can be changed in SAPMF02D. You have access to most of the customer data (everything that is stored in the KNA1 and KNB1 tables). Click on the **Enhancement assignments** button and choose the enhancement you want to use:

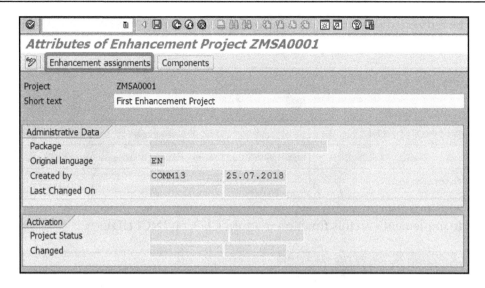

Then, click the **Components** button, as shown in the following screenshot:

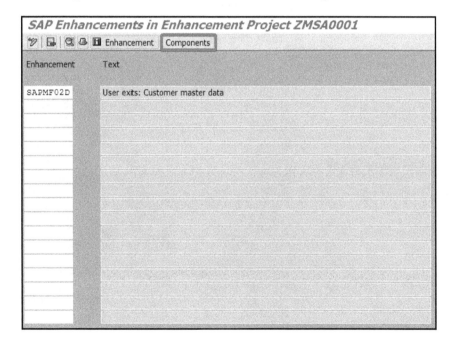

You will be redirected to a screen that shows details of the enhancement. Double-click on the **Function exit** named EXIT_SAPLBPX0_005:

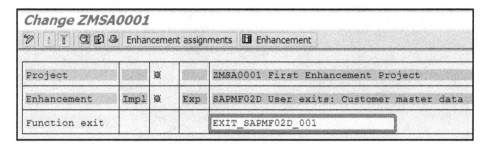

We need to implement z in this function module. Click on **INCLUDE**:

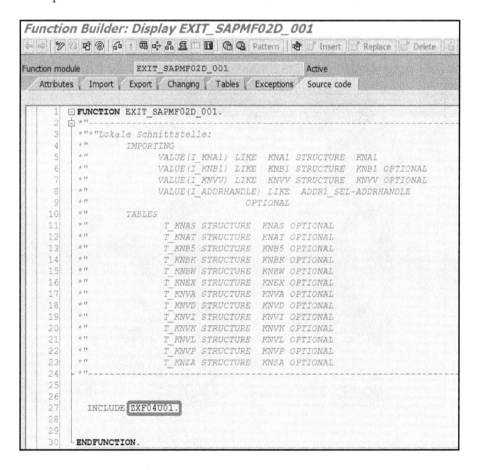

You will be warned that ZXF04U01 is in a reserved namespace. This means that such a name is only used for the implementation of user exits. Hit **ENTER**:

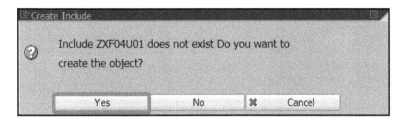

① Program names ZX... are reserved for includes of exit function groups

You will be asked if you really want to create this include. Click **Yes**:

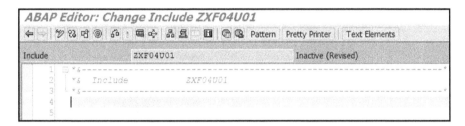

This will create a new **include** and move you to **ABAP Editor: Change Include ZXF04U01**:

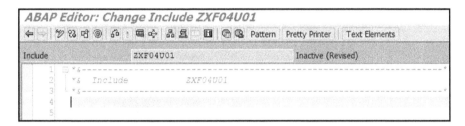

We can write our own logic here, but keep in mind that we only have access to data from function module parameters. It's also recommended to create and attach another Z include for better separation of concepts. For example, it could be ZMSAF04U01 where we put all of our logic. Put the following code in the include before saving and activating it:

```
CONSTANTS: lv_land1 TYPE land1 VALUE 'DE'.

IF i_kna1-land1 <> lv_land1 AND i_kna1-stceg IS INITIAL.
MESSAGE 'VAT number for this country is obligatory' TYPE 'E'.
ENDIF.
```

Click the **Back** button twice (F3) and head to the screen where the enhancement details are—you can see it in the following. Click on the **Active** button to make the enhancement work. You should have three green squares in the third column, as shown in the following screenshot:

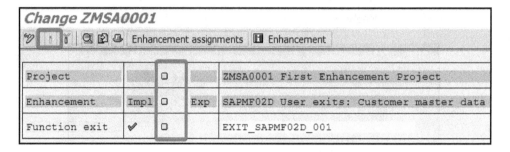

The last thing we need to do is test our new development. Head to the XD01 transaction, choose any **Account group**, and click the green check mark:

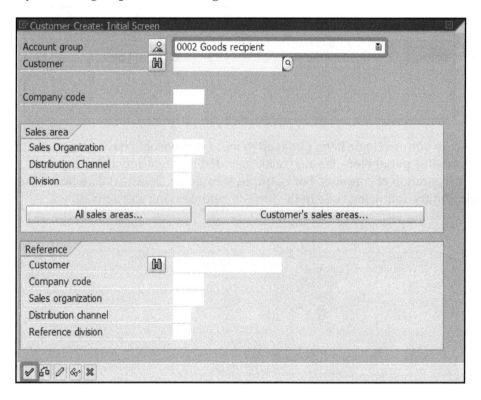

Fill in all the obligatory data on the first screen and click **Save**:

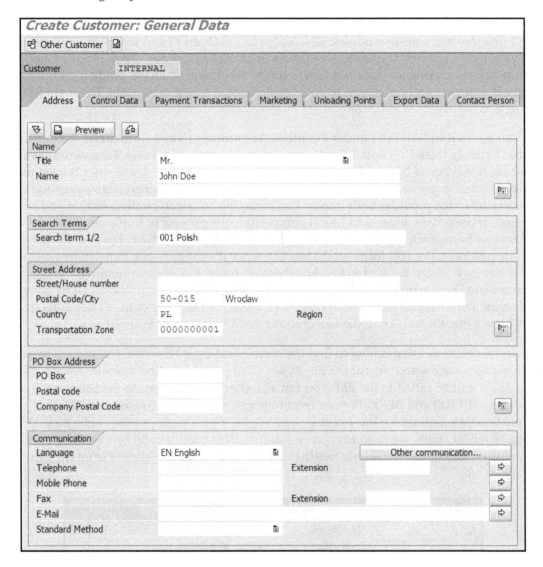

You will get the message that we implemented earlier:

⊗ VAT number for this country is obligatory

When you change the country or fill in a tax number, you will be able to save the customer.

Using BTE to extend FI functionality

BTE is a technique that allows the developer to extend the functionality of (mostly, but not only!) financial accounting modules. BTE is also called Open FI and works more like FQEVENTS in Contract Accounting, or BAdIs in all other modules. Open FI uses function module objects to enhance standard functionality. Basically, you have predefined hooks in standard code that you can assign to your implemented function module. The main BTE transaction is FIBF.

You can access it in SAP IMG under **Financial Accounting (New)** | **Financial Accounting Global Settings (New)** | **Tools** | **Customer Enhancements** | **Business Transaction Events**. There are two types of BTE: publish and subscribe, and processes. The former is used to invoke external processes. You don't have control over what is changed. However, the processes interface provides both import and changing parameter values so that you can influence process data. From a technical perspective, the process of implementing is identical for both. Each type of BTE has three different types: For SAP, For SAP partner, and For customer. We will focus on the last one since it's the only one that can be enhanced by customers. BTE can be used to invoke other processes, too, such as sending **Intermediate Documents** (**IDOCs**), clearing data, and sending notifications. Here, we will implement a notification mechanism that will inform the manager of the FI department every time a document is posted on an amount that's higher than €10,000.

The first problem to solve is how to find the corresponding BTE event. You can try to find this information by searching for the BF_FUNCTIONS_FIND function module. All the BTEs related to it will be called in the FM. You can also check transactions in the **Business Event Repository** (**BERE**) and BERP. For our requirements, we will use BTE event 1030. The sample function module for this event is SAMPLE_INTERFACE_00001030. Let's go to the transaction FIBF. First, we need to create a product. This product will be a container for your custom functionality. Choose **Settings** | **Products** | **... of a customer** from the top menu:

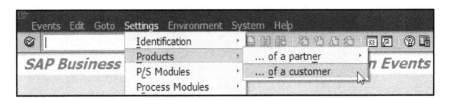

On the next screen, you will see some other **Customer Products** that have been created. Click **New Entries**:

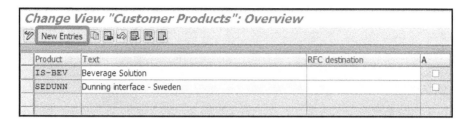

Fill in **Text** with a description of the product. It's important that you mark the checkbox in the last column as this will activate your product:

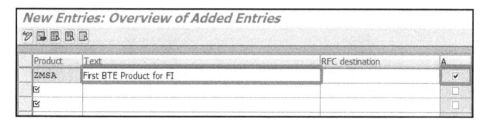

Go back to the main screen of FIBF. Now, choose **Settings | P/S Modules | ... of a customer**:

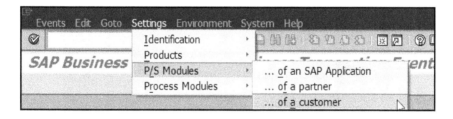

On the next screen, click the **Create Entire** button and fillin all the necessary data. The event number is something that we need to know or find using the debugging technique we described earlier. The **Product** is the object we just created. The next two columns, **Country** and **Application**, are just for the purpose of separation of concerns. You can only filter a process to a specific country or application. The last column allows you to fill in the name of the function module that we will soon create:

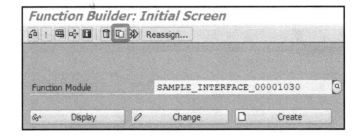

Go to transaction `SE37`. We need to create a function module that will be connected to the BTE event. This object needs to have the same interfaces as the sample BTE function module event. The easiest way to achieve this is to just copy the standard module, `SAMPLE_INTERFACE_00001030` (analogous to other events). Make a copy using the copy button:

Now, open the new function module and pass in the following source code:

```
DATA: ls_mailsubject TYPE sodocchgi1.
DATA: lt_mailrecipients TYPE STANDARD TABLE OF somlrec90 .
DATA: ls_mailrecipients TYPE somlrec90.
DATA: lt_mailtxt TYPE STANDARD TABLE OF soli.
DATA: lv_mailtxt TYPE soli.
DATA: lv_content TYPE string.
FIELD-SYMBOLS: <ls_bseg> TYPE bseg.


LOOP AT t_bseg ASSIGNING <ls_bseg> WHERE dmbtr > 10000.
```

```
     IF <ls_bseg>-dmbtr > 10000.
        CONCATENATE lv_content 'Check position' <ls_bseg>-buzei 'from
document' <ls_bseg>-belnr '<BR>' INTO lv_content SEPARATED BY space.
     ENDIF.
  ENDLOOP.

  CHECK lv_content IS NOT INITIAL.

  CONCATENATE '<HTML><BODY><H1>' lv_content '</H1></BODY></HTML>' INTO
lv_content SEPARATED BY space.

  lv_mailtxt = lv_content.

  ls_mailrecipients-rec_type = 'B'.
  ls_mailrecipients-receiver = sy-uname.
  APPEND ls_mailrecipients TO lt_mailrecipients.

  ls_mailsubject-obj_name = 'Notification Email'.
  ls_mailsubject-obj_langu = sy-langu.
  ls_mailsubject-obj_descr = 'High Amount Document Posted!'.


  APPEND lv_mailtxt TO lt_mailtxt.

  CALL FUNCTION 'SO_NEW_DOCUMENT_SEND_API1'
    EXPORTING
      document_data = ls_mailsubject
      document_type = 'HTM'
    TABLES
      object_content = lt_mailtxt
      receivers = lt_mailrecipients
    EXCEPTIONS
      too_many_receivers = 1
      document_not_sent = 2
      document_type_not_exist = 3
      operation_no_authorization = 4
      parameter_error = 5
      x_error = 6
      enqueue_error = 7
      OTHERS = 8.
```

This code checks for a position where an amount is higher than €10,000 and sends a notification to `sy-uname`. This variable can be easily replaced with a customizing table, which would make more business sense. Save and activate everything. We can test this enhancement in transaction `FB01` (document posting). Open `FB01` and fill in all the fields in accordance with what's shown in the following screenshot:

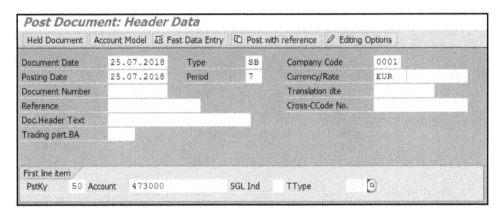

It is highly likely that you will have other accounts, posting codes, and control on your system. Please ask your functional consultant for specific data. Click **Enter** and incorporate the following data into the next screen:

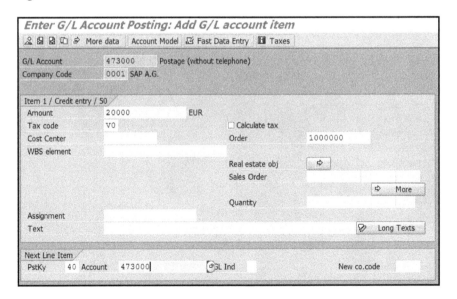

Again, click **Enter**, fill in the last screen, and click **Save**:

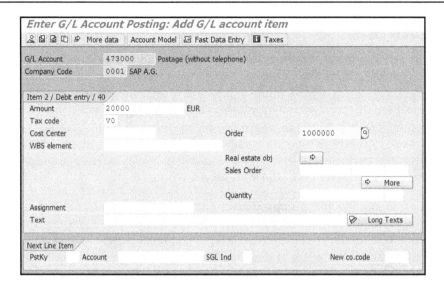

This should post a financial document and run our implementation. If you go to the **SAP Business Workplace** (**SBWP**) transaction, you will see a message notification stating that a high amount of documents have been posted:

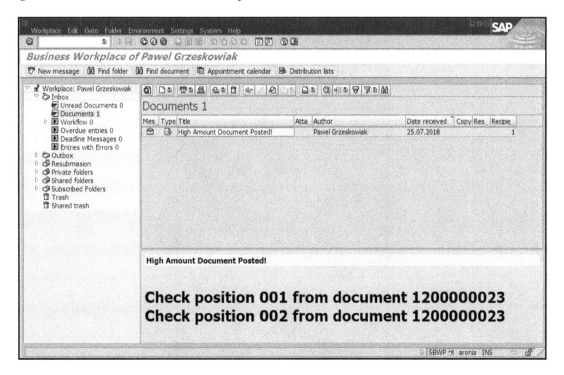

Modifications

Modifications are changes that are made to the SAP standard core code. In order to implement any modifications, it is necessary to generate the access key for the object. It isn't recommended that you use modifications. The main disadvantage of modifications is that they are overwritten during a system upgrade. You can change any SAP standard coding using this method, but it can lead to unpredictable system behavior. Let's say you change the function module to achieve specific business requirements, but this function module can be used in other parts of SAP for other processes. It's really hard to predict the impact of your changes on the operation of the system as a whole.

To solve this problem, SAP has prepared an enhancement approach called user exits. It's a type of modification, but it's used in predefined places so that possible consequences are easier to predict. User exits are represented from a technical perspective as FORM subroutines, and so on these types of modifications are also called FORM exits. In the following example, we will modify the SAP standard using one of the user exits. From a business perspective, this modification will refer to the SD module. SD is the only module where user exits are present. To implement user exits, go to SE80 and open the VMOD package:

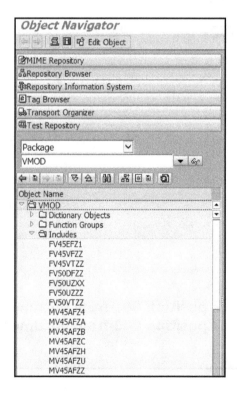

This package contains every user exit. Open any of them and you will see a bunch of form subroutines. SAP took care of describing most of the subroutines. This makes it very easy for you to find the right item to modify. Modifications are available for areas such as a sales order, delivery, billing, and pricing. As an example, open `MV45AFZZ`, in which you will find the `USEREXIT_FIELD_MODIFICATION` subroutine. This can be used to modify the fields of an SD transaction. You can turn off certain fields or fill in a field with data. To create your user-exit implementation, switch the ABAP workbench to edit mode. After hitting the **Display/Change** button, you will see the following screen:

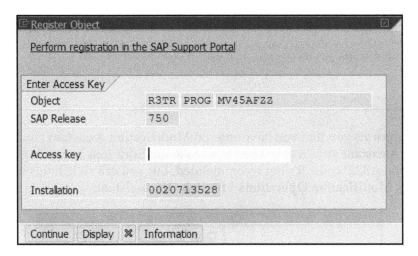

This is the **Access key** popup. In general, in order to modify any SAP standard development object, you need to register this modification on the **SAP Support Portal**. This key can be requested by the system administrator. This mechanism was created to protect the system against too many modifications and to make sure that all modifications are registered in one central place.

After getting the access key from the BASIS team and putting it in the previous window, you will see another popup:

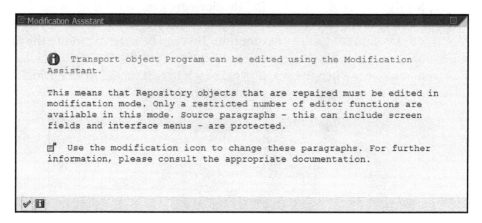

This window informs you that you have entered **Modification Assistant** mode. **Modification Assistant** guides you when you make modifications by putting additional comments in the ABAP code. It's not recommended, but you can switch this mode off by going to **Edit** | **Modification Operations** | **Switch Off Assistant**:

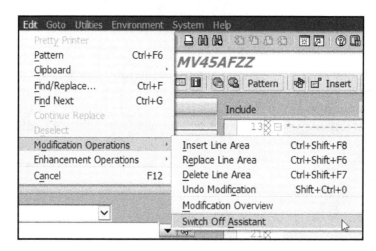

In **Modification Assistant** mode, you have four options to choose from:

Insert allows you to add new code. With **Replace**, you can change the standard SAP code. If you need to delete some standard code, you can use the **Delete** option. Last but not least, **Undo** will take you back a step if you have made a mistake. In this example, we will use the **Insert** option. Clicking **Insert** will create the following code:

```
FORM USEREXIT_FIELD_MODIFICATION.
*{     INSERT          HERK900424

*}     INSERT
```

You can put any code in-between inserted comments based on your customer requirements. In this specific subroutine, we could do something like this:

```
CONSTANTS: cv_augru TYPE C length 10 VALUE 'VBAK-AUGRU'.
 CONSTANTS: cv_tcode TYPE C LENGTH 4 VALUE 'VA01'.

 IF sy-tcode = cv_tcode.
   CASE screen-name.
     WHEN cv_augru.
       IF vbak-augru IS INITIAL.
         vbak-augru = '001'.
       ENDIF.
   ENDCASE.
 ENDIF.
```

This will cause a change in standard field behavior and set a default value in our code field. From a business perspective, this will set a service call as a sales order reason for all the orders that are created in the VA01 transaction.

FQEVENTS

Events is another type of enhancement that can be applied to SAP standard behavior. From a technical perspective, they are very similar to Customer Exits, and are also represented by a function module. Events are used in the FI-CA module and other modules that are integrated into contract accounting, such as convergent Invoicing.

You can implement this type of enhancement in the FQEVENTS transaction:

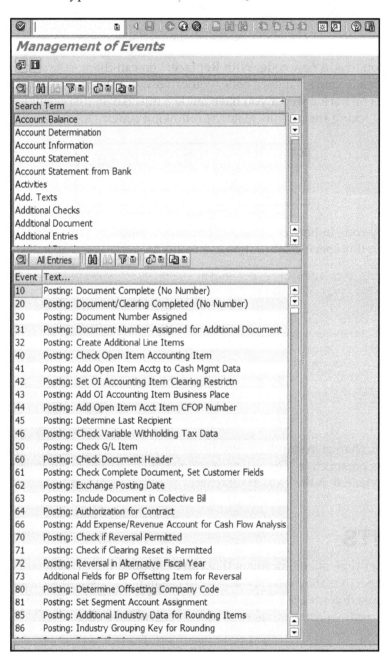

On the left, you can see the navigation menu, where you can find any predefined event. Try to search by description or by area. A typical business requirement is to implement additional logic for the FI-CA posting header field. Go to **Event | 60 (Posting: Check Document Header)**. For every event, there is very clear **Documentation** that explains where this event is triggered and how to use it:

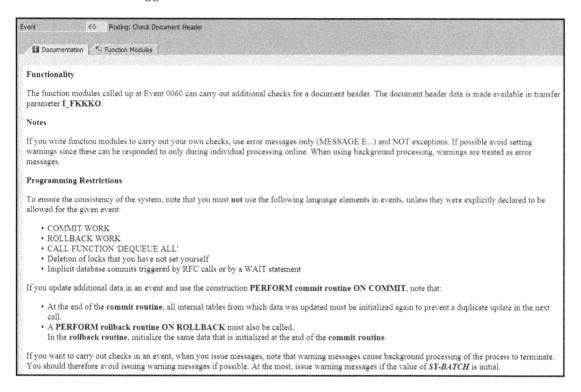

Every event also has a sample function module that the developer should copy in order to provide perfect interface compatibility with **function modules**:

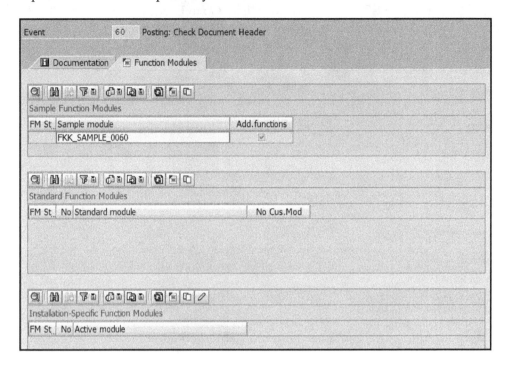

Click on the copy icon:

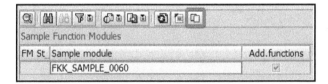

Give a new name to the function module copy and set your function group. It's highly recommended that you create a dedicated function group (or a few of them) just for events in the **Function Module**:

Add a new function module to the **Installation-Specific Function Modules** area by clicking on the pencil icon:

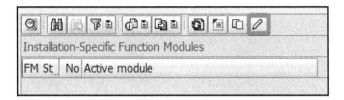

On the next screen, you have to click on the **New entries** button:

As you can see, for each event, it's possible to add a few function modules. **Sequence Number** determines the order of execution. We will add ZFKK_FM_EVENT_0060 here:

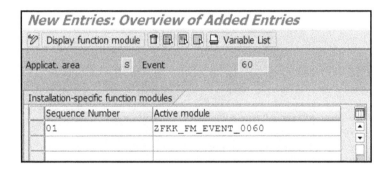

Save your changes and go back to the main screen of the FQEVENTS transaction. Click on the white-blue icon:

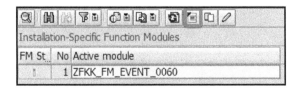

This will bring you to the function module editor, where you can insert any valid ABAP code. You can use something like this:

```
IF i_fkkko-blart = '06' and i_fkkko-abgrd IS INITIAL.
  MESSAGE 'For returns documents return reason is obligatory' type 'E'.
ENDIF.
```

Now, every time someone creates an `FI-CA` document of type 06 (returns) and forgets to fill in the return reason field, they will be informed via an error message.

Appends

Appends are a very important concept and are present in almost every modification project. Appends are used to expand dictionary objects, such as tables, data element text, and search for help. In this section, you will learn how to extend a standard SAP table so that you can store additional client-specific information. Go to transaction `SE11` and open the `KNA1` table (you can use any other table if you so desire). This table stores **General data in Customer Master**:

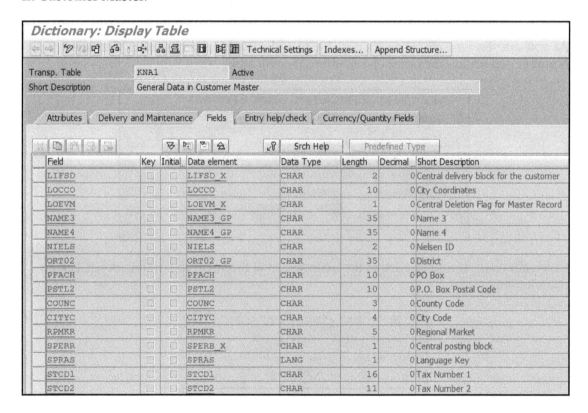

The client wants to have information about customer nationality so that they can adapt their offers to their customers. This isn't part of the standard, so we need to extend this KNA1 table. Click on **Goto** | **Append Structure**:

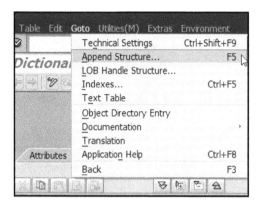

In the popup that appears, choose a name. It's recommended by SAP to start the append structure with double Z. In the case of appends, a single Z is reserved for SAP development:

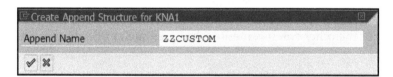

Put in a Nationality field as a field type and activate **append**:

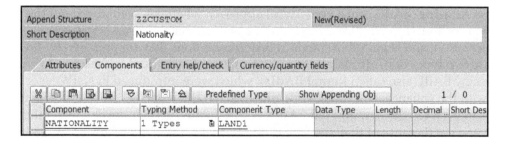

After the activation of the new field and the new append, additional information will be shown in the table:

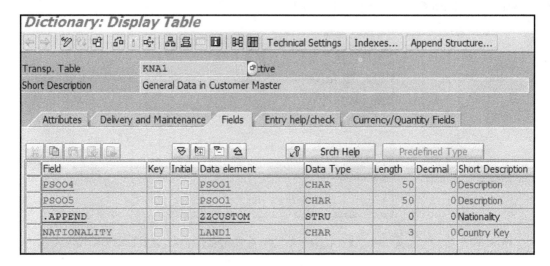

This chapter only covers the append technique, which is nothing more than a placeholder for data. To be able to see this field on the screen and add some sophisticated logic, you will have to read about the other enhancement techniques such as BAdI, that are presented in this chapter.

Classical BAdI

Business Add-Ins (BAdIs) are a very useful approach when you want to extend the standard functionality of SAP systems. BAdI can be understood as an interface awaiting implementation, and is placed in standard SAP transactions that are prepared by SAP. There are two types of BAdI: classic BAdIs, which were introduced in the early 4.6 versions, and the new BAdI (also called **kernel BAdIs**), which were introduced in NetWeaver 7.0 (along with the enhancement framework and switch framework). There are three important differences between the new and old BAdIs. A new BAdIs object is created using the GET BAdI statement (because of that, they are called Kernel BAdIs); old BAdIs are initialized using the get_instance factory method from the cl_exithandler class. In the case of the classic BAdI, a new object is always created in a factory method, whereas kernel BAdIs already provide an initialized instance. This difference is also noticeable in the filtering mechanism. The classic BAdI passes a filter value to the method call, whereas in kernel BAdIs, filtering is executed in the GET BAdI level. There are also significant differences between the management of calls. The old approach only allowed one BAdI call, and call positions were registered centrally.

In the new kernel approach, multiple calls are possible, and the call positions are not registered centrally. Always use the kernel BAdI if possible—in addition to the aforementioned advantages, they are also much faster. In this example, we will implement the CTS_REQUEST_CHECK BAdI, which is capable of extending transport request functionality. Go to SE18 and enter a name in **BAdI Name** and click the **Display** button:

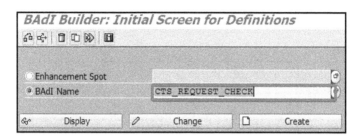

On the BAdI definition screen, choose **Implementation | Create**:

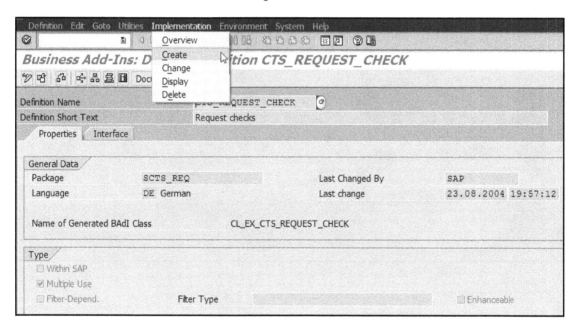

A popup will appear where you have to choose an enhancement name. Then, click on the green checkmark:

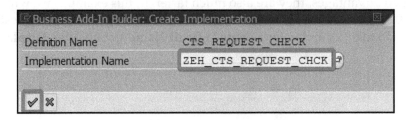

On the next screen, enter **Implementation Short Text**. Then, click the **Activate** button:

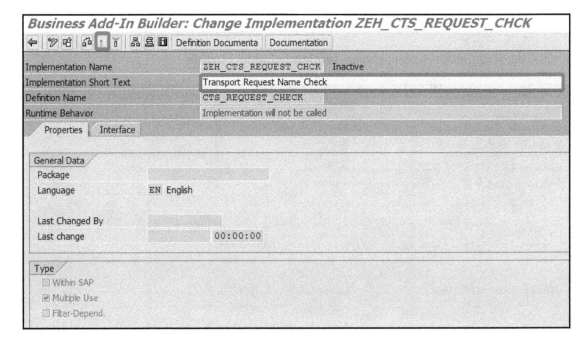

During this process, a new class called `ZCL_IM_EH_CTS_REQUEST_CHCK` will be generated automatically. Go to the `CHECK_BEFORE_CREATION` method of this class and insert the following code:

```
    CASE text+0(3).
      WHEN 'FI:' OR 'SD:' OR 'MM:'.
      WHEN OTHERS.
         MESSAGE 'Name should start from module name (FI:, SD:, MM:)' TYPE
'E'.
    ENDCASE.
```

The `CHECK_BEFORE_CREATION` method is always executed when someone creates a new transport request. To achieve proper naming conventions, we will add an additional check and inform the user that the description is incorrect. You can test this development in transaction `SE10`—just try and create a new transport request.

Enhancement framework and its components

The Enhancement Framework, sometimes referred to as New Enhancement, is a concept that was presented in version 2004 of the SAP system that provides a new, modification-free approach to extending standard SAP functionality. It's the best way to extend development objects, such as function modules, global classes, programs, and Web Dynpro components. The Enhancement Framework is also integrated with the new kernel BAdI enhancement technology, which gives developers a wide and clear tool for extending SAP. There are a couple of benefits of using the **Entity Framework** (**EF**). For example, enhancements can now be grouped together and integrated for specific industry solutions. You can also switch any enhancement on and off using the switch framework mechanism. You also have better support during system upgrades. The downside of EF is that some functionality may require *old* technology to get the full scope of client requirements (for example, table appends).

There are two general types of enhancement supported by the Enhancement Framework: explicated and implicated enhancement. Explicated enhancements are provided by SAP and divided into the `ENHANCEMENT-POINT` and `ENHANCEMENT-SECTION` types. The main difference between *section* and *point* is that section contains some default code, whereas point is empty. Implicit enhancements are similar to `Enhancement-Point` since they are implicit in some specific places, which will be described later in this chapter.

Enhancement sections and Enhancement points

To work with new enhancements, you need to use the enhancement builder, which is part of the ABAP development workbench transaction SE80. If you don't know the name of the ENHANCMENT, try to debug the program you want to modify. In this section, we will focus on the BAPI_SALESORDER_CREATEFROMDAT1 function module. If you open this function, you will find ENHANCMENT-POINT:

```
25  *"------------------------------------------------------------------
26  ENHANCEMENT-POINT BAPI_SALESORDER_CREATEFROMD_G8 SPOTS ES_SAPL2032 STATIC.
27  *$*$-Start: BAPI_SALESORDER_CREATEFROMD_G8---------------------------------$*$*
28  ENHANCEMENT 3  MGV_GENERATED_BAPI_SALESORD002.    "active version
29  DATA: T_MGV_FNAMES1 LIKE MGVBAPIFNAMES OCCURS 0 WITH HEADER LINE.
30  DATA: T_MGV_FNAMES2 LIKE MGVBAPIFNAMES OCCURS 0 WITH HEADER LINE.
31  ENDENHANCEMENT.
32  *$*$-End:   BAPI_SALESORDER_CREATEFROMD_G8---------------------------------$*$*
33
34  ENHANCEMENT-POINT BAPI_SALESORDER_CREATEFROMD_G6 SPOTS ES_SAPL2032.
35  *$*$-Start: BAPI_SALESORDER_CREATEFROMD_G6---------------------------------$*$*
36  ENHANCEMENT 1  MGV_GENERATED_BAPI_SALESORD002.    "active version
37  *{BAPI Begin} generation http://intranet.sap.com/materialversion
```

There are two additional options that can be used both with section and points. STATIC, which is shown in the preceding screenshot, will make the implementation static, which is good for data declaration. Assigning a switch to Enhancements will change its behavior. Even static enhancement will work on the switch status. For non-static enhancement, the switch is obligatory. Turn on EF by clicking on the spiral button:

Put the cursor on the ENHANCMENT-POINT line:

```
ENHANCEMENT-POINT BAPI_SALESORDER_CREATEFROMD_G8 SPOTS ES_SAPL2032 STATIC.
```

Choose **Edit** | **Enhancement Operations** | **Create Implementation**:

You will get a popup that shows all the enhancement implementations. Click on the new icon at the bottom of the window:

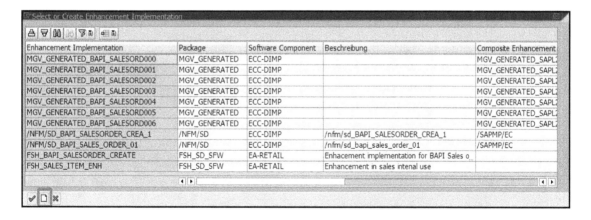

You will see a popup where you need to insert an enhancement name and description:

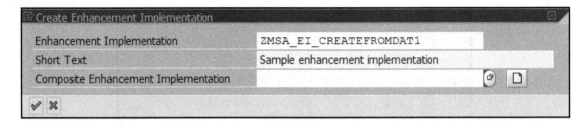

This will create a new section, where you can add specific customer code:

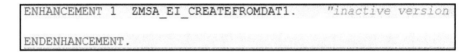

This could be an additional check, additional business logic, or other additional information. In our case, we will fill in some short text with a material name every time this field is empty:

```
FIELD-SYMBOLS: <ls_order_items_in> TYPE bapiitemin.

LOOP AT order_items_in[] ASSIGNING <ls_order_items_in> WHERE short_text IS
INITIAL.
  SELECT SINGLE maktx FROM makt INTO <ls_order_items_in>-SHORT_TEXT WHERE
matnr = <ls_order_items_in>-material AND spras = 'E'.
ENDLOOP.
```

Every enhancement has to be activated in the same way you would activate an ABAP program or include:

Now, every time you use BAPI_SALESORDER_CREATEFROMDAT1, your additional logic will be executed.

Implicit enhancements

Implicit enhancements are spots where you can create your own source code. Those spots are automatically created in pre-defined places. You can find implicit enhancements at the end and beginning of most ABAP development objects (**Includes**, **Reports**, **Function pool**, **Module pool**, and **Function modules**). Implicit enhancements are also available at the beginning and end of FORM subroutines, the methods of all classes, and the visibility areas (public, protected, and private) of the local class. To check all the implicit options that are available in the source code, go to the ABAP workbench (transaction SE80) and choose any of the objects we mentioned previously:

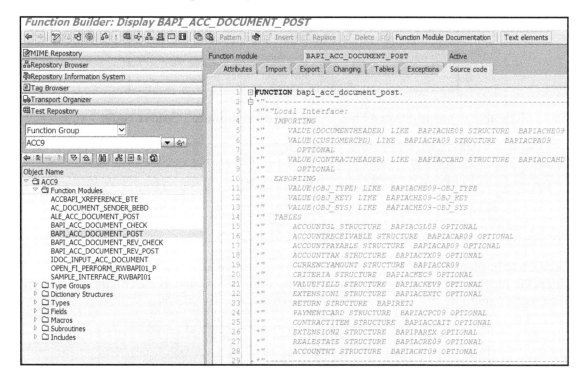

Choose **Edit** | **Enhancement Operations** | **Show Implicit Enhancement** option from the editor:

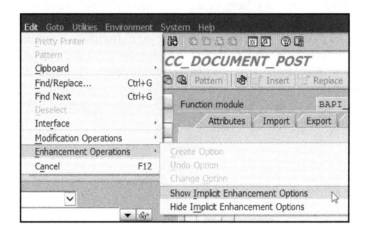

You will be able to see additional lines in the **Function module** | **Source code**:

Let's try to implement implicit enhancement. The BAPI we just created is used to post financial documents. It's the equivalent of transaction FB01. Click on the enhance icon from the toolbar menu:

New options will be shown on the toolbar (**Create**, **Change**, **Replace**, and so on):

Right-click on the first line of code and choose **Enhancements Operations | Create Implementation**:

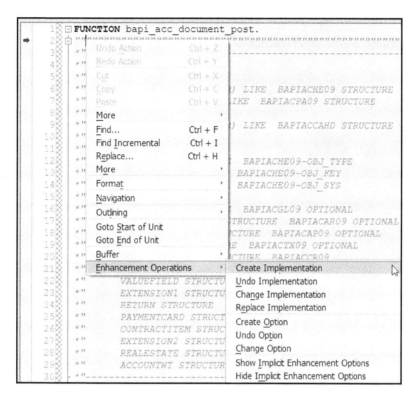

On the next screen, you will be asked to **Choose Enhancement Mode**:

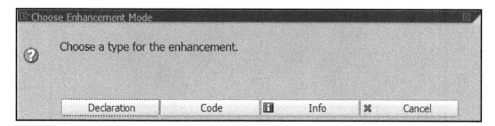

The declaration type is used for static code, such as data declaration, forms, and local class definitions. The declaration is client independent. On the other hand, the code type is used for dynamic enhancements and can be switched on and off using the switch framework. The declaration type of an implicit enhancement doesn't provide the same performance as the code type. Click on the **Declaration** button:

Composite Enhancement Implementation is a higher abstract structuring approach for development. It's similar to package subpackage. Fill in the boxes, just like I have in the following screenshot:

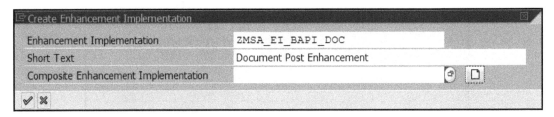

Click on the green check mark button. You should be back inside editor, where you can insert the ABAP code:

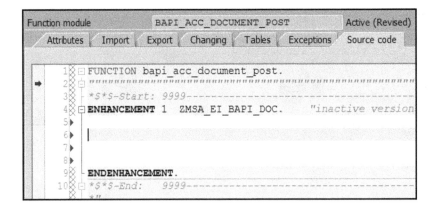

You can put any code here, for example, the code from the BTE example (with some minor modification) and get almost the same result with an entirely different enhancement technology.

Summary

In this chapter, you learned about extending standard SAP system functionality. This multiplicity of options is due to long history of SAP software and various approaches to development over the years. As a developer, you should always try to use the latest approach whenever possible. In spite of such broad knowledge, not all areas have been described. The new HANA and SAPUI5/Fiori technologies also have their own extension techniques, and they are used more and more often. Having acquired the knowledge from this chapter, you should be able to implement even the most complex requirements of an end customer. In the next chapter, we will discuss how do handle exceptions in ABAP programming.

Questions

The following questions will allow you to consolidate the information contained in this chapter:

1. Which of the listed technologies in this chapter is not recommended for use?
2. What is the switch mechanism used for?
3. What is the difference between classical BAdI and kernel BAdI?
4. Which module is used to extend FQEVENT transactions?
5. What is the difference between the enhancement point and the enhancement section?
6. What does the INCLUDE BOUND option do?
7. What technical object is used in customer exit implementation?

Further reading

- **Enhancement techniques for SAP Fiori:** `https://wiki.scn.sap.com/wiki/display/Fiori/SAP+Fiori+-+Extensibility`

- **Business Data Toolset (BDT):**
  `https://help.sap.com/erp2005_ehp_02/helpdata/en/44/bd8d5377a0ec23e10000000a174cb4/frameset.htm`

- **Enhancing WebDynpro:** `https://wiki.scn.sap.com/wiki/display/WDABAP/Enhancing+the+WebDynpro+Component+and+Methods`

11
Handling Exceptions in ABAP

In a perfect world, perfect programs would always behave the way they were intended to. All the data would be consistent, the users would always act properly, and there would be no unexpected conditions. Unfortunately, the perfect world does not exist and even the most elaborate programs may sometimes fail. To minimize losses and prevent damage from spreading any further, developers, users, and system administrators should react to any unexpected circumstances.

This chapter will also describe the classic exception. The information pertaining to the classic exception for the program is important because, in older implementations, they can come across this solution.

This philosophy was also incorporated in the **Systems Applications and Products in Data Processing** (**SAP**) system, through the use of several tools, concepts, and syntax statements. This chapter will describe how to handle improper runtime behavior, both at the programming level and error root causes analysis level.

The following topics will be covered in this chapter:

- Classic exception handling
- Class-based exceptions
- Assertions
- Runtime errors
- ABAP dump analysis tool

Technical requirements

All the code used in this chapter can be downloaded from the following GitHub link: `https://github.com/PacktPublishing/Mastering-SAP-ABAP/tree/master/Chapter11`.

Classic exception handling

As was mentioned in the introduction, when working with the SAP system, it is rather inevitable to find some old code, and it was most likely created with classic exceptions. Although it is not recommended, and even discouraged, to use them on a regular basis in a new development, there are still several cases where it is the only way to communicate and handle the unexpected behavior of the program.

Handling

Prior to the introduction of class-based, object-oriented programming in SAP systems, one of the methods of code modularization was function modules. The reusable code components with a particular task to do were wrapped into pretty simple function calls, and the modules were bundled into function groups. The function modules—despite the fact that they were mostly superseded by the classes and methods—are still necessary when using **Remote Function Call** (RFCs).

Even if the code is well thought out and well written, it is still necessary to ensure that the system will not fail if something unexpected happens. What is even more important, it is required to prevent the database from having inconsistent data, even if processing is interrupted abruptly. To solve this problem, developers were given the appropriate mechanism of communicating failures or problems to anyone using their modules—including the EXCEPTIONS section in the function module interface shown in the following code snippet:

```
CALL FUNCTION 'SAMPLE_FUNCTION'
    EXPORTING
        ...
    IMPORTING
        ...
    TABLES
        ...
    CHANGING
        ...
    EXCEPTIONS
        ...
```

The EXCEPTIONS section of the call is built along similar lines to the preceding ones—it is a list of possible exceptions returned by the function modules, followed by the assignment of a number in the 0-65535 range. A simple list is presented here:

```
CALL FUNCTION 'SAMPLE_FUNCTION'
    some_defined_exception    = 1
    some_other_exception      = 2
    yet_another_exception     = 3
```

As it is possible for the function module to have a long list of possible exceptions—and not all of them can be handled in a meaningful way—we can use a keyword, OTHERS, to assign a single number to all handleable exceptions not mentioned by name. Refer to the following code snippet:

```
CALL FUNCTION 'SAPMLE_FUNCTION'
    EXCEPTIONS
        some_defined_exception = 1
        OTHERS                 = 2.
```

It is important to observe that omitting the OTHERS keyword while not assigning a number to an exception will lead to a runtime error when this particular exception occurs.

Once the function module is executed and the program flow goes back to the caller, the sy-subrc system variable is set. By default, if the flow was not interrupted by any exception, the sy-subrc value is set to 0. In any other situation, the value is set according to the number specified in the EXCEPTIONS section thus letting the developer act accordingly.

The classic exceptions are the natural extension of the function modules interface, but they can also be incorporated into the class methods (although it is not recommended). For the local classes, the exceptions are also defined in a dedicated section as shown here:

```
CLASS lcl_class DEFINITION.
    METHODS
        sample_method
            RETURNING value(arg) TYPE I
            EXCEPTIONS some_exception another_exception
yet_another_exception
ENDCLASS.
```

When defining global classes using the Class Builder, the exceptions are defined on the corresponding screen, accessible via the **Exceptions** button:

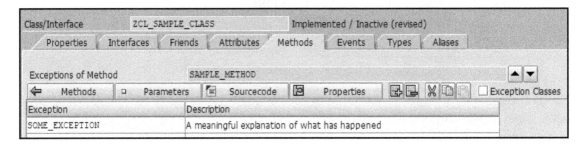

On the new subscreen, the classic exceptions are created simply by declaring their name and adding a meaningful description. As the classic exceptions and class-based exceptions (described further in this chapter) are mutually exclusive, the **Exception Classes** checkbox needs to be left unmarked, as follows:

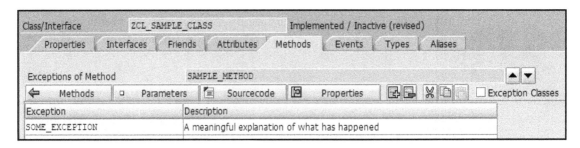

Similar to function modules, when calling the method containing the EXCEPTIONS section, the developer is responsible for assigning appropriate codes (numbers) to all the exceptions declared, similar to the following code snippet:

```
DATA lr_ref TYPE REF TO lcl_class.
DATA lv_result TYPE I.
    ...
CREATE OBJECT lr_ref.
lr_ref->some_method(
    RECEIVING
        arg = lv_result
    EXCEPTIONS
        some_exception        = 1
        another_exception     = 2
        yet_another_exception = 3 ).
```

Once again, should the exception happen while not declared in the call statement, the runtime error will occur and the program will be terminated immediately.

After the method call is completed, the `sy-subrc` variable is set to `0` for success or to any number assigned to the exception that was raised during the execution.

Raising

Classic exceptions should not be considered the exceptions originating from the system core. They are rather a short explanation, or the reason for the premature termination of the method or a function call. Such termination can be the result of preventive steps to avoid system failure, but also—and probably more likely—it is a simple message stipulating that for some reason, the code logic deviates from the designed flow and the valid results cannot be provided.

Due to their logic-specific nature, classic exceptions need to be raised manually in places where they are actually needed. Regardless of whether you're defining a new function module or new class method, there are two ways of raising a classic exception—the first is with the `RAISE` statement:

```
RAISE some_exception.
```

The second one is an addition to the `MESSAGE` statement:

```
MESSAGE 'Some error message'  TYPE 'E' RAISING some_exception.
```

Both statements result in the immediate termination of the current processing block. This termination may have several outcomes, depending on the context. If any of these two statements is executed within the function module or class method, and the caller provided an appropriate `EXCEPTIONS` assignment, the program flow resumes right after the call. If they are executed within a subroutine, the interpreter searches the call stack for the first method or function module that wraps the current context.

If there is neither the former nor the latter, the `RAISE` statement causes a runtime error, whereas `MESSAGE-RAISING` behaves like the standard `MESSAGE` statement. Otherwise, if either function module or class method is found, its interface is checked for the definition of the exception. Provided the definition is present, the execution flow is resumed after the call. In other cases, where the definition is not available, `RAISE` results in a runtime error and `MESSAGE-RAISING` produces a message.

The aforementioned outcomes lead to a recommendation—when the classic exception is required to be raised, it is preferable to use the `MESSAGE-RAISING` clause as it may carry a bit more information (a message) than the `RAISING` clause alone.

Classic exceptions cannot be used alongside class-based exceptions within the same processing block.

Class-based exceptions

As the object-oriented programming philosophy was incorporated into ABAP programming, the exceptions concept had to evolve as well. As programs grew and used more classes and objects, the exceptions were eventually migrated to class-based programming. There was also a more practical reason for this move-defining exception, since an object allows for passing more detailed information on what happened to the caller, thereby letting the developer define better-tailored reactions.

The newly created exception objects—either standard or custom ones—are children of the same master abstract class, CX_ROOT, and therefore all have common attributes: TEXTID, PREVIOUS, and IS_RESUMABLE, and the common methods, GET_TEXT, GET_LONGTEXT, and GET_SOURCE_POSITION.

The CX_ROOT class is the most general exception class and, as such, contains very little information about the specific causes of the exception. Thus, there is a whole hierarchy of subclasses grouped into three elements that make up the first tier —CX_STATIC_CHECK, CX_DYNAMIC_CHECK, and CX_NO_CHECK. This separation of the inheritance tree is done as per the requirements in the declaration and checks are performed.

The requirements mentioned—as well as short recommendations on usage—are as follows:

- Exceptions based on CX_STATIC_CHECK and its subclasses need to be declared in the method interface. The syntax checks checks whether the caller wrapped the call with the appropriate TRY-CATCH block to catch the exception. This type of exception should be used when there is no way to prevent the exception and it needs to be forced to handle the exception by the caller explicitly.
- The exceptions originating from CX_DYNAMIC_CHECK and its children need to be declared in the interface as well. However, there is no syntax check when defining the method call. These exceptions should be raised if the cause is somehow prevented by other means in the application flow, and therefore there is no need to explicitly tell the caller that the exception needs to be handled. More detailed subclasses of this group are, for example, CX_SY_ARITHMETIC_ERROR, CX_SY_CONVERSION_ERROR, or CX_SY_ASSIGN_ERROR.

- The usage of CX_NO_CHECK and its subclasses—as the name suggests—results in exceptions that are not supposed to be declared in the interface but are always propagated. It represents the exceptions that can happen any time and cannot be prevented in any other way. This group contains, for example, CX_SY_REMOTE_CALL_ERROR or CX_BADI subgroups, and CX_SY_ILLEGAL_HANDLER or CX_SY_NO_HANDLER classes.

Although the introduction of standard exception classes is a natural outcome of migrating the ABAP language to object-oriented programming, it is the possibility of creating custom exception classes that make it a powerful tool. The custom exception classes can be created either locally or by using the Class Builder.

The main difference between the custom exception classes and ordinary classes is that the former must be defined as the subclasses of any of the three tier one exception classes (CX_STATIC_CHECK, CX_DYNAMIC_CHECK, and CX_NO_CHECK). Apart from this requirement, they can be freely extended with the properties and methods needed.

Handling

Unlike classic exceptions, class-based exceptions are not a part of the method call. This is partly due to the separation between CX_STATIC_CHECK, CX_DYNAMIC_CHECK, and CX_NO_CHECK—not all of them are required to be handled every time. Similar to other object-oriented languages with the exception mechanism, class-based exceptions are caught with the TRY-CATCH block. In ABAP, however, the aforementioned block is further enhanced with several optional context-control statements, shown in the following code snippet:

```
TRY.
    ...execute standard program flow here...
CATCH [BEFORE UNWIND] some_exception another_exception [INTO oref].
    ...react to the exception here...
[CLEANUP [INTO oref].]
    ...cleanup here before passing the exception...
ENDTRY.
```

The simplest possible declaration of the TRY-CATCH block includes only the following statements with the exception name:

```
TRY.
    ...execute standard program flow here...
CATCH some_exception.
    ...react to the exception here...
ENDTRY.
```

Although this straightforward example is sufficient to pass the syntax check and avoid runtime errors caused by some_exception, it is most likely not enough for proper handling in terms of business context or application logs. In order to get more information from the exception, the INTO oref addition can be used:

```
TRY.
    ...execute standard program flow here...
CATCH some_exception another_exception INTO oref.
    ...react to the exception here...
CATCH yet_another_exception.
    ...react to the exception here...
ENDTRY.
```

This addition causes the exception object thrown to be stored in the oref variable. Keep in mind the hierarchical structure of the exception classes; the oref variable's type must be a superclass of all the exceptions declared in the CATCH statement. Alternatively, it is possible to use DATA(oref) instead, letting the code interpreter decide the variable's type.

 The type of the oref variable declared with DATA(oref) in the INTO clause will be the lowest common superclass of all the exceptions declared in the CATCH statement.

Once the exception object is stored in the variable, it is possible to access its public properties and methods when reacting to the exception. The exact properties and methods are dependent on the type of the exception and can be freely defined when the custom exception classes are used.

If the standard execution block can raise multiple exceptions, and the reaction for any of them must differ, it is possible to use several CATCH statements within one TRY-ENDTRY section, as was also shown in the previous code snippet.

The exceptions mechanism in ABAP is designed this way, so when the exception is raised and the flow control is passed to the CATCH statement, the context in which it was raised is lost by default. Although not so common, there are some situations that require the preservation of the raising context when executing the reaction block. One particular example is when the exception is thrown is resumable and the flow is indeed supposed to be resumed. For these purposes, the BEFORE UNWIND addition was introduced:

```
TRY
    ...execute standard flow here...
CATCH BEFORE UNWIND some_exception INTO oref.
    ...react to the exception here...
    RESUME.
ENDTRY.
```

One more option for flow control when handling exceptions can be added with the CLEANUP statement. This optional keyword can be used when the exception raised is not handled directly by the same TRY-CATCH block, but by some other surrounding block, as in the following code snippet:

```
TRY.
    TRY.
        ...execute standard flow here...
        ...some_other_exception is raised...
    CATCH some_exception.
        ...react to some_exception...
    CLEANUP.
        ...cleanup section...
    ENDTRY.
CATCH some_other_exception.
    ...react to some_other_exception...
ENDTRY.
```

When some_other_exception is raised, it is not caught by the innermost TRY-CATCH section, but by the outermost, so the structure is syntactically correct. The CLEANUP section is executed immediately after the raising context is deleted and before the outermost CATCH section.

If the catching statement is supplied with the BEFORE UNWIND addition, the CLEANUP section is executed after the CATCH section, or, if there is a RESUME statement in the CATCH clause, it is not executed at all.

Similar to the CATCH statement, the CLEANUP section can be further supplied with the INTO oref addition to get a reference to the exception object. This time, however, oref is always of the CX_ROOT type.

Raising

Raising class-based exceptions is only a little bit more complicated than classic exceptions. In this case, the RAISE EXCEPTION statement should be used, with appropriate additions and options when needed.

The appropriate syntax for raising this kind of exception depends on whether the exception object variable was declared prior to raising. In the first scenario, the following syntax is valid:

```
CLASS lcx_exception DEFINITION INHERITING FROM cx_static_check.
ENDCLASS.
...
DATA lx_exception TYPE REF TO lcx_exception.
...
CREATE OBJECT lx_exception.
RAISE EXCEPTION lx_exception.
```

If the object was not declared, the RAISE statement should have the TYPE keyword and should refer to the type instead of the variable, as in the following code snippet:

```
CLASS lcx_exception DEFINITION INHERITING FROM cx_static_check.
ENDCLASS.
...
RAISE EXCEPTION TYPE lcx_exception.
```

The actual values of the exception parameters need to be passed to the exception object during its creation (either with CREATE OBJECT or RAISE EXCEPTION TYPE) through the EXPORTING clause:

```
RAISE EXCEPTION TYPE custom_exception_class
    EXPORTING
        param1 = value 1
        param2 = value 2
        ...
    .
```

The values passed here will be accessible within the CATCH statement of the first surrounding TRY-CATCH block, suitable for catching this type of exception.

If the exception thrown is not meant to stop the execution flow—and it should be possible to resume it when the exception is handled—the optional RESUMABLE clause can be used:

```
RAISE RESUMABLE EXCEPTION TYPE custom_exception_class.
```

The appropriate `CATCH BEFORE UNWIND` block may contain the `RESUME` statement.

Many programs in the ABAP environment utilize messages as a way to communicate their current state and issues to the user, or to store information in logs. Thus, class-based exceptions are also prepared to use this mechanism. As long as the exception class is declared with either the `IF_T100_DYN_MSG` or `IF_T100_MESSAGE` interface, the `MESSAGE` addition can be used.

When constructing custom exception classes, these interfaces are included automatically when the following checkbox is checked:

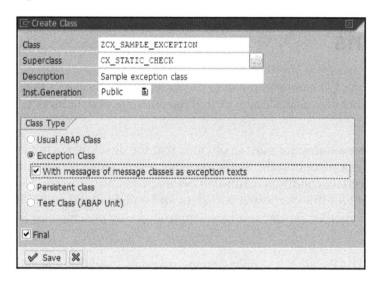

The resulting interfaces tab is as follows:

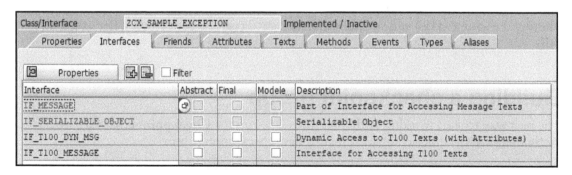

Using the MESSAGE clause similar to the following code snippet will result in the exception object with the fields populated according to the interface rules, with the whole message accessible through the get_text( ) method:

```
RAISE EXCEPTION TYPE sample_exception_class
    MESSAGE
        ID sy-msgid
        TYPE sy-msgty
        NUMBER sy-msgno
        WITH sy-msgv1 sy-msgv2 sy-msgv3 sy-msgv4.
```

Assertions

ABAP programs, as well as pretty much every other program, are more or less based on certain assumptions. For example, the data provided to a method or a function is consistent, that the program behaves as designed, or that the outcome of data processing follows some kind of scheme.

In most cases, these assumptions are so obvious that the developer is not even aware of them when writing a piece of code. Sometimes, however, it may be more important to check whether a certain condition is fulfilled before proceeding further. Using the standard IF-ELSE statement for this purpose is sufficient and will do exactly what is needed. However, there is another shorter and more controlled way of achieving this—with assertions.

The assertion in ABAP code is a simple statement saying *assert that something fulfills a condition*. There is no need to use any sophisticated syntax or build nested IF structures for several conditions. What's more, the assertion mechanism is remotely controlled—particular groups of assertions can be turned on or off when needed (without altering the source code) and several different actions can be performed if the assertion fails.

Building a checkpoint group

The best way to start working with assertions is to run the **Checkpoints that Can Be Activated (SAAB)** transaction and create a new checkpoint group:

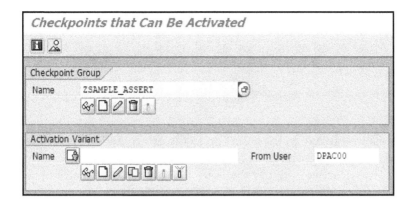

Assign the new group to the appropriate package and transport request. This object should advance to the productive system to handle failed assertions there as well.

The resulting checkpoint group is ready to be used and the preview shows the screen as follows:

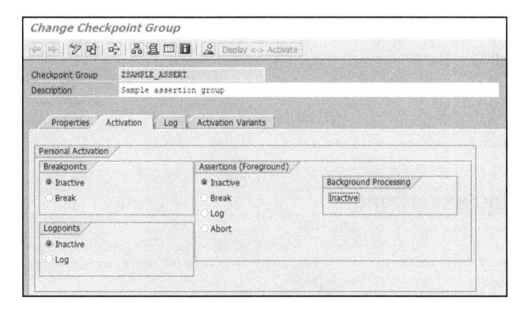

The preceding screenshot shows that the information about the settings is very clear. The user can set them in a simple way. They are also grouped by their characteristics.

Defining assertions

Once the checkpoint group is created, it is time to set up some assertions in the code. To to this, the following syntax is used:

```
ASSERT [ [ ID groupID [ SUBKEY key] ] [ FIELDS field 1 ... ] CONDITION ]
expression
```

The `ID` addition is used to assign the assertion to the group defined in the SAAB transaction and control it remotely. Although it is possible to omit this addition (resulting in an assertion that is always active), should the assertion fail, the runtime error will be triggered by the non-handleable `ASSERTION_FAILED` exception. The `ID` clause can be further specified with the `SUBKEY` addition—it can be followed by any character string and is used to easier identify assertions in the program.

The optional `FIELDS` addition is used to provide a list of fields (variables) that should be passed to the assertion log if the assertion fails.

The `CONDITION` clause is required if either `ID` or `FIELDS` clauses are used. After the `CONDITION`, one defines the logical expression to be checked at runtime.

Using the checkpoint group defined in SAAB, a simple assertion example may appear, similar to the following code snippet:

```
ASSERT ID ZSAMPLE_ASSERT SUBKEY 'date assertion' FIELDS sy-datum sy-uzeit
CONDITION sy-datum < '19990101'.
```

As the year `1999` is obviously in the past, this assertion is meant to fail.

Using assertions

Provided assertions included in the code are assigned to the checkpoint group using the `ID` addition, they are inactive by default. Using the SAAB transaction again, these assertions can be activated temporarily and the required action can be defined. You can choose from four options for foreground processing:

- **Inactive**: The assertions are not checked at all.
- **Break**: Failed assertions open the debugger window.
- **Log**: The values of variables specified in the `FIELDS` addition are logged if the assertion fails.
- **Abort**: The `ASSERTION_FAILED` exception is thrown when the condition is not met and the program is terminated immediately.

The available options are also shown in the following screenshot:

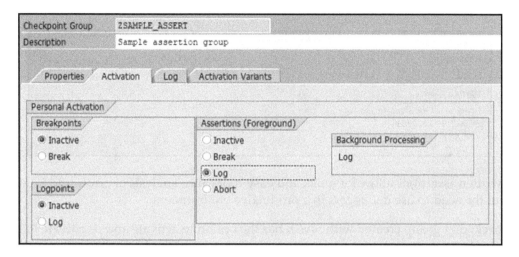

 ABAP programs can be executed as background processes, for which the debugger cannot be opened. Choosing the `Break` option requires additional decisions as to whether background processing should log the assertion failure or whether to abort processing with `ASSERTION_FAILED`.

Once the decision is made and the save icon is pressed, the user is prompted to choose an activation period. The assertions from within the checkpoint group will automatically turn inactive after the specified time.

Executing the code with the assertion in **Log** mode results in a new entry on the **Log** tab:

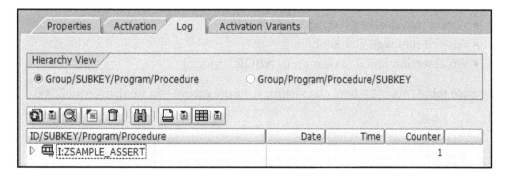

Drilling down the tree eventually shows the details of this particular assertion failure and the values of variables defined in the FIELDS clause:

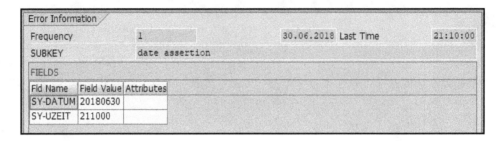

Well-written assertions allow for quick and easy root cause analysis of errors and failures without the need to use debuggers in a productive environment.

The checkpoint group created with SAAB has the option to activate and deactivate BREAK-POINT and LOG-POINT, both assigned to it. The behavior of the former is similar to the assertion in **Break** mode, and the latter to the assertion in **Log** mode, but they don't specify additional conditions.

Runtime errors

A runtime error in an SAP system can have many causes. A runtime error is a problem whose effect is interrupting the program. The most common reasons for this are as follows:

- Non-handled exceptions.
- A handleable exception was not handled.
- A non-handleable exception was raised.
- An exit message was sent.
- An assertion failed (assertion in **ABORT** mode).

The database table SNAPTID lists all existing runtime errors—in total, around 2,000.

ABAP dump analysis tool

ABAP Dump Analysis is used to analyze execution errors in the SAP system. It is a very powerful tool often displayed by developers. The user can run this tool with the ST22 transaction. The tool provides a lot of information that is necessary to repair the existing situation. The selection screen is shown after starting the ST22 transaction. The selection screen is shown as follows:

ABAP Runtime Errors - All Clients

Parameters

Standard

	Today		0	Runtime Errors
	Yesterday		0	Runtime Errors

Own selection

Date		to		
Time	00:00:00	to	00:00:00	
Host		to		
Work Process Index		to		
User		to		
Client		to		
To be stored		to		
Runtime Error		to		
Terminated Program		to		
Exception		to		
Transaction ID		to		
EPP Full Context ID		to		
EPP Connection ID		to		

⊕ Start

These files were investigated for each runtime error:
☐ With Short Text of Runtime Error
☐ Corresponding Application Component (Long Runtime)

☐ Use old dump analysis

Searching for a specific error becomes easier when the developer has as much information as possible; this can narrow down the search area.

The following code will result in a short dump since the division by 0 has not been handled:

```
REPORT ztestdump.

DATA : lv_count TYPE i VALUE 4,
       lv_div   TYPE i,
       lv_denom TYPE i VALUE 0.

lv_div = lv_count / lv_denom.
```

The previous code was presented for demonstration purposes. The error simulated in this program will help the reader understand the ABAP Dump Analysis tool in the SAP system.

Error log

The resulting error log can be analyzed in the transaction described previously. The error log is divided into a tree structure; its main nodes are composed of the following:

- **System Environment**
- **User View**
- **ABAP Developer View**
- **BASIS Developer View**

Each of the preceding nodes contains subnodes containing important information related to the problem.

System environment

There are two subnodes in the **System Environment** node: **User and Transaction** and **System Environment**. The first contains technical information about the system; there is also information about memory usage. In the second section, the user will find information about the **User and Transaction**. In this subnode, the user can find out which user caused the error and on which mandate they were logged in.

User View

In this part, the system informs the user what happened in the system at the time of the error. There is also a suggested way to solve the problem, but this information is not usually sufficient for repair. The sample data provided by the SAP system is shown as follows:

```
What happened?
    Error in the ABAP Application Program

    The current ABAP program "!TESTDUMP" had to be terminated because it has
    come across a statement that unfortunately cannot be executed.
```

```
What can you do?
    Note down which actions and inputs caused the error.


    To process the problem further, contact you SAP system
    administrator.

    Using Transaction ST22 for ABAP Dump Analysis, you can look
    at and manage termination messages, and you can also
    keep them for a long time.
```

The preceding screenshot shows that the information is very general. It is rare that this is sufficient to take appropriate action to repair the system. However, the information provides a general picture of the problem, which is useful.

ABAP developer View

The first set of information contains a brief description of the error. This information (as in this case) is often sufficient to locate the source of the problem. An example message is shown here:

```
Short text
    Division by 0 (type I)
```

The next set of information is more detailed. It contains detailed information about what has happened and in which program. Often, there is also information about the exception that should be used:

```
Error analysis
    An exception occurred that is explained in detail below.
    The exception, which is assigned to class 'CX_SY_ZERODIVIDE', was not caught
     and
    therefore caused a runtime error.
    The reason for the exception is:
    In the current program "!TESTDUMP", an arithmetic operation ('DIVIDE',
    '/', 'DIV', or 'MOD') attempted to use operands of type I to divide
    by 0.
```

Information on where terminated gives information about where the error occurred and in which line of code the program was aborted. The developer also has access to the data included in the system variables. Sample information about the system variables is shown in the following screenshot:

Contents of system fields	
Name	Val.
SY-SUBRC	0
SY-INDEX	0
SY-TABIX	1
SY-DBCNT	0
SY-FDPOS	0
SY-LSIND	0
SY-PAGNO	0
SY-LINNO	1
SY-COLNO	1
SY-PFKEY	
SY-UCOMM	
SY-TITLE	
SY-MSGTY	
SY-MSGID	
SY-MSGNO	000
SY-MSGV1	
SY-MSGV2	
SY-MSGV3	
SY-MSGV4	
SY-MODNO	0
SY-DATUM	20190324
SY-UZEIT	171213
SY-XPROG	RSDBRUNT
SY-XFORM	%_INIT_PBO_FIRST

Some of the most important information provided by this tool is **How to correct the error**. This tells you what can be done to fix the error. This is to avoid repeating problems when using the program. In the following example, the system determines which classes to use to handle the exception. This information is important for both experienced programmers and beginners alike. Often, the information contained in this section allows you to eliminate the error. The use of the exception class is also described in this chapter. An example screen is shown in the following screenshot:

```
How to correct the error
    If the error occurred in your own ABAP program or in an SAP
    program you modified, try to remove the error.


    If the error occures in a non-modified SAP program, you may be able to
    find an interim solution in an SAP Note.
    If you have access to SAP Notes, carry out a search with the following
    keywords:

    "COMPUTE_INT_ZERODIVIDE" "CX_SY_ZERODIVIDE"
    "ZTESTDUMP" or "ZTESTDUMP"
    "START-OF-SELECTION"

    If you cannot solve the problem yourself and want to send an error
    notification to SAP, include the following information:

    1. The description of the current problem (short dump)

        To save the description, choose "System->List->Save->Local File
    (Unconverted)".

    2. Corresponding system log

        Display the system log by calling transaction SM21.
        Restrict the time interval to 10 minutes before and five minutes
    after the short dump. Then choose "System->List->Save->Local File
    (Unconverted)".

    3. If the problem occurs in a problem of your own or a modified SAP
    program: The source code of the program
        In the editor, choose "Utilities->More
    Utilities->Upload/Download->Download".

    4. Details about the conditions under which the error occurred or which
    actions and input led to the error.
```

All parts of the tool shown here are valid, but rarely give sufficient information for repair. The next point, however, is the most useful for everyday work. Users have access to information about the code in which the error occurred. After double-clicking, you can go to the place where it will be modified if the user has permission. The following screenshot shows what it looks like:

```
Source Code Extract

Line  SourceCde

    1 *&---------------------------------------------
    2 *& Report   ZTESTDUMP
    3 *&
    4 *&---------------------------------------------
    5 *&
    6 *&
    7 *&---------------------------------------------
    8
    9 REPORT ztestdump.
   10
   11 DATA : lv_count TYPE i VALUE 4,
   12        lv_div    TYPE i,
   13        lv_denom TYPE i VALUE 0.
   14
>>>>> lv_div = lv_count / lv_denom.
```

The preceding screenshot, along with the code, proves that the tool allows you to easily find the problem in the code.

BASIS developer View

This section describes the problems with BASIS. This is very helpful when the error is related to malfunctions on the kernel side. The user gets information about which program was started during the error. This information is rarely important to the programmer, because in most cases, the problem is programming and the solution consists of modifying the existing code. The sample information is shown as follows:

```
Internal notes
    The termination was triggered in function "AbCaliDivr"
    of the SAP kernel, in line 5006 of the module
     "//bas/722_REL/src/krn/runt/abcalc.c#2".
    The internal operation just processed is "ccqi".
    Internal mode was started at 20190331145850.
```

The preceding screenshot shows that the information in this section is relatively short. However, it offers useful data that the BASIS team can use when the problem and error are on their side.

Summary

This chapter covered the testing exceptions concept of ABAP, types of exceptions that have existed from the beginning, and the types we have now. It also offered recommendations on the proper way of handling exceptions, and those situations when situations it is strongly required and in which it is not recommended.

The next chapter describes testing applications written in the ABAP language. This information is vital for every programmer and for technical consultants who work with the SAP system.

Questions

The following questions will allow you to consolidate the information contained in this chapter:

1. How do we implement the exception class?
2. What is the checkpoint group?
3. What is the ABAP Dump Analysis tool for?
4. What transaction triggers the ABAP dump analysis tool?
5. Why should programmers use error handlers?

12
Testing ABAP programs

Testing is an inherent element of software development. You can risk saying that your software will contain smaller or larger errors without performing the relevant tests. There is very common law about this, called Lubarsky's Law.

There's always one more bug.

– Lubarsky's Law

Fortunately, the SAP environment is equipped with a number of tools that allow for convenient work with both automated tests and static code quality testing. While the ABAP language itself has built-in mechanisms for creating unit tests, SAP has also equipped us with a powerful **extended Computer Aided Test Tool** (**eCATT**) to create complex test scenarios that allow the automation of functional tests.

The availability of this type of tool is very important in a solution that is constantly being developed, and subsequent changes may disturb its stability. Rapid regression tests are the foundation of a modern software development process. In this chapter, we will go through all the important techniques and tools that the technical consultant has at their disposal in the SAP environment.

The following topics will be covered in this chapter:

- Static testing with Code Inspector
- **ABAP Testing Cockpit** (**ATC**)
- ABAP Memory Inspector
- Advanced ABAP Debugger techniques
- Testing with eCATT

Technical requirements

The following requirements need to be met to ensure that all examples from this chapter will work:

- **ATC**: Available with EhP2 for SAP NetWeaver 7.0 support package stack 12 (SAP Basis 7.02, SAP Kernel 7.20) and EhP3 for SAP NetWeaver 7.0 support package stack 5 (SAP Basis 7.31, SAP Kernel 7.20).
- **Debugger scripting**: NetWeaver 7.0 EHP2.
- **eCATT**:
    - **Web Application Server (WAS)** 6.20 or above
    - SAPGUI 6.20 or above
    - R/3 4.6C or above (the target system must have a sufficient support package level–details available in SAP Note 519858–or SAP R/3 Enterprise Release 4.7)

All the code used in this chapter can be downloaded from the following GitHub link: `https://github.com/PacktPublishing/Mastering-SAP-ABAP/tree/master/Chapter12`.

Testing the quality of code

Ensuring the high quality of development is much more important than getting things done quickly and cheaply. In this chapter, you will learn the possibilities that SAP can offer to provide better quality code.

Static testing with Code Inspector and ABAP Test Cockpit

Static testing is a technique by which we can check the defects in software without actually executing it. Many of the mistakes made by developers are repeated from one project to another. SAP created a mechanism and implemented a number of test variants, which allows us to check the overall code quality and avoid certain common mistakes. Static tests allow you to check the name convention, detect potential performance problems, and find uncaught exceptions.

If you do not find a ready variant for the repeated problem that you have identified, SAP also provides the option to create your own implementation:

1. For test purposes, we will create new `ZMSA_R_CHAPTER12_1` report from a report template. In the main section, declare the following variables:

```
DATA: lt_bkpf_users TYPE TABLE OF bkpf.
DATA: users_tab TYPE TABLE OF usr02.
DATA: users_structure TYPE usr02.
DATA: lv_message TYPE char128.
```

2. After the variable has been declared, add the following logic:

```
SELECT DISTINCT usnam FROM bkpf INTO CORRESPONDING FIELDS OF TABLE
lt_bkpf_users WHERE bldat = sy-datum.
    SELECT * FROM usr02 APPENDING TABLE users_tab
      FOR ALL ENTRIES IN lt_bkpf_users
      WHERE bname = lt_bkpf_users-usnam.

    LOOP AT users_tab INTO users_structure.
        CONCATENATE 'Hello financial team member, your last login was
at' users_structure-trdat users_structure-ltime
          INTO lv_message SEPARATED BY space.

    CALL FUNCTION 'TH_POPUP'
        EXPORTING
          client = sy-mandt
          user = users_structure-bname
          message = lv_message.
    ENDLOOP.
```

3. This logic takes all users that created financial documents and sends a notification to them. Now, choose **Program** | **Check** | **Code Inspector** from the top menu:

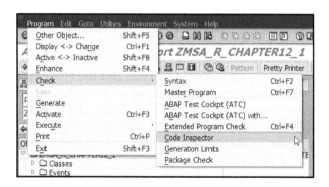

4. **Code Inspector** will give you an overall report of the tests:

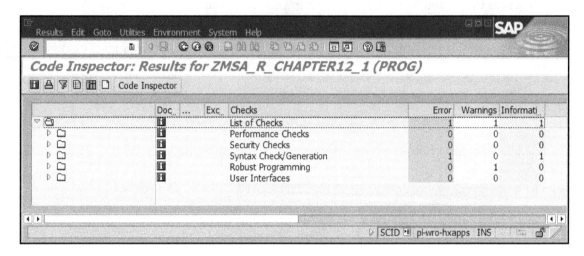

5. We have two errors, one warning error and one information error, and that is just for a default set of rules. If you extend the directory tree, you will see exactly what the problem is:

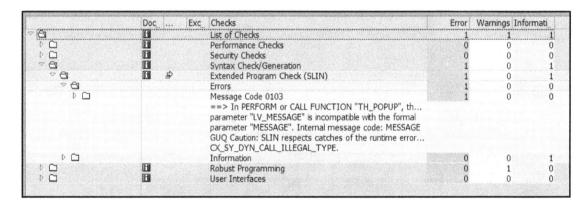

Errors will very often end up with a short dump, so you never should ignore them. Warnings and information errors are less dangerous and the effects are gentler, but they may still cause some performance problems and, in general, they indicate that the quality of the code can be improved. Code Inspector is cool and has a lot of features, but there is an even better test tool. ATC has a powerful functionality that not only allows you to check the code more widely, but it also facilitates the implementation of the testing process in to your daily workflow.

Code Inspector is integrated into ATC, so you can limit yourself to this tool as follows:

1. To run ATC, simply choose **Program** | **Check** | **ABAP Test Cockpit (ATC)**:

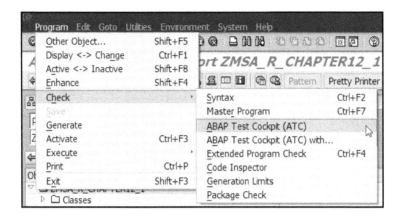

2. This will run the ATC report with a default set of checks. On the next screen, you will see a similar report to the one from **Code Inspector**:

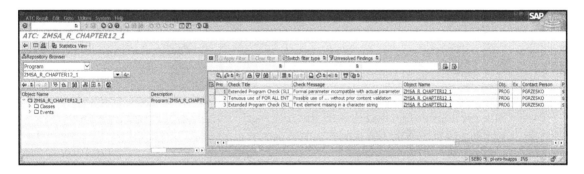

3. To run a custom set of tests, you can choose **Program | Check | ABAP Test Cockpit (ATC)** as shown in the following screenshot:

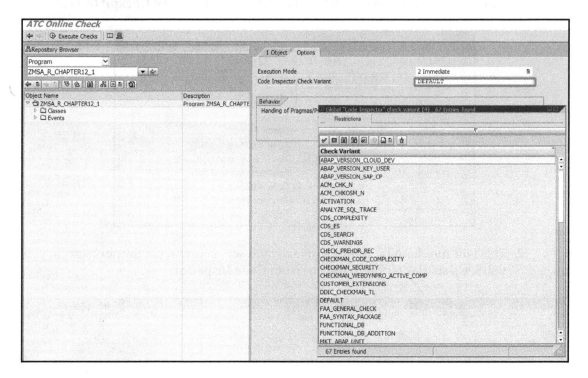

4. You can now choose a **Check Variant** option prepared by SAP. You have a few of these that are related to performance, security, **high-performance analytic appliance (HANA)** readiness, and, of course, a bunch of generic code checks that include best practices. To get even more from ATC, you can go to the ATC transaction itself. You can find tons of useful options here, but probably the most important part is the managing of **Check Variant**. Click on **Mange Check Variants**:

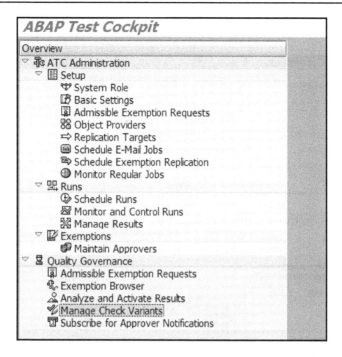

5. This is actually Code Inspector integrated into ATC. You can not only modify existing variants, but also create your own based on the best practices of your company or customer requirements. Click on the **copy** button, as highlighted in the following screenshot:

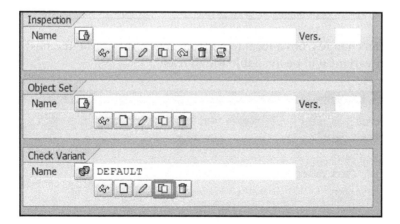

6. Call a new `ZEVENBETTERDEFAULT` variant:

7. Now, click on the **modification** button, as highlighted in the following screenshot:

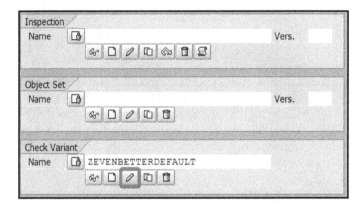

8. You can change from a local to a global check variant on the next screen. The global variant will be available for all users:

You can activate or deactivate specific variants/checks here. You can also change the configuration. You can ask yourself why we need a configuration for a single check, but the answer is very simple. Some checks are client-specific; this could be, for example, a variable naming convention. It's difficult to find two customers that use the same convention for every object.

Activate the **Naming Convention** checks and click on the configurations button, as highlighted in the following screenshot:

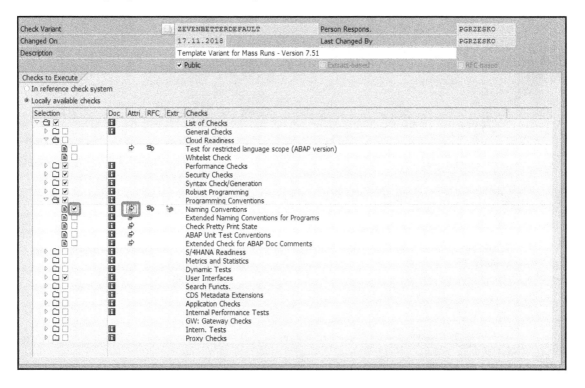

9. You will see tons of options here, but the default settings are sufficient for this example:

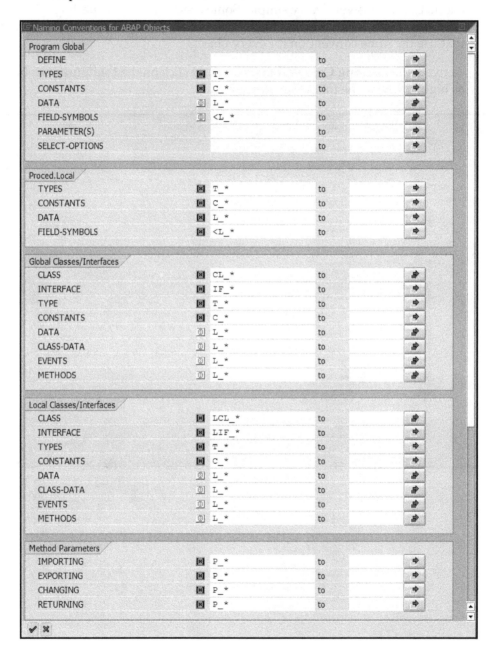

10. Go back to your report and choose **Program | Check | ABAP Test Cockpit (ATC)** with ZEVENBETTERDEFAULT. There will be new warnings related to the naming conversion:

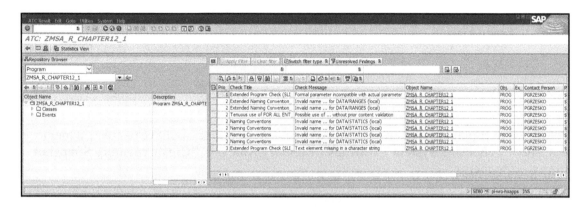

In this subsection, only the basic functionalities of ATC have been presented. Detailed information and advanced settings can be found on the links included in the *Further reading* section.

Testing and troubleshooting

This section is dedicated to all those moments when, despite quality checks and the developer's best efforts, a bug has arisen. The two techniques presented in this section will allow you to more easily solve some of the most frequently encountered problems.

ABAP Memory Inspector

ABAP Memory Inspector is another tool in the developer's toolkit. Its main purpose, as you may guess, is related to memory. Finding memory leaks and predicting memory consumption on the production system may be crucial if you have a system with an enormous amount of data. For this example, we need to create a new ZMSA_R_CHAPTER12_2 report with the following code:

```
REPORT zmsa_r_chapter12_2.

TABLES sscrfields.
DATA: gt_usr TYPE TABLE OF usr02.

SELECTION-SCREEN:
```

```
        PUSHBUTTON 2(10) but1 USER-COMMAND load.
  INITIALIZATION.
    but1 = 'Load Data'.

  AT SELECTION-SCREEN.
    CASE sscrfields.
      WHEN 'LOAD'.
        SELECT * FROM usr02 APPENDING CORRESPONDING FIELDS OF TABLE gt_usr.
    ENDCASE.

  START-OF-SELECTION.
  "do nothing
```

Before we start playing around with ABAP Memory Inspector, we have to create a memory snapshot by choosing **System** | **Utilities** | **Memory Analysis** | **Create Memory Snapshot** from the top menu:

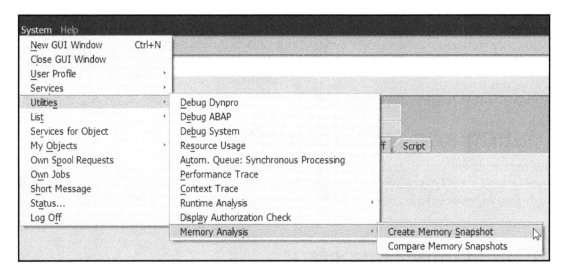

In any transaction, enter /hmusa in the command field:

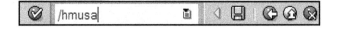

You can also use the CL_ABAP_MEMORY_UTILITIES class in your report and simply call the WRITE_MEMORY_CONSUMPTION_FILE static method. We will use both options, but first, we have to run our report. On the main screen, click the **Load Data** button multiple times, then use method number one. Click on **Load Data** a few more times and save the **Memory Snapshot** again. Go to **Memory Inspector** (the S_MEMORY_INSPECTOR transaction) and you will be able to see your snapshots:

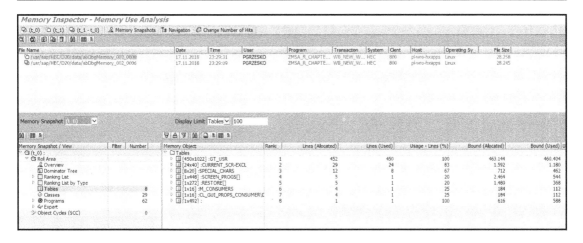

In the bottom section, you can choose, for example, **Roll Area** | **Tables** in order to look at some information about the **Tables** memory consumption. To compare snapshot one with snapshot two, simply choose t_1 - t_0:

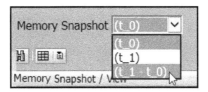

This recalculates the values in the bottom section and displays those parts that have any differences. As you would already suspect, there are differences in the new content of GT_USR table as compared to the GT_USR table in the old snapshot:

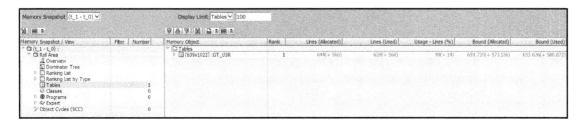

In each column, you can see what exactly has changed. For example, in the **Lines** column in the preceding screenshot, you can see how many rows were added in the GT_USR table between the first and second memory snapshots.

Advanced ABAP debugger techniques

In this section, we will present the operation of one of the more advanced techniques when using the debugger. The debugger allows you to solve problems detected by testers. We will need a new ZMSA_R_CHAPTER12_3 report for this section.

Create a new report from the report template using the following steps:

1. Put the following variable declarations in the main method:

```
DATA: lt_usr TYPE TABLE OF usr02.
DATA: ls_usr TYPE usr02.
DATA: lv_monday TYPE datum.
DATA: lv_sunday TYPE datum.
```

2. After the variable has been declared, add the following program logic:

```
SELECT * FROM usr41 INNER JOIN usr02 ON usr41~bname = usr02~bname
    APPENDING CORRESPONDING FIELDS OF TABLE lt_usr.

LOOP AT lt_usr INTO ls_usr.
  IF ls_usr-bname <> sy-uname.
      CHECK ls_usr-pwdlgndate IS NOT INITIAL.
      CALL FUNCTION 'GET_WEEK_INFO_BASED_ON_DATE'
      EXPORTING
        date = sy-datum
      IMPORTING
        monday = lv_monday
        sunday = lv_sunday.

      IF ls_usr-pwdlgndate >= lv_monday AND ls_usr-pwdlgndate <=
lv_sunday. .
        WRITE /: 'This user last password change was within this
week:', ls_usr-bname .
```

This report reads the currently active user on the system and reports when they last changed their password. It may be difficult to test this program, due to the fact that you may be the only one on the system and the user may never change their password.

3. To test this, we need to somehow manipulate the data. To test the report, we will create a debugger script that will edit values for us. First, we need to set up a breakpoint by clicking on the marked line:

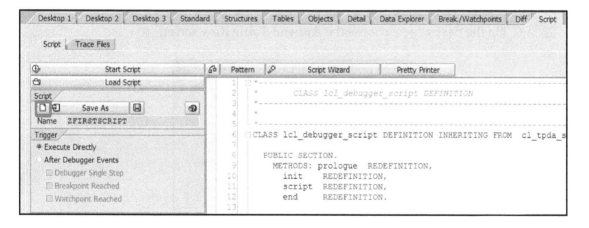

4. Now, run the report. The debugger will start immediately. Go to the **Script** tab and click on the **Create Script** button:

5. On the next popup, fill in the description and name of the script. By default, the script source is set to the database, but you could also set the local file and save everything on the frontend PC. This will allow you to move the script from one system to another. We will create our script by using the script wizard. Click on the **Script Wizard** button:

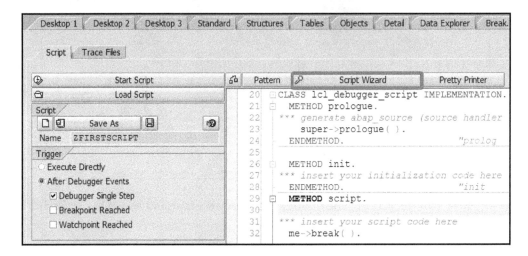

6. On the next screen, choose the **Append Table Row** script:

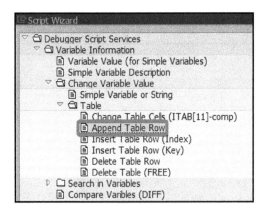

This will add the following code template:

```
CALL METHOD CL_TPDA_SCRIPT_TABLEDESCR=>APPEND_LINE
    EXPORTING
        P_NEW_VALUES_IT =
        P_TABLE_NAME =
        .
```

7. `P_NEW_VALUES_IT` is the table of values that we want to add, and `p_table_name` is the name of the internal table we want to modify. Change the code to get the following:

```
DATA: lt_values TYPE tpda_scr_change_itab_it.
    DATA: ls_values TYPE LINE OF tpda_scr_change_itab_it.

    ls_values-compnr = 2.
    ls_values-value = 'TESTUSR1'.
    APPEND ls_values TO lt_values.

    ls_values-compnr = 39.
    ls_values-value = sy-datum.
    APPEND ls_values TO lt_values.

    TRY.
        CALL METHOD cl_tpda_script_tabledescr=>append_line
          EXPORTING
            p_new_values_it = lt_values
            p_table_name = 'LT_USR'.
      CATCH cx_tpda_sys_symb .
      CATCH cx_tpda_sys_auth .
    ENDTRY.
```

8. Column number 2 refers to the user-name and will have a `'TESTUSR1'` value. Column 39 refers to the password change date. We need to change the trigger to **Execute Directly** and then we can start the script:

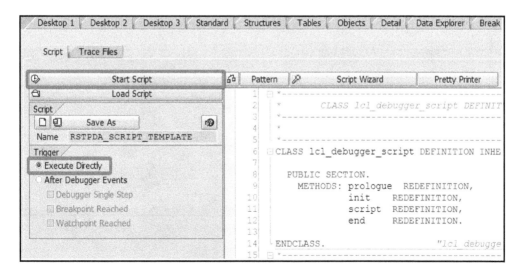

9. If you go to the **Desktop** tab and check the values of the `lt_usr` table, you should now see an additional row:

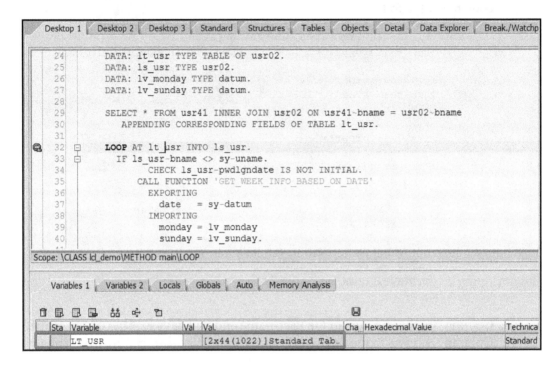

10. If you double-click on the row counts, you will see the exact values that we have added:

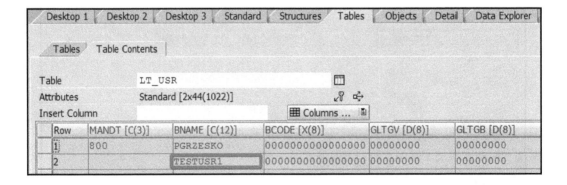

11. If you click on the **Continue** button (or use the keyboard shortcut, *F8*), you will see the following results:

```
Program ZMSA_R_CHAPTER12_3


Program ZMSA_R_CHAPTER12_3

This user last password change was within this week:
TESTUSR1
```

This basic example should give you a basic understanding of debugger scripting, and this technique will now be another useful tool for testing your applications.

Testing with eCATT

eCATT is another tool for testing our software. It is used to automate functional tests and create test scripts, so it is closer to business than technology than it was in the two previous cases. Thanks to eCATT, we can simulate user behavior.

In this section, we will create a simple example of using eCATT for our reports using the following steps:

1. First, create a new ZMSA_R_CHAPTER12_4 report and add the following parameter and variables' declaration:

```
REPORT zmsa_r_chapter12_4.

DATA: lv_result TYPE string.

PARAMETERS: p_num1 TYPE int4.
PARAMETERS: p_num2 TYPE int4 .
PARAMETERS: p_radio1 RADIOBUTTON GROUP rad1.
PARAMETERS: p_radio2 RADIOBUTTON GROUP rad1.
PARAMETERS: p_radio3 RADIOBUTTON GROUP rad1.
PARAMETERS: p_radio4 RADIOBUTTON GROUP rad1.
PARAMETERS: p_result TYPE string NO-DISPLAY.
```

2. In the `AT SELECTION-SCREEN` section, add the following arithmetical operations:

```
AT SELECTION-SCREEN.
       CLEAR: p_result.
       CASE abap_true.
         WHEN p_radio1.
           p_result = p_num1 + p_num2.
         WHEN p_radio2.
           p_result = p_num1 - p_num2.
         WHEN p_radio3.
           p_result = p_num1 * p_num2.
         WHEN p_radio4.
           IF p_num2 IS INITIAL OR p_num2 = 0.
             p_result = 'N/A'.
           ELSE.
             p_result = p_num1 / p_num2.
           ENDIF.
         WHEN OTHERS.
       ENDCASE.
       MESSAGE p_result TYPE 'S'.
```

3. Don't forget to add the parameter's text in the **Text Symbols** menu:

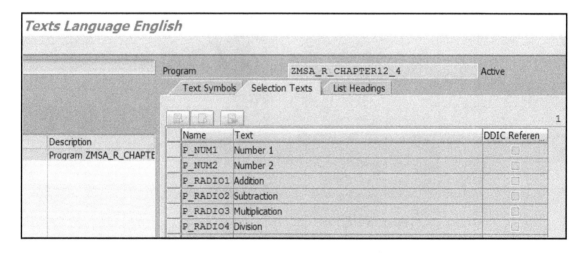

4. We also need to create a transaction code. Go to **Maintain Transaction** (transaction SE93), choose the **Transaction Code** of your choice, and click on the **Create** button:

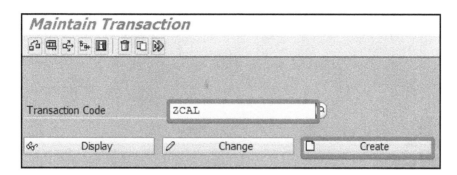

5. In pop-up window, set **Short text** and click the green checkmark button to save:

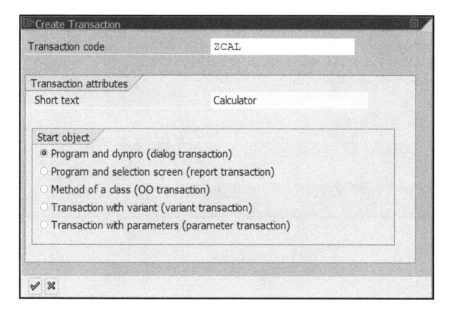

6. Fill in the **Program** name and screen number on the **Create Dialog Transaction** screen:

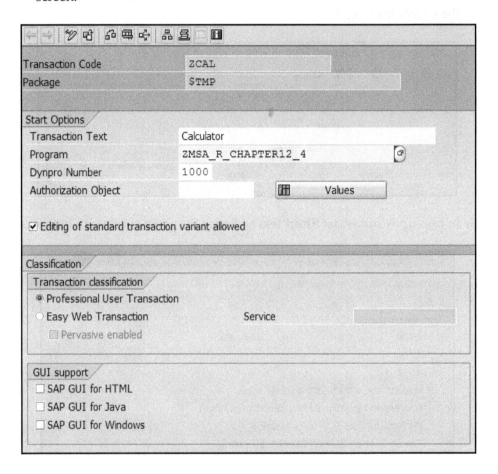

7. Save everything and go to **eCATT** (transaction `SECATT`):

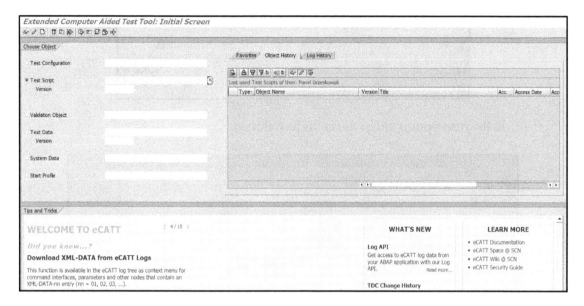

8. We need to create a test script to test the calculator function. We would like to check every `Calculator` function, such as adding and subtracting. Name the **Test Script** as `ZCALTEST` and hit the **Create** button. On the next screen, choose **Title** and **Application Component**, then click on the **save** button highlighted in the following screenshot:

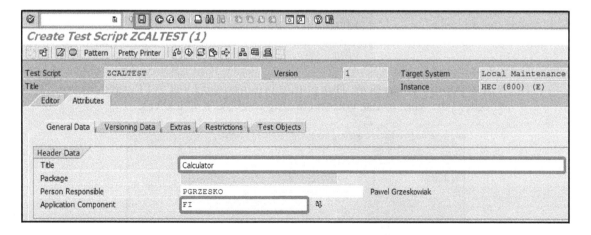

9. Now, we need to use **Pattern** to create a **Test Script**:

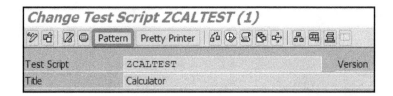

10. In the next popup, fill in the fields as follows:

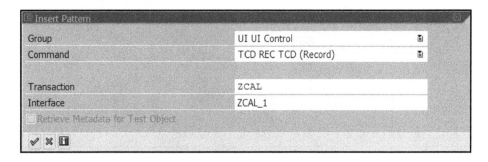

11. Provide the number parameters and click on the **Execute** button:

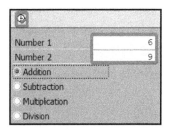

12. A new popup will appear. This popup is generated by eCATT and asks you whether you want to use your recording in eCATT. Click **Yes**:

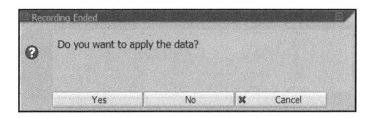

13. In the main screen, click on the **ZCAL_1** interface name on the left-hand side of the screen. This will open the records for you in the middle section. Navigate to the following section:

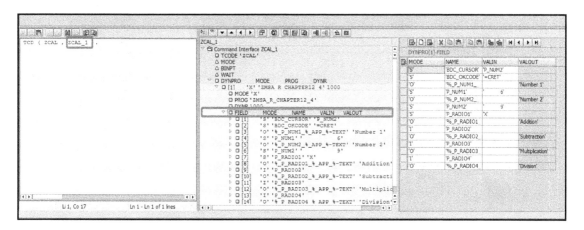

14. We need to modify some parts of the screen to make it more useful. As a start, we will define all of our fields dynamically. This concerns the customization of the number field values and radiobuttons. First, change the static value for the parameter name of the P_NUM1 field:

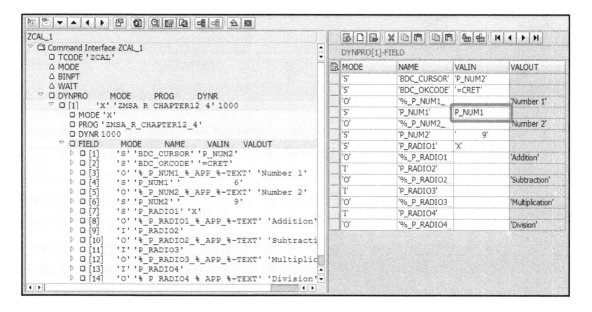

15. You will be asked to create a parameter:

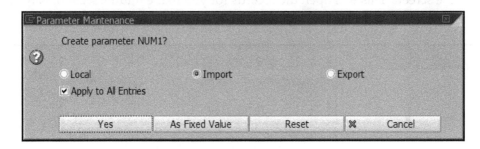

16. Repeat the same steps for **P_NUM2** and the **NAME** of **P_RADIO1**:

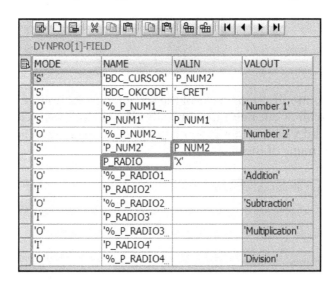

We will have three input parameters, but we need to create something for the results. Click on the **create** button highlighted in the following screenshot, and add the following line:

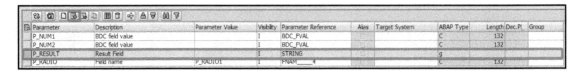

We also need to add the following coding just below the **TCD** record:

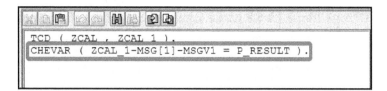

```
TCD ( ZCAL , ZCAL_1 ).
CHEVAR ( ZCAL_1-MSG[1]-MSGV1 = P_RESULT ).
```

17. This will compare the output message of our calculator with the expected result.
    We can test our script now. Save everything and click on the **execute** button
    highlighted in the following screenshot:

On the next screen, we need to go to the **Parameters** tab and fill in the **Parameter Value**:

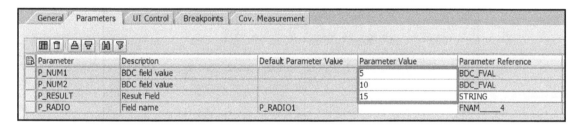

Parameter	Description	Default Parameter Value	Parameter Value	Parameter Reference
P_NUM1	BDC field value		5	BDC_FVAL
P_NUM2	BDC field value		10	BDC_FVAL
P_RESULT	Result Field		15	STRING
P_RADIO	Field name	P_RADIO1		FNAM____4

18. Again, click on the execute button, and you will see the test results:

```
▽ 📘 0000000005 Test Script ZCALTEST Version 1 - SECATT [W/o Interruption] [1 s]
  ▷ 🗶 HEC 800 PGRZESKO (Pawel Grzeskowiak) E 752 pl-wro-hxapps Linux HDB 20.11.2018 12:38:27
  ▷ ⓘ Test Caller
  ▷ 🗗 Start Options XML-DATA-01
  ▽ ▢ ZCALTEST Version 1 [      0,118] My first
    ▷ ▶◻ IMPORT ZCALTEST
    ▷ ▢ TCD    ZCAL    [0,050 / SUT: 0,003 N] Calculator
        S00001 15
    ▷ ▢ CHEVAR ( ZCAL_1-MSG[1]-MSGV1 = P_RESULT )
       ◻▸ EXPORT ZCALTEST
```

19. The green square icon close to CHEVAR means that the test was passed. So far, so good, but we would like to create multiple test examples to automatically test all the other variants. Go back to the main **eCATT** screen and create a new **Test Configuration**:

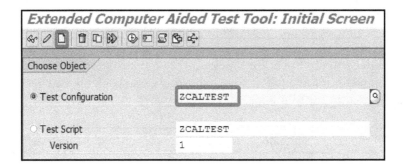

On the first **Test Configuration** screen, fill in the description and area:

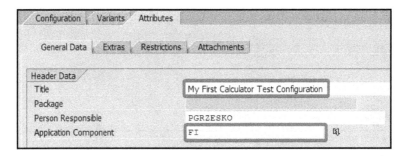

20. Switch to the **Configuration** tab and fill in your **Test Script** name:

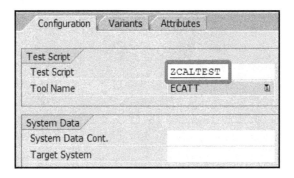

21. Now, switch to the **Variants** tab and add as many examples as you need:

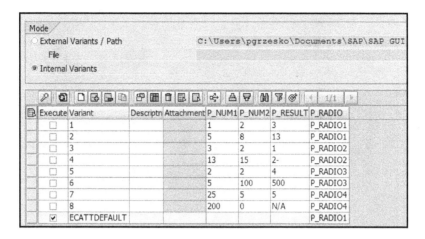

Save everything and execute **Test Configuration**. On the next screen, go to the **Variant** tab and make sure that new variants are active:

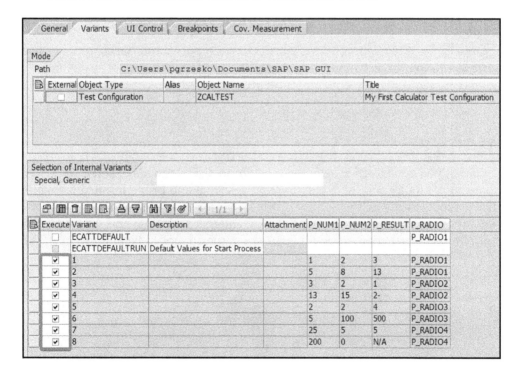

Now, you can execute the test (press *F8*) and check the results:

```
▽ ▲ ▼   2 Expand Levels   ▲   Expand Error   ⚓ ▣   ⊞

▽ 🗓 0000000007 Test Configuration ZCALTEST - SECATT [W/o Interruption] [3 s]
   ▷ ▦ HEC 800 PGRZESKO (Pawel Grzeskowiak) E 752 pl-wro-hxapps Linux HDB 20.11.2018 12:56:17
   ▷ ❶ Test Caller
   ▷ 🖳 Start Options XML-DATA-01
   ▽ 🗒 ZCALTEST  [        2,036]   My First Calculator Test Configuration
      ▷ 🗗 Version Finding -> XML-DATA-05
      ▷ ▢ ZCALTEST  Version 1 [        0,196]   Variant 1
      ▷ ▢ ZCALTEST  Version 1 [        0,063]   Variant 2
      ▷ ▢ ZCALTEST  Version 1 [        0,063]   Variant 3
      ▷ ▢ ZCALTEST  Version 1 [        0,063]   Variant 4
      ▷ ▢ ZCALTEST  Version 1 [        0,132]   Variant 5
      ▷ ▢ ZCALTEST  Version 1 [        0,064]   Variant 6
      ▽ ▢ ZCALTEST  Version 1 [        0,173]   Variant 7
         ▷ ▷▢ IMPORT  7
         ▷ ▢ TCD      ZCAL [0,047 / SUT: 0,003 N] Calculator
              S00001 5
         ▽ ▢ CHEVAR  ( ZCAL 1-MSG[1]-MSGV1 = P RESULT )
              ZCAL_1-MSG[1]-MSGV1  =  5
              P RESULT             =  5
         ▷▶ EXPORT  7
      ▷ ▢ ZCALTEST  Version 1 [        0,238]   Variant 8
```

As you can see, this tool gives you a very transparent report about the current application status. Implementing this type of testing will allow you to avoid a lot of stress and frustration on systems that are already in the production phase.

Summary

In this chapter, you have learned why the most important elements of software development are quality and the ability to analyze errors and problems. SAP provides a broad base of tools to ensure the quality (Code Inspector and ATC) and test your software and speed up the error repair process (eCATT, Debugger Scripting, and ABAP Memory Inspector). In the next chapter, you will learn about the advanced techniques in ABAP Objects.

Questions

The following questions will allow you to consolidate the information contained in this chapter:

1. What is the name of the ATC variant that checks whether the code will work on S4/HANA?
2. Which ATC variant would you use to check code performance?
3. Which ABAP command can you use in code to turn off the ATC checks?
4. What method can you use to add a line to a table in the debugger script?
5. A debugger script can be executed directly or after a debugger step. What debugger steps are available for this purpose?
6. What type of command is used to record the transaction flow in eCATT?
7. What types of dynamic parameters are available for eCATT?

Further reading

You may also want to check out the following:

- **Debugger scripting**: https://help.sap.com/saphelp_nw70ehp2/helpdata/en/68/c9bbb62be34d2eaac1c5d3ccd2ba48/content.htm?no_cache=true
- **ATC**: https://help.sap.com/viewer/ba879a6e2ea04d9bb94c7ccd7cdac446/7.51.4/en-US/491aa66f87041903e10000000a42189c.html
- **eCatt**: https://www.sap.com/documents/2015/07/eac23283-527c-0010-82c7-eda71af511fa.html

13
Advanced Techniques in ABAP Objects

Object-oriented programming (OOP) refers to the process of programming by defining objects, which combines state and behavior (combined data and procedures—in this case, methods). An object program is created as a collection of these objects, which communicate with each other. This approach is different than procedural programming, where data and procedures are not connected. OOP is useful when writing application and code maintenance. With OOP, you can use the same piece of code (a method) in order to program actions that are repeated in the code.

The biggest asset of OOP is its compatibility with the human brain's way of perceiving things, which naturally combines objects with actions.

We will cover the following topics in this chapter:

- Technical requirements
- The creation of global and local classes in ABAP
- The differences between static and instance methods and attributes
- The creation of a nested class
- The event concept
- ABAP Objects design patterns

Technical requirements

ABAP Objects was introduced by SAP as an extension of the ABAP on SAP Basis Release 4.5. In the 4.6 release, SAP provided the complete version of ABAP Objects by introducing inheritance.

All the code used in this chapter can be downloaded from the following GitHub link: `https://github.com/PacktPublishing/Mastering-SAP-ABAP/tree/master/Chapter13`.

Global versus local classes

In ABAP, we can create classes in two ways: locally or globally. The main differences are that local classes can be used only in the program in which the class is created, while a global class can be used in every program or function module. Also, the ways in which these classes are created are different. In a local class, we need to create a definition and implementation of the class in the program, and, in a global class, the definition and implementation are created in the class builder.

We create global classes more often than local classes because it's possible to reuse them. If we want to use a local class in a different program, we need to create the same local class in that program, which is not necessary for a global class.

Creating a local class

To create a class, first we need to create a definition of it. In this definition, we can create types, data, class data, and methods and inheritance.

It is necessary to explain the differences between data and class data. Along with the creation of data, an instance attribute is created. Analogically, with class data, a static attribute in a class is created.

In the following example, there are two different visibility sections: public and private. In general, there are three visibility options in ABAP:

- **Public**: Public methods and public attributes are visible outside the class, and the parameters can also be changed from the outside.
- **Protected**: Protected methods or attributes are visible outside of the class but the values cannot be modified.
- **Private**: Private methods or attributes are neither visible outside of the class, nor can they be modified.

To create a definition of a class, we use CLASS name_of_class DEFINITION.

An example of the definition for the class named cl_auto is as follows:

```
*---------------------------------------------------------------*
*           CLASS cl_auto DEFINITION
*---------------------------------------------------------------*
*
*---------------------------------------------------------------*
CLASS cl_auto DEFINITION.
  PUBLIC SECTION.
    TYPES: t_fuel TYPE i,
           t_brand  TYPE char20,
           t_model  TYPE char20.
    CONSTANTS: tank_cap TYPE t_fuel VALUE 70.
    DATA: brand TYPE t_brand.

    CLASS-DATA: numb_of_cars TYPE i.

    METHODS: refuel IMPORTING iv_fuel TYPE t_fuel
                    EXCEPTIONS no_space,
             constructor IMPORTING iv_brand TYPE t_brand,
             get_fuel_status EXPORTING ev_fuel TYPE t_fuel.

  PRIVATE SECTION.
    DATA: fuel TYPE t_fuel.
    METHODS: check_space IMPORTING iv_fuel TYPE t_fuel
                         RETURNING value(available_space) TYPE t_fuel.

ENDCLASS.                           "cl_auto DEFINITION
```

In the preceding definition, in the PUBLIC section, there are three types: one constant, one instance attribute, one static attribute, and three methods. In the PRIVATE section, there is one instance attribute and one method.

However, the definition is only one part of the class. Equally important is its implementation. To create an implementation, we use the IMPLEMENTATION keyword, as shown in the following code block, which is an example of the implementation of the cl_auto class.

Here is an example of the implementation of the cl_auto class:

```
*-------------------------------------------------------------------*
*       CLASS cl_auto IMPLEMENTATION
*-------------------------------------------------------------------*
*
*-------------------------------------------------------------------*
CLASS cl_auto IMPLEMENTATION.
  METHOD constructor.
    brand = iv_brand.
    ADD 1 TO numb_of_cars.
  ENDMETHOD.                      "constructor
  METHOD check_space.
    available_space = tank_cap - fuel.
  ENDMETHOD.                      "check_space
  METHOD refuel.
    IF check_space( iv_fuel ) >= iv_fuel.
      ADD iv_fuel TO fuel.
    ELSE.
      RAISE no_space.
    ENDIF.
  ENDMETHOD.                      "refuel

  METHOD get_fuel_status.
    ev_fuel = fuel.
  ENDMETHOD.                      "get_fuel_status
ENDCLASS.                         "cl_auto IMPLEMENTATION
```

As presented in the preceding code block, during the implementation, only the implementation of the method is being created, meaning pieces of code will be executed after calling methods.

In this process, no additions (such as the visibility of methods) are needed. All of the parameters are in the definition.

Creating a global class

A global class can be created in an SE24 transaction.

The initial screen of this transaction looks as follows:

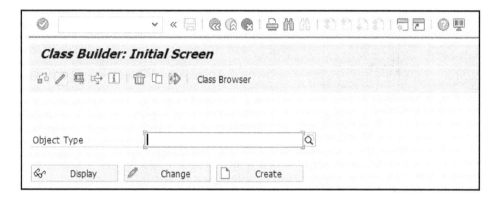

In **Object Type**, we can pass the name of the class that will be created, or pass the name of a class that has already been created in order to edit it. If we want to create the same cl_auto class, we need to rename it, as global classes need to be created with a Z or Y prefix. In our example, the class will be named ZCL_AUTO.

After typing the name of the class, we have to choose whether we want to create a class or an interface.

This selection will be made in the next pop-up window, as presented in the following example. Choose **Class** and click on the **OK** button (interfaces will be discussed later in this chapter):

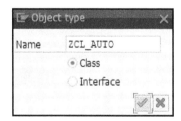

In the next window, we need to add a **Description** and choose the **Class Type**:

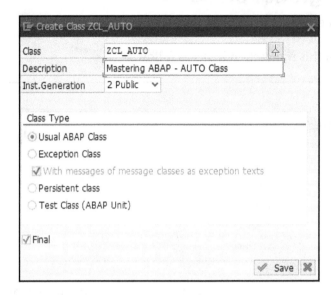

On this screen, inheritance can also be chosen and/or a class can be made a **Final** class. This subject will be covered in detail later in this chapter while discussing nesting. Also, we can choose the **Class Type**, but we'll only discuss Usual ABAP Class; other types of classes will be explained later. Once all the obligatory values have been defined, you can click on **Save**. Then, you need to choose package and transport or local object and a new class will be created.

The next screen looks as follows:

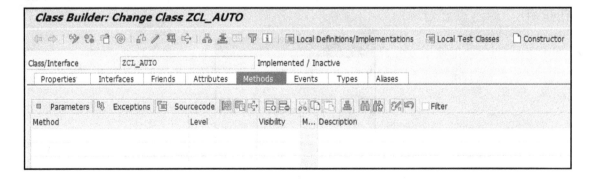

Now, create the **Attributes**, **Methods**, and **Types**.

After the class has been created, the screens will look like the following examples.

An example of **Attributes** is as follows:

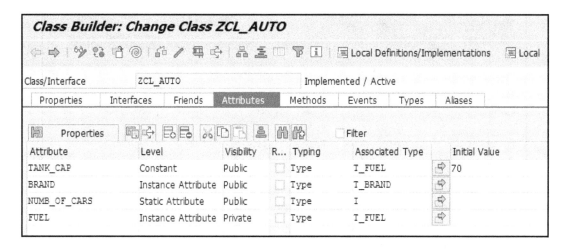

An example of **Methods** is as follows:

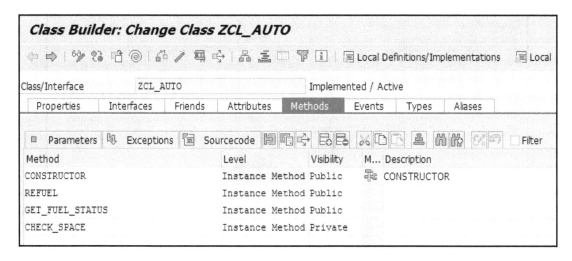

An example of **Types** is as follows:

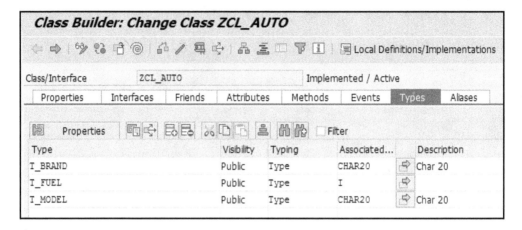

Furthermore, an example of parameters in the **REFUEL** method is as follows. This can be shown after selecting the method and clicking on **Parameter**:

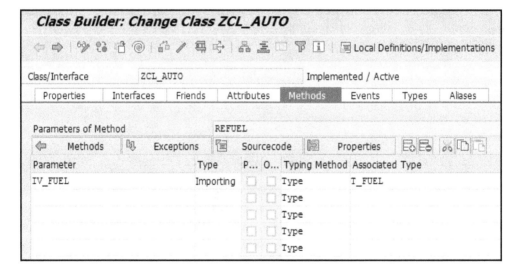

As you can see in the preceding screenshots, all of the properties, such as the type of the parameters or the level of a variable, are defined in this tool. In SE24, we can define all of the things that were previously defined in the local class's definition.

When we want to create an implementation of a method, we can double-click on the name of the method. In the following example, we can see the implementation of the **REFUEL** method:

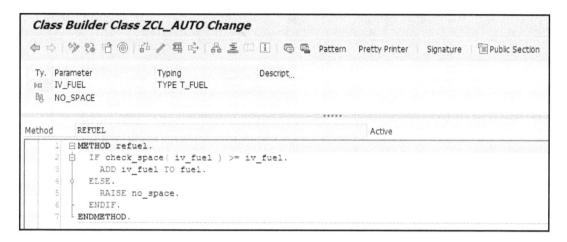

One very useful advantage of the class builder is also showing all of the parameters and exceptions of the displayed method, but that can be toggled on/off by the **Signature** button.

The static method versus the instance method

When we want to create our software in ABAP OOP technology, we need to know the differences between static and instance methods as well. The same is applicable for attributes.

Why are these differences so important? Imagine we have a car and we want to accelerate by 10 km/h. In this case, we would need to press the gas pedal for the car to accelerate. In Objects, we can describe this as using the Accelerate method, which changes the SPEED instance attribute in the instance of the CAR class. This example shows us that an action should not be made without reference to something.

When we speak about static attributes, these can be changed without reference to any object. Also, a static method can be executed without any reference. Instance attributes or an instance method can be used only with reference to the object on which the operation is to be performed.

Instances of the same class can be created multiple times during runtime, but static attributes can be created only once. To call a static method or access a static attribute with its class name directly, we can use the => operator.

For example, if we want to call the CHECK static method of the ZCL_CLASS class without any parameters or exceptions, the code would look as follows:

```
ZCL_CLASS=>CHECK( ).
```

Alternatively, it would look like this to change the NAME static attribute in the same class:

```
ZCL_CLASS=>NAME = "Mastering ABAP".
```

However, if we want to change a static attribute in an object or call a static method in an object, we need to use the -> operator.

The following example is a call for a static method in the GR_OBJECT object. For the CHECK method, this would look as follows:

```
GR_OBJECT->CHECK( ).
```

The code for changing the NAME attribute is shown as follows:

```
GR_OBJECT->NAME = "Mastering ABAP".
```

If we wanted to perform the same operation on instance attributes, the code would look similar, but the first example, with the direct call for a method of a class, would not be able to proceed, as we need to make that call with reference to the object.

For example, if we wanted to call the instance method, we would use the following:

```
GR_OBJECT->INSTANCE_CHECK( ).
```

Before using objects, we need to create an object with reference to the class using a CREATE OBJECT statement. As an example of using this operation, we can use a class from *Creating a global class* section:

```
DATA: lo_auto1 TYPE REF TO zcl_auto,
      lv_fuel TYPE i.

CREATE OBJECT lo_auto1
  EXPORTING
    iv_brand = 'AUDI'.

WRITE: 'Name of car:', lo_auto1->brand.
NEW-LINE.
WRITE: 'Number of cars in class CL_AUTO:', zcl_auto=>numb_of_cars."
```

```
NEW-LINE.
CALL METHOD lo_auto1->refuel
  EXPORTING
    iv_fuel   = 50
  EXCEPTIONS
    no_space = 1.

IF sy-subrc = 0.
  WRITE: 'Car refuelled'.
  lo_auto1->get_fuel_status( IMPORTING ev_fuel = lv_fuel ).
  NEW-LINE.
  WRITE: 'Amount of fuel:', lv_fuel.
ELSE.
  WRITE: 'No space in the tank'.
ENDIF.
```

In the preceding example, we created an object with reference to the zcl_auto class and using all of the defined methods.

Understanding the differences between the static and instance methods and attributes is one of the most important aspects of OOP, which helps to correctly use the possibilities that object-oriented writing offers us.

Nested classes

In ABAP OOP, we can nest classes in three ways:

- A class as an attribute of the class
- Inheritance
- Using interfaces

Interfaces are not really a full class. This is due to the fact that, in interfaces, we have only a definition of a class without any implementation. This is important because interfaces in ABAP allow us to implement multi-inheritance. However, we'll turn to that in a moment, in the *Inheritance* and *Interfaces* section.

All examples will be shown as a global class created in SE24.

A class as an attribute of the class

We can create a class as an attribute of the class. To create that attribute, we need to add an attribute, which is typed as TYPE REF TO. In our example, we'll create an attribute as a reference to the ZCL_ENGINE class:

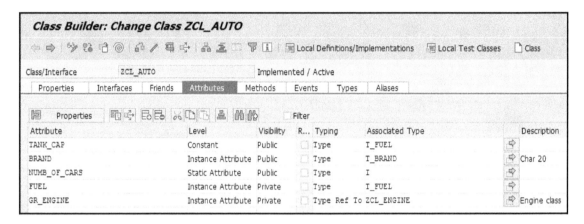

In the preceding example, we created an attribute named GR_ENGINE as an attribute of the ZCL_AUTO class. After the instantiation of ZCL_AUTO and the initialization of its GR_ENGINE attribute, a new object of the ZCL_ENGINE class is created inside ZCL_AUTO. Then, the GR_ENGINE reference can be freely used inside the ZCL_AUTO class's methods, and—if the property is defined as public—outside of it.

The ZCL_ENGINE object is tightly bound to ZCL_AUTO and its lifecycle is limited to the existence of the ZCL_AUTO object—once ZCL_AUTO is destroyed, so is ZCL_ENGINE.

Inheritance

First of all, we need to speak about what inheritance is. Inheritance is one of the features of the OOP paradigm. According to the paradigm, inheritance organizes and supports polymorphism and encapsulation, facilitating the definition and creation of a specialized object based on a more general one.

As an example, I used one of the most commonly used examples of a class named ZCL_CAR. All vehicles have wheels, an engine, and a fuel tank. But, if we speak about a more specific vehicle, for example, a truck, we also want to know how much of a load that truck can carry. So, to create a class for the truck, we can call it ZCL_TRUCK, and we can inherit the ZCL_CAR class, as we have some parameters that the truck also has. We also inherited attributes of the class and methods.

But, remember: we inherited only attributes and methods that have a visibility status that is not private.

We can also use the ZCL_CAR class multiple times. For example, if we want to create the ZCL_BUS class, an attribute that is important, is how many passengers the bus will accommodate. We can inherit the ZCL_CAR class and add this attribute to the class attributes.

Many classes can inherit from another class, but a class can inherit from only one class at a time.

To allow inheritance, when we create the class, we need to unmark the Final checkbox. If the final checkbox is checked, this class cannot be inherited:

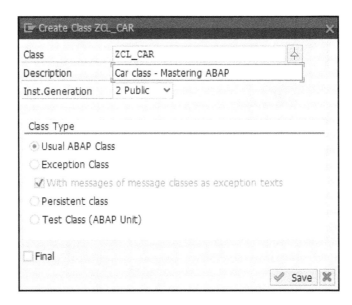

In the `ZCL_CAR` class, attributes look like the following:

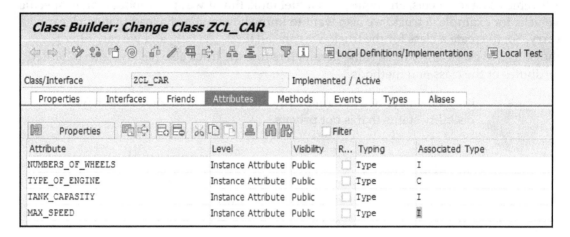

To create inheritance, we need to click on the button within the red box in the following screenshot:

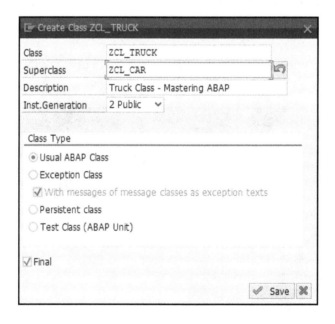

The pop-up window should look like the following example, wherein the name of the inherited class has been entered into the **Superclass** box:

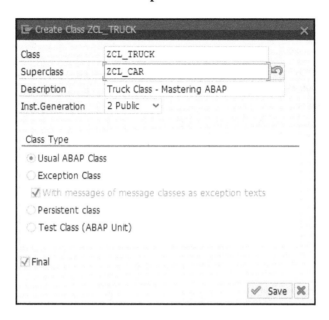

After clicking on **Save**, we can see our class:

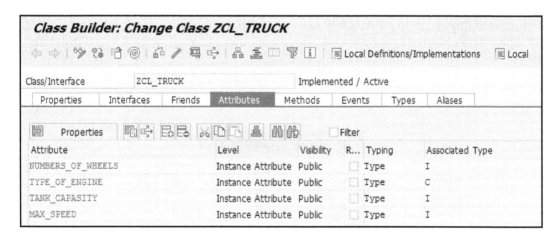

Attributes written in blue are inherited from the ZCL_CAR class and are now parts of the ZCL_TRUCK class, which means we can directly use them in the ZCL_TRUCK class.

Also, methods are inherited. If we want to redefine methods, we need to click on Redefine Method .

For example, for the truck, we need to do something more than for a regular car. After clicking on Redefine Method, we have two possibilities. We can define a whole new method or we can use the code from the superclass. To call the method from the superclass, we need to use the **super|name_of_method** statement.

In the following example, we can see the method from the superclass, as follows:

```
METHOD start_engine.
   CALL METHOD super->start_engine.

ENDMETHOD.
```

Interfaces

As I mentioned previously, interfaces are a special type of class, possessing only definition parts (attributes, the names of methods, and the parameters of methods, but without the implementation of those methods).

Interfaces are important in ABAP OOP because, with them, we can perform some sort of multi-inheritance, which is not possible using just inheritance, described in the previous section.

To create an interface, we need to put the name of the interface in an SE24 transaction (in our example, ZIF_AUTO), and, in the pop-up window, we need to choose the following:

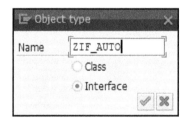

After clicking on **OK**, we need to choose a **Description**, for example, as shown in the following screenshot, and click **Save**:

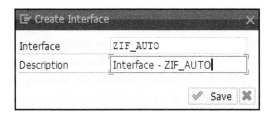

After selecting package and transport or a local package, we get a screen like this:

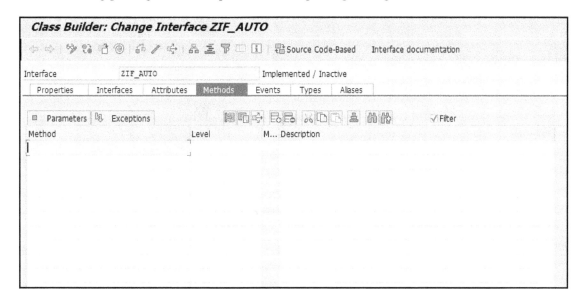

In here, we can define all elements as in a class, but the implementation cannot be created.

If we want to add interfaces to a class, we need to move into the SE24 main window in the class, to the **Interfaces** sub-tab, and enter the name of the interface, as shown here:

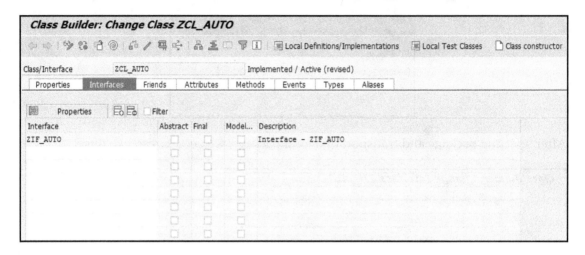

After pressing the **ENTER** button, you can see the method of this interface in the **Method** tab:

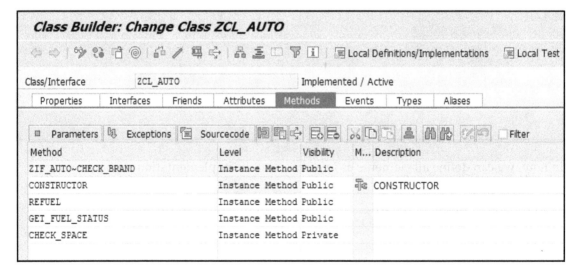

Right now, we can implement something in this method, as in a normal method.

Here, I need to mention aliases in classes. The names of interfaces and the methods of those interfaces can be really long. In order to avoid using long names in code, we can use aliases. To change them, we need to go to the **Aliases** tab and choose a name.

In the following example, I use the name CHECK_BRAND, and when I want to use this method, I can call it by using the name CHECK_BRAND instead of ZIF_AUTO~CHECK_BRAND:

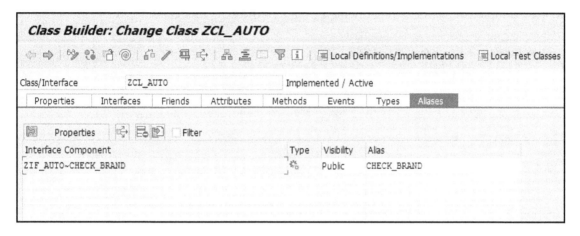

Now, let's have a look at the concept of an event in the next section.

The event concept

Events in ABAP are characterized by occurring at a specified point of time. An event can be executed, for, example when we create a new account or post a document, and, if the event includes changing the status of an object, another interested object will be informed of the situation.

To every event, we can assign a method, which will be called when the event is raised. We can also assign the same event handler to a different object and, thanks to that, the object will be able to react when an event is raised. In contrast to methods that affect only the process in which they are called, an event can cause any number of event handlers to be called globally.

If several event handlers are registered for one event, these are called in the sequence in which they were registered. An event can also have output parameters, which are defined using the normal method. Event handlers can also be called directly. This is helpful when you want an event handler to handle an event without being registered.

To create an event, we have to create it in the **Events** tab in **SE24**.

In the example, we have an event named BROKE in the ZCL_CAR class:

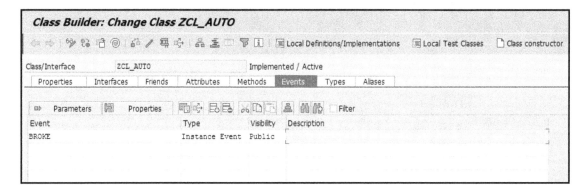

To create a method called when the **BROKE** event is called, we need to create a method or use an existing method. In the preceding example, a method named BROKE_CAR is created.

 The names of a method and an event cannot be the same!

To register this method as a method that's called when the event is raised, we need to click on the Go to **Properties** icon.

In the pop-up window, we need to check the **Event Handler for** checkbox. In the next step, specify the event name and **Class/interface** name and click on **Change**.

In our example, the properties of the method will look as follows:

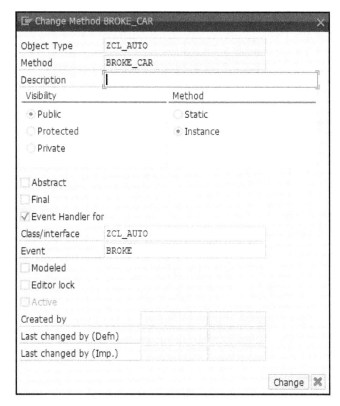

After clicking the **Change** button, the method will be registered as a method called after the event.

Last but not least, is registering the event. To register the event, we need to use the SET HANDLER statement.

For instance, this statement is as follows:

```
SET HANDLER gr_car->broke_car FOR gr_car.
```

But, if we have a class event, the event is registered as follows:

```
SET HANDLER zcl_auto=>broke_car .
```

When a handler is created, the event can be raised and the class to which it was set will react by calling the method assigned to the event.

To raise the event, use the RAISE statement, for example:

```
RAISE EVENT broke_car.
```

ABAP Objects design patterns

One of the most important things when speaking about OOP is design patterns. But what are design patterns? A design pattern is a universal, tested-in-practice guide for frequently occurring, repetitive design issues.

 Design patterns are a description of a solution, not the implementation of a solution.

Design patterns can be described using four basic elements:

- The name of the pattern
- **Problem**: How to recognize situations when we should use a particular pattern to ensure the use of a pattern is justified
- **Solution**: Describes elements of a solution, their relations, connections, and duties
- **Consequences**: A list of advantages and disadvantages of a pattern

Design patterns can be divided into three sets according to their purpose:

- **Creational**: Describes the process of creating a new object, the initialization, and the configuration of objects or classes
- **Structural**: Describes the structure of related objects
- **Behavioral**: Describes the behavior of cooperating objects

Over the next few pages, I will describe two design patterns of each type presented above.

Prototype - creation pattern

The purpose of the **Prototype Pattern** is to offer the option of creating multiple classes based on one class: a prototype. This pattern can be created when we want a large number of objects of the same type or when we need to create a collection of almost the same object.

Here's an example implementation of a prototype in ABAP:

The `zcl_car` class is the class that creates an abstract definition of new cars:

```
CLASS zcl_car DEFINITION ABSTRACT.
   PUBLIC SECTION.
     METHODS:
       clone ABSTRACT
         IMPORTING
                      iv_color         TYPE string
         RETURNING VALUE(ro_object) TYPE REF TO zcl_car.

   ENDCLASS.                    "zcl_car_data DEFINITION
```

In the following class, is the definition of every prototype with the implementation of how a car should be built:

```
CLASS zcl_car_detail DEFINITION INHERITING FROM zcl_car.
   PUBLIC SECTION.
     METHODS: clone REDEFINITION.
     METHODS: constructor
       IMPORTING iv_type TYPE string.
     DATA: type_of_car TYPE string,
           color_car   TYPE string.
   ENDCLASS.                    "zcl_car_Detail DEFINITION
   CLASS zcl_car_detail IMPLEMENTATION.
     METHOD constructor.
       super->constructor( ).
       type_of_car = iv_type.
     ENDMETHOD.                 "create_car
     METHOD clone.
       DATA: lr_car TYPE REF TO zcl_car_detail.
       CREATE OBJECT lr_car
         EXPORTING
           iv_type = me->type_of_car.
       lr_car->color_car = iv_color.
       ro_object = lr_car.
     ENDMETHOD.                 "clone
   ENDCLASS.                    "zcl_car_detail IMPLEMENTATION
```

What follows here is the implementation of the `factory` class. This class *produces* a new car from the definition of the `zcl_car_detail` class:

```abap
CLASS zcl_factory DEFINITION.
    PUBLIC SECTION.
      METHODS:
        get_car
          IMPORTING iv_name        TYPE string
                    iv_color       TYPE string
          RETURNING VALUE(rv_car) TYPE REF TO zcl_car,
        constructor.
    PRIVATE SECTION.
      TYPES:
        BEGIN OF ts_prototype,
          name      TYPE string,
          prototype TYPE REF TO zcl_car,
        END OF ts_prototype,
        tt_prototypes TYPE STANDARD TABLE OF ts_prototype.
      DATA lt_prototypes TYPE tt_prototypes.
ENDCLASS.                    "zcl_factory DEFINITION
CLASS zcl_factory IMPLEMENTATION.
  METHOD constructor.
    DATA ls_prototype TYPE ts_prototype.
    ls_prototype-name = 'Car1'.
    CREATE OBJECT ls_prototype-prototype TYPE zcl_car_detail
      EXPORTING
        iv_type = 'Car1'.
    APPEND ls_prototype TO lt_prototypes.
  ENDMETHOD.
  METHOD get_car.
    READ TABLE lt_prototypes WITH KEY name = iv_name ASSIGNING FIELD-
SYMBOL(<fs_prototype>).
    IF sy-subrc = 0.
      rv_car = <fs_prototype>-prototype->clone( iv_color ).
    ENDIF.
  ENDMETHOD.
ENDCLASS.                    "zcl_factory IMPLEMENTATION
```

The main program to use the factory class is presented here:

```abap
START-OF-SELECTION.
  DATA: lr_factory TYPE REF TO zcl_factory,
        lr_car     TYPE REF TO zcl_car.
  CREATE OBJECT lr_factory.
  lr_car = lr_factory->get_car( EXPORTING iv_name = 'Car1' iv_color =
'Blue' ).
```

The following are the advantages of the Prototype Pattern:

- New instances are created more quickly.
- Code is more organized and easier to read.

The following are the disadvantages of the Prototype Pattern:

- Excessive use of this pattern may cause the linking of objects that are not connected.
- There is no easy way to modify the output of objects.

Singleton - creation pattern

The **Singleton Pattern** is a creational pattern used for creating one instance of a class and to use that instance as a global point of access. This means that the instance of this class cannot be created more than once. If we want to create a new instance of this class, we first need to destroy the previous instance.

But, sometimes, the Singleton pattern is treated as an anti-pattern. Why? Singleton as a pattern is not a problem but it is often badly used. Programmers use singleton like a global variable. Singleton also makes code harder to refactor and maintain. Sometimes, we find out that we need more than one instance, but we cannot create them because a Singleton Pattern has been used. In that case, it may turn out that it is necessary to redesign the whole program in order to implement the desired change.

To create a singleton class, we need to avoid initiating the class outside of a class. How can we achieve that?

We need to create a private instance constructor. So, if a developer wanted to use this constructor, it would be impossible, as this method is private and can be used only inside this class. But that's not everything. To create an instance of this class, we also need a static constructor. As we know, a static constructor is run only once at runtime, when any static method of a class is called. So, we need to call an instance constructor inside of the static constructor.

An example of implementing the Singleton pattern in ABAP is as follows:

```
CLASS zcl_singleton DEFINITION CREATE PRIVATE.
 PUBLIC SECTION.

 CLASS-DATA: lr_singleton TYPE REF TO zcl_singleton.

 CLASS-METHODS: class_constructor,
```

```
run.

PRIVATE SECTION.
METHODS constructor.

ENDCLASS.

CLASS zcl_singleton IMPLEMENTATION.
METHOD class_constructor.
   IF zcl_singleton=>lr_singleton IS NOT BOUND.
     CREATE OBJECT zcl_singleton=>lr_singleton.
    ENDIF.
ENDMETHOD.

METHOD run.
ENDMETHOD.

METHOD constructor.
WRITE: 'Singleton instances created'.
ENDMETHOD.
ENDCLASS.

START-OF-SELECTION.
zcl_singleton=>run( ).
```

The following are the advantages of the singleton pattern:

- The user is neither involved nor responsible for creating a class instance.
- Instance creation is done only once, which saves time if the procedure is time-consuming.
- The number of instances is controlled by the class itself.

The following are the disadvantages of the Singleton Pattern:

- Testing singleton is sometimes troublesome
- Code pieces are linked together more, which may contradict the separation of concerns rule.
- It binds together instance management and business process handling.
- It is often misused as a global variable in the form of a class.

Facade - structural pattern

The **Facade pattern** can be used to create a single point of access to a complex system by issuing a simplified, structured programming interface that facilitates its use. It is frequently used when we want to hide some part of implementation from the user, for example, when they want to create an order.

The user sees only the interface used to create orders, but in the backend, classes and methods are necessary to process this order, for example, as follows:

- Checking the availability of the product
- Filling in the form
- Paying the check
- Creating data for the delivery

The facade pattern is built with these three elements:

- **A complex system**: In our example, this is a system to create an order.
- **Facade**: A class whose one and only purpose is to communicate with other classes via the backend, which has references to those classes.
- **Client**: Any code interested in using a complex system.

An example of the facade pattern in ABAP follows here:

1. The interface is created. This interface will be used by the facade to connect with the classes behind the facade:

```
INTERFACE lif_order.
    METHODS: create_order.
ENDINTERFACE.
```

2. Create a definition of the classes that will be using the interface and aliases, in order to shorten the interface methods' names:

```
CLASS zcl_check DEFINITION.
    PUBLIC SECTION.
      INTERFACES: lif_order.
      ALIASES: create_order FOR lif_order~create_order.
    ENDCLASS.
    CLASS zcl_fill_form DEFINITION.
      PUBLIC SECTION.
        INTERFACES: lif_order.
        ALIASES: create_order FOR lif_order~create_order.
    ENDCLASS.
    CLASS zcl_pay DEFINITION.
```

```
      PUBLIC SECTION.
        INTERFACES: lif_order.
        ALIASES: create_order FOR lif_order~create_order.
    ENDCLASS.
    CLASS zcl_create_delivery DEFINITION.
      PUBLIC SECTION.
        INTERFACES: lif_order.
        ALIASES: create_order FOR lif_order~create_order.
    ENDCLASS.
```

3. The following code shows the definition of the facade itself:

```
CLASS zcl_facade DEFINITION.
    PUBLIC SECTION.
      METHODS: process_order.
    PRIVATE SECTION.
      DATA: lr_check TYPE REF TO zcl_check,
            lr_fill  TYPE REF TO zcl_fill_form,
            lr_pay   TYPE REF TO zcl_pay,
            lr_deliv TYPE REF TO zcl_create_delivery.
    ENDCLASS.
```

4. The next code block is an example of the implementation of methods that the facade is connected to:

```
CLASS zcl_check IMPLEMENTATION.
    METHOD lif_order~create_order.
      WRITE: / 'Check availability of product: OK '.
    ENDMETHOD.
  ENDCLASS.
  CLASS zcl_fill_form IMPLEMENTATION.
    METHOD lif_order~create_order.
      WRITE: / 'Filling the form: OK'.
    ENDMETHOD.
  ENDCLASS.
  CLASS zcl_pay IMPLEMENTATION.
    METHOD lif_order~create_order.
      WRITE: / 'Pay the check: OK'.
    ENDMETHOD.
  ENDCLASS.
  CLASS zcl_create_delivery IMPLEMENTATION.
    METHOD lif_order~create_order.
      WRITE: / 'Create data for delivery: OK'.
    ENDMETHOD.
  ENDCLASS.
```

5. The implementation of the main facade class is as follows:

```
CLASS zcl_facade IMPLEMENTATION.
   METHOD process_order.
      CREATE OBJECT: lr_check, lr_fill, lr_pay, lr_deliv.
      lr_check->create_order( ).
      lr_fill->create_order( ).
      lr_pay->create_order( ).
      lr_deliv->create_order( ).
   ENDMETHOD.
ENDCLASS.
```

6. An example of implementing the main app using facade is as follows:

```
START-OF-SELECTION.

   DATA: gr_facade TYPE REF TO zcl_facade.
   CREATE OBJECT gr_facade.
   gr_facade->process_order( ).
```

The following are the advantages of the facade pattern:

- It separates the user from the complex implementation of the system; the user does not directly use any of the system elements, thanks to making the connection easier to maintain.
- It separates applications into layers, limiting the dependencies between them.
- It may prevent the unintended use of sensitive parts of the system.

The following is a disadvantage of the facade pattern:

- Failure of the interface (caused, for example, by high load) can make the whole system unusable. There are, however, protective measures against this.

Decorator - structural pattern

The **Decorator design pattern** allows the dynamic assignment of new behaviors to a given object. Decorators give flexibility similar to that offered by inheritance, but they provide much-extended functionality. When used, inheritance objects can be changed only before running a program. However, the decorator can change an object during runtime, because the decorator can change the operations of any component by using the additional code in relation to the decorated object being called.

The following is an example of decorator implementation.

1. Define the abstract definition of a document:

```
CLASS doc_output DEFINITION ABSTRACT.
   PUBLIC SECTION.
     METHODS:
       doc_output ABSTRACT.
   ENDCLASS.
```

2. In the following fragment of code is the definition and implementation of the standard SD document:

```
CLASS sd_doc_output DEFINITION INHERITING FROM doc_output.
   PUBLIC SECTION.
     METHODS:
       doc_output REDEFINITION.
   ENDCLASS.
   CLASS sd_doc_output IMPLEMENTATION.
    METHOD doc_output.
      WRITE: / 'Standard SD doc output'.
    ENDMETHOD.
   ENDCLASS.
```

3. In the following code block, we are creating the definition and implementation of the decorator:

```
CLASS zcl_decorator DEFINITION INHERITING FROM doc_output.
   PUBLIC SECTION.
     METHODS:
       constructor
         IMPORTING ir_decorator TYPE REF TO doc_output,
       doc_output REDEFINITION.
   PRIVATE SECTION.
     DATA: lr_decorator TYPE REF TO doc_output.
   ENDCLASS.
   CLASS zcl_decorator IMPLEMENTATION.
    METHOD constructor.
      super->constructor( ).
      me->lr_decorator = ir_decorator.
    ENDMETHOD.
    METHOD doc_output.
      CHECK lr_decorator IS BOUND.
      lr_decorator->doc_output( ).
    ENDMETHOD.
   ENDCLASS.
```

4. Now create the first decorated class, as follows:

```
CLASS zcl_inquiry DEFINITION INHERITING FROM zcl_decorator.
  PUBLIC SECTION.
    METHODS: doc_output REDEFINITION.
ENDCLASS.
CLASS zcl_inquiry IMPLEMENTATION.
 METHOD doc_output.
   WRITE: / 'Generating Inquiry'.
 ENDMETHOD.
ENDCLASS.
```

5. And now create the rest of the decorated classes (created in a similar way to the first one), as follows:

```
CLASS zcl_contract DEFINITION INHERITING FROM zcl_decorator.
  PUBLIC SECTION.
    METHODS: doc_output REDEFINITION.
ENDCLASS.
CLASS zcl_contract IMPLEMENTATION.
 METHOD doc_output.
   WRITE: / 'Generating Contract'.
 ENDMETHOD.
ENDCLASS.
 CLASS zcl_sched_agree DEFINITION INHERITING FROM zcl_decorator.
  PUBLIC SECTION.
    METHODS: doc_output REDEFINITION.
ENDCLASS.
CLASS zcl_sched_agree IMPLEMENTATION.
 METHOD doc_output.
   WRITE: / 'Generating Scheduling Agreements'.
 ENDMETHOD.
ENDCLASS.
CLASS zcl_sales_order DEFINITION INHERITING FROM zcl_decorator.
  PUBLIC SECTION.
    METHODS: doc_output REDEFINITION.
ENDCLASS.
CLASS zcl_sales_order IMPLEMENTATION.
 METHOD doc_output.
   WRITE: / 'Generating Sales Order'.
 ENDMETHOD.
ENDCLASS.
CLASS  zcl_deliv_doc DEFINITION INHERITING FROM zcl_decorator.
  PUBLIC SECTION.
    METHODS: doc_output REDEFINITION.
ENDCLASS.
CLASS zcl_deliv_doc IMPLEMENTATION.
 METHOD doc_output.
```

```
            WRITE: / 'Generating Delivery document'.
          ENDMETHOD.
        ENDCLASS.
```

6. The following code shows the definition and implementation of the main class, where all of the decorated classes are created:

```
CLASS zcl_main DEFINITION.
  PUBLIC SECTION.
    CLASS-METHODS:
      run.
ENDCLASS.
CLASS zcl_main IMPLEMENTATION.
 METHOD run.
    DATA: lr_decorator       TYPE REF TO doc_output,
          lr_decorator_inq   TYPE REF TO doc_output,
          lr_decorator_cont  TYPE REF TO doc_output,
          lr_decorator_sched TYPE REF TO doc_output,
          lr_decorator_sales TYPE REF TO doc_output,
          lr_decorator_deliv TYPE REF TO doc_output.
    CREATE OBJECT lr_decorator TYPE sd_doc_output.
    CREATE OBJECT lr_decorator_inq TYPE zcl_inquiry
      EXPORTING
        ir_decorator = lr_decorator.
    CREATE OBJECT lr_decorator_cont TYPE zcl_contract
      EXPORTING
        ir_decorator = lr_decorator.
    CREATE OBJECT lr_decorator_sched TYPE zcl_sched_agree
      EXPORTING
        ir_decorator = lr_decorator.
    CREATE OBJECT lr_decorator_sales TYPE zcl_sales_order
      EXPORTING
        ir_decorator = lr_decorator.
    CREATE OBJECT lr_decorator_deliv TYPE zcl_deliv_doc
      EXPORTING
        ir_decorator = lr_decorator.
    lr_decorator->doc_output( ).
    lr_decorator_inq->doc_output( ).
    lr_decorator_cont->doc_output( ).
    lr_decorator_sched->doc_output( ).
    lr_decorator_sales->doc_output( ).
    lr_decorator_deliv->doc_output( ).
  ENDMETHOD.
ENDCLASS.
```

7. Finally, the following fragment of code is used to start the main class:

```
START-OF-SELECTION.
  zcl_main=>run( ).
```

The following are the advantages of the Decorator pattern:

- This approach is more flexible than inheritance, as decorators may be applied dynamically on demand.
- It breaks up functionality into separate classes, which makes coding simpler.

The following are the disadvantages of the Decorator pattern:

- It results in a great number of small objects, similar to each other. This may lead to problems with understanding the relations between them.
- It becomes difficult, or even impossible, to compare decorated objects, as the result of decoration is different than the source object.

Observer - behavioral pattern

The observer pattern consists of an object that we call the *observed object*, and a number of observer objects. There is a one-to-many relationship here. The object is observed by the data manager, who informs all the observers about changes in the data that it contains. It is the only rightful owner of this data.

When observers get information that the data has changed, they collect it from the observed object and update the data of the observers. The observer itself can decide whether it wants to continue observing an object, but the observed object can also remove it from the list of observers. The observer does not know any other observers; they are independent of each other. Any modification of one observer does not affect the others.

The pattern is characterized by the ease with which new followers can be added. We'll create a new class that will implement the observer interface. The observing object itself can be observed (composition).

The observer pattern works wherever the state of one object depends on the state of another object.

An example of observer implementation in ABAP is presented below and starts with the definition of the application simulation:

```
CLASS zcl_app DEFINITION.
    PUBLIC SECTION.
        CLASS-METHODS: run.
    ENDCLASS.
```

The definition of observer is shown here:

```
CLASS zcl_observer DEFINITION.
    PUBLIC SECTION.
        TYPES:
          BEGIN OF t_user,
            username TYPE string,
          END OF t_user,
          tt_user TYPE TABLE OF t_user.
        DATA: lt_user TYPE tt_user.
        METHODS: create_doc IMPORTING doc_type TYPE string,
          constructor.
        EVENTS: new_document_created EXPORTING VALUE(doc_type) TYPE string.
    ENDCLASS.
```

In the following fragment of code is the abstract definition of users:

```
CLASS zcl_user DEFINITION ABSTRACT.
    PUBLIC SECTION.
        METHODS: on_notification_received ABSTRACT FOR EVENT
new_document_created OF zcl_observer
        IMPORTING doc_type.
    ENDCLASS.
```

The next code block defines two separate classes for creating users:

```
CLASS zcl_user1 DEFINITION INHERITING FROM zcl_user.
    PUBLIC SECTION.
        METHODS on_notification_received REDEFINITION .
    ENDCLASS.
CLASS zcl_user2 DEFINITION INHERITING FROM zcl_user.
    PUBLIC SECTION.
        METHODS on_notification_received REDEFINITION.
    ENDCLASS.
```

The implementation of the observer class is presented in the following code:

```
CLASS zcl_observer IMPLEMENTATION.
    METHOD create_doc.
        RAISE EVENT new_document_created EXPORTING doc_type = doc_type.
    ENDMETHOD.
```

```
    METHOD constructor.

      DATA: ls_user TYPE t_user.

      CLEAR ls_user.
      ls_user-username = 'user1'.
      APPEND ls_user TO lt_user.

      CLEAR ls_user.
      ls_user-username = 'user2'.
      APPEND ls_user TO lt_user.

    ENDMETHOD.
  ENDCLASS.
```

The implementation of the first and second classes for creating users is as follows:

```
CLASS zcl_user1 IMPLEMENTATION.
    METHOD on_notification_received.
      WRITE: / 'Notification User1 - New document', doc_type .
    ENDMETHOD.
  ENDCLASS.
  CLASS  zcl_user2 IMPLEMENTATION.
    METHOD on_notification_received.
      WRITE: / 'Notification User2 - New document', doc_type.
    ENDMETHOD.
  ENDCLASS.
```

The following fragment is the penultimate step – the implementation of the simulation app:

```
CLASS zcl_app IMPLEMENTATION.
    METHOD run.
      DATA: lr_observer TYPE REF TO zcl_observer,
            lr_user1    TYPE REF TO zcl_user1,
            lr_user2    TYPE REF TO zcl_user2.
      CREATE OBJECT: lr_observer.
      CREATE OBJECT: lr_user1.
      CREATE OBJECT: lr_user2.
      SET HANDLER lr_user1->on_notification_received FOR lr_observer.
      SET HANDLER lr_user2->on_notification_received FOR lr_observer.
      lr_observer->create_doc( 'Order' ).
      lr_observer->create_doc( 'Invoice' ).
    ENDMETHOD.
  ENDCLASS.
```

And last but not least, here's the fragment of code to start the app:

```
START-OF-SELECTION.

    zcl_app=>run( ).
```

The following are the advantages of the observer pattern:

- The observer and observed object are not tightly coupled; they can be extended independently.
- The assignment of the observer to the observed object is created dynamically at runtime.
- The observed object does not need to implement an additional subscription mechanism.

The following is the disadvantage of the observer pattern:

- Observers are created independently and are not aware of each other. This may lead to unexpected side effects.

Strategy - behavioral pattern

The strategy pattern is a family of algorithms. The algorithms are created as separate program classes, fully interchangeable during runtime. At the top, we have a class that chooses an algorithm (but only one), which will be executed. When using this pattern, adding a new algorithm is as simple as creating a new implementation of the interface.

Modifying the algorithm just involves a modification of the proper method, as all algorithms are encapsulated into one method per algorithm. The strategy does not use inheritance, but only the implementation of the interface, so unnecessary linking is not created between the algorithm and methods using the algorithm. Using this method of behavior modification, the factory pattern is very useful for creating a proper class.

The strategy can be used whenever we need to solve a problem in many different ways.

The following is an example implementation.

Firstly, create an interface, which will be implemented in a strategy:

```
INTERFACE lif_vat.

  TYPES: t_price TYPE p LENGTH 10 DECIMALS 2.

  METHODS: calculate_vat
    IMPORTING
              iv_price               TYPE t_price
    RETURNING VALUE(rv_gross_price) TYPE t_price.
ENDINTERFACE.
```

Now create a definition and implementation of `material`, for which VAT will be calculated using various strategies:

```
CLASS zcl_material DEFINITION.

  PUBLIC SECTION.

    TYPES: t_price TYPE p LENGTH 10 DECIMALS 2.

    METHODS: constructor
      IMPORTING iv_vat TYPE REF TO lif_vat.

ENDCLASS.

CLASS zcl_material IMPLEMENTATION.
  METHOD constructor.

    DATA: lv_gross_price TYPE t_price.

    lv_gross_price = iv_vat->calculate_vat( iv_price = 1000 ).

    WRITE: / 'Material gross price:', lv_gross_price.

  ENDMETHOD.
ENDCLASS.
```

The definition and implementation of the first strategy are as follows:

```abap
CLASS zcl_vat7 DEFINITION.
  PUBLIC SECTION.

    INTERFACES lif_vat.

    ALIASES: calculate_vat FOR lif_vat~calculate_vat.

ENDCLASS.

CLASS zcl_vat7 IMPLEMENTATION.
  METHOD calculate_vat.

    rv_gross_price = iv_price + ( iv_price * '0.07' ).

  ENDMETHOD.
ENDCLASS.
```

The second strategy can be defined and implemented as follows:

```abap
CLASS zcl_vat32 DEFINITION.

  PUBLIC SECTION.

    INTERFACES lif_vat.

    ALIASES: calculate_vat FOR lif_vat~calculate_vat.

ENDCLASS.

CLASS zcl_vat32 IMPLEMENTATION.
  METHOD calculate_vat.

    rv_gross_price = iv_price + ( iv_price * '0.32' ).

  ENDMETHOD.
ENDCLASS.
```

The following fragment of code creates a definition and implementation of the main application:

```abap
CLASS zcl_mainapp DEFINITION.
  PUBLIC SECTION.
    CLASS-METHODS run.
ENDCLASS.
```

```
CLASS zcl_mainapp IMPLEMENTATION.
  METHOD run.

    DATA: lr_vat7     TYPE REF TO zcl_vat7,
          lr_vat32    TYPE REF TO zcl_vat32,
          lr_material1 TYPE REF TO zcl_material,
          lr_material2 TYPE REF TO zcl_material.

    CREATE OBJECT: lr_vat7,
                   lr_vat32.

    CREATE OBJECT lr_material1
      EXPORTING
        iv_vat = lr_vat7.

    CREATE OBJECT lr_material2
      EXPORTING
        iv_vat = lr_vat32.

  ENDMETHOD.
ENDCLASS.
```

The last step is to start the main application, as follows:

```
START-OF-SELECTION.

  zcl_mainapp=>run( ).
```

The following are the advantages of the strategy pattern:

- Less conditional programming.
- Implementation is determined at runtime.
- It simplifies the process of adding new implementations.
- It allows the debugging of each strategy, making it easier to test them.

The following are the disadvantages of the strategy pattern:

- It adds another layer of complexity.
- The implementation of a single functionality is spread over several objects.

Summary

Using ABAP Objects can be really helpful in day-to-day work. This way of programming offers the possibility of creating code in small functional parts, which can be helpful when code needs to be refactored or when the code will be reused in many different places. In this chapter, we learned all about how to create different classes in ABAP, the differences between static and instance methods and attributes, the concept of an event, and ABAP Objects design patterns.

In the next chapter, we will focus on how to integrate SAP systems into third-party systems.

Questions

The following questions will allow you to consolidate the information contained in this chapter:

1. What are the main differences between global and local classes?
2. What are the differences between a class and an interface?
3. What are design patterns?

14
Integrating SAP with Third-Party Systems

This chapter focuses on how to build a stable and error-free connection of a **Systems Applications and Products in Data Processing** (**SAP**) system using non-SAP software. The method of solving this task may vary significantly depending on multiple factors, from the number of funds available to the customer to the level of the developer's proficiency. Here, we will try to clarify the range of options that a typical developer has.

The following topics will be covered in this chapter:

- Ways of connecting with legacy systems
- The **Intermediate Document** (**IDoc**) in SAP:
    - Differences between IDoc and **Electronic Data Interchange** (**EDI**)
    - The **Application Link Enable** (**ALE**) framework
- Running programs remotely through the **Business Application Programming Interface** (**BAPI**)
- SAP Gateway
- **Open Data Protocol** (**OData**)
- Developing our first OData application

Technical requirements

The following requirements need to be met to get all of the examples in this chapter to work:

- **For working with OData services**: You will require SAP NetWeaver Gateway, which is included in SAP NetWeaver 7.40+ (the minimum components are `SAP_GWFND` or `GW_CORE` with `IW_FND`)
- **For IDoc**: IDocs from SAP systems Release 3.1x or higher is supported
- **For ALE**: ALE is available with SAP Release 3.0

All the code used in this chapter can be downloaded from the following GitHub link: `https://github.com/PacktPublishing/Mastering-SAP-ABAP/tree/master/Chapter14`.

IDoc

In this section, we will describe a very important part of the SAP system—IDoc. IDoc is frequently used with the SAP system; it is a very friendly technology that does not cause many difficulties during implementation. There are also other integration possibilities that will be described later in this chapter. A user of the SAP system must be familiar with IDoc because it is likely that they will encounter this solution on a daily basis.

IDoc overview

IDoc is a standard data structure that is used to exchange information between any two processes in SAP system applications and external systems. IDocs are used for asynchronous transactions. The structure of an IDoc structure is very similar to XML. An IDoc can be triggered in the EDI subsystem or in the SAP system. In the case of the inbound process, EDI converts data and the IDoc is created in SAP. When the process is successful, IDoc is available for other types of processing in an SAP system. An Outbound IDoc is triggered in SAP and is sent to the EDI subsystem. Once there, it is usually converted to XML format. Then, the EDI subsystem sends a message to the target system.

The construction of IDoc

An IDoc consists of three blocks, as follows:

- The Control Record
- The Data Record
- The Status Record

The **Control Record** contains information such as the type of IDoc, the port of the partner, the type of message, the sender and receiver, and more. The **Data Record** is a block that contains the application data. The **Status Record** gives data about the status of the IDoc (for example, the IDoc created, and whether the recipient exists).

The structure of IDoc is displayed in the following diagram:

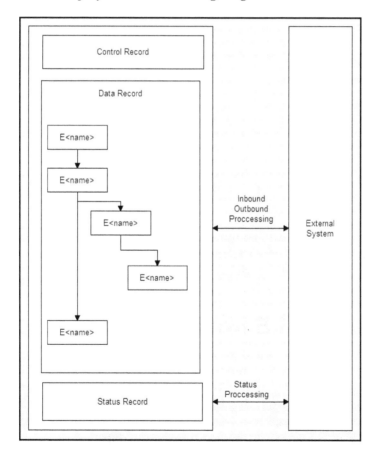

The structure that is shown in the preceding diagram is very well designed and can be widely used for business processes. If you need to expand the structure, then the designer does not have to learn about a very complex and scattered object. This is a big advantage of using IDoc.

The EDI system

The EDI system is used to exchange business documents. EDI reduces errors and processing time when transferring data between two systems.

ALE

ALE is a tool that is used for exchanging data between the SAP R/3 system and an external system. This functionality consists of three layers:

- The application layer
- The distribution layer
- The communications layer

Here, the application layer provides an interface in which to initiate and receive data from or to other systems.

The distribution layer restricts and changes data based on rulesets. Rulesets can be custom configurations or predefined; this is sometimes needed in order to connect to different versions of the SAP system.

In the communications layer, ALE communication can be synchronous and asynchronous. This layer performs a **Remote Function Call** (**RFC**). It uses the RFC destination defined by the client model and port for this purpose.

Differentiating ALE from EDI

Both ALE and EDI technologies are used to support data transfer. ALE is SAP's most frequently used technology for transferring data between SAP systems. EDI is a widely available technology that can be used to connect a SAP system with an external system. The main difference between the two is that EDI is used for external communication, while ALE is used for internal connections. From a technical point of view, EDI transfers data using file ports, whereas ALE uses memory buffers to transfer the data.

BAPI

BAPI is a standard interface that is available in every SAP system. This interface has been designed to access data from the third system (SAP ERP, SAP CRM, other systems). BAPI is a remotely activated function module and can be called by applications that are implemented, for example, in Java. Additionally, the BAPI architecture allows the use of business logic, validation, and checking permissions, which are available in the business object level. BAPI is registered in the **Business Object Repository** (**BOR**).

Implementing BAPI

BAPI is relatively easy to implement. However, the programmer must remember some important rules when creating the interface. We will describe these rules next.

The first step of implementing BAPI is to create a function module in SE37 Tcode (transaction code). To do this, navigate to **Function module** | **Attributes**, and select the options that are displayed in the following screenshot:

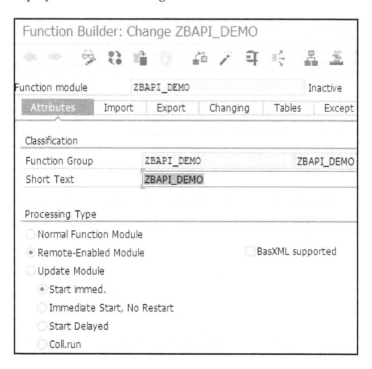

If a user requires input data for the correct operation of business logic, then the developer can add it in the **Import** tab:

> Correct entry of information about the input data requires checking the **Pass value** checkbox.

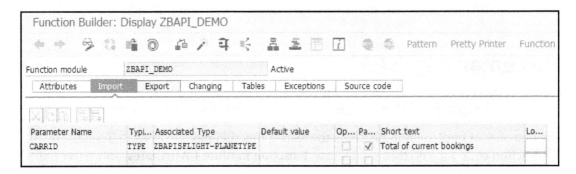

An example of an import table is shown in the preceding screenshot. **BAPIRET2** is a standard structure that is available in every SAP system. A structure could include warning and error messages—this helps us find the cause of the error. On the other hand, it can be used to get success information to confirm the accuracy of program results as follows:

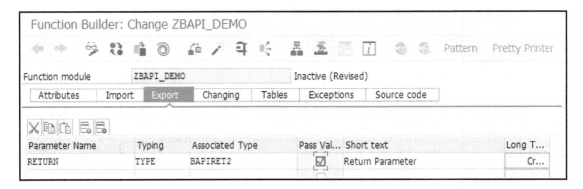

A developer must declare what data will be returned by the BAPI module. In this example, it will be a table, as demonstrated in the following screenshot:

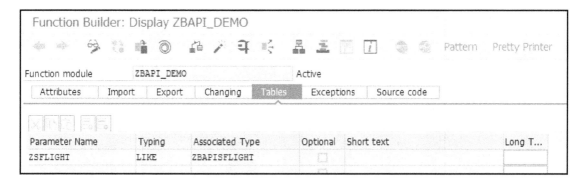

>
> To be able to declare an output table, its type must always start with ZBAPI. This rule is, by default, not validated at this step, but it will be verified later, preventing the successful creation of BAPI.

In the **Source code** tab, we implement the appropriate code. An example code is shown in the following code snippet. The user also has the option of using modern techniques based on object-oriented programming:

```
FUNCTION zbapi_demo.
*"----------------------------------------------------------------
*"*"Local Interface:
*"  IMPORTING
*"     VALUE(CARRID) TYPE  ZBAPISFLIGHT-PLANETYPE
*"  EXPORTING
*"     VALUE(RETURN) TYPE  BAPIRET2
*"  TABLES
*"      ZSFLIGHT STRUCTURE  ZBAPISFLIGHT
*"----------------------------------------------------------------

  CLEAR zsflight .
  SELECT planetype seatsmax_b seatsocc_b seatsmax_f seatsocc_f
    FROM sflight INTO TABLE zsflight
    WHERE carrid EQ carrid.

  IF sy-subrc NE 0.
    CLEAR zsflight .
  ENDIF.


  ENDFUNCTION.
```

Enabling **Release** will make it possible for you to use the function module in BAPI. To do this, you must pass the following path (**Function Module** | **Release** | **Release**):

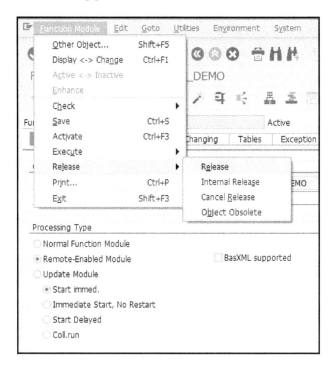

The next step is to create a business object in SW01 Tcode, as follows:

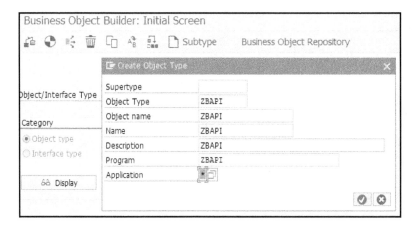

In the resulting screen, click on the **Utilities** drop-down menu and check what methods are provided by default. There should be two methods that are available when creating the BAPI. Next, navigate to **Utilities** | **API Methods** | **Add Method**:

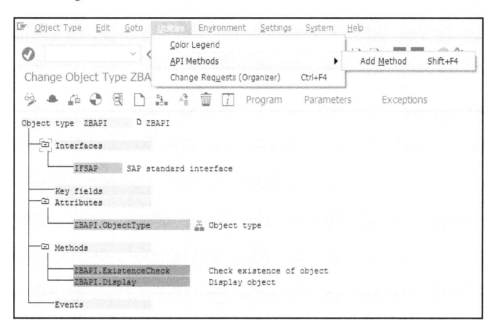

In the next window that appears, enter the name of the method created in the previous steps:

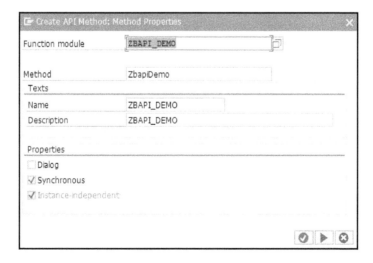

Then, set **Object Type** to the **To implemented** status, as demonstrated in the following screenshot:

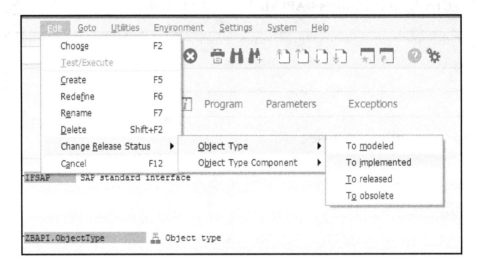

Next, set the **Object Type** component to the **To modeled** status:

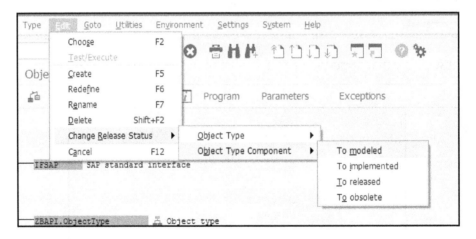

Finally, generate a BAPI that will be visible to external sites, as demonstrated in the following screenshot:

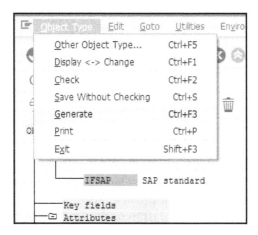

This preceding BAPI example shows that the implementation is not difficult. Similar types of implementation are very frequently used in project work and, as a result, each programmer should have a basic knowledge of BAPI implementations, at the very least.

SAP Gateway

In the previous sections, we covered several efficient and reliable ways of connecting to and from external systems. However, all of these methods share one major flaw – they each require you to expose your system containing business-critical data to third-party systems. Assuming that any system, which is administered by some other entity, will behave according to your established rules of privacy and security is neither recommended nor safe. In order to address this issue and separate the most vital part of the landscape from a potentially dangerous environment, SAP introduced a middleware solution called SAP NetWeaver Gateway (which is available in SAP NetWeaver 7.0 or later releases).

Deployment variants

For older versions (that is, below 7.4) of SAP NetWeaver, the Gateway solution consists of three core parts: GW_CORE, IW_FND, and IW_BEP. Since version 7.4, all of these components have been bundled into one–SAP_GWFND–thereby, reducing the effort of installation. Due to its middleware nature and its component-based architecture, the SAP Gateway can be deployed in SAP landscape in several ways, depending on the infrastructure and the system's ability. We describe the three standard variants in the following sections.

Embedded

The most straightforward way of deploying SAP Gateway is to simply install all the components inside the core system. This is the simplest way to utilize all the tools that have been delivered with the solution without the need for investing in infrastructure. However, this variant does not scale up well. Other drawbacks are that all processing and connections are handled by the core system itself, which increases the system load and the security increase is not significant. On the other hand, this is the fastest solution, as all the required data is in place and there is no need to redirect any requests or calls.

Hub

The recommended way of deploying SAP NetWeaver Gateway is the hub infrastructure. In this scenario, Gateway is split into two systems–the backend server, containing all the business data and processing logic (with IW_BEP or SAP_GWFND installed), and the frontend server for registering services and acting as a single point of entry (with GW_CORE and IW_FND, or SAP_GWFND installed). Using a separate application server for Gateway purposes has significant advantages over the embedded solution. First of all, it introduces an additional layer of security between external systems and business-sensitive data. The core system is not exposed to the non-governed environment and all the incoming calls are guaranteed to be preprocessed and inspected. The frontend server reduces the core system load as well, thanks to the prehandling of authorizations. It requests preprocessing and rejects invalid ones even before they hit their destination. It also introduces the ease of scalability through the very simple registration of another SAP system with their own services and allows a separate maintenance cycle for each and every system. It does, however, extend the call processing time slightly, as it needs to pass the additional system twice.

Hub (with development)

In some special cases, it may be impossible to deploy the `IW_BEP` (or `SAP_GWFND`) component to the backend system, due to restrictive policies, or even system incompatibility. In such situations, the hub variant can be modified by transferring the processing logic to the frontend server and calling the backend system with backward-compatible methods (for example, RFC calls). This modification keeps the security and load-reduction benefits, but requires a bigger development and maintenance effort, as the frontend server is not aware of the backend's dictionary entries, which must be in sync.

Regardless of the deployment variant selected, the core functionality of SAP Gateway are services that use the OData protocol. The protocol itself and how to build an OData service in SAP Gateway will be described in more detail in the following sections.

 Another communication interface introduced by SAP NetWeaver Gateway is WebSocket, and its more general implementation–`TCP/IP` socket. Neither of these, however, are covered in this book.

Main tools

SAP NetWeaver Gateway is not just another system in the landscape, with some additional classes, interfaces, and dictionary entries, but it also consists of a set of tools that can be used to administer core functionalities. These tools are available both through transactions and **SAP Project Reference Object** (**SPRO**) entries. We will discuss several of these tools in the following sections.

Gateway Service Maintenance

The central service maintenance tool is available after running the `/IWFND/MAINT_SERVICE` transaction, or by navigating to **SAP Netweaver | SAP Gateway | OData Channel | Administration | General Settings | Activate and Maintain Services** in SPRO. Once the application is launched, it offers various functionalities, either directly from the cockpit, or by direct navigation to separate tools.

The majority of the screen lists all of the services that are registered in the system, as shown in the following screenshot:

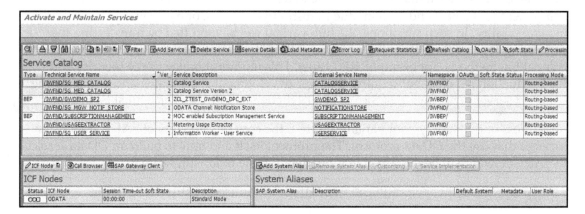

Once the chosen service is selected, the bottom part of the screen displays registration details such as the type of service (for example, OData or SData) or remote systems to which the incoming requests are passed. The buttons ribbon at the top of the screen allows you to check the details of the service, load metadata, check service consistency and availability, and more.

Gateway Client

In order to test any of the registered services, or call external systems using HTTP calls, you can use the `/IWDNF/GW_CLIENT` transaction, as shown in the following screenshot:

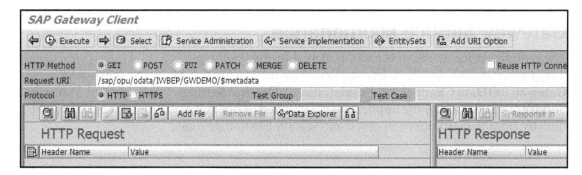

Provided that the URI field is supplied with a relative path (for services on the Gateway system) or an absolute path (for external services) and all the request parameters are set (namely, **Protocol, HTTP Method**, and headers), pressing **Execute** sends the request body (which is defined in the left-hand side) and the result is displayed in the right-hand side. The Gateway Client is particularly useful when the system is isolated from any external REST-testing tools, as it allows you to check the consistency of the services directly in the SAP system environment.

This tool is also accessible directly from the **Service Maintenance** cockpit by selecting the desired service and clicking on the **Gateway Client** button. Entering a transaction this way causes the URI field to be prepopulated with the appropriate value.

Error Log

Since even well-written programs can occasionally lead to some errors, it is necessary to keep track of them in order to analyze and repair the code. The same rule applies to the SAP Gateway, but also there is another threat – incoming requests from external sources may sometimes be malformed, or missing some important data. In order to distinguish backend-related errors and front-facing ones, there are two separate dashboards that you can use. /iwbep/error_log is used on the backend system, whereas /iwfnd/error_log is used on the frontend system (although they may be available on both):

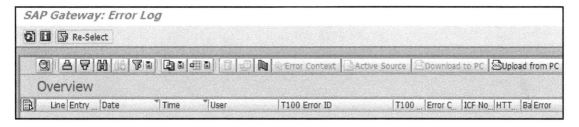

Depending on the log security level, the dashboards contain a list of errors with variably detailed descriptions (on productive systems, the logs are most likely set to hide any business-critical data). Apart from that, basic information such as username, date and time, error type, and service name are always visible.

Gateway Service Builder

Although services can be built manually from scratch, there is also a dedicated tool that can be used to make this process faster, easier, and more reliable. Known as Gateway Service Builder, it is accessible through the `SEGW` transaction:

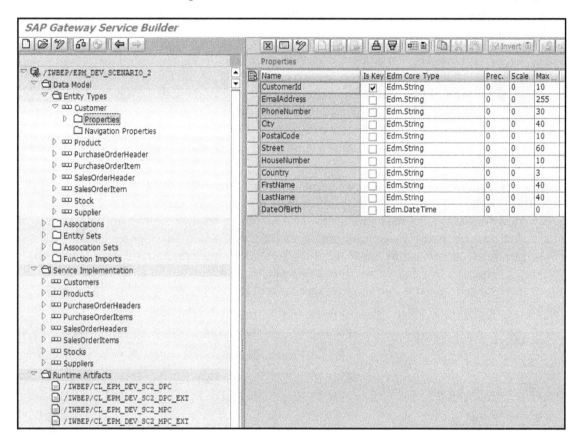

A more detailed description of this tool is presented in the *Developing our first OData application* section. But to summarize its purpose, it allows you to create and edit OData services using automated procedures, check for consistency of provided configuration, and finally, register the service.

The OData protocol

The natural consequence of the release of SAP NetWeaver Gateway was a need to choose a communication protocol that could be handled by the new system. Since the main idea behind the Gateway was to enable non-SAP solutions to easily communicate with the SAP system, without knowledge of **Advanced Business Application Programming Objects (ABAP)** coding or the database structure, the protocol had to be light, fast, and accessible. Coincidentally, parallel to the development of the Gateway, the first version of Microsoft's Astoria project was also introduced, which fit these needs. SAP joined the efforts with Microsoft and several other companies in an attempt to improve this standard, and eventually, this led to what is now known as OData. The OData protocol was then submitted to the **Organization for the Advancement of Structured Information Standards (OASIS)** consortium, which is now responsible for its development and the currently released version, 4.01.

The OData protocol is a RESTful protocol, which allows you to query services without needing to consider request structures and headers. Because of their RESTful nature, these services are not expected to keep track of ongoing sessions and previous requests – each and every call is treated as a completely independent one. Therefore, the limitation of having concurrent sessions running has a smaller impact on the overall efficiency, compared to RESTless protocols.

Characteristics

The OData protocol, in its simplest implementation, supports four basic **Create**, **Read**, **Update**, and **Delete** (**CRUD**) methods. Each of these represent the respective HTTP methods: POST, GET, PUT/MERGE, and DELETE. Furthermore, each resource, which can be manipulated by the aforementioned methods, is uniquely identified by the **Unique Resource Identifier** (**URI**). Both the request and response bodies can be either in XML or in JSON format (the former may contain more information, whereas the latter is much lighter). Some simple requests using this protocol are presented in the following code snippet.

The following code snippet results in the creation of a new flight from London to Paris:

```
POST /Flights
{
    "Destination":"London",
    "Departure":"Paris"
}
```

The following code snippet returns the complete list of `Flights`:

```
GET /Flights
```

The following code snippet returns the details of a particular flight:

```
GET /Flights(id='000001')
```

The following code snippet changes a single property (`Destination`) of a chosen flight:

```
PUT /Flights(id='000001')
{
    "Destination":"London"
}
```

The following code snippet removes the flight specified:

```
DELETE /Flights(id='000002')
```

As you can see, the resources are identified by a collection name, `Flights`, and a key `id` property. Depending on the needs, the resources can be identified by more than one key property. However, if defined, then all key properties need to be supplied in order to manipulate a single entry. If there is a need to fetch more than one entry that fulfills a specific condition, then the `$filter` addition can be used:

```
GET /Flights?$filter=Destination eq 'London'
```

The preceding code returns all flights that are scheduled to land in `London`.

Additional options for manipulating the results are as follows:

- `$orderby`: To set sorting
- `$top` and `$skip`: To fetch a specific range of the records
- `$count`: To obtain only the number of records instead of the full data
- `$select`: To choose which properties of the record should be transferred
- `$search`: To return the records matching a certain condition (the result is highly dependent upon the specific implementation)
- `$expand`: To allow the fetching of additional nested data, which is in line with the main results

As mentioned previously, it is possible to define the service with a nested structure of related information. For example, in the case of a unique flight, it may be useful to identify the crew assigned to it. In order to fetch all flights with their corresponding crews, the following query can be used:

```
GET /Flights?$expand=Crew
```

Additionally, the following query can be used to obtain only the crew of the single flight (without the flight details):

```
GET /Flights(id='000001')/Crew
```

The service definition

The OData protocol is a highly standardized protocol, and so is the definition of the service. In order to consume the service, there is actually no need to go through sophisticated documentation containing lots of nuances. All the information that is required is available with one simple call:

```
GET /$metadata
```

The response to this call includes the full list of available collections, properties, associations, navigation, and more. A short example of such a response (from the SAP system) is presented in the following screenshot:

```
▼<edmx:Edmx xmlns:edmx="http://schemas.microsoft.com/ado/2007/06/edmx" xmlns:m="http://schemas.microsoft.
  ▼<edmx:DataServices m:DataServiceVersion="2.0">
    ▼<Schema xmlns="http://schemas.microsoft.com/ado/2008/09/edm" Namespace="Z_ODATA_SERVICE" xml:lang="pl"
      ▼<EntityType Name="Material" sap:content-version="1">
        ▼<Key>
          <PropertyRef Name="MANDT"/>
          <PropertyRef Name="MATNR"/>
        </Key>
        <Property Name="MANDT" Type="Edm.String" Nullable="false" MaxLength="3"/>
        <Property Name="MATNR" Type="Edm.String" Nullable="false" MaxLength="18"/>
        <Property Name="MTART" Type="Edm.String" MaxLength="4" />
        <Property Name="MBRSH" Type="Edm.String" MaxLength="1" />
        <Property Name="MATKL" Type="Edm.String" MaxLength="9" />
      </EntityType>
     ▼<EntityContainer Name="Z_ODATA_SERVICE_Entities" m:IsDefaultEntityContainer="true">
        <EntitySet Name="MaterialSet" EntityType="Z_ODATA_SERVICE.Material" sap:content-version="1"/>
      </EntityContainer>
      <atom:link xmlns:atom="http://www.w3.org/2005/Atom" rel="self"
      <atom:link xmlns:atom="http://www.w3.org/2005/Atom" rel="latest-version"
    </Schema>
  </edmx:DataServices>
</edmx:Edmx>
```

As you can see here, the SAP OData implementation returns the metadata file in a certain structure. First, there is a definition of each and every entity with all its properties (including key, navigation, and ordinary properties). Then, it defines the associations between the entities. Additionally, in `EntityContainer`, there is a list of collections named `EntitySets`, collection associations (`AssociationSets`), and function imports, which are additional custom actions that cannot be described using the typical structure.

> OData services in SAP follow the `http://schemas.microsoft.com/ado/2008/09/edm` schema, which relates to the **Entity Data Model** (**EDM**). In general, OData services are based on AtomPub, therefore, other naming conventions and schemas can be used.

In the next section, we will demonstrate how you can use the SAP system to generate metadata file that describes the service, and how to handle simple requests.

Developing our first OData application

In `Chapter 8`, *Creating Stunning UI5 Interfaces*, there is a short introduction to SAPUI5 application development. The integral part of such an application is a connection to some sort of data storage, where the business information is saved, and it is being read from and manipulated. For these applications, the most common data storage is the SAP system and the data exchange is handled by the OData services. In the previous example, the application was designed to use the OData service named **ZODATA_SERVICE**. Now, we will demonstrate how you can create it.

Design time

The first step in the creation of any OData service is a good design. The better the service is modeled before the initial draft, the less complicated the coding will be. What is important to remember during the design phase is that each and every piece of information has to be uniquely identified with the key, and nested structures inherit the key of the parent, simultaneously adding their own. This will be demonstrated in the following examples.

The `ZODATA_SERVICE` service, which is used in the sample SAPUI5 application, needs to have at least one collection (entity set) available at `/FlightsSet`. Additionally, it has to be filterable with the `DepartureAirport` property, and the following properties should be provided for display purposes: `DestinationAirport`, `FlightDate`, and `FlightTime`. While it is more convenient to pass the date and time values together as a timestamp, in order to display values more clearly, two separate fields will be used.

Even though the sole purpose of this service is to serve data to the SAPUI5 application, there is no limitation to its interface, as it can be consumed by any number of different applications or, more generally, clients. Therefore, the service will be extended to also show the crew, which is assigned to the specific flight. The crew details will consist of simple `FirstName` and `LastName` properties, followed by `Role` to indicate the actual responsibilities of the crew during the flight.

Having designed the service shape, the SEGW transaction can be launched, and modeling can be started. First, using the **New Project** button, instantiate the project and assign it to the appropriate transport request:

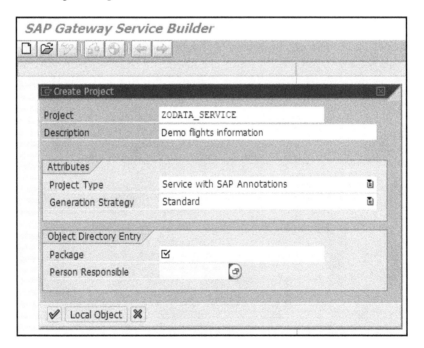

The empty tree structure is shown, as demonstrated in the following screenshot:

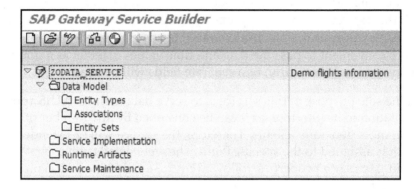

In many cases – including this one – the service has to be built from scratch. There are, however, situations when an automated process can be used. By clicking on the right mouse button on the **Data Model** node of the tree, you can import premodeled data from file, make a clone of the existing project, and generate a new one that is based on the RFC or BOR interface.

Using the right mouse button on the **Entity Types** node, press **Create**, and a new entity can be created. In this scenario, two entity types are needed: **Flight** and **CrewMember**. By checking **Create Related Entity Set**, the collections of **Flight** and **CrewMember** can be created in parallel:

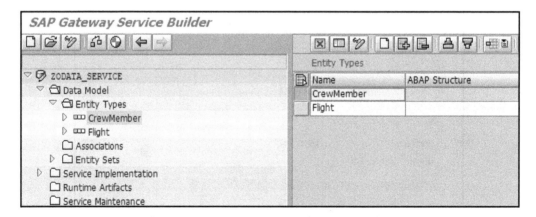

Following this, you will be required to provide the **ABAP Structure** field for each row. The **Flight** entity can be supplied with the `SFLIGHT_T` structure, whereas the **CrewMember** entity requires a custom structure, using the `CARRID (S_CARR_ID)`, `CONNID (S_CONN_ID)`, `FLDATE (S_DATE)`, `MEMBERID (CHAR10)`, `FIRSTNAME (AD_FNAME)`, and `LASTNAME (AD_LNAME)` fields.

Using the right mouse button on the **CrewMember** and **Flight** nodes of the tree, import the relevant properties of the ABAP structures into the OData services. Bear in mind that, while this is a very useful automation tool, these structures can sometimes be very long and not all values are required.

That said, as a creator, you are allowed to define key fields, rename the properties, and change the descriptions. The target properties for **CrewMember** are as follows:

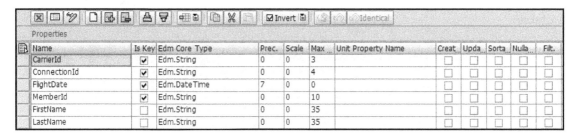

Name	Is Key	Edm Core Type	Prec.	Scale	Max	Unit Property Name	Creat	Upda	Sorta	Nulla	Filt.
CarrierId	✔	Edm.String	0	0	3						
ConnectionId	✔	Edm.String	0	0	4						
FlightDate	✔	Edm.DateTime	7	0	0						
MemberId	✔	Edm.String	0	0	10						
FirstName	☐	Edm.String	0	0	35						
LastName	☐	Edm.String	0	0	35						

Additionally, the target properties for **Flight** are as follows:

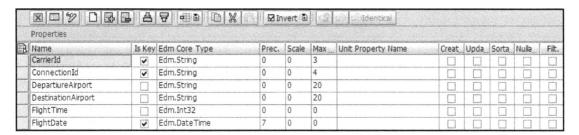

Name	Is Key	Edm Core Type	Prec.	Scale	Max	Unit Property Name	Creat	Upda	Sorta	Nulla	Filt.
CarrierId	✔	Edm.String	0	0	3						
ConnectionId	✔	Edm.String	0	0	4						
DepartiureAirport	☐	Edm.String	0	0	20						
DestinationAirport	☐	Edm.String	0	0	20						
FlightTime	☐	Edm.Int32	0	0	0						
FlightDate	✔	Edm.DateTime	7	0	0						

There is still one section, which has not been maintained yet – the **Creatable**, **Updatable**, **Sortable**, **Nullable**, and **Filterable** columns. Apart from the **Nullable** column, which has to be unchecked for key properties, all can be freely set and have a purely informational role. It is, however, good practice, to set them accordingly in order to inform the service consumer about their capabilities. As this simple service will not have many functionalities, check the **Filterable** checkbox at **DepartureAirport** so that it is kept in line with the SAPUI5 application.

During the design time, a decision about showing the flight's crew was made. Therefore, we need to create a navigation from the flight to the crew members subset. In order to achieve this, we need to set the association between **Flight** and **CrewMember** by using the right mouse button on **Associations** and pressing **Create**. In the pop-up window, **Principal Entity** and **Dependent Entity** need to be pointed to, and an **Association Name** defined. As the flight cannot be started without at least a pilot, the **Cardinality** 1..n is the most suitable:

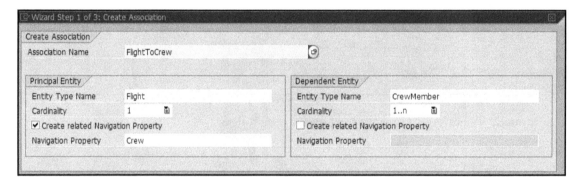

Then, in the subsequent popup, align the keys of the entities. This is where you can clearly see that the dependent (nested) entities need to have the whole parent's key and at least one unique key property.

In the third window, the corresponding association set is created.

Once the association is ready, the **Flight** entity is enhanced using **Navigation Properties**, as shown in the following screenshot:

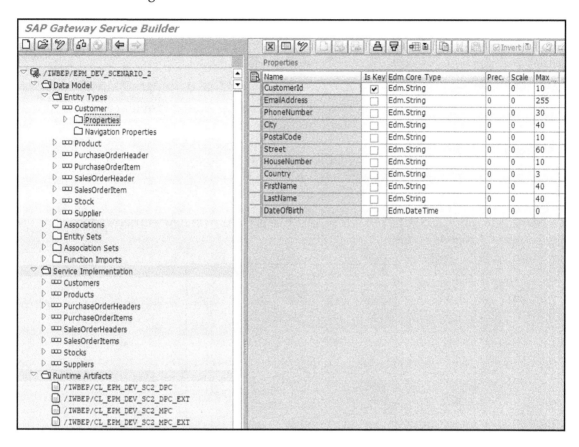

At this moment, the service model can be validated using the **Scale** button (the fifth from the left) in order to check its consistency

As the OData service works with EDM types on one side and SAP dictionary types on the other, it is sometimes impossible to match them exactly. This is why it is quite common to see a list of warnings during the validation process. At this stage, it is the designer's and developer's responsibility to decide whether the warning can be neglected.

Successful validation allows the generation of runtime objects using the **Generate Runtime Objects** button. When the process is started for the first time, the pop-up window is shown, asking for the names of the classes to be generated, the model name, and the service name. Automatically generated class names are usually a good choice unless a specific naming convention is required. However, **Technical Service Name** (even in the simplest scenario) is mapped directly to **External Service Name**, therefore, it is a good idea to give it a meaningful name.

The pop-up window asks for two classes for **Model Provider** and two classes for **Data Provider**. This is due to the SEGW extensibility for the custom code. The base classes are directly affected every time the runtime objects are re-generated, therefore custom coding should not be performed within their bodies. The `*_EXT` classes, on the other hand, are open for manual extending and enhancing.

Once the generation is completed, the project tree is filled with new entries under the **Runtime Artifacts** node:

Now, using the `/IWFND/MAIN_SERVICE` transaction and the **Add Service** button, the newly generated service can be registered and published, as follows:

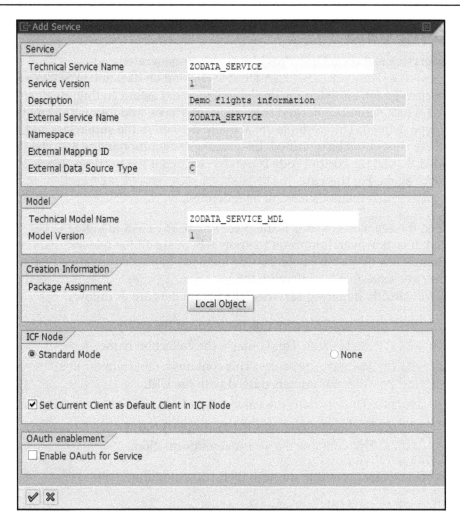

Then, the metadata file can be opened calling the following code:

```
[hostname]/sap/opu/odata/sap/ZODATA_SERVICE/$metadata
```

Alternatively, it can be called through `/IWFND/GW_CLIENT`.

Providing data

During the service creation, a **Data Provider** class was generated called `ZCL_ZODATA_SERVICE_DPC_EXT`. Double-clicking on its name in SEGW results in opening the class editor, allowing the implementation of custom coding. By default, the generated class has methods inherited from eight interfaces, and four CRUD methods for each entity type defined. The methods are actually defined in the superclass and their definition there should not be modified. Instead, the redefinition in the `EXT` class is recommended, so that the custom code is not overwritten if the runtime objects are generated once again. For this case, the `FLIGHTSET_GET_ENTITYSET` and `CREW_GET_ENTITYSET` methods need to be redefined.

Depending on the actual needs, this is the place where any custom logic can be implemented. It is, however, important to know where are all the relevant parameters are stored. Although few of the parameters of the methods interfaces are already marked as obsolete (they are accessible directly with the `io_tech_request_context` methods), they can be found in already deployed services. The parameters are as follows:

- `IV_ENTITY_NAME`: This contains the name of the entity.
- `IV_ENTITY_SET_NAME`: This contains the collection name.
- `IT_FILTER_SELECT_OPTIONS`: This contains a table similar to `SELECT-OPTIONS` of filter parameters passed with the URI.
- `IS_PAGING`: This contains the values of the `$top` and `$skip` parameters.
- `IT_KEY_TAB`: This contains all the key property values.
- `IT_ORDER`: This contains the `$orderby` information.

All of the properties are accessible through their corresponding methods:

```
io_tech_request_context->get_entity_type_name( ).
io_tech_request_context->get_entity_set_name( ).
io_tech_request_context->get_filter( ). "returns filter object
io_tech_request_context->get_top( ).
io_tech_request_context->get_skip( ).
io_tech_request_context->->get_source_keys( )
io_tech_request_context->->get_converted_source_keys( )
io_tech_request_context->get_orderby( ).
```

Once the appropriate data fetching, storing, or updating has taken place, the relevant data needs to be returned with ET_ENTITYSET, or ES_ENTITY (for single rows). These ABAP table and structure are then processed by SAP Gateway OData framework and converted to appropriate response sent to the caller, for example, the SAPUI5 application.

Summary

In this chapter, we learned the most commonly used ways to integrate SAP with third-party systems. In short, combining the SAP system with other systems is a very important issue. There are many ways in which to connect SAP with other systems. The information contained in this chapter allows for the exchange of information and data in the SAP system. It is important for the user to be aware of the situation in which the particular technology should be used.

The next chapter describes the possibilities of using background jobs. This is an important topic for anyone who currently works with or will work with the SAP system.

Questions

The following questions allow you to consolidate the information contained in this chapter:

1. What are the ways to connect with other systems in SAP?
2. How does the OData service work?
3. What is the difference between ALE and EDI?

15
The Background Processing of ABAP Programs

This chapter uncovers all the ins and outs of background data processing in **Systems Applications and Products in Data Processing** (**SAP**) that you can face and the approaches that you can use to handle them. This technique is mainly used for transferring data from non-SAP systems to SAP systems, or between SAP systems that have no direct link to each other. Additionally, it can be applied to the mass processing of data in any transaction. This chapter describes tools that are very important in everyday work. A lot of processes are based on background work and, for the most part, they are the foundation of a well-functioning enterprise.

The following topics will be covered in this chapter:

- Background processing in SAP
- Recording batch input sessions

Technical requirements

The information presented in this chapter requires the SAP system. Basic programming knowledge is also required, which will facilitate the understanding of the described solutions.

All the code used in this chapter can be downloaded from the following GitHub link: `https://github.com/PacktPublishing/Mastering-SAP-ABAP/tree/master/Chapter15`.

Background processing in SAP

The SAP system was production management, through to human resources and financial accounting, and up to customer relationship management and data analytics. While the areas where the SAP system is useful and able to handle the majority of tasks are vast, sometimes, another tool is already deployed in the enterprise environment and, from a business perspective, it is not advised to replace it. In such cases, there appears to be no other option than to integrate the SAP system with a third-party solution.

There are many different scenarios that involve integration, including overnight data exchanges, synchronizations, reacting to live events, and more. Eventually, most of these scenarios will require some data to be imported to the SAP system. The optimistic scenario is pretty straightforward; that is, the data can be sent through any available interface and then simply propagated to an appropriate SAP internal table; however, this rarely occurs.

It is more likely that the external system will have some data in its structure. However, from the SAP perspective, even a single record may need to be stored in several tables, lots of events may need to be triggered, and some additional values might need to be calculated. While it is possible to write an appropriate program, the development effort can easily become overwhelming compared to the potential profits.

Fortunately, if there is a suitable transaction in the SAP system, which could handle most of the logic, then it is very tempting to use this as a quick start, and then do the final polish with some custom development. This will ensure that all the data is well propagated with the currently implemented rules in the SAP system and that all the required events are triggered accordingly.

There is, however, another hurdle when using transactions. Most transactions are designed to handle a single entry and each record needs to be processed separately. The manual import of a large dataset, with all the necessary processing, can take lots of time, effectively blocking the user from performing any other action.

When integration is launched for the first time, an initial data load is usually required, which tends to be in the form of a large dataset. Running transactions on each and every record can be tedious work, but running a custom ABAP report can also lead to a dead end, as the processing of hundreds or thousands of records can take so much time that it exceeds the internal limit for a standard user. There is, however, a specially designed set of tools that can overcome all of these issues.

The first problem to be tackled is the execution time limit. Because the SAP system is designed as a transaction-based system and there are a limited number of sessions running in parallel, the single-transaction execution time limit is a natural consequence of keeping the system stable and responsive. Therefore, by using reports and transactions through SAP GUI, users are prevented from keeping the system busy for too long at once. There is, however, a specially delegated set of threads for launching long-running processes without consuming the daily resources of the system. These are called **background jobs** and they can be triggered in a number of ways.

Background remote function call

Provided that the logic that needs to be executed is wrapped in a remote-enabled function module (RFC), you can use a dedicated API for the background processing of **Remote Function Calls** (**RFCs**). As the descendant of the **transactional RFC** (**tRFC**) and its successor, the **queued RFC** (**qRFC**), **Background Remote Function Call** (**bgRFC**) provides a method of executing code using units and queue mechanisms. These queues, as the name suggests, are meant to keep an order of the execution of units. These units are logically connected bundles of function calls and they are somewhat similar (but not necessarily identical) to **Logical Units of Works** (**LUWs**). There are several options available for developers when using bgRFC.

Notably, you must decide between two different unit types: **T-type** units and **Q-type** units. T-type units are similar to tRFCs, in that the units are processed without preserving the calling order; in comparison to this, Q-type units are more like qRFCs, in that the units are guaranteed to be processed in the calling order. The exact moment of unit execution is not known; it depends on the queue scheduler, which is responsible for maintaining the unit's dependencies and optimization, and for launching the execution itself.

There are also two queue types that use separate schedulers: the inbound queue (with the inbound scheduler) and the outbound queue (with the outbound scheduler). The key difference between the two is that the inbound queue is designed to be executed in the local system (leveraging the possibility of parallelization and load balancing between the application servers), whereas the outbound queue is meant to be executed on remote systems (where it can be used to dispatch the data to several systems).

The type of queue (and, thus, the scheduler) is dependent on the destination defined, as one destination can only have one type of scheduler assigned.

Apart from the configuration of the schedulers and destinations (which is administrative work and is beyond the scope of this book), the development process is rather straightforward. The only limitation is that there cannot be explicit or implicit COMMIT WORK within the code that is executed as a unit. Some basic examples of bgRFC usage are displayed in the following two code snippets.

The following code block calls the Q bgRFC type on an inbound queue:

```
DATA: lr_destination TYPE REF TO if_bgrfc_destination_inbound,
      lr_unit TYPE REF TO if_qrfc_unit_inbound,
      lv_qname TYPE qrfc_queue_name,
      lv_destination_name TYPE bgrfc_destination_inbound.

lv_Destination_name = 'SAMPLE_DESTINATION'.
lr_destination = cl_bgrfc_destination_inbound=>create( lv_destination_name
).
lr_unit = lr_destination->create_qrfc_unit( ).

TRY.
    CALL FUNCTION 'SAMPLE_RFC_FUNCTION' IN BACKGROUND UNIT lr_unit.
    CALL FUNCTION 'ANOTHER_RFC_FUNCTION' IN BACKGROUND UNIT lr_unit.
    lr_unit->add_queue_name_inbound( 'QUEUENAME' ).
    COMMIT WORK.
    CATCH cx_bgrfc_error INTO DATA(lx_error).
ENDTRY.
```

The following code block calls the T bgRFC type on an outbound queue:

```
DATA: lr_destination TYPE REF TO if_bgrfc_destination_outbound,
      lr_unit TYPE REF TO if_trfc_unit_outbound,
      lv_destination_name TYPE bgrfc_dest_name_outbound.

lv_destination_name = 'SAMPLE_DESTINATION'.
lr_destination = cl_bgrfc_destination_outbound=>create( lv_destination_name
).
lr_unit = lr_destination->create_trfc_unit( ).

CALL FUNCTION 'FUNCTION_1' IN BACKGROUND_UNIT lr_unit.
CALL FUNCTION 'FUNCTION_2' IN BACKGROUND_UNIT lr_unit.

COMMIT WORK.
```

As you can see in the previous two code snippets, calling either unit type in either queue is relatively simple. In both cases, you are required to create an instance of the appropriate destination, and then create at least one unit that the `CALL FUNCTION` statement will refer to. For Q-type units, there is an additional requirement to provide at least one queue name in which the unit is supposed to be processed. It is also possible to provide more than one queue name to a single unit.

In these instances, the scheduler will dispatch all the calls registered to the unit between the available queues, while keeping the dependencies (that is, order) between each and every call.

When the administrator creates a bgRFC destination, one part of the process is to define the name prefixes that are allowed for queues. In order to check what prefixes are allowed for a specific destination, you can use the `SBGRFCCONF` transaction.

While monitoring and maintaining queues are not within the scope of this chapter, developers may also need to check what the current state of a specific queue is in order to see whether there are any locks that prevent the units processing. In order to do this, there is a dedicated monitoring tool, which is available in the `SBGRFCMON` transaction:

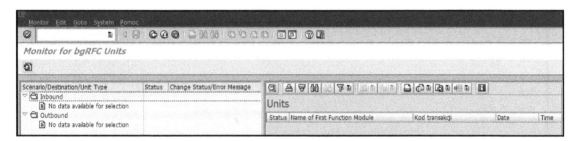

In the left-hand pane of the tool, you can see that there is a tree that shows all the queues that are currently being processed. After selecting a queue, the right-hand pane shows the units that are registered in this specific queue, with corresponding information about the function module that needs to be launched. If there is any problem with the unit processing (for example, if the unit contains a function module that is not remote-enabled), then the locked queue will be highlighted with a red icon and an explanation of the lock.

Scheduling background jobs

Background processing using the bgRFC framework is both powerful and simple to use. However, it still requires user interaction in order to launch the code that registers the calls in the queues. Another drawback is that only remote-enabled function modules can be used in this scenario, so not every piece of code can be executed this way. If either of these obstacles is thrown into the development process, there is another mechanism provided by SAP that removes both problems – the background job scheduler.

Creating a background job

Background jobs can be created using the SM36 transaction.

A batch job in SAP is a scheduled background program. It is used when the user wants to perform a task that requires a large number of resources. To create a batch job (definition scheduled background program), the user must use the SM36 transaction. After using this transaction, the following screen will appear:

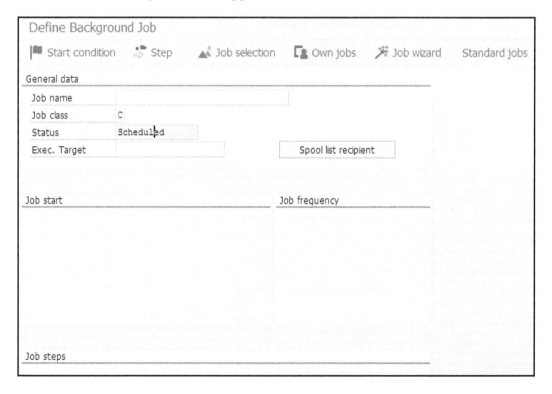

Note that there is no naming convention regulated by SAP: the job name can be any suitable or descriptive text. The **Job class** parameter defines the priority of execution and **Exec. Target** (execution target; this is optional), as the name suggests, is the name of the SAP instance that the job should be run from. Once the fields are filled, the initiator of the job needs to be defined in the pop-up screen that opens after pressing the **Start Condition** button:

Background jobs are grouped into three categories, as follows:

- **High/critical priority**: The tasks specified in this class have a higher priority. The user must carefully choose this category because overly large layers of this type of process can be problematic. The tasks of this class are carried out first. This refers to jobs with high priority whose execution is absolutely necessary for further processing.
- **Medium priority**: When all the tasks of the highest class are carried out, then the processes of the medium class are carried out. It has been assumed that the tasks of this class are carried out cyclically.
- **Low priority**: The tasks in this class have the lowest priority. They will only be executed if all the remaining task classes are empty. This priority is the default class.

 To set the high and medium priorities, the user must have the appropriate permissions. The authorization object is being checked(background processing, background administrator).

There is also a distinction between the statuses that the tasks are currently in. These statuses are as follows:

- **Schedule**: This is the initial status of creating a batch job. It means that the task creation process was initiated.
- **Released**: In this status, all criteria have been correctly filled out. The task is ready to be run by the user; it will not be launched.
- **Ready**: This status means that the task scheduler puts the job in the queue as it waits for the job to be released in the background.
- **Active**: This informs you that the process is being done in the background. It is not possible to change the status at this stage.
- **Finish**: This informs you that the task was completed without errors.
- **Canceled**: This informs you that the background process was interrupted due to an error, or that the administrator was forced to terminate without success.

Creating a new **Background Job** is very simple, despite the extensive features. First, determine the name of the process, and then enter the name in the **Job Name** field. Next, navigate to the **Step** menu; the location of this menu button is shown in the following screenshot:

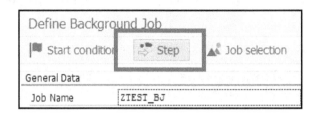

The SAP system calls a window in which the process creator can determine what tasks will be performed in the background. It has three options, as follows:

- ABAP programs
- External commands
- External programs

In order to demonstrate how to use this tool to run in the background of ABAP programs, we have written the following line of code. This is a simple update of the data contained in the `sflight` table. Programs that are launched in the background can be more extensive. The program code shown below takes a line from the `sflight` table for the `carrid` and `connid` conditions. The program will then change the price and will update the database.

```
REPORT zbackround_job.

DATA: lt_line TYPE TABLE OF sflight,
      ls_line LIKE LINE OF lt_line.

SELECT SINGLE * FROM sflight INTO ls_line WHERE carrid EQ 'AA' AND  connid
EQ '0017'.
 IF sy-subrc EQ 0.
   ls_line-price = 700.
   UPDATE sflight FROM ls_line.
 ENDIF.
```

 It is natural that the implemented program must be activated in order to be able to use it.

Returning to creating a process in the background, users must enter the name of the program to be executed, as shown in the following screenshot:

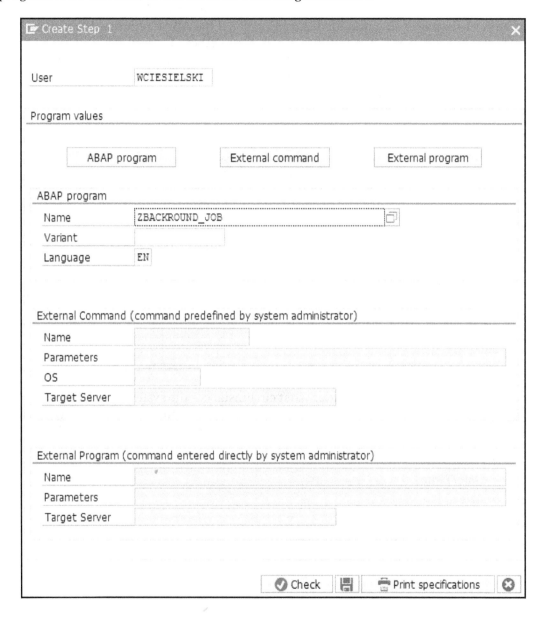

In the preceding screenshot, you can see that we need to provide a **User** name on whose behalf the job will be executed, as well as the type and corresponding parameters. For **ABAP Programs**, the suitable parameters are, for example, simple reports, with, optionally, a **Variant** or **Language** value provided. Additionally, if the ABAP report needs to print any data, there is an additional Print specifications button that can be used. This function allows for defining an appropriate printing device to be used in this particular step. The **External Command** and **External Program** sections are related to host operating system methods and commands, and they are not supposed to be used by ABAP developers. This section should be managed by system administrators.

With the **Check** button, the user can check whether the entered data is correct. It can also introduce variants depending on the needs of the process. If there is no error, then the creator should save the setting (that is, click on the save button). After successfully saving, a list of processes in a job is displayed. The information on this list helps you determine what will happen in the background. An exemplary **Step List Overview** example is shown in the following screenshot:

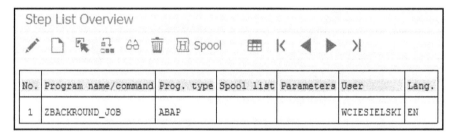

It is very important to determine under what circumstances the system is to trigger the background process. There are many possible variants of commissioning, depending on the business and technical requirements. The following scheduling options are available:

- **Immediate**
- **Date/Time**
- **After Job**
- **After Event**
- **At operation mode**

For the example shown, the program will be executed for a specific date. Then, you can decide whether the job should be scheduled to start immediately after saving (that is, as soon as the required resources are available for the job with a defined priority), at a defined date and time, after another job, and so on.

In addition to this, the job can be scheduled to be launched at specific intervals (using the **Periodic Job** checkbox and the **Period values** button), which is another advantage over bgRFCs. The job start condition can be further restricted (using the **Restrictions** button), for example, to cancel execution on Sundays or other holidays. An example of the execution time setting can be seen in the following screenshot:

After entering the correct data, you should save the task. At this point, the status of the task changes and will be performed in the future. As mentioned before, a job can take many steps. You can also see information on how many steps are included in the scheduled task, as shown in the following screenshot:

When working with the SAP system, it is very important to check if and how the tasks in the background have been performed. The system offers the appropriate transactions indicating what planned processes have taken place in the background. To call the program that was previously described, the user must run SM37 transactions. After starting this transaction, the system shows the selection window.

In the selection screen, you can select the name of the program and the user who launched the background activity. If you enter *, all the entries will be found, by default, for the SAP system. A helpful selection criterion is the ability to filter according to the status of tasks. You can also search for the date range, and the name of the program that can be executed in any of the steps:

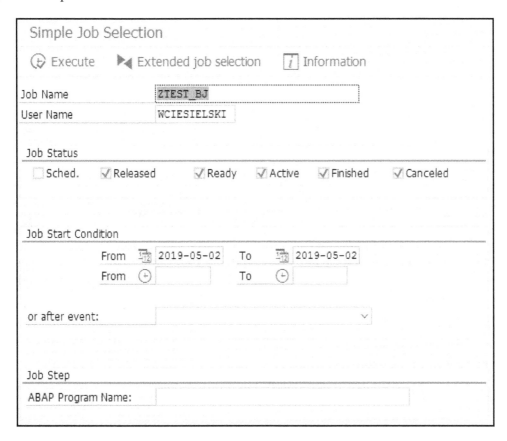

After completing the appropriate criteria, press the *F8* button. The system then routes the user to a window describing the processes carried out. For the preceding example, the system generated the following list:

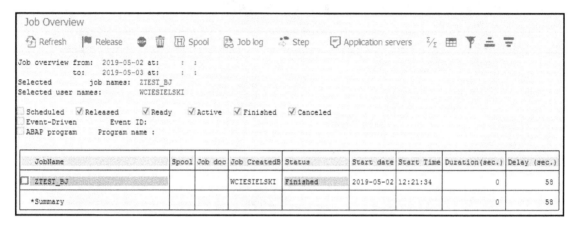

The information provided by the system is very useful for everyday work. There is information about the time the task was started, and the status of the process execution. The tool can also be used to test system performance. The last column contains information about the time the task was completed. Pressing the Job log button will cause, the system will show the logs generated during the task execution. An example log is shown in the following screenshot:

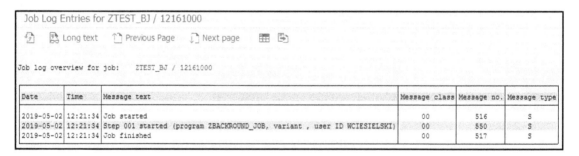

Naturally, in complex business processes, the logs are much more extensive.

Recording batch input sessions

At the beginning of this chapter, we mentioned that using transactions to enter data has its advantages (they allow triggering of all system logic) and disadvantages (they are mostly designed to enter one record at a time).

There is, however, a possibility of leveraging the good sides of a transaction and, by doing so, limiting the drawbacks. By good side, we mean that transactions can be automated. In the SAP system, there is a dedicated toolset named **Batch Data Collection** (**BDC**), which allows for recording the transaction's usage, and then replaying it on a suitable dataset, without the need of user interaction on each and every screen. The recording tool is available as a SHDB transaction, or by navigating to **System | Services | Batch Input | Recorder**:

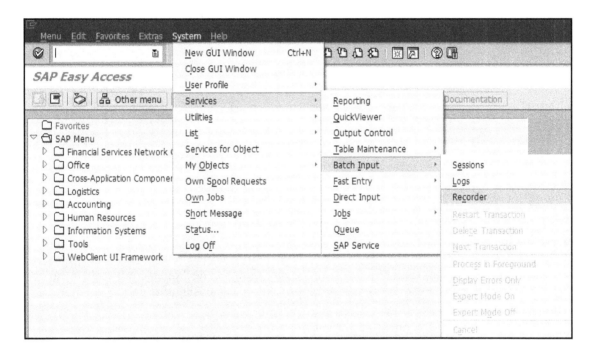

The tool's main list displays the recording that is currently present (that is, saved) on the system. In order to create a new one, you can click on the **New recording** button and the following pop-up box appears:

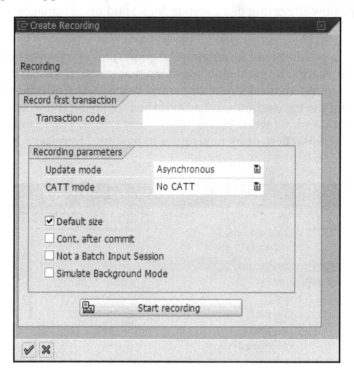

There are several fields and options that need to be filled before starting the recording process. First, the recording name needs to be provided; note that there are no particular naming rules. Then, the starting **Transaction code** field needs to be provided. It is possible to record more than one transaction during the recording as the **Transaction code** input field requires only the first one's name. After providing this basic information, further configuration is possible.

Next, the update mode can be set, and there are three options available:

- **Asynchronous (default)**: Update function modules are executed in the "update" work process (UPD).
- **Synchronous**: Similar to asynchronous, but all COMMIT WORK statements are treated like COMMIT WORK AND WAIT.
- **Local**: Update function modules are executed in the same work process as the main program (similar to the SET UPDATE TASK LOCAL directive).

By default, the recording stops when the `COMMIT WORK` statement is reached. Marking the "Cont. after commit" checkbox overrides this rule, allowing you to make multiple commit recordings. The **Simulate Background Mode** option calls an additional check for using the recording in the background mode – this option is relevant for this chapter.

Pressing the **Start recording** button launches the transaction specified in **Transaction code**. Then, the whole process of entering data into the transaction has to be executed by the user with one restriction: pressing the back button will stop the recording.

Once the execution is complete, pressing the back button will stop the recording, and you will be presented with the list of all the values provided on each subsequent screen, as shown in the following screenshot:

Line	Program	Screen	St..	Field name	Field value	
1			T	MM03		
2	SAPLMGMM	0060	X			
3				BDC_CURSOR	RMMG1-MATNR	
4				BDC_OKCODE	=ENTR	
5				RMMG1-MATNR	MZ-PROC-MC-HT-3104	
6	SAPLMGMM	0070	X			
7				BDC_CURSOR	MSICHTAUSW-DYTXT(02)	
8				BDC_OKCODE	=ENTR	
9				MSICHTAUSW-KZSEL(01)	X	
10				MSICHTAUSW-KZSEL(02)	X	
11	SAPLMGMM	4004	X			
12				BDC_OKCODE	=BABA	
13				BDC_SUBSCR	SAPLMGMM	2004TABFRA1
14				BDC_SUBSCR	SAPLMGD1	1002SUB1
15				BDC_CURSOR	RMMG1-MATNR	
16				BDC_SUBSCR	SAPLMGD1	2001SUB2
17				BDC_SUBSCR	SAPLMGD1	2561SUB3
18				BDC_SUBSCR	SAPLMGD1	2007SUB4
19				BDC_SUBSCR	SAPLMGD1	2005SUB5
20				BDC_SUBSCR	SAPLMGD1	2011SUB6
21				BDC_SUBSCR	SAPLMGD1	2033SUB7
22				BDC_SUBSCR	SAPLMGD1	0001SUB8
23				BDC_SUBSCR	SAPLMGD1	0001SUB9
24				BDC_SUBSCR	SAPLMGD1	0001SUB10

This scenario can be adjusted, if necessary, by simply editing it or using the Export/Import options. Once it is ready and saved, there are a number of options available for further processing using the corresponding buttons:

- **Session**: This generates the batch input session based on the data provided, for example, for test purposes.
- **Program**: This generates an ABAP report to be launched with the data from the recording (then, it needs to be modified to use variable data), or with the data from a file; all the required OPEN, READ, and CLOSE statements are generated automatically as well.
- **Test data**: This generates a sample file with a single record (based on the data provided during the recording) with all relevant data, which can be used to create tests.
- **Function module**: This generates a function module with all the relevant fields so that it can be used for data imports, for example, from an external system as an RFC.

Summary

This chapter revealed all the ins and outs of background data processing in SAP that you can face, along with the approaches that are used to handle with them. This technique is used mainly for transferring data from non-SAP systems to SAP systems, or between SAP systems without any direct link to each other. Additionally, it can be applied to the mass processing of data in any transaction.

In the next chapter, we will describe the performance and optimization of the ABAP code. These themes will make working with the system easier and the code that is created more efficient.

Questions

The following list contains questions that will help the reader to consolidate knowledge.

1. What transaction can a user use to schedule the job in the background?
2. What status must a job be in for it to be done in the background?
3. When can the user set a higher priority for a background job?

16
Performance and Optimization of ABAP Code

The SAP system, in its out-of-the-box variant, is a complex environment built to run various types of industries. This complexity and all custom adjustments developed to tailor the system to customer specific needs, if not handled properly, may lead to low performance and thus make users frustrated because of long-running processes.

Software should be created in such a way as to waste as few resources as possible. Implementing the code in this way allows the user to easily add new functionalities. To help them with this mission, there are several tools (SAT, SE30, ST12) that allow for easy, yet detailed analysis of the program's flow and efficiency.

This chapter will cover the following topics:

- Ways of measuring ABAP programs performance
- ABAP runtime analysis
- ABAP trace analysis
- ABAP SAT transactions
- Best practice techniques

Technical requirements

All the code used in this chapter can be downloaded from the following GitHub link: `https://github.com/PacktPublishing/Mastering-SAP-ABAP/tree/master/Chapter16`.

Ways of measuring ABAP programs performance

As you can easily imagine, poorly written code is sometimes clearly visible at first glance. Making loops with repeated access to the database or reading plenty of data while using only a minute part of it is something that a mature developer avoids intuitively. However, sometimes, the performance bottlenecks and memory management issues are not that obvious.

In complex, multi-level transactions, with various events, nested calls, and tens of screens and subroutines, it is nearly impossible to point out the root cause of performance problems by simply looking at the code or debugging the code step by step. Moreover, when the code is developed by someone else and the logic is not clearly documented, it may turn out that the issue is in a completely different part of the program.

The process of analyzing the program flow, without tedious debugging and checking which part of the code calls another part, can be automated by using several tools delivered with the SAP system. In this chapter, three of them will be covered in detail: the old ABAP Runtime Analysis (SE30), ABAP Trace Analysis (ST12) and the new **ABAP Runtime Analysis (SAT)**. Although the first one, in terms of functionality, is replaced by the SAT transaction, for the sake of backward compatibility, you should be familiar with it as well.

The aforementioned tools are designed to deliver as much information about the execution runtime as possible, starting from the listing of consecutive calls to functions and subroutines, through internal tables and memory variables usage, down to database operations or kernel methods execution. Equipped with this set of transactions, it can become relatively easy to track and eliminate problems that make programs run slowly or to identify when and where the particular methods are called to check if they are suitable extension points.

ABAP runtime analysis

The first tool, which is shown in the following screenshot, is **ABAP Runtime Analysis**, available as a transaction SE30. Since NetWeaver 7.0, when accessing this t-code, the user is prompted that there is a new transaction (SAT) serving the same purpose and that should be used instead. This new SAT transaction will be described later in this chapter, and here, for backward-compatibility, the old one is described.

The initial screen after launching the transaction shows several parameters, as shown in the following screenshot:

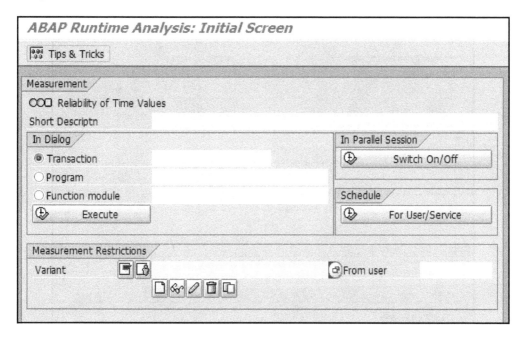

Firstly, the user can provide a short description that will identify the measurement and thus make it easy to find afterward. Then, in the **Measurement Restrictions** section, you can define the **Variant** of execution. The variant can limit (or extend) the results in several ways. At first, the measurement can be limited to particular programs or subroutines by listing them, as shown in the following screenshot:

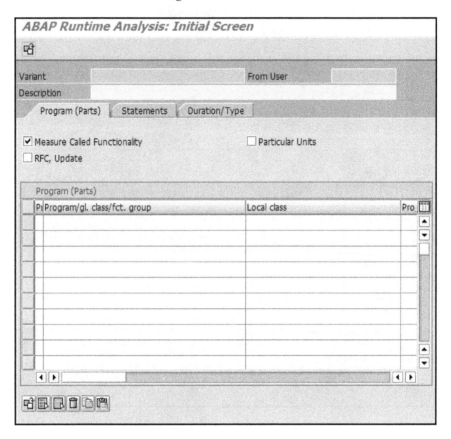

The checkboxes toggle the following options:

- **Measure Called Functionality**: This tells the tool to show not only calls performed directly by the analyzed tool, but also makes a drill-down analysis of sub-calls on deeper levels.
- **Particular Units**: This option leaves the measurement execution start and end in the hands of the user; the measurement has to be triggered either by using /ron (and stopped by /roff) or by the menu option in transaction. This can be particularly handy if only one specific section of the program flow needs to be analyzed.

- **RFC, Update**: This indicates whether RFC calls should be analyzed as well. If the calls are executed in different application servers, the results will be stored on these servers.

On the second tab, **Statements**, the series of checkboxes defines which hotspots of the program should be registered and analyzed. This list allows for fine-tuning of the analysis, so that only the parts of interest are transferred to the result log. The available hotspots are bundled into seven groups, namely: **Modularization Units**, **Screen**, **Internal tables**, **Database accesses**, **Data transfer**, **Generation/Loading**, and **Miscellaneous**.

For easier analysis, the checkboxes should be marked only next to the element that is in fact needed. This will keep the analysis results smaller and more focused on the actual target. The available list is shown in the following screenshot:

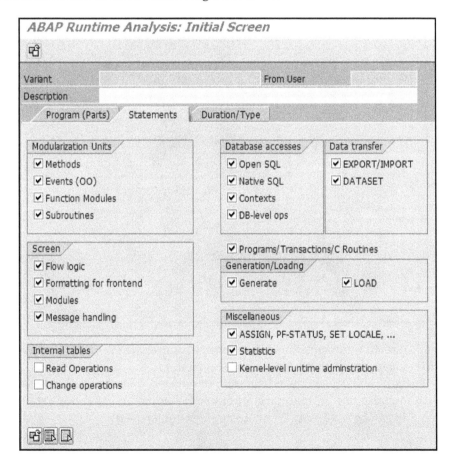

As mentioned previously, the user can freely select what parts of the executed code should be analyzed. In the case of complex programs with various calls, the resulting file can very easily grow to a huge volume or can take a lot of time. The third tab, shown in the following screenshot, is there to address this issue. It is possible to define both the maximum file size (**Max. size of file**) and **Maximum runtime**:

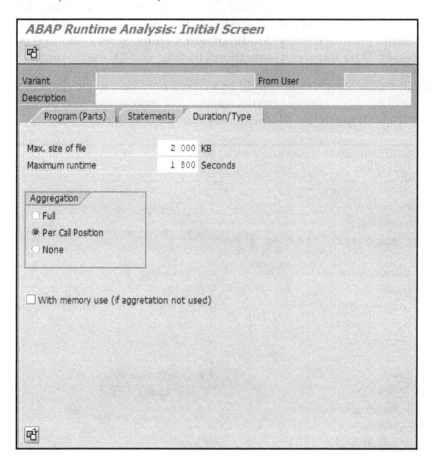

The **Aggregation** section informs the tool whether to aggregate (**Per Call Position**) the results, so that each call will be presented once, even if it is called several times; or not (**None**). The **Full** option is obsolete and should not be used. The checkbox on the bottom—**With memory use (if aggretation not used)**—adds memory usage statistics on the results screen and can be used only when no aggregation is used.

Once the execution variant is defined, back on the first screen, there are three ways of triggering the measurement. The first option—located in section named **In Dialog**—launches a specific transaction, program, or function module directly in the same session and gathers data for analysis until the execution ends (unless the **Particular Units** checkbox was marked in the **Variant**).

The second option is available via the **Switch On/Switch Off** button, which allows you to make a measurement in the **In Parallel Session** section, and allows you to make a measurement on the work process running in a different session on the same **Application Server**. This option can be used for finding potential problems in long-running background processes. After pressing this button, the list of active work processes is shown. By selecting a specific row and pressing the preceding buttons, the measurement can be started and ended manually.

The third option, the **For User/Service** in **Schedule** section, allows for measurement scheduling to be triggered for a specific user, session number, process category, and object. Once scheduled (with expiration date and time), the measurement will take place as soon as the conditions are met.

Regardless of the execution type, the measurement results are stored in separate files and are accessible at the bottom of the initial screen:

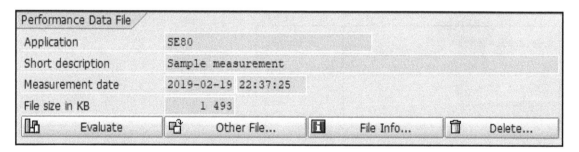

Using the **Other File** button, you can select the interesting measurement results, and then go to the preview by using the **Evaluate** button (or remove using **Delete**).

The overview screen of the evaluation shows the summary of execution, with the chart showing the distribution of the runtime between ABAP code, database access, and system procedures:

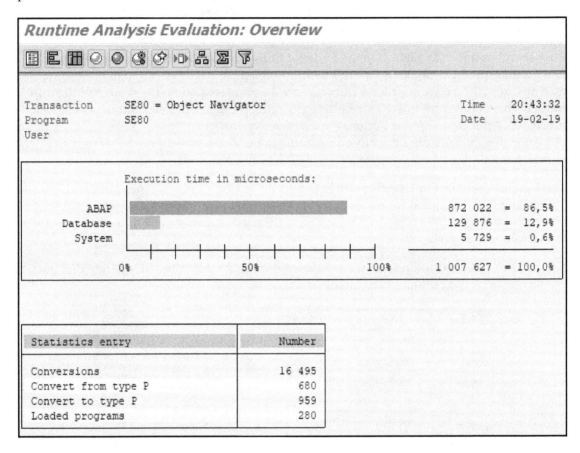

Depending on the defined variant, the detailed results can be shown in several ways, using the buttons at the top of the screen:

- **Hit list**: This shows a plain list of all hotspots.
- **Group hit list**: This shows a list of all hotspots grouped by type:

Runtime Analysis Evaluation: Group Hit List

No.	Gross	Net	CALL METHOD
1	938 278	15	CL_WB_STARTUP=>START
1	937 442	34	CL_WB_STARTUP=>START_INTERNAL
1	934 507	39	CL_WB_MANAGER=>IF_WB_MANAGER~SET_WORKSPACE
1	934 335	63	CL_WB_MANAGER=>PROCESS_REQUEST_QUEUE
8	850 246	233	CL_WB_MANAGER=>PROCESS_WB_REQUEST
1	643 702	7	CL_WB_NAVIGATOR_VIS_AS_DYNPRO=>DO_THE_NAVIGATION
1	643 693	34	CL_WB_NAVIGATOR=>DO_THE_NAVIGATION
1	640 115	6	CL_WB_INITIAL=>IF_WB_PROGRAM~PROCESS_WB_REQUEST
1	640 109	7	CL_WB_INITIAL=>DISPLAY
1	457 779	1 005	CL_WB_INITIAL=>SHOW_CONTROLS
1	456 741	5	CL_WB_INITIAL=>SHOW_WB_PICTURE
1	455 539	455 420	CL_GUI_PICTURE=>LOAD_PICTURE_FROM_URL
7	204 160	70	CL_WB_NAVIGATOR=>DO_THE_NAVIGATION
1	159 739	15	CL_WB_REP_BROWSER_RADA=>IF_WB_PROGRAM~PROCESS_WB_REQUEST
1	84 662	43	CL_WB_REP_BROWSER_RADA=>DISPLAY
1	82 004	51	CL_WB_REP_BROWSER_VIS_RADA=>IF_WB_REPBROWSER_VIS~SHOW
1	75 053	7	CL_WB_REP_BROWSER_RADA=>GET_OBJECT_TREE_FROM_REQUEST
1	74 317	13	CL_WB_OBJECT_TREE_RADA=>CREATE_FROM_TREENAME
1	73 632	40	CL_WB_OBJECT_TREE_RADA=>CONSTRUCTOR
1	66 017	132	CL_WB_REP_BROWSER_VIS_RADA=>SHOW_TREE
1	59 588	46	CL_WB_BROWSER_SELECTION1=>IF_WB_BROWSER_SELECTION~SHOW_SELECTION
518	59 550	1 027	CL_WB_REGISTRY=>INITIALIZE

No.	Gross	Net	RAISE EVENT
1	58 961	8	CL_WB_MANAGER=>IF_WB_MANAGER~MANAGER_FINISHED
1	2 692	5	CL_GUI_CONTAINER_BAR_WB=>EMPTY
4	110	30	CL_GUI_CONTAINER_BAR_WB=>CLICKED
1	24	2	CL_WB_WINDOW_EVENTS=>WINDOW_ACTIVATED
1	7	4	CL_WB_MANAGER=>IF_WB_MANAGER~MANAGER_PBO_PROCESSED

- **Database hit list**: This shows list of database tables accessed during the measurement:

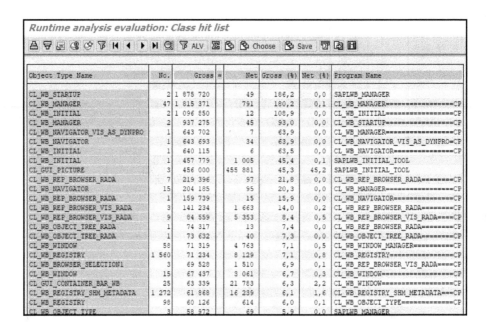

Tab./View	#Acces	Runtime	Class	Buffering	SQL tab.	Description	Package
EUOBJT	4	15 055	TRANSP	Single rec		Workbench: Development Objects	SEU
SEOCOMPO	192	11 428	TRANSP			Class/Interface component	SEO
SEOSUBCODF	36	10 451	TRANSP			Definition class/interface subcomponent	SEO
SEOCOMPODF	60	10 084	TRANSP			Definition class/interface component	SEO
OBJH	4	8 822	TRANSP	Single rec		Object: Header	SCTS_OBJ
BDSPHIO2	63	6 855	TRANSP			BDS: Instances of Physical Information Objects	SBDS
SEOSUBCO	64	4 395	TRANSP			Class/interface subcomponent	SEO
EUOBJEDIT	8	3 336	TRANSP	full		Workbench: Assignment Development Object Type -> Editor	SEU
OBJT	4	3 131	TRANSP			Description of Type T Objects (Separate Transaction)	SCTS_OBJ
BDSPHF2	32	2 756	TRANSP			BDS: Files of Physical Information Objects	SBDS
EUOBJ	6	2 672	TRANSP	full		Workbench: Development Objects	SEU
WBTOOLTYPE	160	2 156	TRANSP	full		Visualization types for tools	SWBM_INTERNAL
SEOSUBCOTX	36	2 003	TRANSP	generic		Class/interface subcomponent short description	SEO
BDS_CONN05	20	1 957	TRANSP			BDS: Link Table Default for Undefined Classes	SBDS
EUOBJV	4	1 946	VIEW	full		Generated Table for View	SEU
RSEUMOD	2	1 833	TRANSP			Settings for ABAP Workbench	SEU
BDSPHPR2	20	1 822	TRANSP			BDS: Attributes of Physical Information Objects	SBDS
BDSPHRE2	20	1 734	TRANSP			BDS: Outgoing Relationships of Physical Information Objects	SBDS
WBREGISTRY	4	1 716	TRANSP	full		Registry ABAP Workbench	SWBM_INTERNAL
BDSCHKO2	20	1 688	TRANSP			BDS: Check out Data for a Physical Information Object	SBDS
BDSLOIO2	5	1 604	TRANSP			BDS: Instances of Logical Information Objects	SBDS
BDSLOIOT2	20	1 596	TRANSP			BDS: Descriptions of Logical Information Objects	SBDS
TOLE	216	1 592	TRANSP	full		OLE Applications	SOLE
SEOCOMPOTX	64	1 429	TRANSP	generic		Short description class/interface component	SEO
DIRTREE	7	1 288	TRANSP			Tree administration	SEU

- **Class hit list**: This shows a list of classes used during the measurement, and can be further broken down into static methods and events:

Runtime analysis evaluation: Class hit list

Object Type Name	No.	Gross =	Net	Gross (%)	Net (%)	Program Name
CL_WB_STARTUP	2	1 875 720	49	186,2	0,0	SAPLWB_MANAGER
CL_WB_MANAGER	47	1 815 371	791	180,2	0,1	CL_WB_MANAGER================CP
CL_WB_INITIAL	2	1 096 850	12	108,9	0,0	CL_WB_INITIAL=================CP
CL_WB_MANAGER	2	937 275	45	93,0	0,0	CL_WB_STARTUP=================CP
CL_WB_NAVIGATOR_VIS_AS_DYNPRO	1	643 702	7	63,9	0,0	CL_WB_MANAGER================CP
CL_WB_NAVIGATOR	1	643 693	34	63,9	0,0	CL_WB_NAVIGATOR_VIS_AS_DYNPRO=CP
CL_WB_INITIAL	1	640 115	6	63,5	0,0	CL_WB_NAVIGATOR===============CP
CL_WB_INITIAL	1	457 779	1 005	45,4	0,1	SAPLWB_INITIAL_TOOL
CL_GUI_PICTURE	3	456 000	455 881	45,3	45,2	SAPLWB_INITIAL_TOOL
CL_WB_REP_BROWSER_RADA	7	219 396	97	21,8	0,0	CL_WB_REP_BROWSER_RADA========CP
CL_WB_NAVIGATOR	15	204 185	95	20,3	0,0	CL_WB_MANAGER================CP
CL_WB_REP_BROWSER_RADA	1	159 739	15	15,9	0,0	CL_WB_NAVIGATOR===============CP
CL_WB_REP_BROWSER_VIS_RADA	3	141 234	1 663	14,0	0,2	CL_WB_REP_BROWSER_RADA========CP
CL_WB_REP_BROWSER_VIS_RADA	9	84 559	5 353	8,4	0,5	CL_WB_REP_BROWSER_VIS_RADA====CP
CL_WB_OBJECT_TREE_RADA	1	74 317	13	7,4	0,0	CL_WB_REP_BROWSER_RADA========CP
CL_WB_OBJECT_TREE_RADA	1	73 632	40	7,3	0,0	CL_WB_OBJECT_TREE_RADA========CP
CL_WB_WINDOW	58	71 319	4 763	7,1	0,5	CL_WB_WINDOW_MANAGER==========CP
CL_WB_REGISTRY	1 560	71 234	8 129	7,1	0,8	CL_WB_REGISTRY================CP
CL_WB_BROWSER_SELECTION1	3	69 528	1 510	6,9	0,1	CL_WB_REP_BROWSER_VIS_RADA====CP
CL_WB_WINDOW	15	67 437	3 061	6,7	0,3	CL_WB_WINDOW==================CP
CL_GUI_CONTAINER_BAR_WB	25	63 339	21 783	6,3	2,2	CL_WB_WINDOW==================CP
CL_WB_REGISTRY_SHM_METADATA	1 272	61 868	16 239	6,1	1,6	CL_WB_REGISTRY_SHM_METADATA===CP
CL_WB_REGISTRY	98	60 126	614	6,0	0,1	CL_WB_OBJECT_TYPE=============CP
CL_WB_OBJECT_TYPE	3	58 972	69	5,9	0,0	SAPLWB_MANAGER

- **Instance hit list**: This shows all objects used during execution, and can be further broken down into instance methods used and events fired:

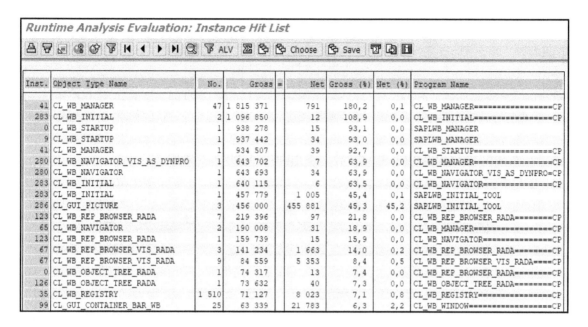

Runtime Analysis Evaluation: Instance Hit List

Inst.	Object Type Name	No.	Gross	=	Net	Gross (%)	Net (%)	Program Name
41	CL_WB_MANAGER	47	1 815 371		791	180,2	0,1	CL_WB_MANAGER==================CP
283	CL_WB_INITIAL	2	1 096 850		12	108,9	0,0	CL_WB_INITIAL==================CP
0	CL_WB_STARTUP	1	938 278		15	93,1	0,0	SAPLWB_MANAGER
9	CL_WB_STARTUP	1	937 442		34	93,0	0,0	SAPLWB_MANAGER
41	CL_WB_MANAGER	1	934 507		39	92,7	0,0	CL_WB_STARTUP==================CP
280	CL_WB_NAVIGATOR_VIS_AS_DYNPRO	1	643 702		7	63,9	0,0	CL_WB_MANAGER==================CP
280	CL_WB_NAVIGATOR	1	643 693		34	63,9	0,0	CL_WB_NAVIGATOR_VIS_AS_DYNPRO=CP
283	CL_WB_INITIAL	1	640 115		6	63,5	0,0	CL_WB_NAVIGATOR==================CP
283	CL_WB_INITIAL	1	457 779		1 005	45,4	0,1	SAPLWB_INITIAL_TOOL
286	CL_GUI_PICTURE	3	456 000		455 881	45,3	45,2	SAPLWB_INITIAL_TOOL
123	CL_WB_REP_BROWSER_RADA	7	219 396		97	21,8	0,0	CL_WB_REP_BROWSER_RADA========CP
65	CL_WB_NAVIGATOR	2	190 008		31	18,9	0,0	CL_WB_MANAGER==================CP
123	CL_WB_REP_BROWSER_RADA	1	159 739		15	15,9	0,0	CL_WB_NAVIGATOR==================CP
67	CL_WB_REP_BROWSER_VIS_RADA	3	141 234		1 663	14,0	0,2	CL_WB_REP_BROWSER_RADA========CP
67	CL_WB_REP_BROWSER_VIS_RADA	9	84 559		5 353	8,4	0,5	CL_WB_REP_BROWSER_VIS_RADA====CP
0	CL_WB_OBJECT_TREE_RADA	1	74 317		13	7,4	0,0	CL_WB_REP_BROWSER_RADA========CP
126	CL_WB_OBJECT_TREE_RADA	1	73 632		40	7,3	0,0	CL_WB_OBJECT_TREE_RADA========CP
35	CL_WB_REGISTRY	1 510	71 127		8 023	7,1	0,8	CL_WB_REGISTRY==================CP
99	CL_GUI_CONTAINER_BAR_WB	25	63 339		21 783	6,3	2,2	CL_WB_WINDOW==================CP

- **Method hit list**: This show static class method calls:

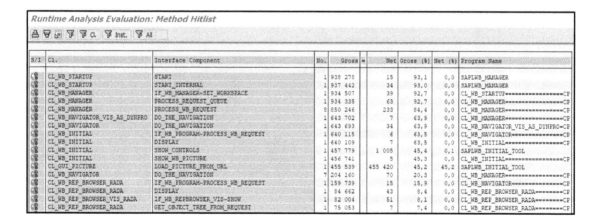

Runtime Analysis Evaluation: Method Hitlist

S/I	Cl.	Interface Component	No.	Gross	=	Net	Gross (%)	Net (%)	Program Name
	CL_WB_STARTUP	START	1	938 278		15	93,1	0,0	SAPLWB_MANAGER
	CL_WB_STARTUP	START_INTERNAL	1	937 442		34	93,0	0,0	SAPLWB_MANAGER
	CL_WB_MANAGER	IF_WB_MANAGER~SET_WORKSPACE	1	934 507		39	92,7	0,0	CL_WB_STARTUP==================CP
	CL_WB_MANAGER	PROCESS_REQUEST_QUEUE	1	934 335		63	92,7	0,0	CL_WB_MANAGER==================CP
	CL_WB_MANAGER	PROCESS_WB_REQUEST	8	850 246		233	84,4	0,0	CL_WB_MANAGER==================CP
	CL_WB_NAVIGATOR_VIS_AS_DYNPRO	DO_THE_NAVIGATION	1	643 702		7	63,9	0,0	CL_WB_NAVIGATOR_VIS_AS_DYNPRO=CP
	CL_WB_NAVIGATOR	DO_THE_NAVIGATION	1	643 693		34	63,9	0,0	CL_WB_NAVIGATOR==================CP
	CL_WB_INITIAL	IF_WB_PROGRAM~PROCESS_WB_REQUEST	1	640 115		6	63,5	0,0	CL_WB_INITIAL==================CP
	CL_WB_INITIAL	DISPLAY	1	640 109		7	63,5	0,0	CL_WB_INITIAL==================CP
	CL_WB_INITIAL	SHOW_CONTROLS	1	457 779		1 005	45,4	0,1	SAPLWB_INITIAL_TOOL
	CL_WB_INITIAL	SHOW_WB_PICTURE	1	456 741		5	45,3	0,0	CL_WB_INITIAL==================CP
	CL_GUI_PICTURE	LOAD_PICTURE_FROM_URL	1	455 539		455 420	45,2	45,2	SAPLWB_INITIAL_TOOL
	CL_WB_NAVIGATOR	DO_THE_NAVIGATION	7	204 160		70	20,3	0,0	CL_WB_MANAGER==================CP
	CL_WB_REP_BROWSER_RADA	IF_WB_PROGRAM~PROCESS_WB_REQUEST	1	159 739		15	15,9	0,0	CL_WB_NAVIGATOR==================CP
	CL_WB_REP_BROWSER_RADA	DISPLAY	1	84 662		43	8,4	0,0	CL_WB_REP_BROWSER_RADA========CP
	CL_WB_REP_BROWSER_VIS_RADA	IF_REPBROWSER_VIS~SHOW	1	82 004		51	8,1	0,0	CL_WB_REP_BROWSER_RADA========CP
	CL_WB_REP_BROWSER_RADA	GET_OBJECT_TREE_FROM_REQUEST	1	75 053		7	7,4	0,0	CL_WB_REP_BROWSER_RADA========CP

- **Events hit list**: This shows events fired during runtime:

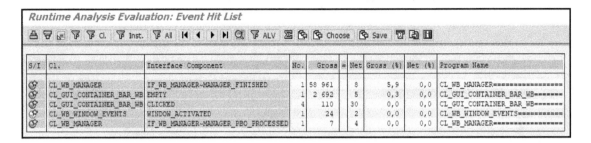

- **Internal table hit list**: This shows internal table accesses:

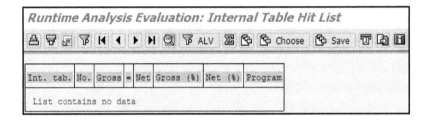

- **Call hierarchy**: This shows a list of all the hotspots, structured into a nested tree of calls to track the program flow:

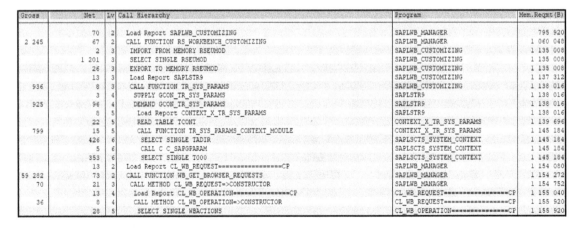

- **Statistics**: This shows summarized data for different hotspot groups.

On most of the screens, there is a button that opens the source code of the specific call; therefore, it can easily guide the developer where to make changes in the code.

ABAP trace analysis

The next tool available for trace analysis is Single Transaction Analysis, available at the ST12 transaction. Similarly to ABAP Runtime Analysis, described in the previous part, this transaction also welcomes the user with a configuration screen, containing several parameters, as shown the following screenshot:

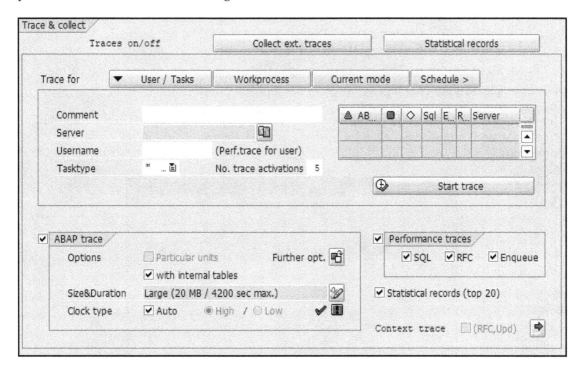

The main section, namely **Trace for**, is suitable for defining the target of the trace with four categories:

- **User/Tasks**: This allows for enabling a trace for a specific user, on a specific server, optionally limiting the scope to a specific task type—**Dialog**, **Batch job**, **Update**, **Incoming RFC call**, **HTTP request/BSP**, **SMTP request**, or **Shared obj. area contr**.
- **Workprocess**: This allows the user to trace a particular work process currently running on the system
- **Current mode**: This runs a particular transaction or program with a trace enabled; tracing ends simultaneously with the transaction.

- **Schedule**: This allows scheduling the trace for a specific timeframe; the scheduled trace can be enabled for background jobs, work processes, or for a particular user and task type, therefore running it when it is actually useful.

Selecting one of the first three options, you are presented with further options of what is meant to be collected—it should be either **ABAP trace**, **Performance trace**, or both. The exposed parameters for the former include the following:

- **Options**: This determines whether the trace should be for particular units, and whether to collect internal tables information as well.
- **Size&Duration**: This limits the output file to a specific size, or the trace time.
- **Clock type**: This sets the interval for collecting data.

The **Further ABAP trace options** button opens the pop-up dialog, shown in the following screenshot, with additional limitation options to make the trace contain only relevant information:

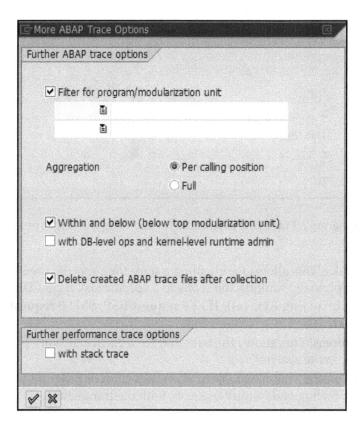

The available options for **Performance traces** configuration cover whether or not to collect the following information:

- **SQL**: Database accesses
- **RFC**: Remote function calls
- **Enqueue**: Database table enqueues and dequeues

Once the user has decided what to collect, the trace collection will start after pressing the **Start trace** button, and will continue until the trace size or the execution time is exceeded. The user ends it manually or leaves the transaction (in **Current** mode). Then, the asynchronous collection of the trace takes place and the list of all collected traces is shown on the main screen:

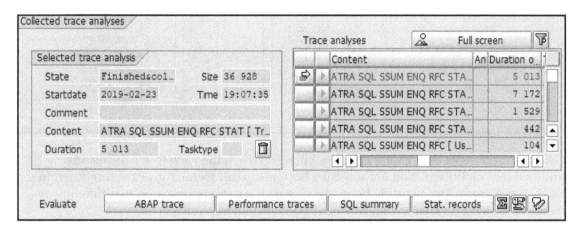

Choosing the trace that is of interest to the user, and pressing one of the buttons on the bottom, leads to the trace results. The available results types are as follows:

- **ABAP trace**
- **Performance traces**
- **SQL summary**
- **Stat. records**

The **ABAP trace**, by default, shows the list of calls in order of their execution, as shown in the following screenshot:

Call	No.	Gross	=	Net	Gross (%)	Net (%)	Program (called program)
Runtime analysis	1	1 528 829		0	100,0	0,0	
CALL TRANSACTION SE80	1	1 528 656		1 132	100,0	0,1	Testframe
Program SAPMSEU0	1	1 527 524		233	99,9	0,0	
System Event <Generic Identifier>	5	1 523 213		39	99,6	0,0	SAPMSEU0
Dynpro Entry PROCESS DARK	1	1 522 909		64	99,6	0,0	SAPMSSY0
PAI Dynpro 1000	2	1 522 662		11	99,6	0,0	SAPMSSY0
CALL FUNCTION WB_NEW_WORKBENCH_START	1	1 522 544		33	99,6	0,0	SAPLWB_MANAGER
CALL METHOD CL_WB_STARTUP=>START	1	1 422 895		12	93,1	0,0	CL_WB_STARTUP============
CALL FUNCTION WB_MANAGER_START	1	1 422 882		12	93,1	0,0	SAPLWB_MANAGER
CALL SCREEN 0200	1	1 422 870		51	93,1	0,0	SAPLWB_MANAGER
Dynpro Entry <Generic Identifier>	2	1 422 819		127	93,1	0,0	SAPLWB_MANAGER
PAI Dynpro 0200	2	1 422 192		9	93,0	0,0	SAPLWB_MANAGER
Module PAI MANAGER_START	1	1 422 126		8	93,0	0,0	SAPLWB_MANAGER
CALL METHOD CL_WB_STARTUP=>START_INTERNAL	1	1 422 116		6	93,0	0,0	CL_WB_STARTUP============
CALL METHOD CL_WB_MANAGER=>IF_WB_MANAGER~SET_WORKS	1	1 418 711		19	92,8	0,0	CL_WB_MANAGER============
CALL METHOD CL_WB_MANAGER=>PROCESS_REQUEST_QUEUE	1	1 418 597		20	92,8	0,0	CL_WB_MANAGER============
LOOP AT ME->REQUEST_QUEUE	1	1 334 057		42	87,3	0,0	CL_WB_MANAGER============

Trace analysis 2019-02-19(1) - ABAP Trace Per Call

Transaction SE80 = Object Navigator   ABAP   1 401 410 = 91,7%
Traced user   Database   121 976 =   8,0%
                                            System   5 443 =   0,4%
Execution times in microseconds   Total   1 528 829 = 100,0%

Using the buttons at the top of the screen, you can switch the view to see the results grouped into modularization units, see the bottom-up call hierarchy, or the top-down tree for a chosen entry. The available hierarchies show the same information in different ways, therefore making it easier to find the required information.

> The ABAP trace is particularly useful for identifying all custom code logic that is executed with the main programs.

The **Performance trace** shows database calls alongside the results (number of records made) and the duration of the processing, therefore allowing the identification of database or time intensive calls, or checking from what tables the transaction takes the information. The results are presented as a simple list, as shown in the following screenshot:

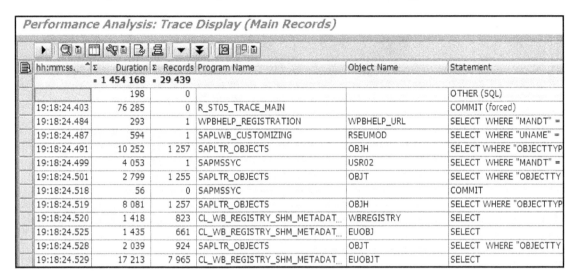

Performance Analysis: Trace Display (Main Records)

hh:mm:ss...	Duration	Records	Program Name	Object Name	Statement
	1 454 168	29 439			
	198	0			OTHER (SQL)
19:18:24.403	76 285	0	R_ST05_TRACE_MAIN		COMMIT (forced)
19:18:24.484	293	1	WPBHELP_REGISTRATION	WPBHELP_URL	SELECT WHERE "MANDT" =
19:18:24.487	594	1	SAPLWB_CUSTOMIZING	RSEUMOD	SELECT WHERE "UNAME" =
19:18:24.491	10 252	1 257	SAPLTR_OBJECTS	OBJH	SELECT WHERE "OBJECTTYP
19:18:24.499	4 053	1	SAPMSSYC	USR02	SELECT WHERE "MANDT" =
19:18:24.501	2 799	1 255	SAPLTR_OBJECTS	OBJT	SELECT WHERE "OBJECTTY
19:18:24.518	56	0	SAPMSSYC		COMMIT
19:18:24.519	8 081	1 257	SAPLTR_OBJECTS	OBJH	SELECT WHERE "OBJECTTYP
19:18:24.520	1 418	823	CL_WB_REGISTRY_SHM_METADAT...	WBREGISTRY	SELECT
19:18:24.525	1 435	661	CL_WB_REGISTRY_SHM_METADAT...	EUOBJ	SELECT
19:18:24.528	2 039	924	SAPLTR_OBJECTS	OBJT	SELECT WHERE "OBJECTTY
19:18:24.529	17 213	7 965	CL_WB_REGISTRY_SHM_METADAT...	EUOBJT	SELECT

The buttons at top of the screen allow for quick navigation to **Data Dictionary** (**DDIC**) information about the objects or to a particular ABAP statement in the source code.

The **SQL summary** contains detailed information about database operations with detailed explanations about how the statement was resolved internally by the database, as shown in the following screenshot:

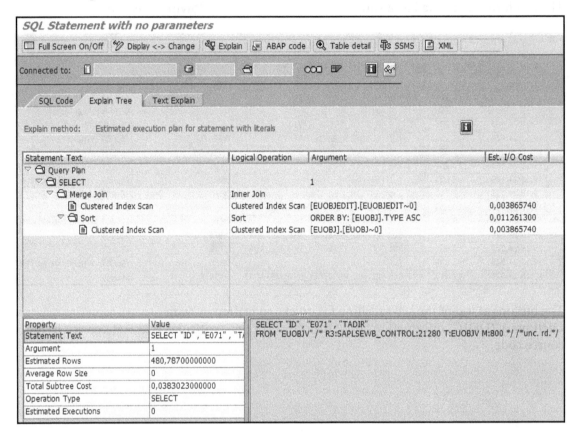

ABAP SAT transactions

The SAP system provides improved programming tools with new versions. Also, the topic of performance is not treated indifferently. In the NetWeaver 7.0 EhP2 version, a new tool named SAT has been added. The transaction that runs this runtime analysis is also SAT. SAT is a developed and improved version of the SE30 program.

It is a tool that allows you to run any programs, function modules and transactions to evaluate the analysis. This allows for better optimization and allows you to find the causes of errors. Using this tool allows you to constantly improve programs, and increase the business suitability of the process by accelerating it.

After starting the SAT transaction, the user will see the following screen:

As you can see, the tool at the beginning seems complicated because it has a lot of options. However, using it is easy. A very big advantage of this tool is the storage of measurement results in the database. This means that it is possible to examine traces from any application server in the system.

The **Data Formatting** checkbox allows for the presentation of measurement results in the internal table. The measurement variant is available in the **Settings** area. This is a very important part of working with the SAT transaction. The basic variant should not be used; the user should always create his own variant. To do this, click on **creating**. It is important that **Explicit Switching On and Off Measurement** is selected in the window. The system will open a new screen, in which the user can define a variant. This screen is as follows:

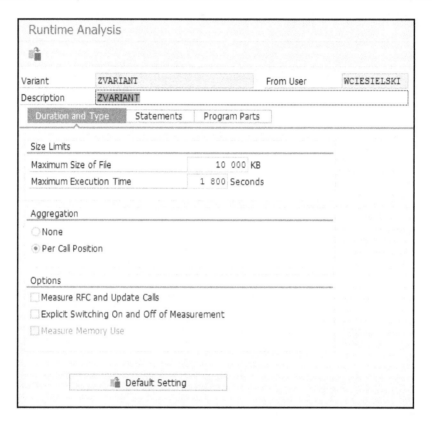

The use of the appropriate variant is intended to obtain the necessary tracking data while limiting the use of memory. This is of great importance in the study of complex processes. One way to reduce the size of the trace file can be found on the **Duration and type** tab by setting the appropriate aggregation.

It is also good practice to limit the variant for specific classes, function groups, and programs. The user can set it in the **Program Parts** section, and check the **Limitation on Program Components** box. An example window is as follows:

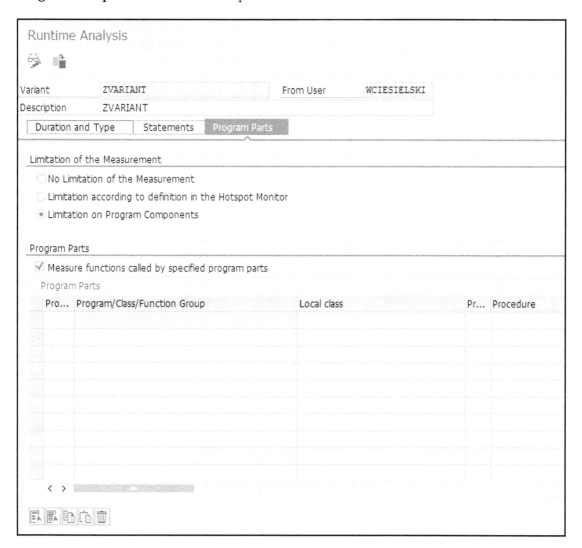

Also important are the settings in the **Statements** tab, which show what should be examined:

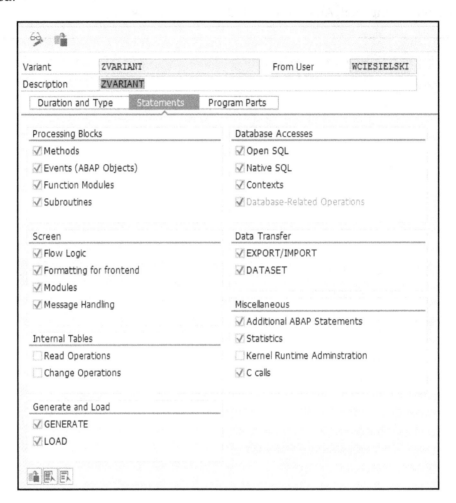

To run real-time tests, press the following button:

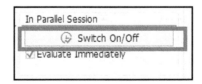

After starting, the user can follow what program is being executed. This allows the user to find problems in the code, such as infinite loops. An example is shown here:

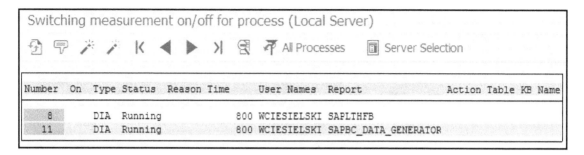

To run the SAT for a specific program, a standard `SAPBC_DATA_GENERATOR` program is used. Go to the menu, as shown in the following screenshot:

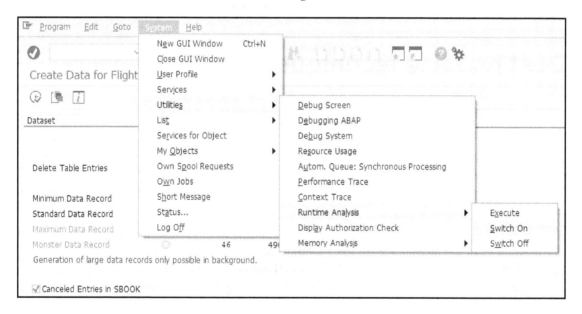

An example of a trace result is shown in the following screenshot:

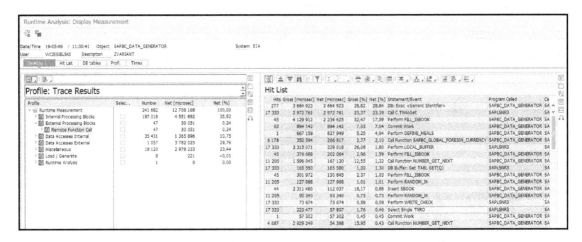

Best practice techniques

Using best practices allows the programmer to create modern code. Programs become optimal and the product life cycle is extended. This part of the chapter will describe techniques that help create high-quality code.

The first topic is the proper naming of all objects while creating and modifying business processes. The exact rules are described in this book in previous chapters. Using an appropriate naming makes it easier in the future to expand programs and look for errors in them.

The next point is to clean variables using the `clear` function. A program that has been used many times may not always return the variables to the correct state. Clearing the content allows you to be sure that incompatible data will not be transmitted. After many operations, such as reading from the database or reading the table, check the `sy-subrc` system variable. If it is not equal to `0`, it means that there is no data that the program has asked for. There is no need to execute further parts of the code that uses the downloaded data.

In order to speed up the search from the database and improve performance, you can use the secondary index. In select queries, you also need to maximize the `where` statements.

Using the field symbol speeds up the operation of the program. It is a very convenient form of variable storage. If an internal table with a large number of records is used during the process, the program should use a binary search to find records. This is due to the specific operation of a binary search. To maximize performance before the binary search operation, table sorting should be performed.

In every language, the program weighs well-formatted code. Also in the SAP environment, the programmer should take care that their code is well formed. What's more, the ABAP editor offers a Pretty Printer tool that automatically adjusts the code. The programmer can adapt it to his own needs and requirements defined by the company's policy.

To configure the tool, the user must enter the **Settings** menu in the edited program. The access path is shown in the following screenshot:

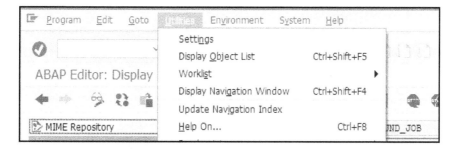

Next, in the window, select **ABAP Editor** and **Pretty Printer**. This choice is shown in the following screenshot:

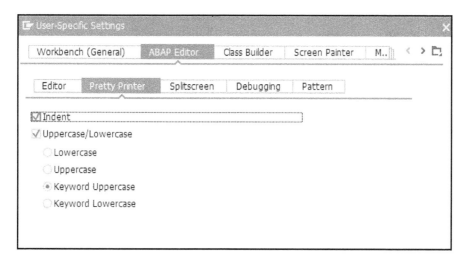

As shown in the preceding screenshot, there are options for how the code should behave after using this tool. The programmer can determine when uppercase letters will be used and add automatic indents. Launching this tool during the code implementation is done by using the **Pretty Printer** button or the *Shift + F1* shortcut.

It is used to compare possible implementations. To use it, use the SE80 transaction and then move the combination, as follows:

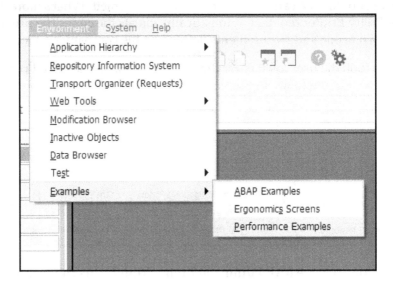

The user gets sample code comparisons. After they are done, the **Measure runtime** button will get information about the time of the execution. An example window is shown in the following screenshot:

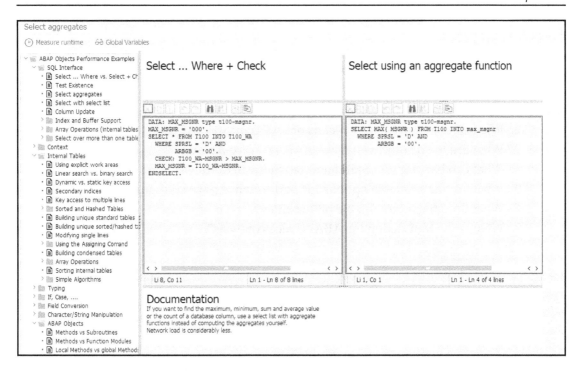

The tool can be useful for both novice programmers, as well as those experienced users who want to use the results to improve performance.

Summary

This chapter provided a thorough review of the available ABAP toolset for testing the performance of ABAP apps and tuning their execution. It also gave some best practice tips and tricks for internal ABAP statements, and focuses on tracing and tuning OpenSQL selections. After reading this chapter, you should know how to check the various parameters of your ABAP programs, find performance bottlenecks, spot extensive database usage, and be able to correct these issues.

Questions

The following questions will help you to consolidate the information contained in this chapter:

1. Which transaction is better: SE30 or SAT? Why?
2. What can be examined by means of SAT transactions?
3. What are the results available for ABAP Trace Analysis?
4. What can be set in the **Statement** tab in the SAT transaction?
5. What are the available options for performance trace configuration?
6. What does the internal table hit list show?
7. What is the transaction for ABAP Trace Analysis?

Assessments

Answers

This chapter contains the answers to the questions that are at the end of each chapter. These answers will help the reader to test their knowledge of each chapter. Understanding the content of the chapters is very important for further development and working with the SAP system.

Chapter 1 - Creating Custom Code

1. Working with Agile speeds up product creation and organizes the creation process. It determines what is important in the project. In this approach, people are very important.
2. The following are the principals of the Agile Manifesto:
    1. Individuals and interactions over processes and tools
    2. Working software over comprehensive documentation
    3. Customer collaboration over contract negotiation
    4. Responding to change over following a plan
3. The logical model contains information on data storage, but there is no information on how it will be stored. The physical data design model includes changing the logical database design to a physical layer.
4. Enhancement and custom development.
5. The motto is *doing, not talking*. It is coherent because design thinking is about testing real prototypes, instead of just talking about them.
6. The categories are as follows:

    - Documentation on the high-level architecture
    - Documentation where we have to describe the whole system, from the high-level architecture to the smallest details

7. There are various aspects. The ones that apply to SAP development include comprehensibility, conciseness, consistency, maintainability, testability, reliability, and security.

8. Loose coupling allows for easier maintenance.

Chapter 2 - The Basic Structures of ABAP

1. They must start with the Z or Y characters.

2. A field symbol is an instrument in which applications are created with elasticity. Field symbols do not have any memory; instead, they point to a memory location.

3. The elementary types in the SAP system are C, N, D, T, I, F, P, STRING, and XSTRING.

Chapter 3 - Database Access in ABAP

1. You need a list of the selected fields, the tables from which data will be selected, and the names of the variables to where data will be downloaded.

2. The three ways are: FOR ALL ENTRIES, SELECT...ENDSELECT, and JOIN.

3. The ways to read data from tables are as follows:

   - Get only the required rows from a table.
   - Get only the required columns from a table.
   - Do not use more reads than necessary.
   - Use local buffers and indexes.

Chapter 4 - Import and Export to Document Formats

1. You can use CL_GUI_FRONTEND_SERVICES to upload files from the presentation layer to the application layer.

2. The setting of a multiselection parameter controls whether the user can choose one or more files.

3. The `ARCHIVFILE_CLIENT_TO_SERVER` function can upload files from the presentation layer to the application server.

4. The purpose of the parameters is as follows:

   - `ASC`: data will be transferred as ASCII text.
   - `BIN`: data should be transferred unconverted in binary format.
   - `DAT`: data will be transported as unconverted ASCII text, where the different columns are separated by the tabulator.

1. The `CG3Z` transaction allows the user to upload a file to the application server.
2. The file will be saved in the default root folder, `DIR_SAPUSERS`.
3. The two languages are: Desktop Office Integration or Object Linking and Embedding.
4. The `ole2incl` type-pool needs to be included.

Chapter 5 - Exposing Data to Print Forms

1. The container for ABAP code is *Command Lines*.
2. In Smartform, you have to add empty rows using *Command Lines*. In Adobe Form, you can set a minimum number of rows in the table settings.
3. Adobe Forms supports FormCalc and JavaScript.
4. Transaction SE78 allows the uploading of additional graphics to the server.
5. When an object is set to a position, it will stay in the same place, no matter what. The object status will be placed according to the available space.
6. Changes to the structure of the form are not allowed (except for the form field and data values).
7. Adobe can get input from a user and store that information in a system.

Chapter 6 - ABAP and XML

1. The `import_from_file` method will parse the XML stream.
2. The `Display` method prints an XML file onscreen.
3. The constant that describes the JSON format can be found in the `IF_SXML` interface, in the `CO_XT_JSON` attribute.

4. No, it's not possible to do that.
5. ST supports only XML to ABAP and ABAP to XML; XSLT supports any XML transformation.
6. No, it's possible only using XSLT.
7. Put the following tag at the beginning of the file: `<?xml version="1.0" encoding="UTF-8"?>`.

Chapter 7 - Building User Interfaces

1. The two categories are Selection Screen and Classic DynPro.
2. In **Parameters**, you have the ability to input only one values, and in **Select-Options**, you can input multiple values.
3. The name of the Custom Container needs to be written in capital letters, and needs to be exactly the same onscreen and in the code.

Chapter 8 - Creating Stunning UI5 Interfaces

1. Although there are available tools for Eclipse IDE, it is recommended to use WebIDE from SAP (either the Cloud or Personal editions).
2. According to the development rules, all texts displayed in the applications should be stored in an i18n file. Then, the translation process requires only the generation of a new i18n file, with appropriate language suffix and translated texts inside. When using a fully integrated cloud version of WebIDE, this can be performed with the use of Translation Hub.
3. MVC is a paradigm that introduces the separation of concerns in applications. It states that the model (M), view (V), and controller (C) should be maintained separately, making the whole process of development and maintenance easier and cheaper.
4. The toolset includes mock servers, OPA5 for intergration tests, and QUnit for unit tests.

Chapter 9 - Business Object Processing Framework

1. To enhance the BO standard, you can use a BOBX transaction.
2. The BOBF transaction is used for SAP internal uses.
3. The association's entity is used to create a relation between two BOPF objects.
4. There are two different types of association: general and composite.
5. To save data to the database, we have to use Transaction Manager.
6. The main BOPF exception is /bopf/cx_frw.
7. The configuration object is used to get BO metadata.

Chapter 10 - Modification and Customization Techniques

1. The techniques are Changes and modification.
2. With the switch mechanism, you can switch enhancement on and off without making any change to the code.
3. Classical: objects are created by the factory method; filters are passed into implementation; classical BAdI can be called only once; and the calling position is registered centrally.
   New: This is created by GET BADI; filters are used when an object is created; and multiple calls are possible and are not centrally registered.
4. It's used for the FICA module.
5. A SECTION contains default code and POINT does not.
6. If INCLUDE BOUND is used, the enhancement will be called from every main program that uses this include method.
7. For customer exit implementation, we use function modules.

Chapter 11 - Handling Exceptions in ABAP

1. Exception classes are implemented in the Class Builder just like usual classes. The difference is that it has to be marked as an exception class, and it must inherit from one of the standard exception classes.

2. It is an object that groups breakpoints and assertions in order to manage them centrally. It allows for quick activation/deactivation, behavior configuration, and log checks.

3. ABAP Dump Analysis is used to analyze execution errors in the SAP system.

4. ABAP Dump Analysis is launched after using the st22 transaction.

5. Despite the exception, the program does not end its work in an unexpected way. Dumps will not appear.

Chapter 12 - Testing ABAP Programs

1. This variant is called S4HANA_READINESS.

2. PERFORMANCE_CHECKLIST can be used to check code performance.

3. Using SET EXTENDED CHECK OFF will turn off extended checks.

4. You can use append_line from cl_tpda_script_tabledescr.

5. Those steps are: Debugger Single Step, Breakpoint Reached, and Watchpoint Reached.

6. To record, the TCD REC transaction can be used.

7. Either the Local, Import, or Export parameters.

Chapter 13 - Advanced Techniques in ABAP Objects

1. The global class can be used in the code all over the system. The local class can be used only in the code where it is defined.

2. Interfaces cannot have an implementation of methods. Only definitions are allowed.

3. Design patterns are universal, tested in practice for frequently occurring and repetitive design issues.

Chapter 14 - Integrating SAP with Third-Party Systems

1. The user can connect with other systems using the following technologies: IDoc, EDI/ALE, BAPI, OData, or Gateway.
2. The OData service works as a RESTful service, offering basic CRUD methods. From the consumer's perspective, it provides uniquely identified data according to the OData specification. From the system's perspective, it usually consists of model-provider classes and data-provider classes, where the latter is responsible for business logic implementation.
3. The main difference between the two is that EDI is used for external communication, while ALE is used for internal connections. From a technical point of view, EDI transfers data using file ports, whereas ALE uses memory buffers to transfer the data.

Chapter 15 - Background Processing of ABAP Programs

1. Users can schedule the job in the background with the SM36 transaction.
2. Ready: This status means that the task scheduler puts the job in the queue while it waits for the job to be released in the background.
3. To set the **High** and **Medium** priorities, the user must have the appropriate permissions.

Chapter 16 - Performance and Optimization of ABAP Code

1. SAT–it is a modern replacement of SE30 offering better configuration options and more transparent result analysis
2. Using this tool allows you to constantly improve programs and increase the business suitability of the process by accelerating it.
3. The ABAP Trace Analysis offers the list of calls executed during runtime, alongside the execution times and counters.

4. In the **Statement** tab, the user can set what should be checked during the operation of the ABAP SAT Transaction tool.

5. Users can decide whether to collect information about database accesses, remote function calls, and enqueues/dequeues on database tables.

6. It shows accesses to internal tables during program execution.

7. SAP Trace Analysis runs through ST12 transactions.

Additional tutorials

This part contains additional tutorials that can help the reader to learn and work with the system. These tutorials lead the reader through the creation of functionality, step by step.

Creating a report from the template

This tutorial shows how to create a report from a template. The following steps will guide the reader through the creation process:

1. Go to ABAP Workbench (transaction SE80), choose **Program** from the development object list, and choose a name. We've used ZMSA_R_CHAPTER0_0:

2. You will be asked whatever you want to create new object. Click **Yes** on the popups that will appear:

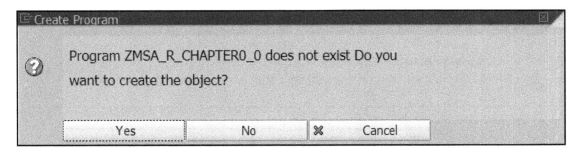

3. Give a program name and click the green check mark on the popups that will appear:

4. Add the following code into the editor window and activate reporting:

```
CLASS lcl_demo DEFINITION CREATE PRIVATE.
  PUBLIC SECTION.
    CLASS-METHODS main.

  PRIVATE SECTION.
ENDCLASS.

CLASS lcl_demo IMPLEMENTATION.
  METHOD main.
  ENDMETHOD.

ENDCLASS.
START-OF-SELECTION.
lcl_demo=>main( ).
```

Uploading graphics to SE78

The SAP system allows you to upload images. This is a useful functionality used for many purposes (such as SmartForms). The following is a tutorial that shows how to add a picture to the SAP system:

1. Go to **Administration of Form Graphics** (transaction SE78). Choose the BMP folder from the tree on the left-hand panel and enter a new image name:

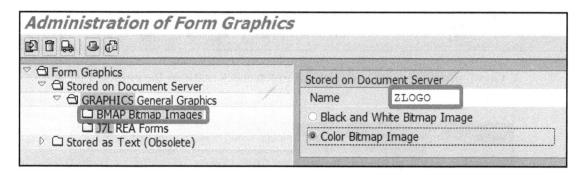

2. Choose **Import** from the **Graphic** menu:

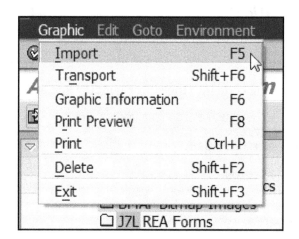

3. In the popup, fill in the **Description** and enter the path in the **File name** field of the image file:

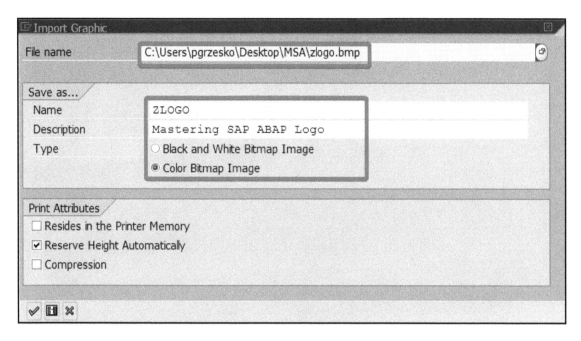

4. After clicking the green check mark, the image will be uploaded to the server.

At the time of writing, you can use the ZLOGO image in all forms and in all transactions that require it.

Another Book You May Enjoy

If you enjoyed this book, you may be interested in this book by Packt:

SAP Business Intelligence Quick Start Guide
Vinay Singh

ISBN: 9781789346206

- Work with various tools to create interactive data visualization and analysis
- Query, report, and analyze with SAP Business Objects Web Intelligence
- Create a report in SAP Crystal Reports for Enterprise
- Visualize and manipulate data using an SAP Lumira Storyboard
- Deep dive into the workings of the SAP predictive analytics tool
- Deploy and configure SAP BO Intelligence platform 4.2

Leave a review - let other readers know what you think

Please share your thoughts on this book with others by leaving a review on the site that you bought it from. If you purchased the book from Amazon, please leave us an honest review on this book's Amazon page. This is vital so that other potential readers can see and use your unbiased opinion to make purchasing decisions, we can understand what our customers think about our products, and our authors can see your feedback on the title that they have worked with Packt to create. It will only take a few minutes of your time, but is valuable to other potential customers, our authors, and Packt. Thank you!

Index

control record 439
Create, Read, Update, and Delete (CRUD) 453
customer exits 305, 306, 307, 308, 309, 310, 311
Customer Exits (CMOD) 305
customer exits, types
  about 305
  function exits 305
  menu exits 305
  screen exits 305
  table exits 305

D

data declaration
  about 41
  field symbol 43, 44
data definition language (DDL) 48
Data Dictionary (DDIC) 228, 501
Data Dictionary
  about 25
  data elements 30
  domains 27, 29
  search help 34, 37
  structures 32
  table types 37
data manipulation language (DML) 48
data record 439
Data Types 26
data
  changes, identifying 76
  changes, saving 76
  reading, from several tables 70, 72, 74
  selecting, from database 58
database management systems (DBMSes) 20
database
  about 37, 40, 41
  data, selecting 58
  designing 19
dataset
  creating 77
  deleting 79
  optimization 79
  updating 78
Decorator design pattern
  about 425, 427, 428, 429

advantages 429
disadvantages 429
design patterns
  elements 418
  purpose 418
design thinking 13
design thinking, process
  empathy 13
  ideas 13
  problem, defining 13
  prototypes 14
  tests 14
Desktop Office Integration (DOI) 93, 94
Development and operations (DevOps) 22
development tools 251

E

EDI system
  using 440
EDI
  versus ALE 440
enhancement framework
  about 331
  explicated framework 331
  implicated enhancement 331
enhancement points 332, 333, 334
enhancement sections 332, 333, 334
entities, Business Object Processing Framework (BOPF)
  actions 289
  associations 289
  determinations 289
  nodes 288
  queries 289
  validations 289
Entity Data Model (EDM) 456
error log, nodes
  ABAP Developer View 359, 360, 361, 362
  about 358
  BASIS Developer View 362, 363
  System Environment 358
  user View 359
event concept 415, 417, 418
extended Computer Aided Test Tool (eCATT)
  about 365

www.ingramcontent.com/pod-product-compliance
Lightning Source LLC
Chambersburg PA
CBHW060638060326
40690CB00020B/4437